The Israeli Settler Movement

The Israeli settler movement plays a key role in Israeli politics and the Arab-Israeli conflict, yet very few empirical studies of the movement exist. This is the first in-depth examination of the contemporary Israeli settler movement from a structural (rather than purely historical or political) perspective, and one of the few studies to focus on a long-standing, radical right-wing social movement in a non-western political context. A trailblazing systematic assessment of the role of the settler movement in Israeli politics writ large, as well as in relation to Israel's policy towards the West Bank, this book analyzes the movement both as a whole and as a combination of its parts (i.e. branches) - institutions, networks, and individuals. Whether you are a student, researcher, or policymaker, this book offers a comprehensive and original theoretical framework alongside a rich empirical analysis which illuminates social movements in general, and the Israeli settler movement in particular.

Sivan Hirsch-Hoefler is a Senior Lecturer in the Lauder School of Government, Diplomacy, and Strategy at the Interdisciplinary Center (IDC) Herzliya, Israel. Her work focuses on the processes underpinning political extremism, notably right-wing extremism.

Cas Mudde is Stanley Wade Shelton UGAF Professor of International Affairs at the University of Georgia, and Professor II at the Center for Research on Extremism (C-REX) at the University of Oslo. His other books include *The Far Right Today* (2019) and *Populist Radical Right Parties in Europe* (Cambridge, 2007), which won the Stein Rokkan Prize in 2008 and was named an Outstanding Academic Title by Choice in 2008.

The Israeli Settler Movement

Assessing and Explaining Social Movement Success

Sivan Hirsch-Hoefler

The Interdisciplinary Center (IDC), Herzliya

Cas Mudde

University of Georgia

CAMBRIDGE
UNIVERSITY PRESS

CAMBRIDGE
UNIVERSITY PRESS

Shaftesbury Road, Cambridge CB2 8EA, United Kingdom

One Liberty Plaza, 20th Floor, New York, NY 10006, USA

477 Williamstown Road, Port Melbourne, VIC 3207, Australia

314–321, 3rd Floor, Plot 3, Splendor Forum, Jasola District Centre, New Delhi – 110025, India

103 Penang Road, #05–06/07, Visioncrest Commercial, Singapore 238467

Cambridge University Press is part of Cambridge University Press & Assessment, a department of the University of Cambridge.

We share the University's mission to contribute to society through the pursuit of education, learning and research at the highest international levels of excellence.

www.cambridge.org
Information on this title: www.cambridge.org/9781316503461

DOI: 10.1017/9781316481554

First published 2021
First paperback edition 2024

A catalogue record for this publication is available from the British Library

ISBN 978-1-107-13864-3 Hardback
ISBN 978-1-316-50346-1 Paperback

Edan, Lior, and Neta

Contents

Figures

Preface

Almost ten years have passed since we started the journey that resulted in this book. We signed the advance contract with Cambridge University Press in early 2015, after having debated the idea and outline for at least several years. Much has happened since then, and yet so little has changed with regard to the topic of this book. Across Western democracies, center-left parties have been decimated (with a few notable exceptions), while far-right parties and politicians have become part of the mainstream. Premiers and presidents have come and gone, but one has remained the same: Benjamin Netanyahu, Israel's prime minister since 2009.

Both of us have been fascinated by the Israeli settler movement for a long time. Cas wrote a course paper about Gush Emunim as an undergraduate student at Leiden University, in 1991, while Sivan wrote a PhD on the settler movement (*Settle for Nothing: The Action Strategies of the Israeli Settlement Movement*) at the University of Antwerp between 2004 and 2008. While the settler movement has always remained a hot issue in the Israeli and international media, almost universally presented as exceptionally successful, academic research on the movement remained limited in number and scope. Most studies of the settler movement focus on only one aspect (e.g., ideology/religion) or group (i.e., Gush Emunim). Our interest has always been, first and foremost, on the *success* of the settler *movement*. That is why this book approaches the Israeli settler movement from a social movement perspective.

Writing about a highly controversial and topical issue is challenging in many different ways. For instance, while "settler" is the common English term for (Israeli) Jews "settling" in the territories that Israel captured in the Six-Day War of 1967, equivalents of "colonist" are more common in other languages, like Dutch or German. Similarly, the territory that is being "settled" is described in many different terms, all reflecting, consciously or unconsciously, a certain normative or political position. Religious Jews refer to the West Bank as "Judea and Samaria." Opponents of Israel's presence refer to the "occupied territories," while others prefer the supposedly neutral term "territories." We have tried to find a balance between commonality, factuality, and neutrality, using "occupied territories," "settlers," and "West Bank" – except when we cite individuals and sources using other terminology.

Another challenge was the ever-shifting political context and development, particularly in Israel and the United States, the two most important countries for this study. As we were finishing the manuscript, the issue of annexation took the Israeli political debate by storm. Long considered taboo outside of some radical fringes, annexation of the settlements, or the Jordan Valley, is now openly propagated by the two biggest parties in Israel. At the same time, the United States, under President Donald Trump, shifted decades of foreign policy, when Secretary of State Mike Pompeo recently declared that the United States had concluded that "the establishment of Israeli civilian settlements in the West Bank is not, per se, inconsistent with international law."

By the time you read this book, Netanyahu might no longer be Israeli prime minister and Trump might no longer be US president. But if they still are, what seemed impossible only a year ago could become reality in the near future: the annexation of the (key) settlements in the West Bank, supported by the United States (which will veto any UN Security Council resolutions). Fortunately, our book focuses more on the past and present than on the future, trying to assess and explain the success of the settler movement *up to this point in time*. It does not claim to predict the future but will hopefully help understand it – irrespective of the political fate of Netanyahu and Trump in 2020.

Over the years we have been lucky to receive a tremendous amount of support from many colleagues near and far. Each of them, through his or her academic work, has offered invaluable critiques, feedback, and evaluations of our work. In particular, we would like to thank (in alphabetical order) Shaul Arieli, Lihi Ben-Shitrit, Daphna Canetti, Ehud Eiran, Gilad Hirschberger, David Meyer, Ami Pedahzur, Maoz Rosenthal, Natasha Roth-Rowland, Brent Sasley, Dahlia Scheindlin, Sidney Tarrow, and Yael Yishai. We owe a great debt of gratitude to Mabelle Kretchner, Guy Freedman, and Hannah Broad for their devoted, efficient, and valuable research assistance for this project. For the flaws that remain, obviously we alone are responsible.

We are grateful for the participants who answered the survey questionnaires, and especially the interviewees who were kind enough to invite Sivan to their homes and, more importantly, into their hearts and minds. It was a journey among people of strong convictions and opinions. Each of them provided a unique opportunity to better understand this fascinating yet complex phenomenon. It enabled us to hear and learn only a *little* of so much. This book does not purport to enumerate *all* features and frictions of the Israeli–Palestinian conflict. Rather, as suggested by the late great Israeli writer Amos Oz, it seeks the listening ear of those whose opinions differ from our own.

We have profited from assistance from various institutions, most notably B'tzelem, the Israel Central Bureau of Statistics, and Peace Now. In addition, we are grateful for the generous resources and support provided to us by the Israel Institute; the Lauder School of Government, Diplomacy and Strategy at IDC-Herzliya; and the School of Public and International Affairs of the University of Georgia. These resources enabled us to work on the book and present drafts to colleagues around the world.

More than anyone else, we would like to thank our families for their enduring support during this long and often torturous project. This book could not have been written without the encouragement of and distractions by Itai, Itamar, Joe, Maryann, and Yotam. Their support made our work an arduous journey at times but always a pleasant one. We dedicate this book to the three children born in the time that it was written: Edan, Lior, and Neta.

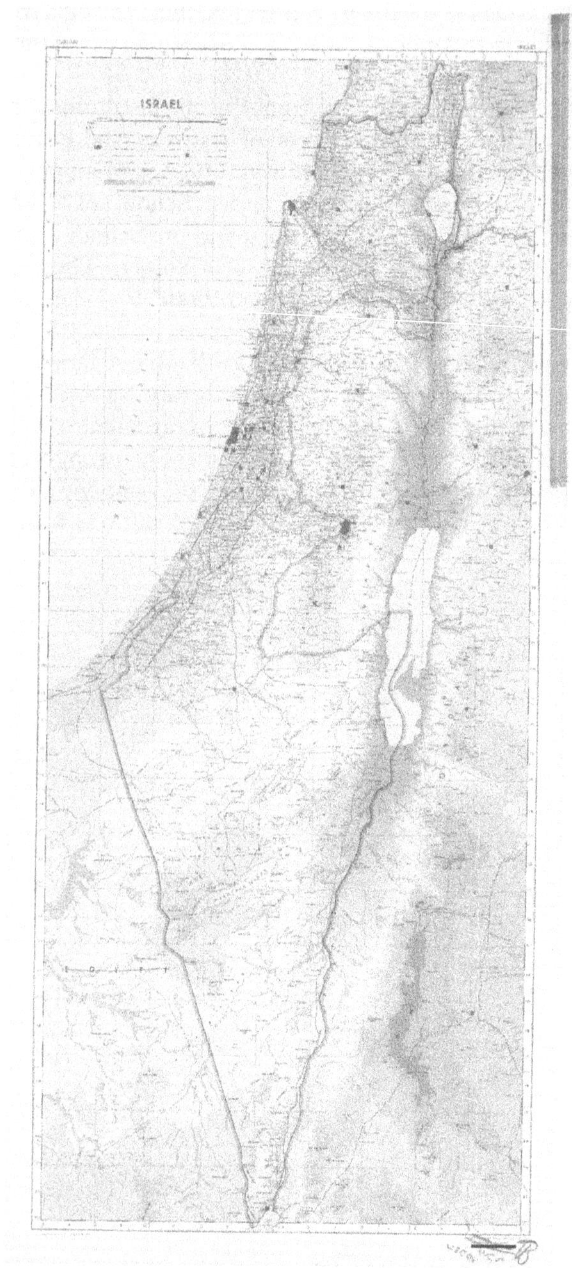

Map of Israel. Source: The Survey of Israel

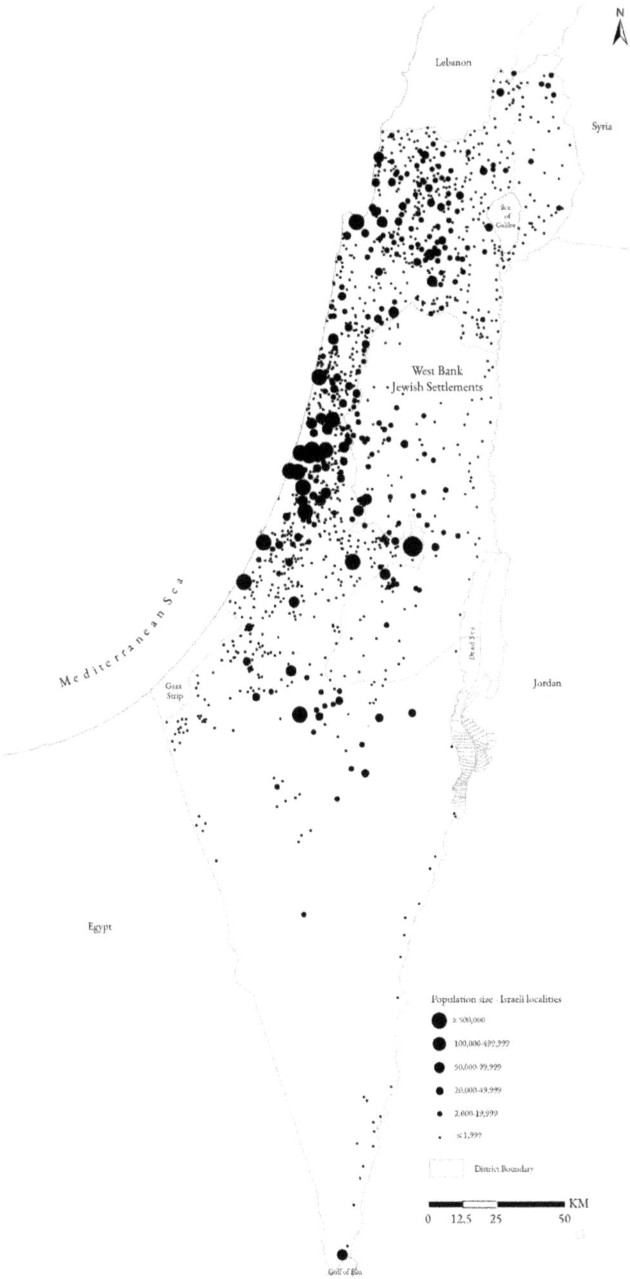

Distribution of localities, by population size 2018. Source: Israel Central Bureau of Statistics

Introduction

> Fifty years ago, the State of Israel was able to return to Judea, Samaria and the Jordan Valley. Fifty years have passed, and we are stronger and certainly much more successful. We will have all the international support when we have the confidence. We need to know that this is our land. We will never return to the '67 borders.
>
> Former Deputy Foreign Minister Tzipi Hotovely (Likud)
> (*Arutz Sheva*, March 28, 2017)

The Israeli settler movement is not only one of the most enduring social movements in recent history, having been active for over fifty years now, but it is also widely seen as one of the most successful. Observers on both sides of the highly polarized issue of Israel's politics in the West Bank agree on little, but all accept that the settler movement is one of the most important actors on this issue. For example, Likud member and then-Knesset Speaker Reuven Rivlin, who has served as President of Israel since 2014, has thanked the settlers for keeping Zionism alive (*Kikar Hashabat*, August 3, 2011), while Labor Party Member of Knesset (the Israeli Parliament) Stav Shaffir has argued that the left-wing camp should learn from the settler movement, because, although accounting for only a tiny percent of the population, they have managed to establish facts on the ground so that the next generation will grow up in a messianic and extremist society (*At Magazine*, August 1, 2018). Meron Benvenisti (2009), a political scientist who was deputy mayor of Jerusalem under Teddy Kollek from 1971 to 1978, is perhaps most blunt in his assessment of the success of the settler movement, arguing that, through its numbers and political savvy, it has already won because there no longer is either a physical or legal distinction between the State of Israel and the occupied territories.

Israel's rule over the West Bank is now in its sixth decade and a solution to the Israeli–Palestinian conflict has never seemed more distant than it does today. As part of his all-or-nothing campaign for the April 2019 elections, Prime Minister Benjamin Netanyahu promised to annex all

Jewish settlements in the West Bank if reelected, then reiterated and elaborated on the promise in the lead-up to the September elections of 2019, adding a plan to annex parts of the Jordan Valley. Rather than showing outrage or shock, leaders of his main opponent party, the recently formed Blue and White (*Kahol Lavan*) political alliance, responded by accusing Netanyahu of stealing their idea, stating that, for Blue and White, the Jordan Valley will remain in Israeli hands.

This once again placed the fight over the future of the occupied territories, over the Jewish settlements, and over relations with the Palestinian population at the top of the Israeli political agenda, where it has been since the late 1960s. The settler movement has played a central role in shaping the discourse around the occupation, even though the settlers are a small minority, never exceeding 5 percent of the total Israeli population. This book aims to provide a first comprehensive assessment and explanation of the success of the settler movement.

The guiding principles of the settler movement are pioneering and settling, the realization of the dream of *Eretz Yisrael* (Greater Israel or Land of Israel), and service to the "Jewish People" by defending the country and promoting its national interest. The standard bearer for these ideas was initially *Gush Emunim* (Bloc of the Faithful), a national-religious movement that operated primarily in the 1970s and provided the main ideological foundation for Jewish settlement across the Green Line – the demarcation line between Israel and its Arab neighbors set out in the 1949 Armistice Agreements following the 1948 Arab–Israeli War, which with some exceptions still functions as the de facto border of the State of Israel.

At the center of the worldview of Gush Emunim was a belief in the holiness of Jewish law and of the Land of Israel, as formulated by Rabbi Abraham Isaac Kook and his son Rabbi Zvi Yehudah Kook,[1] and a belief that the Land of Israel and the Jewish People constitute a single entity, as promised by God. Its vision was to expand the boundaries of the State to those of the biblical Land of Israel, and to build a Third Temple on the site of the destroyed First and Second Temples, which would serve as the national and religious center for the Jewish people. Gush Emunim believed its role was not just to settle the land, but also to instill its pioneering ideology in society and culture at large, and to lead a historic renewal of Zionism, which they believed to have been waning since the 1950s (Aran 1991; Chapman & Benson 2015; Don-Yehiya 1987; Weissbrod 1982).

Along the way, the settler movement has radically increased its numbers, from a couple of hundred in 1967 to almost half a million settlers today.[2] The settler population has also diversified, including now both religious and secular families seeking a better quality of life – often with the active support of the Israeli state, whose substantial subsidization of building and infrastructure across the Green Line stands in contrast to its increasingly neoliberal policies in Israel proper. Through the years, the settlers' struggle has taken many forms and has included various strategies and activities, including illegal ones. Five decades have passed since the first appearance of the modern settler movement in the form of Gush Emunim, and since then, articles and books have been written about the subject, and discussions have taken place in varied public and academic arenas. But many key questions regarding the settlers, the patterns of their struggle throughout the years, and, specifically, their actual impact on the Israeli political agenda and policies in the West Bank have remained largely unanswered.

Our book aims to make three important contributions to the academic literature. First, it is the first study to systematically and empirically assess the political success of the Israeli settler movement. Second, it develops an original and comprehensive theoretical framework to assess and explain political success of social movements in general. Third, it broadens the study of social movements by focusing on the Israeli settler movement, which is atypical in at least three ways: it is (a) a longstanding social movement, with (b) a (radical) right-wing ideology, which operates in (c) a non-Western context.[3]

Structure of the Book

In the first chapter, we discuss the broader academic literature on social movements, focusing particularly on the issue of assessing and measuring success, and present our original and comprehensive theoretical framework. Chapter 2 provides a historical background and contemporary political context to our case study, the Israeli settler movement, by laying out the history of the settlement process in Israel in general, and the West Bank and Gaza Strip in particular, as well as the national and international political context in which the settler movement has operated since its inception. In Chapter 3 we introduce the Israeli settler movement itself. After a concise history, and an overview of the prime ideological currents, we describe the movement in terms of our theoretical framework, most notably the three different branches and their main modes of action.

In Chapter 4 we assess the success of the Israeli settler movement, focusing specifically on the link between aspects of success and types of political arena. Here, we show how success in terms of policy is achieved mainly within the arena of the state, in terms of resources in all three realms but primarily in the state, and in terms of support in all three realms but predominantly society. Chapter 5 focuses on explanations for success, in which we delve further into the theoretical connection between the different branches and repertoires of actions, with institutions focusing on moderate actions (collaboration with and capture of the state), networks employing all three repertoires but with radical actions at the center, and influencers focusing also on moderate actions (capture of the state and influencing society).

In Chapters 6 and 7 we address the assessment and explanation of success (and failure) in a holistic manner, which allows us to focus on the *interactions* between the different branches and actions. The first of the two chapters addresses an example of settler movement *success*, in the form of the settlement of Ariel, one of the largest and most normalized in the West Bank. The next chapter focuses on one of the most damaging examples of *failure*, that is, the disengagement from Gaza, which helps us identify the limitations to the successful mobilization strategies of the settler movement.

Chapter 8 concludes the book with a summary of our original theoretical framework, of the overall assessment of the success of the Israeli settler movement, and of the explanations for its success. It ends with a discussion of how our framework and study contribute to the broader literatures on both social movements and Israeli politics.

1 Theoretical Framework

A fundamental aspect of the study of social movements is the analysis of their success. However, before one can engage in such an assessment, we must first understand what success means in the context of social movements. For decades, scholars of collective action have paid only scant attention to the outcomes and political success of movement activities (Bosi et al. 2016; Giugni 2008), a fact that may be explained, at least in part, by the conceptual and methodological difficulties inherent in the task of explaining success (Amenta & Young 1999; Earl 2000).

A large part of the academic literature on social movement success is deeply intertwined with related – but not identical – terms, such as *impact* (Burstein & Linton 2002; Escobar et al. 2018), *influence* (Cress & Snow 2000; Ganz & Soule 2015; Olzak & Soule 2009), *consequences* (Amenta et al. 2010; Lyman 2016), and *outcomes* (Amenta et al. 2018; Andrews 2004; Bosi & Uba 2009; Diani 1997; Earl 2013; Giugni 2007; Thomas et al. 2018; Tilly 1999). Methodological difficulties include the problem of causal attribution, the small number of subjects, time reference and effect stability, goal adaptation and subjectivity, interrelated effects, and indirect and unintended outcomes (see Bosi et al. 2016; Giugni 1998; McAdam 1989; Rucht & Ohlemacher 1992). Finally, one of the key challenges of the field is that most insights have been derived from the US context, leaving unclear how these insights can be applied to other national and regional contexts, including outside the Western world (Giugni 2008: 1583). In short, there is no scholarly consensus on how to define or measure social movement success (Alvarez et al. 2018; Bosi & Uba 2009).

Despite a still relatively limited, albeit rapidly growing, number of scholars who explicitly and systematically address the success of social movements, the field provides valuable works and useful insights into the question, offering means to assess when and how movements influence the political process and its outcomes (see Alvarez et al. 2018; Amenta 2014; Giugni 1998, 2007; McAdam 2017; Roggeband & Klandermans 2017; Uba 2009; Yates 2015). We aim to integrate, systematize, and elaborate upon these insights to construct a comprehensive theoretical framework for assessing and explaining social movement success and to test it on the specific case of the Israeli settler movement.

This chapter starts with a discussion of how the literature on social movements addresses the issue of success. After identifying the key frameworks and variables for assessing and explaining political success, we present our own theoretical framework. We argue that political success of social movements is multifaceted, encompassing policies, resources, and support, and is best analyzed through the individual contributions of the three essentially separate but intimately connected *branches* of a social movement (institutions, networks, and influencers), each of which specializes in a specific *repertoire of actions* (combining moderate, radical, or extreme actions) and targets specific *political arenas* (state, civil society, and society at both the national and international levels). In the following sections we present the various parts of our theoretical framework.

1.1 Defining Social Movement Success

Conceptualizing success in relation to social movements is no simple task. The range of outcomes attributed to social movements varies widely, from "state-level policy decisions to the expansion of a movement's social capital to changes in participants' biographies" (Cress & Snow 2000: 1064). Most research in this realm "focuses on the determinants of policy outcomes and ... is geared towards assessing whether, when, and how movements influence the policy process and its outcomes" (Giugni 2008: 1583). Many scholars offer broader definitions, which extend beyond policy outcomes to include attainment of tangible benefits that meet the organization's goals; formal acceptance by political elites; legitimization of the movement's goals; and transformation of the individual or group consciousness (Bell 2014; Jenkins & Klandermans 1995; Kolb 2007). In all these cases, success can be whole or partial, gauged by the attainment of some, but not all, of the movement's stated objectives (Gamson 1975). Still another approach conceptualizes success as the movement's survivability and longevity, in contrast to material gains or policy change (Meyer 2004; Van Dyke & Amos 2017).

More recently, social movement scholars have attempted to rectify the subjective nature of measuring success by designating distinct categories for measurement. Specifically, the means by which the social movement achieves its outcomes can be understood and conceptualized in the context of three sets of outcomes identified in the social movement literature: (a) attainment of goals (also known as policy success); (b) mobilization of resources; and (c) acceptance by society. In this book, we adopt this multifaceted approach to political success, focusing on both institutional and noninstitutional changes and outcomes.

The primary indicator of political success is whether the social movement manages to attain its stated goals, in whole or in part (e.g., Banaszak 1996; Bosi et al. 2016; Burstein et al. 1995; Kitschelt 1986; Kriesi 1995; Rochon & Mazmanian 1993). Thus, the first outcome type defines success in terms of *policy* gains and changes (Amenta & Caren 2004; Klandermans 2016). Most contemporary scholars of social movements working within the US context analyze to what extent the goals of social movements and advocacy organizations are realized in Congress through policy change and the development and funding of programs (Burstein & Linton 2002; Gamson 1975). These institutional changes include what Felix Kolb (2007) has termed "substantive change" – that is, changes in the political agenda and public policy, and/or changes in political institutions and the policymaking process.[1] Scholars have also distinguished between short-term gains (changes in political decisions), medium-term gains (major changes in policy and in its bureaucratic enforcement and implementation), and long-term gains (changes in the distribution of public goods) (Jenkins 1982).

A second set of outcomes treats success as a measure of a movement's ability to garner *resources*. The literature generally focuses on two specific, tangible types of resources: members and money (e.g., Alvarez et al. 2018; Amenta & Caren 2013; McAdam 2017; Thomas et al. 2018). In a democratic system, mobilizing relatively large numbers of committed people is often necessary to win new collective benefits. Resource mobilization theory (RMT) is a useful tool to assess the success of social movement organizations in these terms, because it shows how organizational resources are translated into concrete, quantifiable gains for the organization's adherents. It holds that successful social movement organizations – that is, those that maximize their resources – also contribute to the sustainability of their internal organizational structure by realizing their purpose as a function of collective action.

The third set of outcomes measures success in terms of *support* – that is, whether, and to what extent, the social movement and its goals are accepted by society, at both the elite and mass levels (e.g., Amenta & Caren 2013; Luders 2010; Melucci 1989; Staggenborg 2015). There is evidence that the success of social movements can be significantly enhanced when they seek other political groups as allies (Jenkins & Klandermans 1995; Klandermans 2016). Such alliances provide access to elites and enhance the movement's image in society (Giugni et al. 1999). For instance, social movements benefit substantially from obtaining the support of a major political party (Jenkins & Klandermans 1995: 289). Such connections not only bolster the movement's image but also improve outcomes in the first two areas (resource mobilization and policy change) – for example, by increasing the movement's inclusion in the national discourse and in political circles, by encouraging officials to aid its constituents, and by increasing its general leverage over political processes.

William Gamson (1990) offers important insights into the process of institutional acceptance, a modified version of "inclusion," whereby a challenger is recognized as a legitimate representative of a previously underrepresented constituency, which can lead to collective benefits. In other words, the political system becomes biased in favor of the movement. Gamson distinguishes between three categories of political influence: participatory gains, material gains, and discursive gains. Participatory gains refer to the challenger's acceptance by the political elite and the latter's recognition of the social movement as a player within the political sphere. Material gains denote the elite's acceptance of new policies promoted by the efforts of the social movement. Finally, discursive gains reflect the elite's acceptance of the movement's "narrative and social orientations" and the assimilation of these cultural ideologies or opinions into the collective consciousness (Khalfa 2009: 28–29).

Although the abovementioned theoretical framework emphasizes the differences between each category, success is also affected by interactions between the various factors. That is to say, the parameters that define the success of a social movement are inextricably intertwined, with one measure affecting the outcomes of the others. We acknowledge that the different dimensions of success (policies, resources, support) are not exhaustive, but we also believe that even this relatively simple framework, which broadens the conceptualization of success beyond policy gains, can help uncover important processes and determinants of social movement achievements.

1.2 The Three Branches of Social Movements

The organizational infrastructure of a social movement ultimately determines how groups within it best survive and empower themselves, and, more importantly, the degree to which this involves the pursuit of political objectives. Yet most studies of the political effectiveness of social movements ignore variation in the achievements of different organizational subgroups and goals.

We treat social movements not just as unitary actors but also as pluralistic entities composed of institutions, networks, and influencers, with organizational objectives that may be complementary or contradictory. We argue that social movement scholars should look more closely at the impact of organizational diversity on various movement-related outcomes (see also Clemens & Minkoff 2004; Taylor & Van Dyke 2004) and, specifically, at how a *range* of mobilizing structures, including decentralized and informal as well as centralized and formal ones, affects the strategies and the success of social movements (Staggenborg 2013).

Historically, the nexus of organizational scholarship and social movement theory has been a rich area of inquiry, and each field has learned a great deal from the other. Social movement researchers have borrowed insights from organizational ecologists to help explain the organizational forms and network dynamics of social movements. Likewise, scholars of organizations have drawn on social movement theory to describe how movements impact basic organizational processes. However, as Sarah Soule (2013) has recently asserted, this relationship has become lopsided, with social movement scholarship moving away from explicitly utilizing organizational scholarship (see also Caniglia & Carmin 2005; Clemens & Minkoff 2004; Minkoff & McCarthy 2005). Social movement scholars have become more interested in loosely structured networks of social movement participants, who seem to deliberately eschew formal organizations (Roggeband & Duyvendak 2013). In reality, however, "social movements [assume] various organizational forms ... including hierarchy, decentralized networks, and a spontaneous, leaderless form without much organization at all" (Campbell 2005: 67).

Scholarship suggests that contemporary social movements are likely to be diverse, with informal networks of activists coexisting alongside more formal organizations. How this manifests in the real world is still largely an open question. How does such heterogeneity affect the movement's ability to act in different public spheres? Are movements with organizational diversity more successful? Are they more likely to be repressed? In general, it is assumed that social movements comprised of diverse groups, with multiple and sometimes competing leaders or centers of influence, and with some form of integration across organizations, are better tasked to achieve the goals of the movement (Gerlach & Hine 1970). However, while social movement scholars assert that organizational diversity is important to movement processes and outcomes, very few have actually studied this empirically.

We know that some degree of organization is a "structural necessity [enabling the] step up from loosely-related protest events to sustained collective action, one of the distinguishing features of social movements" (Klandermans 2001: 273). A movement, if it is to be sustained for any length of time, requires leadership, administrative structure, incentives for participation, and means for acquiring resources and support – in short, some sort of organization (McAdam & Scott 2005). However, as argued by Dieter Rucht (2013), the generic notion of "structure" in social movements needs to be unpacked.

Social movements are complex entities, composed of many organizations and agents pursuing different strategies (Della Porta & Diani 1999; Gamson 1990; Klandermans 2016). These can vary dramatically in their mobilizing configurations, the number and strength of the actors they incorporate, and the extent to which they are coordinated (McCarthy 1996). According to RMT, a social movement consists of an array of interrelated *individuals*, social *networks*, and formal or informal *institutions* acting together in a coordinated way to achieve some shared goals (Pagnucco 1996; Shannon 2011). Importantly, groups choose organizational configurations that reflect and support their actions, behaviors, and identities (Rohlinger 2002; Staggenborg 2015).

Social movement organizations are organized elements within social movements. They are social structures characterized by both internal divisions of labor, where different organization members work in tandem to reach the organization's goals, and external divisions of labor, where different organizations take responsibility for different subgoals, strategies, and tactics (Della Porta & Diani 1999; Edwards & McCarthy 2004; Morris & Staggenborg 2004). It is assumed that social movements are most viable when they encompass a number of organizations fulfilling varied functions and dealing with different strategic possibilities (Zald & Ash 1966). However, despite attempts to create a sense of solidarity and mutual aims, social movements are seldom internally cohesive, with a range of affiliated organizations working in tandem toward the same ends. Instead, they tend to fracture internally along a variety of axes (Gupta 2002). Therefore, rather than one homogeneous unit for analysis, we shift our focus toward an analysis of the social movement as a multifaceted "network of networks" by highlighting the various formal and informal groups within it. Specifically, to gain greater insight into the structure of the movement, to capture the process that links resources, tactics, and political ties, and to achieve the movement's goals, an analysis of the main *branches* of the movement is essential.

Individuals and organizations can be categorized into three branches according to their organizational structure, ranging from strongly hierarchical and formalized organizations to extremely decentralized and informal circles of friends: the centralized branch (*institutions*), the decentralized branch (*networks*), and the individual branch (*influencers*). The centralized branch consists of highly structured and institutionalized organizations, often subsidized by the state and sometimes even officially connected to the state. The decentralized branch comprises a broad range of informal and formal groups, which can be subsidized but are clearly delineated from the state. Finally, the individual branch consists of prominent influencers, who can be members of groups or organizations within the other two branches but whose actions are primarily individual and their relevance is based on their own personal reputation rather than that of the group(s) they belong to – one can think of athletes, intellectuals, movie stars, pundits, singers, and so on.

Each branch has a specific role to fulfill within the broader social movement. The key role of the centralized branch (institutions) is collaborative – that is, working with(in) the state to further the social movement's goals. By contrast, the decentralized branch (networks) is figuratively positioned in opposition to the state. Its main role is to apply pressure, either pushing the state to advance the social movement's goals or pushing back against state actions that could impede them. Finally, the main role of the individual branch (influencers) is to influence elite and public opinion, primarily through the media, to become more supportive of the social movement and its goals. It should be clear that these branches are fluid and dynamic; the categories are neither mutually exclusive nor collectively exhaustive. The relationships between the different branches can vary. Influencers, networks, and institutions may coordinate and even collaborate, either on an ad hoc basis or in a more structured way.

The Israeli settler movement operates within a multiform, or polymorphic, framework – that is, it consists of interrelated institutions, networks, and influencers who share the common goal of the settlement enterprise but disagree on the best means to achieve this. The configurations and interactions of the different types of actors create their own order rather than having an organizational order imposed upon them. Hence, rather than developing a strict typology of mutually exclusive and distinct categories, we discuss the three key branches of social movements and examine their main areas of activity and the ways they seek to gain political influence.

1.2.1 Institutions

Resource mobilization theories of collective action have long highlighted the dominant role of formal, centralized organizational structures (Olzak 1989). Ironically, however, leading proponents of RMT, when defining social movements, did not directly refer to organizations as a constitutive element but rather spoke generally of structural relations within such movements. A good example is Rucht's (2013) description of structure as a pattern of more or less stable relationships within and between various elements of a larger entity.

Social movement organizations are formal groups that mobilize human and material resources and activate and coordinate strategic action within the broader social movement (Smith 2005). They vary in their degree of *formalization*, or the presence of formally defined roles, rules, and criteria of membership, and *centralization*, or the degree to which decision-making power is concentrated (Gamson 1990). Specifically, institutions, defined in a narrow way, are usually associated with characteristics such as formal membership criteria, a clear division of roles and internal functions, a mission statement, and legal status (Rucht 2013: 170). The relationship between institution leaders and members is formalized and can be expressed vertically or hierarchically, such that the lines of command are clear and the roles are well defined and handed down by the leadership (Willems & Jegers 2012).

The chief benefit of a centralized organizational structure is that it can broadly maintain the goals and momentum of the social movement even when the economic or political climate may not be favorable or hospitable to other organization types (Staggenborg 1988, 2015). Furthermore, institutions are usually more accessible to outsiders, especially when they have newsletters, offices, spokespeople, and websites. This means they are better placed to fundraise, which ensures the continuation of the organization and increases awareness of its aims. Although many contemporary social movements eschew formal organizations, institutions are far from moribund. Several studies have shown that they remain a vital mode of organization within social movements of varying sorts (Earl 2010; Polletta et al. 2013; Soule 2013; Vermeulen 2006; Walker et al. 2011).

1.2.2 Networks

Informal, loosely connected groups exist side by side with institutions within a multi-organizational field (Diani 2013). Alberto Melucci (1989: 71) describes movements as consisting of "submerged networks" that emerge from time to time for collective action, while Mario Diani (1992: 13) sees movements as "networks of informal interaction" among individuals and groups that engage in political or cultural conflict and share a collective identity. Networks have become the prime mode and structure of organization within social movements (Castells 1996).

A number of scholars posit the idea of a shift from the dominance of formal organizations to more informal, sometimes temporary or issue-specific networks (Bauman 2000; Dalton 2008; Roggeband & Duyvendak 2013; Schudson 2006; Zukin et al. 2006). The argument is that contemporary activists are likely to prefer diffuse and decentralized networks over formal organizations (Duyvendak & Hurenkamp 2004; Taylor 2000). They explicitly reject a hierarchal structure of governance, instead creating alternative structures that offer participants many access points. In such networks, so the theory goes, decisions are made spontaneously, in contrast to the top-down, elite-driven manner predominating in social movement institutions.

These so-called light communities are informal, open, and temporary, compared with traditional organizations, resulting in loose ties, short-term engagements, and low levels of identification (Roggeband & Duyvendak 2013: 97). They are often characterized by interactions that are flexible in both form and content, with spontaneous exchanges of information, resources, and so on replacing formal divisions of labor and with ad hoc or short-term coordination by operational equals replacing an overarching hierarchy (Diani 2013; Rucht 2013). This pattern of autonomous structures frees the collective actors to a large extent from the cumbersome "coalition work" (Staggenborg 1986: 387) that characterizes many other groups. However, sometimes these networks become internally differentiated, establishing committees, subgroups, task forces, and so on, which focus on specific functions, thereby forming extremely complex structures. In addition, while these nonhierarchical structures sometimes compete for scarce resources, they also may fall naturally into an implicit division of labor, reducing competition between them and allowing for more fruitful cooperation.

Networks provide the channels through which social movement frames, repertoires, and sometimes even triggers are diffused to a wider population of potential participants (Andrews & Biggs 2006; Hedström et al. 2000; Krinsky & Crossley 2014; Oliver & Myers 2003). The decentralized networks often rely on grassroots outreach and volunteers, as opposed to the more formalized relationships in institutions. Indeed, they may attract more participants than institutions do, because the costs (financial, social, time) of engagement in these networks are much lower than in institutions, which may entail dues-paying, regular meetings, and other commitments (Roggeband & Duyvendak 2013). Furthermore, decentralized networks may result in better deliberative practices, more innovative tactics, and political leaders who are more representative and accountable (Polletta 2002). Some even argue that this type of mobilizing structure may be harder for governments to suppress and may be more successful at infiltrating the national consciousness and discourse.

1.2.3 Influencers

The last branch is the least well-known and understood. Influencers are individual actors who work outside formal institutions and hierarchical leadership structures (Phillips 2011), and sometimes even outside the loose networks described earlier. Some influencers create their own loose networks using online forums, blogs, and open databases (Roggeband & Duyvendak 2013). While social movements have always had influencers – think of Harry Belafonte and the US civil rights movement – social media has amplified both the number and reach of influencers. For example, when international pop star Ariana Grande retweets an anti–animal-abuse tweet by People for the Ethical Treatment of Animals (PETA), she not only reaches a much larger audience (in December 2019 she had an estimated 68.4 million followers on Twitter versus PETA's 1.1 million) but also a very different audience (e.g., younger, less political).

While influencers can be linked to movement organizations, be they formal or informal, their political significance does not derive from the organization. Rather, they act as independent individuals, or small groups of people (often spousal teams or a few friends), using their individual reputation and skills to advance the goals of the movement. The most important influencers are celebrities, such as actors, authors, journalists, singers, and sports personalities, whose personal audiences often reach far beyond that of the social movement. A second group of influencers are individuals and groups who work together to create groups, including businesses that promote the movement's ideology and goals. Finally, a third group includes influencers in key state positions, from generals to judges, who do not represent social movement organizations, but do support the movement and its goals, in word and, often also, deed.

1.3 Repertoire of Actions

Few social movements aim to fulfill only one solitary political goal. Similarly, few employ only one type of strategy to achieve their goals. Social movements make use of a broad range of actions, the so-called action repertoire, to further their goals. This also applies to the different branches of the social movement. Given the various roles that they perform within the broader movement, each branch specializes in a different set of actions from the broader action repertoire. Branches often apply more than one action strategy at any given time. In some cases, such multifaceted or "hybrid" strategies (Burstein & Linton 2002) involve both collaborative and confrontative elements.

Scholars have devoted much attention to determining how different *modes of collective action* have a positive or negative influence on the success of a social movement. Doug McAdam and Yang Su, for example, identify two competing theoretical models that outline the relationship between the mechanisms employed by collective action groups and policy change. The first is through *threat or disruption*, which social movement organizations use to facilitate change by causing disorder in the public realm so as to "achieve bargaining leverage" (2002: 23). The second is *persuasion*, in which advocates of social change try to achieve their goals by affecting public opinion. In democratic systems, expression of opposition is an inherent tool for a population that wishes to protest a policy it considers unfair or unjust.

Democracies offer their citizens a variety of means to express their discontent under the protection of the law, such as petitions, demonstrations, and lobbying. This type of activism, often termed *moderate* (or conventional), refers to actions sanctioned by laws and regulations in relation to a contentious policy issue (Shuman et al. 2016). These tactics emphasize working within the political framework and a "willingness to bargain and compromise with opponents" (Karapin 2010: 46). Overall, participation in moderate opposition has increased in most Western countries since the 1970s. This trend can be explained by the growing acceptance of moderate forms of action (notably nonviolent protest), on the part of governmental authorities, free access to legitimate means of participation (which were not available in the past), and familiarity with conventional forms of collective action (Tarrow 1998: 95–98).

Yet moderate activism may seem futile for a population determined to stop a policy from being implemented by any means necessary. Sometimes, activists are tempted to engage in unlawful behavior, which entails acts that are against the law and are intended to affect public policy by way of illegitimate (threat of) force (Kaase & Marsh 1979). Unlawful activism varies in the degree to which it violates the law and can range from relatively mild infractions, such as blocking roads, to extreme acts of violence, sabotage, and terrorism (e.g., Hirsch-Hoefler et al. 2016; McAdam & Tarrow 2000; Tausch et al. 2011; Wright et al. 1990).

It is therefore useful to differentiate not only between legal and illegal actions, but also between violent and nonviolent actions. Within the tactical repertoire, scholars identify three broad types of collective action – moderate and legal, illegal but nonviolent, and illegal and violent – which they refer to under various sets of names (Taylor & Van Dyke 2004; Tarrow 1998; Wang & Soule 2016).[2] We largely follow this distinction, but prefer the following terminology for the trilogy: moderate, radical, and extreme. Moderate activism, that is, actions that are legal and nonviolent, was already discussed before, so we now focus only on radical and extreme actions.

Radical action is illegal but nonviolent. Roger Karapin (2010: 46) describes this type of action as "the disruption of political or economic routines in nonviolent ways in order to get public attention, gain public support, influence elites, seize control of important resources, spur broad policy debates, and gain policy reforms." Radical activities may include blockades, housing takeovers, sit-ins, and illegal encampments. Such actions can be taken in response to an organization's lack of resources or simply because of a belief that they are the best means to achieve the movement's goals (Cross 2013; McCarthy & Zald 1977; Cloward & Piven 1977; Tarrow 1998).

The last category, *extreme* action, is both illegal and violent. There is some debate within the literature over what exactly constitutes "violence." For some, violence includes a broad range of actions, including (threats of) physical attacks on both human beings and property (Taylor & Van Dyke 2004). For others, violence should only be used for (threats of) harm to human beings, not properties (or innate objects). We agree with this stricter approach to violence, and therefore categorize property destruction (including arson and vandalism) as radical actions, and only consider (threats of) physical attacks on human beings as violence and therefore as extreme actions.

That said, the boundaries are not always so clear, as certain acts of vandalism can have (intended or unintended) threats to the safety of human beings – for example, a Molotov cocktail at a car (with someone in it) or an arson attack on someone's house (even if the person is not at home at that moment). Sometimes the attack is clearly aimed at a property but includes a threat to a person (e.g., a note at the scene that reads "next time we will wait till you at home"). This is the case, for example, with the bulk of actions that constitute the contested term of "ecoterrorism" (Hirsch-Hoefler & Mudde 2014).

The repertoire of actions forms a pyramid (see figure 1.1), with a base comprising legal political actions (*moderate*), a middle layer of illegal but nonviolent actions (*radical*), and an apex of illegal and violent actions (*extreme*) (see also McCauley & Moskalenko 2017; Moskalenko & McCauley 2009). The more extreme the action, the less activists and organizations participate. For the great majority of activists and organizations, the use of illegal tactics, and particularly the use of violence, is a red line that cannot be crossed. In fact, very few people in social movements – usually 1 or 2 percent – endorse or engage in extreme activities (Barnes et al. 1979; Weisburd 1989). This observation affirms the well-known participation paradox: the more intensive a form of political participation,

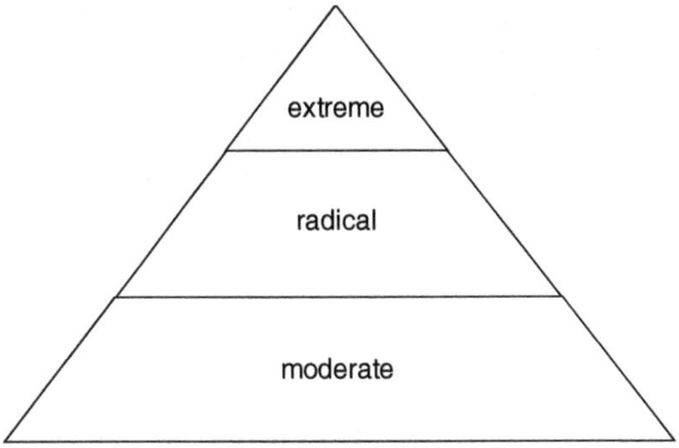

Figure 1.1 Repertoire of actions

in terms of the risks and resources it involves, the more skewed its distribution across the population (Verba et al. 1995).

Agencies of collective action, that is, organizational structures through which people commonly mobilize for political expression (Norris 2004), are important for explaining modes of action and opposition. Studies have found that the type of organizational structure can have direct implications for tactical decisions and, in accordance, the mode of collective action employed. That is, aspects of an organization's formal or informal structure may place limits on the use of some tactics and increase the likelihood of others. In particular, in social movements dominated by networks, involving loose coalitions that are relatively flat and horizontal, activists may be exposed to a range of political ideas that they would not otherwise encounter – and as such, are at greater risk of becoming radicalized (Della Porta & Haupt 2012). Accordingly, while institutions are more likely to use a moderate, nonconfrontational repertoire of actions, which often engage directly with the state and remain within the law, networks are more likely to use a more confrontational, that is, radical or even extreme, repertoire of actions (Della-Porta & Diani 1999; Edwards & McCarthy 2004; Tilly 1995; Verba & Nie 1972).

The repertoire of actions used by different bodies within a social movement can also be affected by factionalism. Social movements, especially when they grow and expand, are likely to fracture into distinct groups and subgroups, which may disagree on both conceptual – for instance how to define the problem – and practical issues – including the actions they believe can legitimately be employed to achieve the movement's goals (Balser 1997; Blee & Taylor 2002). Different subgroups can also part ways because of bureaucratization and professionalization, produced by the need for skills in accounting, and fundraising and lobbying (McCarthy

& Zald 1977: 1234). These practical exigencies can give rise to different worldviews as well as differences in the modes of action considered legitimate. Hence, a social movement may have a moderate camp, which aims to reform the social system using actions drawn from the repertoire of traditional bureaucracies, alongside a radical camp, which strives to restructure rather than reform the social system (Wrenn 2016: 2).

1.4 Political Arena

The success of the settler movement is often stated without much knowledge about what the movement has actually achieved. One reason for this may be that success on the part of social movements tends to be defined rather narrowly, in terms of whether a given action influences key decision makers – or, in the case of the settler movement, in terms of settler numbers and settlement counts. Another reason may be that we tend to judge the success of social movements based on a biased "sample," with both researchers and the media focusing on actions and movements that are unusually visible (Gamson 1975, 1990). Moreover, scholars use different reference points, including standards and case selection, and often overstate the scope of their findings. The result is that most studies represent only part of the story.

In fact, social movements are generally neither wholly successful nor entirely unsuccessful. Rather, they negotiate their course through assorted ups and downs in a variety of arenas. Hence, only by examining outcomes in a range of arenas can we reach a realistic understanding and assessment of the success of a social movement. Following Marco Giugni and his collaborators (1999), we suggest that success should be assessed in three interlinked arenas: the state, civil society, and the public – each has both a national and an international dimension. Gains in each realm contribute in some way to the success of the broader movement, and actors that fail in one arena can still prosper overall.

We challenge contemporary research to offer a more precise understanding of the interaction between these three realms by unpacking more specific relationships and processes of influence. By doing so, we also hope to strengthen the recent engagement between scholars who study social movements, civil society, and institutional state organizations (see Weber & King 2014).

1.4.1 The State

The first political arena that social movements try to influence is the state. The state apparatus comprises various sets of actors, including governments, bureaucracies, and the judiciary at the supranational, national, and subnational levels (Meyer & Reyes 2010). Social movements that gain access to the policymaking process can successfully influence policies through formal political institutions (Andrews 2001; Zald 2017). The state is also crucial for the access to resources it provides. These resources can manifest themselves in many ways, including concrete assets, such as financial support granted as part of the political process, and more figurative resources, such as legitimacy by way of favorable political conditions (Cress & Snow 2000; Edwards & Marullo 1995; Snow et al. 2004).

Political opportunity plays an integral role in resource mobilization, allowing social movements to bolster their impact and resources (including financial resources, benefits, and manpower) by leveraging political conditions to obtain support from the state or institutional actors (Amenta et al. 1992; Cloward & Piven 1977; Goldstone & Tilly 2001; Lipset & Marks 2000; Skocpol 1992). Thus, social movements must form coalitions with members of the political establishment (civil servants and other appointed or elected officeholders), winning support from within the establishment by adopting organizational forms that fit current political conditions, or even becoming part of the establishment itself (Roggeband & Klandermans 2017; Snow et al. 2004; Tilly 1975).

Social movements can influence state bureaucracies through different mechanisms, ranging from open collaboration to open opposition. Given that opposition is inherently reactive, this path will mainly prevent things from happening. But social movements can also use threats of opposition to pressure the state into implementing certain policies (Quadagno 1992). Collaboration can be both active and reactive, aimed at furthering or preventing policies. Theoretically, there are different levels of collaboration, depending on the level of openness and shared purpose between the movement and the state. For example, in the case of infiltration, or "capture," social movements try to influence states covertly, for instance, by changing the institutional environment through the policies and regulations that affect organizations. In contrast, in the case of co-optation, it is often states that try to covertly influence the social movement.

Social movement institutions are most likely to collaborate with or be co-opted by the state for at least three reasons. First, their organizational rationale mirrors that of the state. Indeed, the defining characteristic of institutions is the subjugation of the individual to the impersonal rational rules and hierarchies of bureaucratic rule (Weber & King 2014: 487). Second, states often require a high level of organization to implement their policies. And third, the state is one of the few actors that can guarantee institutions the resources they need to sustain themselves. In sharp contrast, networks are more likely to work through pressure, that is, through (the threat of) opposition, mostly directed at forcing the state to (not) implement certain policies (Wapner 1995; Yates 2015). Influencers, for their part, are uniquely suited to infiltrate, for example, as bureaucrats or educators. However, whether through infiltration or co-optation, influencers will often have only limited impact in the state arena, as they can only influence a small subsection of the larger project – apart from some very highly placed bureaucrats.

Success in the state arena can range in importance from the most insignificant, such as winning "a specific state policy decision with no long-term implications for the flow of benefits to the group," to the highest realization of group goals, with actions that provide "continuing leverage over political processes" (Giugni et al. 1999: 31). In fact, there are many possible manifestations of "success," even in terms of a social movement's policy impact. For example, some scholars examine passed legislation (Burstein 1979), while others measure public spending on a particular policy (Giugni 2004). One useful measure by which to score the success of social movements with respect to the state is whether the state provides movement actors with open access, that is, openings in the political opportunity structure (Tarrow 1994).

As noted by David Meyer and Daisy Reyes (2010: 221), "political opportunities affect the social movement's potential to mobilize, advance particular claims, cultivate alliances, employ particular strategies and tactics, and influence mainstream institutional politics and policy." Such political opportunities include (1) ties and collaboration with state actors; (2) access to the electoral and judicial processes; (3) socialization of citizens, most notably through the educational system; and (4) budgetary subsidies made in response to the movement's professed needs. Increased political opportunities are thus both an outcome measure for social movement success, and an antecedent of it. Indeed, gaining access to the policy process is the most effective way for social movement organizations to have an impact on policy outcomes, because authorities are often more willing to offer inclusion in the process than they are to accept social movement demands for policy change (Rochon & Mazmanian 1993). However, specific characteristics of social movements shape their ability to achieve favorable policies, and to influence institutional priorities and resources (Harrison 2016: 536).

Characteristics of the state bodies with which social movements interact can also influence the relationship and, therefore, their impact on policy outcomes. The literature identifies three vital intraorganizational factors that shape how organizations implement social movement policies: (1) ideological commitment to movement policies – whether relevant staff exhibit a "pro- or anti-movement orientation" (Zald et al. 2005: 275); (2) organizational capacity to respond to movement demands; and (3) surveillance and sanctions that compel compliance. State bureaucracies are shaped not only by rational decisions about efficiency but also by norms, shared meanings, and pressure from movements and politicians (DiMaggio & Powell 1983). Thus, to fully explain social movement policy outcomes further, the beliefs of state representatives – and how they apply them – are key variables.

There is evidence that social movement activities that respond to the electoral concerns of elected officials can have a particularly potent impact. Officeholders are most likely to pay attention to groups whose members vote and participate in politics. In accordance, social movement organizations are most likely to influence policy when "they change their activities in ways that attract legislators' attention, and when the attention-getting activities in turn lead legislators to worry that if they do not respond to the organizations' demands, their chances of reelection will suffer" (Burstein & Linton 2002: 387; see also Amenta & Poulsen 1996). Another effective tactic is to provide elected officials with information and resources (e.g., members, money, and media access) relevant to the officials' reelection (Lohmann 1993).

In this book, we will analyze the role of the settler movement and its supporters within state organizations, and in particular in the administration of the occupied territories. In doing so, we will consider both the *direct* and *indirect* impact of the settler movement on the state bureaucracy. The former refers to the organizations' impact on the final stage of legislative activity, when policy changes are, or are not, enacted into law. The latter refers to organizations' success in getting issues on the political agenda, influencing how issues are framed, providing information, and affecting public opinion. We thereby distinguish between the overall long-term goal of the settler movement (i.e., the realization of *Eretz Yisrael*) and more concrete short- and medium-term goals (such as the building, expansion, legalization and protection of concrete settlements).

1.4.2 Civil Society

The state is not the sole antagonist or contested site for social movements. They also operate outside the formal political system, targeting other forms of authority (Baron 2003; Bartley 2007; Weber & King 2014). Thus, social movement scholars have begun to expand their domain of interest, turning from an exclusive concern with "public politics" to various forms of "private politics," that is, means and modes of interorganizational conflict resolution in which public authorities have only a limited role (De Bakker et al. 2013: 576; see also Armstrong & Bernstein 2008). Social movement research has increasingly broadened from state-oriented action to, more generally, conceptions of conflict or collaboration with different types of institutional and noninstitutional targets, including civil society associations (Alexander 2006; Meyerson & Scully 1995).

The civil society arena is largely defined by what it is not. It is the amorphous space between state and society (Kopecký & Mudde 2003). Civil society thus includes a broad range of political actors and structures and should not be perceived as homogeneous or unitary. An active civil society is broadly considered a measure of democratic success (Foley & Edwards 1996; Putnam 1993), although recent research has problematized this relationship. From Weimar Germany to twenty-first-century Egypt, (fragile) democracies have been challenged, and defeated, by highly active civil society groups (Berman 1997). Moreover, in some cases in postcommunist Eastern Europe, "civil society" has been detrimental to democracy, while "uncivil society" has been beneficial (Kopecký & Mudde 2003).

Social movements that focus on civil society strive to garner collective benefits outside the realm of state legislation or policy. Building ties with civil society groups, whether through memberships or partnerships, enables networking, cooperation, and collaboration to achieve mutually beneficial ends (Caniglia et al. 2015; Putnam 1995). As Anthony Oberschall (2012: 189) has argued, "when favorable changes in public policy and legislation occur, the social movement input is one component of a larger coalition of political groups, lobbies and supportive publics, all of which were crucial for success."

For social movements, three specific non-state actors are of particular importance: political parties, nongovernmental organizations (NGOs), and the media (Benford & Snow 2000; Melucci 1996). All three are imperative to furthering the cause of any social movement, albeit via different processes. Logically, social movements will try to influence civil society actors who share, at least in part, their ideology and interests; see, for example, the relationship of US civil rights organizations to black churches during the 1950s and 1960s (Morris 1999). In fact, in some cases, social movements will not even have to influence these actors, which chose to advocate for their shared agenda anyway.

The bridge or conduit between the formal activity of the state and the informal political activity of social movement organizations is political parties. Although conceptualized in a variety of ways, the most concise definition comes from the late Italian political theorist Giovanni Sartori (1976: 63), who defined a political party as "any political group identified by an official label that presents elections, and is capable of placing through elections candidates for public office." Some scholars exclude parties from the sphere of civil society, arguing that they are part of the state (Carothers & Barndt 1999). However, despite growing connections between them (Katz & Mair 1995), political parties are, for the most part, distinguishable and formally independent from the state. For social movements, they are particularly important as policymakers. While the state *implements* policies, political parties actually *introduce* them, through their actions in executives and legislatures (Burstein & Linton 2002).

Scholars who examine the interactions between social movement organizations and other political actors often employ a *political opportunity structure* (POS) framework to see how and to what degree different institutions influence and benefit from mutual cooperation. The framework examines the importance of the political context and the opportunities it offers social movements, including the configuration of power within the party system. For example, Hanspeter Kriesi and his collaborators (1992) have suggested that the need for social movements to engage in mobilization is directly related to political tendencies on a linear, left–right spectrum. Practically, this means that if a left-leaning party dominates the government, social movements with similar views have less need for mobilization, as they foresee greater chances of reform in their favor. The flip side is that social movements whose views clash with those of the government have greater need to mobilize supporters. Thus, political parties act not only as a channel between non-institutional action and governmental processes, they also magnify or minimize the need for internal mobilization, depending on the party's current electoral fortunes.

Given that most political parties are, first and foremost, driven by the need to maximize their electoral support, the branch of social movements that should hold the largest influence over them is the institutions (Tarrow 1994). The greater the electoral power of social movement institutions, based on the number of voters they can mobilize, the greater their potential influence. Examples, in the US context, include the American Association for Retired People (AARP) and the National Rifle Association (NRA), who have a large and highly mobilized membership (as well as significant financial resources), making them formidable players within US politics. Networks have less power, because they represent constituencies outside the established political organizations, which have the most significant and direct ability to affect politics (McCarthy & Zald 1977). Similarly, most influencers have limited power, because their (increasingly online) followers are not easily mobilized in the real political world.

Influencers can have an impact through infiltration, and to a certain level, co-optation, but only if they achieve a particularly powerful position within a party (Waddock 2017). Influencers require capital, information, labor, and skills. While holding some of these resources themselves, they often complement them by accessing their contacts (Greve & Salaff 2003). In general, the relationship between influencers and political parties is symbiotic: political parties offer influencers complementary resources to produce and deliver their goods or services (Teece 1987), and can provide influencers with increased visibility and legitimacy. In turn, influencers afford political parties access to people and organizations by fostering connections and leveraging new media platforms.

Nongovernmental organizations range from small, poorly funded local groups formed around specific issues like the local playground to global behemoths like Amnesty International and Greenpeace. Social movements mainly reach out to NGOs to increase their resources, including finances and personnel. Nongovernmental organizations and social movements, however, often occupy the same conceptual playing field, leading to tensions, politically and organizationally, in their interactions with each other and with third-party actors. Indeed, as Alejandro Bendaña (2006: 1) argues, social movements can end up "absorb[ing] and reorient[ing] NGOs," or conversely, experiencing an "NGO-ization of movements and politics." That is, interactions between the two can result in the assimilation of NGOs into social movements, or the effective professionalization of social movements to resemble NGOs, as manifested in their organizational frameworks and modes of action.

Inherently, social movements and NGOs have different bottom lines, and therefore work to achieve their goals via different means. NGOs are intrinsically dedicated to "policy advocacy [and] service delivery and monitoring" (Bendaña 2006: 7), and are characterized by a certain (though limited) accountability and transparency. Social movements are mass or popular movements that owe accountability only to their constituents. Yet although the fundamental construction of NGOs and social movements differ, they share the desired outcome of (not) changing social, political, and economic policies.

Despite the tension between social movements and NGOs, their shared interests mean that they can achieve the most when they act together, such "that none loses its autonomy and each contributes according to their particular strengths" (Bendaña 2006: 18). Social movements can attract mass constituency support, a feature that most NGOs frequently lack. For their part, NGOs can give social movements legitimacy in the eyes of the political elite and the "neutral" public, and can open channels to the government. Partnerships between NGOs and social movements can come to fruition either incrementally or as a "single process of elaborating common national and international projects" (Bendaña 2006: 18). The formation of such coalitions can help social movements expand beyond their core constituencies to include grassroots members, civil servants, and the political elite.

We can assume a natural tendency toward "like to like," meaning that individuals and groups will gravitate toward structurally similar individuals and groups. For example, social movement institutions are likely to pursue collaborative efforts with more organized NGOs, whereas informal networks will tend to engage with less organized groups. Likewise, influencers will most frequently collaborate with other influencers. However, this tendency for organizationally analogous actors to seek one another out is ameliorated by the possibility of dual membership. In other words, given that the goal of movement organizations is resource mobilization, the "like to like" tendency is mitigated by a more primary urge to enlist maximum capital. When informal networks determine that they can bolster their group's potential for success, it is commonplace for them to seek partnerships with structurally dissimilar groups.

The media are of primary interest due to its influence on public opinion and its power to help set the political agenda (King et al. 2017; McCombs 2013; Soroka 2003). The media – particularly television, the press, and online outlets – are also a malleable organizing tool, one that evolves in accordance with the changing (and sometimes conflicting) needs of activists. Studies have shown that the media can facilitate connective engagement and protest mobilization, enabling grassroots campaigns to build quickly and effectively (Hensby 2017). When a social movement challenges a cultural code, a change in the media arena both signals and spreads the change (Gamson 2004). Additionally, mass media also play a key catalyzing role in public protest, as all players in the policy process accept their pervasive influence. As such, media coverage can greatly influence "the nature, development and ultimate success of social protest" (Corbett 1998: 42).

The media are not a neutral actor, but part of the dominant power structure, and act as a "gatekeeper" of content (Corbett 1998: 43). That is, traditional news outlets can pick and choose what content they wish to disseminate or suppress. As such, the media also control which social movement institutions they respond to. Social movement institutions, for their part, can develop structural relationships of collaboration and interdependency with media organizations, for example, by providing them with access, information, and talking heads. Social movement networks mainly try to influence the media by creating "newsworthy" events. Influencers, finally, can impact specific media by either working for them, as journalists, or by functioning as "experts" on issues related to the broader political agenda of the social movement.

Not only do media outlets play a crucial role in determining whether a particular social movement is newsworthy, they also have a huge hand in the narrative of certain movements (Breuer et al. 2015). By presenting an organization as sympathetic, aggressive, or victimized, the media can affect the resource and constituency mobilization of the group. In this respect, getting noticed by the media has traditionally been most important for small, resource-deprived groups, who have few other instruments of mobilization. In fact, the success of a social movement is often indicated by its "ascension to a permanently newsworthy status" (Roscho 1975: 101).

Regardless of a social movement's size or degree of formality, the media are an indispensable arbiter in a social movement's interaction with the public. This gives media actors a huge amount of control over the framing of the public discourse. It is still unclear what this means in the age of social media. Developments in communication, and changes in how people connect with information sources, have created new opportunities for engaging and mobilizing mass audiences, both online and offline. Unlike traditional forms of collective action, social media do not rely so strongly on organizational resources. Rather, they transmit ideas and messages virally through networks such as Facebook and Twitter – what Bennett and Segerberg (2012, 2015) refer to as "connective action" logic. Following this logic,

> activists can disseminate first-hand accounts of events via social networking sites – events which previously might have received one-sided coverage in the mainstream media or no coverage at all. Moreover, these sites are extremely popular, enabling activists to connect with like-minded people across the globe, as well as open their campaigns out to wider, less-politicized audiences (Hensby 2017: 468).

Mark Tremayne (2014), for example, has argued that the proliferation of social media content created for Occupy Wall Street was a key driver of the movement's upward "scale shift" to a worldwide phenomenon.

On the other hand, studies have demonstrated that the media have the power to severely limit the information that audiences receive and can eliminate alternative solutions to political problems from public debate (Happer & Philo 2013). Moreover, repeated exposure to media messages can have a reinforcing effect on public opinion. In experimental research, individuals who were more exposed to a specific media message were increasingly less open to new information, and less flexible in assimilating any new information that filtered through. This was evident even if the message was inaccurate (Happer & Philo 2013). Therefore, the increased proliferation of messages by members of social movement networks across social media could have a significant effect on public opinion, building public support that can be translated into resource mobilization. This brings us to the third political area, the public.

1.4.3 Society

Social movements mainly meet society in the public arena, in a battle over public opinion, or *public values*, in what is amorphously termed "culture." Culture can be conceived of as "the norms, values, traditions, artifacts, and expectations [that operate] within a community" (Fine 1995: 127). Cultural context is imperative in the formation and framing of social movements, which are, in fact, *cultural* movements. Not only do cultural cues define the figurative bounds of social movements, but they are also in constant interaction with the movement organizations – dynamically framing and reframing the boundaries as cultural pressures and themes shift (Snow et al. 1986; Snow & Benford 1992).

Despite conceptual and methodological dilemmas, which make this a particularly challenging area of inquiry, social science research has made significant advances in identifying and demonstrating specific cultural outcomes related to the success of social movements (Hart 1996). These include changes in *public opinion*, changes in *cultural products* and everyday practices (e.g., in language, music, fashion, visual culture, the academy, and literature), and the (re)emergence of (new) communities and/or *identities* (d'Anjou 1996; d'Anjou & Van Male 1998; Earl 2013; Gamson & Modigliani 1989; Melucci 1989; Rochon 1998).

The public arena is where individuals and groups meet and exchange views concerning their interests, while at the same time deliberating, raising objections, and making suggestions concerning public issues (Habermas 1989). Within this more general space of the public arena exists the space of public opinion, which denotes the collective expression of citizens' views on issues of public concern, and which serves as a means of regulating the activities of formal, institutional bodies. Public opinion can be expressed informally or, as in the case of elections, formally (Habermas & Lennox 1974). In general, the public sphere operates as the broker between society and the state, and is thus pivotal in relaying the desires and opinions of the masses to the political elite and state institutions.

Ralph Turner and Lewis Killian (1987: 158) maintain that the public arena comprises a set of discursive groups, namely a group of people interested in an issue, "with a view to registering a collective opinion which is expected to affect the course of action of some decision-making group or individual." Gamson suggests straightforwardly that the public arena can be conceived of as a forum in which public discourse is carried out (in Snow et al. 2004). This discourse is carried out by individuals or collective actors in a myriad of different *public galleries*, including the mass media, parliaments, and social media. These actors take on a performative role in the public forum in order to foster resource mobilization by appealing to the masses to gain legitimacy.

The public arena is indispensable to social movements, because it is the most open space in which social movements operate: "It is the space where people come together as citizens and articulate their autonomous views to influence the political institutions of society" (Castells 2008: 78). In addition to being crucial for solidifying constituents' affective attachment to the social movement, organizations that know how to successfully co-opt public opinion can garner resources to maintain and perpetuate the movement, and push civil society and the state to further their cause (Keane 2018; Schurman 2004).

Accordingly, to the extent that social movements are conceived of as vehicles for social change, the effects these challengers have on belief systems and ideologies, as well as on "the practices and culture of mainstream institutions," become a yardstick for social movement success (Giugni et al. 1999: 34). Moreover, the creation of (new) collective identities can serve as proxy gains within the public framework. In fact, Gamson's (1975) well-known definition of movement success includes public acceptance or recognition, in the sense that the movement's objectives become part of the public agenda, as a core component. Some of the biggest achievements of social movements lie in broadening the public discourse. Bringing public attention to the claims of the social movement can itself have an enormous effect, in particular if the movement does so by inventing new tactics (Zimmermann 2015).

At least within a democratic context, though to some extent even in authoritarian settings (Geddes & Zaller 1989; Soroka & Wlezian 2010), politics is largely a struggle over public opinion. Electoral competition means that officials seeking reelection – indeed, all candidates seeking office – must respond to the public, which may lead them to promote policies that accord with public opinion, even, in some cases, regardless of their own personal views (Burstein & Linton 2002; Parinandi & Hitt 2018). Social movement mobilization can serve a key role in this process by providing decision makers with information on public preferences (Uba 2009). Hence, political actors try to influence not just what people think about a certain issue, but also what issues they think about. In other words, social movements aim not only to make people see their point of view on a specific issue, but also to make people consider that issue to be of vital importance (Benford & Snow 2000).

Although much of the debate on movement outcomes has focused on the role of public opinion, the empirical evidence is still inconsistent (Burstein & Linton 2002; Giugni 2004; Soule 2004). This may be in part due to differences in the measures used to assess the impact of social movements on public opinion. Importantly, the role of public opinion also varies across measures of organizational resources and activity (Parinandi & Hitt 2018; Uba 2009). For example, while institutions have sometimes been included in analyses of a social movement's impact on public opinion, much less attention has been paid to networks or influencers.

Social movement organizations can influence the public sphere, and by extension, public opinion, in different ways – both *indirectly*, through the state and civil society organizations (like schools and the media), and *directly*, through their own political campaigns. Their level of organization and resources means that institutions are likely to have more sustained influence on both issue salience and issue positions. In contrast, networks mainly have a short-term agenda-setting function, through well-mediatized actions. Influencers normally have only a limited impact on both aspects, barring some exceptional individuals and events. Examples are influencers who reach a broader audience in another capacity than social movement activist and use that position to change opinions about the movement's cause. This includes celebrities who speak out for a cause, like US actress Angelina Jolie on human rights, Canadian actress Pamela Anderson on animal rights, or Swedish teenager Greta Thunberg on the environment.

The phenomenon of celebrities and cultural icons using their agency to advance a social cause or agenda has in fact become a fixture of the social movement landscape (Wilson et al. 2015). Zeynep Tufekci (2013) has suggested that recent developments in media ecology add to the development and production of "attention" as an asset for social movements, with it becoming an invaluable resource for gaining traction, soliciting new membership, and presenting preferred frames. The result is that celebrities are increasingly useful as movement advocates. Equally, the movement serves the celebrity in a reciprocal relationship, keeping the spotlight on that individual. David Meyer and Joshua Gamson (1995: 181) have even suggested that it is far more anomalous to see a celebrity "*without a* cause" these days.

The specific areas in which celebrities' contributions to social movements appear to be most significant are resource mobilization and collective identity. The resource that celebrities offer to social movements is visibility. This is primarily realized on the media stage, where the public is informed by news outlets and sources as to what is important: "Once an individual has been certified as newsworthy, he or she has been empowered, within limits, to make news" (Gitlin 1980: 146). Celebrity icons and personalities are intrinsically newsworthy, and therefore their association with a movement or cause imbues it with their status and media attention. In fact, while experts may have more knowledge about a particular cause, celebrities have exponentially more access to the public eye and therefore serve as an attractive and efficient pathway. Celebrity participation in a protest or rally on behalf of a given movement organization will also have a reinforcing effect for the constituency. This combination then catalyzes a positive loop for the movement's resource mobilization; the presence of a celebrity attracts media and strengthens constituent support at events or rallies, which then furnish larger attendance and further justification of the event as "newsworthy."

1.4.4 International Arena

There has been a significant increase in transnational activity among social movement organizations over the last 50 years (Della Porta & Tarrow 2005). Transnational activism refers to an appeal to international support networks on behalf of actors who may be too weak to progress their own cause on the domestic arena, or who seek to leverage their movement with international pressure. Sidney Tarrow (2005) argues that with the rise of internationalism, transnational activist networks have provided domestic activists with added resources and legitimacy, especially if the international actors come from the political elite. The intersection of globalization and internationalization has resulted in a surge of transnational activists, who are conceived of as actors or groups that act both within multiple counties in order to catalyze resource mobilization – in particular by eliciting support from external, international allies.

Cultural, geopolitical, and social paradigm shifts have affected social movements' institutional and cultural environments, such as the transformation of the media system, globalization of the economic system, and the presence of political authorities on the international level (Della Porta & Tarrow 2005). These global forces encompass information exchange, global cultural and policy diffusion, and the interdependence of trade and production (Almeida & Chase-Dunn 2018). It is important to note that the relationship between transnational allies is generally mutually beneficial. In other words, activists tend to engage international actors or groups whose own ideologies or driving tenets align with their own, or who stand to benefit from a symbiotic alliance.

Building alliances with international actors can be a potent tool for social movements, because it multiplies opportunities for mobilizing support and resources. That is, the international arena provides new space for lobbying and alternative paths of access to political processes (Passy 1999; Smith 1999). Clifford Bob (2005) suggests that disadvantaged movements around the globe increasingly seek out the assistance of international organizations, both governmental bodies and NGOs, precisely because they feel they lack the resources and influence to successfully fight for change on their own. The European Union (EU), for example, provides a supranational forum where advocacy groups can present their grievances while also generating momentum through formal policy-making channels (Ruzza 2004; Tarrow 2005; Zippel 2004).

Whereas groups lacking transnational contacts might find themselves either ignored or repressed by their own national governments, those whose struggles are recognized by international actors can gain political leverage in their domestic contexts. Margaret Keck and Kathryn Sikkink (1998) describe this strategy of using the international stage to influence the behaviors of national governments as a "boomerang effect." Certification by international actors or institutions, whether transnational citizens' groups or international agencies, has important effects on national political struggles, as it demonstrates the movement's claims are viewed as legitimate by those outside the country in question. This can enhance activists' sense of efficacy and can help local groups mobilize resources from the transnational activist community. International allies, in turn, can contribute significantly to the success of a social movement by creating pressure from above and below the national state. Thus, by participating in the international arena, social movements can "bypass their state and directly search out international allies to try to bring pressure on their states from the outside" (Keck & Sikkink 1998: 12).

What is novel about these international alliances is the ability of national social movements, including from relatively small countries, to persuade, pressure, and exert leverage over much more powerful organizations and governments. Alliances with international actors – including international NGOs, governmental organizations, social movements, and professional bodies and conferences – provide vital resources for domestic social movements, and help spread the movement's ideas, practices, and frames from one country to another. In creating these networks with international actors, social movements try not only to influence policy outcomes but also the nature of the debate, building legitimacy, awareness, and a voice for the social movement from the outside (Tarrow & McAdam 2005). Social movements can also bolster their cause by challenging international institutions to intervene in problems or domestic conflict and mobilizing resources, including money, information, and activists for the movement's project and activities.

The boundary-less nature of online media has made the transnational approach more efficient and feasible (Bennett 2003). The Internet has broken the monopoly of communication once held by traditional elites, such as governments, churches, or political parties. Activist websites assembled by the independent media as well as movement-specific Facebook sites and free international messaging applications (such as Skype, WhatsApp, Twitter, and Telegram) perform a broker role for social movements by connecting organizations and individuals globally (Della Porta et al. 2006; Horstink 2017; Juris 2005). These websites and digital messaging applications offer logistic information in multiple languages for coordinating local events as well as transnational campaigns (Almeida & Lichbach 2003; Howard 2010).

Social media platforms, in particular, have served as outlets for social movements to propagate ideas, mobilize members for collective action, and coordinate activism. Online websites, for example, create opportunities for interaction and connection, often featuring numerous international and interorganizational hyperlinks (Burris et al. 2000; Daniels, 2009). As Francesca Polletta (1999: 3) notes: "Free spaces supply the activist networks, skills, and solidarity that assist in launching a movement." The Internet has also simplified the process for appealing to international support in circumstances where information would not be diffused by official channels (Karolak 2017). Furthermore, it enables individuals to become political broadcasters and voice their opinions on an equal footing with any other user, thereby allowing marginalized groups to become (more) vocal and reach international audiences (Karolak 2017). As such, social media have further democratized the various arenas in which social movements operate.

1.5 Internal and External Antecedents of Political Success

Social movement scholarship has identified both internal and external factors that impact social movement success. Among the most oft-mentioned internal factors are the movement's tactical repertoire and organizational infrastructure. The main external factors are the political opportunity structure and public acceptance (McAdam 2017).

1.5.1 Internal Factors

It seems obvious that the tactics adopted by any organization, group, or movement will have an effect on the group's ability to achieve its goals.

Early work on the impact of social movements emphasized the advantages of radical action strategies (e.g., Gamson 1990; Piven & Cloward 1993). Yet findings on the effectiveness of different tactical repertoires are mixed and inconclusive at best. Social movements do not exist within a vacuum. Their actions, be they moderate, radical, or extreme, are limited and influenced by other players in the sociopolitical system. That is, the application of violence is a dynamic result of differing opportunities and limitations that the contemporary political opportunity structure offers protesters and law-enforcement alike (Tarrow 2011). For example, with the normalization of protest in Western democracies, people have come to see peaceful protests (demonstrations, marches, rallies) as a legitimate way of expressing demands (Norris et al. 2005), whereas illegal and violent acts have become less accepted (Della Porta & Diani 1999; Tarrow 1994).

Decision makers within social movements must weigh the costs and benefits of moderate versus radical or extreme modes of action. Studies have found that in the United States, social movements which opted for more moderate, insider tactics were more successful in generating Congressional support (e.g., Gamson 1990; Santoro & Fitzpatrick 2015; Soule et al. 1999). Radical, disruptive actions have the advantage that they can garner the attention of target authority figures and can serve to mobilize a sympathetic audience (Bearman & Everett 1993). But disruptive, radical modes can also undermine a movement's cause by alienating the movement's support base if it goes too far, particularly when it veers into the territory of violent acts (Biggs & Andrews 2015; Elsbach & Sutton 1992; Johnson et al. 2006; Kanter & Troup 2018).

Social movement organizations that have a cause with broad appeal are more likely to use radical disruptive methods, but less likely to resort to extreme (violent) measures. In contrast, organizations with narrow appeal are more likely to opt for extreme means. This is because more-niche organizations inherently have a smaller support base, making them less dependent upon broader support but more dependent upon attention-grabbing tactics to arouse media attention (Wang & Piazza 2016). When the target of the organization is the government, there is a success trade-off when employing violent tactics. Extreme actions are likely to lead to the marginalization of protestors, and it can alienate elected officials and potential sympathizers (McAdam & Su 2002). Hence, social movements may choose nonviolent actions over violent ones to gain recognition as respectable players who should be listened to (Tilly 1999, 2008).

While there is considerable debate on the effectiveness of different types of actions, most scholars agree that social movements are more successful when they employ a *variety of tactics*, that is, when they draw from a broad tactical repertoire rather than a more narrow one (e.g., Fishman & Everson 2016; McCammon 2012; Taylor & Van Dyke 2004; Tilly et al. 1975). For example, they point to the success of the women's movement in the second half of the twentieth century, which incorporated both moderate and radical protests (Gelb & Hart 1999; Rupp & Taylor 1987; Staggenborg 1991). Several scholars have noted that cultural change is particularly likely to follow "moments of madness," that is, a snowball effect where more and more organizations engage in various collective actions (Koopmans 1993; Kriesi et al. 1992; Tarrow 1993).

Successful social movements also engage in novel or "hybrid" tactical actions to enhance their effectiveness and survival over time (Dalton et al. 2003; Katzenstein et al. 1998; McAdam 1983; Meyer & Tarrow 1998). Novel tactics can refer to a range of activities, including art, protest music, speak-outs, street performances, and theater. Although social movements are often reluctant to stray from familiar tactics, there is evidence that organizations willing to try novel tactics often enjoy more successful policy outcomes (Snow et al. 2004; Wang et al. 2018). However, in practice, a movement's pool of viable tactics can be constrained by the resources and opportunities available. That is, a group's choice of particular actions will reflect a combination of external factors and internal conditions, including the political opportunity structure and the group's internal preferences, organizational identity, and resources (Balser & Carmin 2002; Jasper 1997; Meyer 2004; Tarrow 1998; Zald & Useem 1987).

Another factor that underpins the success of social movements is their *organizational size and infrastructure* (Andrews 2004; Ganz 2010). Larger organizations can be more sustainable, as their size bolsters the organization both internally, by affirming the commitment of the organization's constituency, and externally, by empowering outsiders to join. Large protest activities have the aesthetic benefit of being attention grabbing. For example, Aldon Morris (1993) cites the size of the civil rights movement as one of the key elements behind its success in influencing public opinion and political institutions. Not only do large membership and protest participation numbers attest to the legitimacy of the movement, in that they convey broad appeal, but numerical superiority has greater "disruptive potential" (Snow et al. 2004: 281). The structure of an organization, whether formal or informal, also plays a role in determining the degree of success the organization can attain. In fact, structuralist theory holds that the structure of social movement organizations explains the greatest variation in the outcome of campaigns both within and across movements (Krause 2011).

Some studies have found that organizational form can influence a movement's ability to facilitate policy change (Jenkins & Klandermans 1995). Several scholars have identified typologies of organizational forms based on dimensions such as bureaucratization, centralization, formalization, and professionalization – all of which can inform the success potential of social movement organizations (Gamson 1975; Mirowsky & Ross 1981; Staggenborg 2015; Wrenn, 2016). Bureaucratization or formalization are the common terms scholars employ to describe increasing control or rigidity in the management and upkeep of the organization's administrative aspects and internal infrastructure. While some degree of administrative formalization may be useful, too much bureaucratization makes organizations "more oligarchical and rigid, less democratic and spontaneous," and increases their reliance on ambiguous sources of authority (Corbett 1998: 44–45). Although research suggests that less centralized, more informal networks are more likely to succeed (Breines 1982; Gerlach & Hine 1970), there is also evidence that bureaucratization can contribute positively to movement sustainability (Kielbowicz & Scherer 1996). In particular, having a clear organizational infrastructure can help social movements maintain a presence in the mass media, and therefore, in the public eye – thus making them more relevant to policymakers. In short, movement success requires different organizational competencies and forms in order to mobilize support from state authorities, civil society, and the public.

1.5.2 External Factors

Among the external factors most relevant to the mobilization and success of social movements is *political context* (Jenkins 1995). Social movements, like other aspects of society, are influenced and informed by existing power relations and political structures (McAdam 1982, 2017). The political opportunity approach to the study of social movements examines the openness of the political system – that is, limitations to formal political access, the level of stability afforded by political alliances, the availability of potential partnerships, and political conflicts among elites (Tarrow 1994). Studies show that the openness of the political system and governmental institutions' tendency to inhibit challenger groups strongly inform which tactics social movement organizations select, and ultimately help shape their outcomes (Meyer 2004; Tarrow 1998).

It should be emphasized that political opportunity structures may constrain as well as empower social movements. In some cases, the political context is such that social movement activities are met with public outcry, including condemnation and countermobilization, both within the state and internationally (Alimi & Hirsch-Hoefler 2012). Likewise, a social movement can give rise to or strengthen opponents as well as allies. For example, the activities of the settler movement have produced opposing responses in three different arenas: Jewish Israeli (e.g., Peace Now, B'Tselem), Palestinian (inside both Israel and the West Bank), and international (notably the EU, UN, and the United States – both at the government and civil society level). It has also for at least the last decade, but arguably about two decades, come to increasingly divide Jewish communities outside Israel (primarily in the United States).

The final factor that contributes to social movement success is the *framing narrative* of the organization, or its "cultural resonance" (Snow et al. 2004: 282). The tactics of social movement organizations are not exclusively a function of cost–benefit analysis, but also reflect and reinforce the group's ideological/cultural identity (Dalton 1994; Polletta 2016; Snow & Benford 1988, 1992). Social movements construct and adapt their identity in order to appeal to their own constituencies, to the wider public, and to institutional operatives that can help them achieve their goals. As such, the specific framing that an organization chooses to identify can affect the success of both the specific organization and the broader movement. Group ideology can also serve as a frame of reference for either justifying or delegitimizing violent means of facilitating social change. As noted by Ted Gurr (1970: 194), one of the main functions of political ideology is to provide "norms about the desirability of political violence."

While the choice of frame is largely an internal factor, it is significantly influenced by the broader political context. In particular, a social movement will be more successful if it can design a narrative that resonates with the cultural ideology of the mainstream public (Baumgarten & Ullrich 2016). This is what Ruud Koopmans and Paul Statham (1999) have termed the "discursive opportunity structure," sometimes also referred to as "cultural opportunity structure," that is, "political-cultural or symbolic opportunities that determine what kind of ideas become visible for the public, resonate with public opinion and are held to be 'legitimate' by the audience" (Kriesi 2004: 72).

A large component of the junction between cultural resonance and social movement organization and mobilization is consciousness-raising. Consciousness-raising is akin to public support capital and is often a top priority of first-generation activists in any given movement (McGehe et al. 2014: 143). Raising public awareness of a social movement can heighten its success by reinforcing individuals' connection to and enlisting participation in the social movement (Eisenstein, 2001). By increasing participation and membership the social movement increases its visibility and legitimacy, thereby bolstering perceptions of the organization and its chances of success. While consciousness-raising usually reinforces individual participation, it can also strengthen public support by eliciting sympathy for a cause, which, while not always culminating in active participation, can facilitate further awareness of the social movement (McGehe, Kline & Knollenberg 2014).

1.6 Conclusion

The question of success is at the heart of most research of social movements, and yet very few studies explicitly define what "success" constitutes and how best to assess it. Building upon the existing literature, we have developed an original and comprehensive theoretical framework in which the key concepts of *success* and *social movement* are deconstructed into separate components, which will allow us, and others, to assess success in a more fine-grained manner without losing track of the overall assessment.

Table 1.1 provides a visual representation of our theoretical framework for the assessment and explanation of the success of social movements. It distinguishes four categories, where the first, the dimensions of success, is crucial to *assessing* success. Specifically, after having established the main goal(s) of the social movement on the basis of its own documents and statements, we argue that its success must be assessed vis-à-vis three separate but related areas: policies, resources, and support. Has the social movement been able to advance policies that further its main goal(s)? Has it been able to mobilize resources to strengthen and sustain the social movement itself? And has the social movement created support for its goal(s) among the elites and masses?

The other three categories – the types of movement branches, actions, and political arenas – help us to better *explain* the (lack of) success of a social movement. To better understand *how* social movements do (not)

Table 1.1 *Theoretical framework of social movement success*

Success	*Movement branches*	*Repertoire of actions*	*Political arenas*
Policies	Institutions	Moderate	State
Resources	Networks	Radical	Civil society
Support	Influencers	Extreme	Society

achieve success, we propose to look at the movement as the sum of three branches. Institutions constitute the most formalized, organized, and centralized branch of the movement. Not all social movements have institutions, particularly not at the beginning, but many of the more successful ones do. Networks are less formalized and institutionalized and operate in a more decentralized manner, with fluid memberships and organizations. Influencers, finally, are individuals who play an important role irrespective of their organizational connections in the movement. Their influence is based on their personal appeal, related to activities outside the realm of the social movement (e.g., actors, artists, athletes).

Social movements employ different types of activities, legal or illegal, violent or nonviolent. The most common type of action is moderate and includes all activities that are legal and nonviolent, such as demonstrations, lobbying, and mass media communications. Illegal actions are divided into nonviolent (radical) actions, such as blockades or sit-ins, and violent (extreme) actions, notably (threats of) physical attacks on persons. In most cases, a minority of social movement activists and groups are involved in radical actions and only a tiny portion engages (also) in extreme actions (see Figure 1.1).

Finally, social movements try to achieve success by influencing different political arenas, both at the national and international level. The first arena is the state, which includes the government, legislature, judiciary, bureaucracy, and military. The second is civil society, most notably political parties, NGOs, and the media. Third, and final, is the public, most notably public opinion. Obviously, the three arenas are closely related; for example, governments and legislatures are mostly occupied by leading members of political parties, who are very sensitive to public opinion. Moreover, the three arenas exist at both the domestic and foreign level, and interconnect in many different ways. A foreign government can subsidize a domestic NGO or domestic parties can try to influence international public opinion.

It is important to note that our theoretical framework is not an alternative to existing (meta)theories like POS or RMT. Rather, it is consistent with them, but elaborates upon them. It allows a more fine-grained analysis of resource mobilization of the social movement as a whole, by distinguishing the activities of its different, constituent branches. Similarly, there are interesting interactions between POS theory and our theoretical framework. The political opportunity structure describes the political context in which social movements operate, providing challenges and opportunities not just for the movement as a whole, but also for its individual branches. For instance, a more open political opportunity structure, in which the state (and major parties) are sympathetic to the goals of the social movement, encourages collaborative behavior and moderate actions, strengthening the power of the institutions within the broader social movement. In contrast, a more closed political opportunity structure, and particularly a hostile state (and major parties), will encourage more radical, and perhaps even extreme, actions, increasing the importance of the networks.

2 History of the Settlements

Israel launched its settlement project in the West Bank,[1] categorized by much of the international community and at times by Israel itself as "occupied" – later the Israeli government would come to call it "disputed"[2] – shortly after its military occupied the region during the 1967 Six-Day War. In addition to annexing East Jerusalem and surrounding areas as well as the Golan Heights, Israel has allowed and initiated a scattered network of 127 settlements and some 100 outposts in the West Bank (excluding East Jerusalem), covering 1 percent of its territory (Arieli 2013).[3] As of the end of 2018, some 427,800 Jewish settlers live there, making up 13 percent of the total population of the West Bank, but just 4.7 percent of the Israeli population.

The territorial and demographic implications of the Six-Day War continue to divide Israeli society. Many Israelis want to maintain an Israeli presence in the West Bank, believing that this serves the state's strategic and security interests or that the West Bank is part of the historical "Land of Israel" (*Eretz Yisrael*). Many other Israelis believe that Israel should withdraw from the West Bank, either because they consider the occupation illegal and/or immoral, or simply because it too costly – particularly after the various Palestinian civil uprisings, notably the First Intifada (1987–91) and the Al-Aqsa Intifada or Second Intifada (2000–5).

This chapter provides a concise history of the Israeli settlement of Gaza and the West Bank, outlining the main periods of settlement activity. In addition to chronicling the slow but steady growth of settlement and settlers, we also shortly explain the way in which the Jewish settlements (in the West Bank) are administered by the State of Israel and discuss the broader international political context in which the settlement, and the Israeli occupation of the West Bank (as well as of East Jerusalem and the Golan Heights), operate.

2.1 The Israeli Settlement of Gaza and the West Bank

From the First Aliyah (1881–1903)[4] to Israel's independence in 1948, Jewish "pioneers" settled on the plains of *Eretz Yisrael* and invested their resources outside the Arab-populated West Bank. The earliest settlements, those constructed up through World War I, were built without regard to defense. But a series of Arab attacks in 1929, and even more the Arab revolt of 1936–39, which was directed against Jewish settlements as well as the British administration, led to the prioritization of security needs in both the form of Jewish settlements and their locations (Troen 2011).

Since the 1880s, Zionist settlement had been characterized by a clustering of small communities into a discernible N-shaped pattern across the landscape of Palestine – running north up the coast, southwest along the Jezreel and Beit She'an Valleys, and then north along the shores of Lake Tiberias. This N-shaped pattern arose organically, based on the willingness of absentee Arab landowners to sell their holdings in the thinly populated plains and valleys to Jews. But from the 1930s onward, this pattern was deliberately strengthened for both strategic and demographic reasons by the leaders of the *Yishuv*, the local Jewish population before the establishment of the state. Central planning ensured that settlements protected the Zionist enterprise as a whole, not merely the particular community. Their locations were chosen based on the idea that the people who lived within them would be responsible for establishing and defending the borders of the Yishuv (Troen 2011). This logic continued to shape the defense of the state after Israel was established, with new communities established along the borders and in strategic areas where the Jewish population was sparse (Troen 2016).

Yishuv-era Zionism was highly centralized and encouraged *halutzim* (the pioneering settlers) to sacrifice their private interests for the sake of the common good. Newly established communities tended to be small and often adopted a socialist or even communist ideology.[5] Prior to the creation of the State of Israel, new settlements were often formed as *kibbutzim*, fully collective communities characterized by joint ownership of most if not all property. By the 1950s, the kibbutz model was mainly supplanted by the *moshav*, a form of settlement that blended private property with cooperative features. These forms of settlement were suited to homogeneous communities and aimed to serve national purposes (Troen 2011).

The story of the United Nations (UN) Partition Plan for Palestine, Israel's Declaration of Independence in May 1948, and the war with the Arab states that followed has been told elsewhere (Lustick 1993; Morris 1987; Shlaim 2015). For present purposes, what matters is that the Armistice Agreements, signed in January 1949 between Israel and its Arab neighbors (Lebanon, Syria, Jordan and Egypt), created the de facto borders of the new state, based on the position of Israeli forces when the war ended. The lines demarcating Israel's borders with Syria, Jordan, and Egypt came to be known collectively as the Green Line. Two parts of British Mandatory Palestine on the other side of the Green Line came under Arab rule: Egypt took control of the Gaza Strip, and Jordan annexed the area known as the West Bank. The independent Arab state envisioned under Partition never came to fruition.

It should be stressed that, prior to 1948, the philosophy behind the settlement of what would become Israel, as well as the continued settlement of the nascent state until 1967, was in large part secular. The connection of the Jewish people to the "Land of Israel," mythically forged in biblical times and nurtured in Jewish prayer and practice through millennia of exile, was transformed into a purely nationalist (as opposed to religious) ideology by, first, the Yishuv leadership and, later, the Israeli state. At the same time, what would become the post-1967 settler movement also had clear religious roots, particularly visible in a group of Ashkenazi yeshiva students who took the name *Gahelet* – a Hebrew word meaning "ember," and an acronym for "corps of Torah-learning *halutzim* [pioneers]" (see in more detail in Chapter 3).

After the founding of the State of Israel, new Jewish communities continued to be planned largely along the ideological–security lines established earlier. At this stage, however, most were essentially urban communities located in rural settings, built to house workers who would commute to work in local industrial zones or nearby cities. In terms of their location, the goal was now to maintain control over areas within the new state with majority Arab populations, such as the hilltops of the Galilee. As Ilan Troen (2011) has noted, these new towns would later serve as a model for Jewish settlements across the hilltops of the West Bank.

The Six-Day War resulted in total Israeli control over the territory of the former British Mandate (see Figure 2.1), and therefore, over a large Arab–Palestinian population. It de facto transformed Israel into a "communal state" (Kimmerling 1993), consisting of three separate communities: the Jewish community; the Arab–Israeli community, which has Israeli citizenship; and the Palestinian community residing in the occupied territories across the Green Line, who are not citizens of Israel.[6]

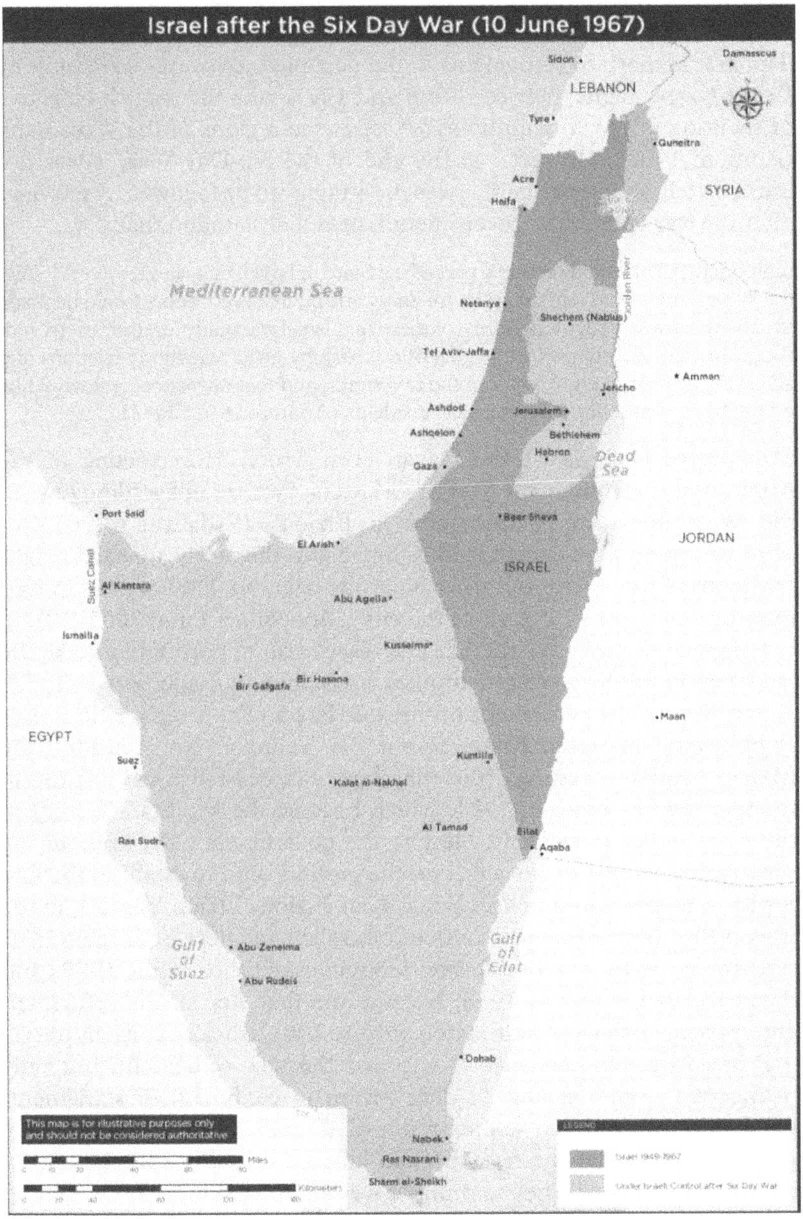

Figure 2.1 Israeli control before and after the Six-Day War[7]

2.1.1 *The Beginnings: 1967–1977*

The first authorized settlements in the occupied territories were built by Labor governments, between 1968 and 1977, with the explicit objective of securing a Jewish majority in key strategic regions of the West Bank (Admoni 1992). However, at the end of the Six-Day War, it was not immediately apparent that this was the strategy to be followed. A few days after the war ended, the government issued a declaration that

> united Jerusalem would remain a part of the State of Israel; that, as a temporary step, the West Bank would remain under military control; that every effort would be made to achieve a constructive long-term solution; that Israel was ready for discussions with King Hussein of Jordan with the goal of establishing good neighborly relations and achieving economic unity between the two states; and that any agreement would be on the basis of autonomy for the local residents (Admoni 1992: 20–21).

Minister of Defense Moshe Dayan even wrote, at a meeting of the Ministerial Committee for Security Matters, "we are not settling Jews in the West Bank, in Hebron, and in Etzion" (Pedahzur 1996: 46). However, Jews were encouraged to move into the newly annexed neighborhoods of Jerusalem. Less than a decade later, 50,000 Jews had moved into the newly annexed parts of the city (Mnookin & Eiran 2005: 19).

Religious Zionists saw the Six-Day War as an opportunity to take the next step in fulfilling the redemption envisioned by Rabbi Zvi Yehudah Kook, that is, the settlement of Greater Israel. The charismatic son of Rabbi Abraham Isaac Kook, Rabbi Zvi Yehudah Kook headed the Mercaz HaRav Yeshiva, the flagship national-religious institution founded by his father in 1924, which became the key brain factory of the early settler movement. Despite the government's declaration, the settlers decided to "create a fact on the ground" and to establish the first Jewish settlement in the West Bank, Kfar Etzion (Etzion Village), in the Etzion Bloc (Gush Etzion), south of Jerusalem and near Bethlehem. The settlement, on the site of a former kibbutz established in the 1940s and destroyed in the war of 1948, became the first step in the settlement enterprise, which would ultimately involve Israeli society in its entirety.

Prime Minister Levi Eshkol opposed the new settlement, but only halfheartedly, later saying, "I didn't want to confirm their settlement, but I didn't want to refuse their request" (Pedahzur 1996: 194). Eshkol was well aware that the reestablished kibbutz would not be the end of settlement activity: "They said that it was an outpost but I know that, in time, kids turn into goats" (Admoni 1992: 36–37). Minister of Agriculture Haim Givati raised objections to the choice of site on strategic grounds, pointing out that "we should decide whether the Etzion Bloc is the first place we should settle, as we have certain goals there, and political, settlement and occupation considerations, among others" (Eldar & Zertal 2004: 20). Nonetheless, Government Decision 839 declared that "an outpost would be established at the Etzion Bloc" (Eldar & Zertal 2004).

Despite Eshkol's warning that "establishing facts" would erode the authority of the government if not do greater damage (*Annals of the Knesset*, August 17, 1968), he and his government were creating the foundations for the settlement enterprise in the occupied territories. Eshkol even requested that the Director of the World Zionist Organization (WZO), an international nongovernmental organization (NGO) promoting Zionism that was cofounded by Theodor Herzl, enlist the aid of a "Department for Settlement" in establishing new settlements in the territories. This led to the founding of HaMarchiv, a government company for settlement within and outside of Israel (Admoni 1992).[8]

Other prominent Labor Party politicians were involved in the settlement project too. In September 1967, MK Shimon Peres drafted a fourteen-point document in which he discussed his proposal to unite the *Rafi*, *Mapai*, and *Ahdut HaAvoda* (Labor) political parties. The ninth item specified that "places which had been left in the past would be reestablished" (Eldar & Zertal 2004: 24). The places he cited were Beit HaArava, Kalia, Hebron, and the Etzion Bloc. Two additional Labor ministers waved the settlement flag: Yigal Allon, a legendary commander of the *Palmach*, the underground army of the Yishuv, and Yisrael Galili. The two represented the settlers in the government, and aided them in gaining the stamp of approval for their settlement activities (Eldar & Zertal 2004).

Allon believed that territory was the only true guarantor of peace and security for Israel. In July 1967, he presented the Israeli government with a plan for dividing the West Bank, creating an independent Palestinian state and ensuring Israel's territorial security. It involved keeping Jerusalem and Gaza under Israeli control, along with parts of the West Bank comprising the Jordan Valley and the eastern parts of the Judean Desert and Samaria. The following year he presented a modified version of the plan, whereby the western portion of the West Bank, which was densely populated by Palestinians, would be returned to Jordan (Arieli 2013). The government did not officially approve or reject the plan, but it would form the basis for (ultimately ineffective) secret talks between Israel and Jordan's King Hussein in September 1968. The settlers, for their part, rejected the principles underlying the Allon Plan, which limited the establishment of settlements to the Jordan valley and an area around Jerusalem.

Soon after the establishment of the Kfar Etzion settlement, the idea of settling in Hebron – a city with a Jewish history dating back to biblical times – began to be discussed. Elyakim Haetzni, one of the nonreligious founding fathers of the settler movement, told Rabbi Moshe Levinger, a religious Zionist and soon to be a central figure in the settler movement leadership, that Israel's first Prime Minister, David Ben-Gurion, had asked the head of the Hebron Yeshiva in Jerusalem "why we haven't yet gone there [to settle in Hebron]," and had said "we must do so at once" (Ozeri 1977:15, quoted by Zertal & Eldar 2007: 17).

In the spring of 1968, Rabbi Levinger and a group of other settler leaders requested permission to hold a Passover Seder (the Passover ceremonial feast) at the Park Hotel in Hebron, saying they would leave the city the next day. They did not. Rather, they announced that they were "the first group to renew the Jewish community in Hebron" (Pedahzur 1996: 233). A few days later, Allon visited Hebron to express his support, providing the settlers with a car and other supplies (Eldar & Zertal 2004: 32). The following month, the government formally authorized Moshe Dayan, Minister of Defense, to ensure the security of the Levinger group (Sternhell 1998: 334); and in February 1970, it approved the establishment of Hebron Illit (Upper Hebron), the settlement which would become known as Kiryat Arba (Admoni 1992: 60–61).

Important in itself, the settlement of Kiryat Arba is also worth noting because it created a new settlement group, the Elon Moreh group, which believed that the time had come to settle the hills of Samaria (the northern West Bank) as well as Judea (the southern West Bank). Once again, the settlers' strategy was to establish a physical presence on the ground. In 1974, under the (first) government of Yitzhak Rabin, several attempts were made to settle in Sebastia (Tel Shomron), but each time the efforts resulted in eviction. In an attempt to change the government's decision, the Elon Moreh group adopted a new strategy: establishing a "work camp" in the area, which would allow them to live and work at the site, and thereby to create a "fact on the ground." Under an agreement with the government, a contingent from Sebastia established a camp in Kadum, an old army base. By June 1976, thirty families had settled in Kadum. One year later, the army camp had acquired a dining room, synagogue, and study hall as well as electricity supply and public bus service from Tel Aviv – along with formal status and a new name, Kdumim (Newman 1981).

A similar "work camp" at Ofra, north of Jerusalem, was approved by Minister of Defense Peres in April 1975 (Eldar & Zertal 2004; Segal 1987). A number of settler organizations and institutions, including the Yesha Council and the *Nekuda* magazine (see Chapter 3), were later located at Ofra (Lustick 1988). During this period, the Rabin government also agreed to the establishment of what was to become the city of Ma'ale Adumim (Demant 1988: 363). The Labor-led government further confirmed the building of Elkana in Western Samaria, two weeks before the election upheaval of May 1977, which brought Likud to power. Another decision adopted in principle by this government was the creation of Ariel, which eventually became the capital of Samaria (see Chapter 6).

In sum, despite the initial reservations of some Labor leaders, including Rabin, the Labor-led coalitions that governed Israel between 1967 and 1977 not only failed to prevent the rise of the settler movement, but often actively encouraged it. During the deliberations over Sebastia-Kdumim, representatives of the Labor party, along with international Jewish leaders, called on the Rabin–Peres government to promote settlement in the northern West Bank. By the time of the May 1977 election, 4,400 settlers were living in thirty-eight agricultural settlements in the West Bank and the Gaza Strip (excluding East Jerusalem). Most of the West Bank settlements were in the Jordan Valley and the Etzion Bloc, but the movement to populate the northern West Bank (Samaria) had also begun.

2.1.2 *The Expansion: 1977–1992*

Following the election of Israel's first right-wing government in 1977, the settlers assumed that now they could work with the government (Naor 1993). Indeed, one of Prime Minister Menahem Begin's first actions was to visit the Camp Kadum outpost and declare that there would be many more Elon Moreh's (Newman 2005). While Begin explained to the settlers that the time was not right for a discussion in the government, he also validated the settlers' strategy, advising them to "go to the area spontaneously and get organized on the ground. After that, it will be easy for me to say, 'You have won, my sons!'" (Eldar & Zertal 2004: 86).

In July 1977, the government authorized a "Settlement Committee, run jointly with the Zionist administration, to decide on the establishment of new settlements" (Government Decision 803; Arieli 2017). This committee, headed by Minister of Agriculture Ariel Sharon, would be responsible for decisions on the location of new settlements, as well as land apportionment, infrastructure, and building expenses. Sharon regarded control of the highlands of the West Bank and the western slopes of Samaria as crucial to securing the defense of the densely populated coastal plain, and to supplying strategic depth in the east (Arieli et al. 2009: 3).[9] The plan he submitted to the security cabinet in September 1977 called for the establishment of urban settlements, as opposed to the agricultural settlements established by the Labor-led governments in the Jordan Valley, Etzion Bloc, and Gaza Strip. Sharon favored urban settlements because they were relatively easy to set up, and because they would be attractive to segments of the population less enamored by the agricultural traditions of the labor movement. The government approved the plan the next month.

The new settlements, and their locations on the map, clearly indicated the new primacy of political and security considerations. Likud's aim was to ensure "maximum Jewish presence" throughout the occupied territories, and effectively create a net of civil command posts, meant to guarantee Israeli control (Feige 2002: 147). During Likud's seven years in power, Sharon established sixty-seven Jewish settlements in the West Bank. In addition, the Likud government initiated a substantial program of land expropriation in the territories, creating areas which were then defined as state land (Eldar & Zertal 2004: 140). This led to a growth of the settler population in the West Bank from approximately 4,400 in 1977 to about 16,200 in 1981.

The settler movement underwent a shock in 1982, when Israel evacuated the Yamit settlement in the Sinai Peninsula under the Camp David Accords of 1978, whereby Israel returned the Sinai to Egypt in exchange for peace with that country. While most Yamit residents evacuated peacefully, a few offered violent resistance, encouraged and joined by settler leaders and activists from elsewhere in the country. The forced removal of the resistors in April 1982 was a traumatic experience for the settlers, and indeed, the country.

Yet even after Camp David and the subsequent withdrawal from Yamit, the Likud-led government continued to establish new settlements in the West Bank and Gaza Strip. For example, in December 1978, just a few days after the end of the Camp David talks, the settlement of Elon Moreh was established in the Samarian highlands. More than half of all the settlements existing today (59 percent) were built between 1977 and 1983 by the government of Menachem Begin. Although other Israeli governments also promoted the building of new settlements, the greatest number was founded in 1983, a total of nineteen in one year. Settlement activity continued under the national unity government formed in 1984. Indeed, it was agreed that five to six new settlements would be established each year. Ultimately, thirteen new settlements were established between 1985 and 1990, and the number of settlers doubled from 44,200 to 78,600.

Begin's government, followed by subsequent Likud-led governments, also provided financial incentives for Jews to move to the West Bank, with the aim of expanding the settler population beyond the relatively small number of citizens motivated by national-religious claims to settle the whole of *Eretz Yisrael*. As Begin's Construction and Housing Minister, Sharon actively recruited new types of settlers by granting mortgages at low interest rates (Eldar & Zertal 2004). The lure of a higher standard of living at lower cost led to a significant change in the profile of the settlers, with many now comprising new immigrants and young couples for whom territorial considerations were relatively unimportant.

In 1990, the number of settlers increased by 8,600, and in subsequent years the number was 10,000 and more annually. On the eve of the 1992 elections, which brought about the fall of Likud and the installment of Rabin's second government, the number of settlers in the territories – not including East Jerusalem – stood at 101,100, living in 120 settlements. As Yaakov Katz, assistant to Sharon in settlement matters, boasted: "There is no tree that we did not sit under . . . 40 thousand apartments and 20 thousand trailers were built in the settlements by Ariel Sharon, so that they can never be removed" (*Yediot Aharonot,* July 11, 2003). Importantly, the purpose of all this settlement activity was not only to ensure Israel's security, by creating strategic depth, but also to solidify the country's hold on territory that was part of biblical and historical Israel as well as to preempt the creation of a Palestinian state.

2.1.3 The Years of Trouble: 1992 to the Present

The Labor government that came to power in 1992 was the first in which no Cabinet member represented the interests of the settlers. The new government promised that "no new settlements would be established, and existing settlements would not be expanded" (*Annals of the Knesset,* July 13, 1992). However, two restrictions were added to this statement: first, it would not apply to greater Jerusalem, and second, "the government would continue to build in the occupied territories to answer the needs of 'natural growth' of the existing population" (Eldar & Zertal 2004). Under the rubric of "natural growth," Israeli governments set up new settlements, disguised as new neighborhoods of existing settlements (Eldar & Zertal 2004). The government also allowed existing settlements to expand by establishing a "Committee for Exceptions," which had the authority to recommend settlement expansion. The Committee comprised the Director General of the Ministry of Construction and Housing, the Accountant General of the Ministry of Finance, and the Defense Minister (Eldar & Zertal 2004: 178).[10] Through this committee, grants for construction were extended to "special cases," where the cessation of building would cause direct damage to the citizens residing in a given area.

The decision to establish the Committee for Exceptions sat uneasily alongside Prime Minister Rabin's campaign promise to cease the settlement project, but was emblematic of his ambivalent attitude toward the settler movement (Eldar & Zertal 2004). On the one hand, Rabin had expressed the view that continued settlement construction went against Israeli interests, while, on the other hand, he established a committee with the explicit purpose of bypassing this decree.

In January 1993, the Rabin government began negotiations with Palestinian partners that resulted in two sets of agreements, the Oslo Accords, signed in September 1993 (Oslo I) and September 1995 (Oslo II). Under the Accords, the newly created self-government over parts of the West Bank and Gaza Strip, as an interim step toward a final settlement of the Israeli–Palestinian conflict. In both the negotiations preceding the Accords, and the discussions that followed, Israel refrained from making any concessions with regard to the settlements (Hirschfeld 2000: 133).

The Rabin government avoided a firm commitment to freezing settlement construction, continued to expand the settlements in the name of "natural growth," and approved 4,000 new residences in existing West Bank settlements (Aronson 1996). Under the Labor governments of Rabin and (his successor) Peres, the number of settlers in the West Bank grew by 30 percent, from 111,600 in 1993 to 144,500 in 1996. Likewise, the WZO Settlement Division continued to expand and strengthen the settlement enterprise. However, the signing of the Oslo Accords led many settlers to perceive the government in general, and Rabin in particular, as traitors. Their response had two particularly violent manifestations. In February 1994, a US–Israeli terrorist from Hebron, murdered 29 Muslim worshippers and injured 125 others at the Tomb of the Patriarchs in Jerusalem. And in November 1995 Prime Minister Rabin was assassinated by a law student from Bar-Ilan University, an admirer of the Hebron terrorist[11] – both are revered within broad parts of the Israeli far-right.

In the next few election cycles, the settler vote played a role in the country's right-wing shift, although not as important as the influx of more than half a million Jews from the former Soviet Union in the early 1990s. They massively supported the right-wing parties in June 1996, contributing to the election of Benjamin Netanyahu as prime minister. Yet the Wye River Agreement of October 1998, signed by Netanyahu and Yasser Arafat and aimed at rebooting the Oslo II Accord, led to disillusionment among the settlers. In the elections of 1999, 18 percent of settlers voted for Labor's Ehud Barak rather than Netanyahu (Eldar & Zertal 2004). Faced with the prospect of further withdrawal from portions of the West Bank, they responded by establishing new "facts on the ground," setting up eight new outposts. During Barak's term, 1,924 housing units and 3,500 public buildings were constructed in the settlements, as the number of settlers in the West Bank grew by another 12 percent (*Haaretz*, September 12, 2000; Eldar & Zertal 2004: 238–239).

At the Camp David Summit of July 2000, Prime Minister Barak called upon the Palestinians to give up any claim to four settlements and areas – Ariel, the Etzion Bloc, Ma'ale Adumim, and Givat Zeev – in return for Israel relinquishing claim to Palestinian neighborhoods in East Jerusalem and parts of the Old City as well as territorial exchange in the Gaza Strip (Eldar & Zertal 2004: 242). However, the failure of the summit, and the subsequent outbreak of the Second Intifada, helped Sharon win the elections of March 2001 and become prime minister. Under him and his successor Ehud Olmert, the population of the Jewish settlements grew by some 100,000.

Sharon was known as the father of the settlement project, who had established dozens of settlements specifically to disrupt the territorial contiguity of Palestinian-populated areas, and thereby to forestall any possibility of a viable independent Palestinian state. But in 2003 he underwent an apparent change of heart. In December, he presented his government with a plan under which Israel would unilaterally withdraw from the Gaza Strip and the northern part of the West Bank. Although the plan was rejected in a referendum of Likud party members, in May 2004, it was approved by the Knesset in October 2004, and was executed in August 2005 (see Chapter 7).

The so-called Disengagement was a traumatic process for the country. Some 9,000 people, mostly families with children, were removed from their homes, communities, schools, and, in some cases, places of work. The settlers felt deeply betrayed by the government, which had supported their movement for decades. In addition, religious settlers believed that the evacuation of Jewish settlements was a serious violation of religious norms, with renunciation of any part of the Land of Israel considered on par with the sins of murder, apostasy, and incest (Shechory & Laufer 2011; Weisburd & Lernau 2006). But as Israel evicted its settlers in the Gaza Strip, the settler population in the West Bank continued to grow (see Figure 2.2). By the end of 2007, the Jewish population in the West Bank had reached 276,100, representing 5 percent of the Israel's Jewish population and almost 4 percent of the total population.

Netanyahu learned his lesson after his defeat to Barak. Never again would he fail to treat the national-religious (as well as ultraorthodox) constituencies in Israel as strong potential political allies. His subsequent governments, from 2009 onward, have seen increased settlement development. At least ten new settlements were approved in the West Bank between 2009 and 2013. During that same period, 5,302 tenders for housing units were approved for the West Bank and East Jerusalem. In 2014, this number was 4,485 (*New York Times*, March 12, 2015). The settlements also receive disproportionate funding in comparison to Israel

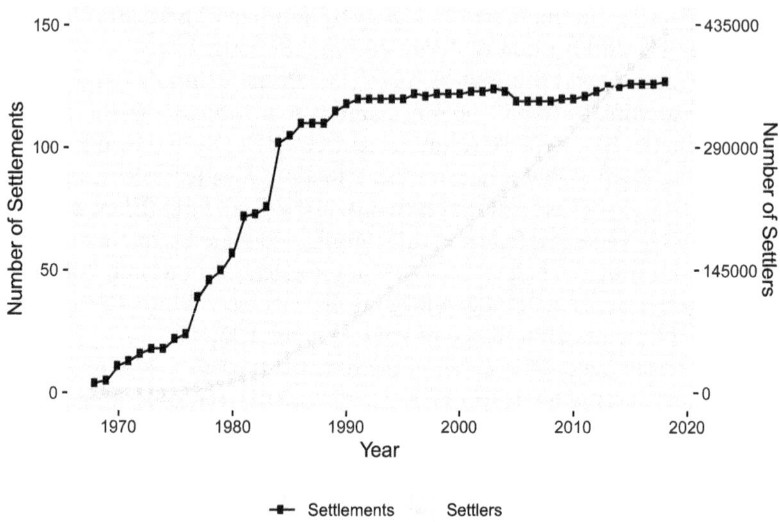

Figure 2.2 Number of settlers and settlements in the West Bank, 1967–2018[12]

within the Green Line. For instance, in 2014 the Netanyahu government spent approximately USD 950 per West Bank resident, more than double that spent on residents of Tel Aviv or Jerusalem (see Chapter 4).

In sum, all Israeli governments supported settlement activity, whatever their political persuasion. With the rise of the Likud governments, however, settlements were established over a broader territory, including areas with dense Palestinian settlement. Moreover, in the past fifty years, despite ongoing negotiations and the fact that Israel has surrendered (or offered to surrender) land and settlements in the Sinai II Agreement (1975), the Camp David Accords (1978), the "Autonomy Plan" for the West Bank (1978), Oslo I and II (1993, 1995), Gaza (2005), and in outpost demolitions, the settler population in the West Bank has more than doubled, at a growth rate much higher than that of the general Israeli population (see Figure 2.2).

In terms of their physical form, the settlements can be categorized broadly into four main types: urban suburbs, settlement blocs, villages, and outposts. The urban suburbs are towns and cities in the Jordan Valley, close to Tel Aviv and Jerusalem, which offer an attractive option for commuters. Settlement blocs comprise large or medium-sized cities

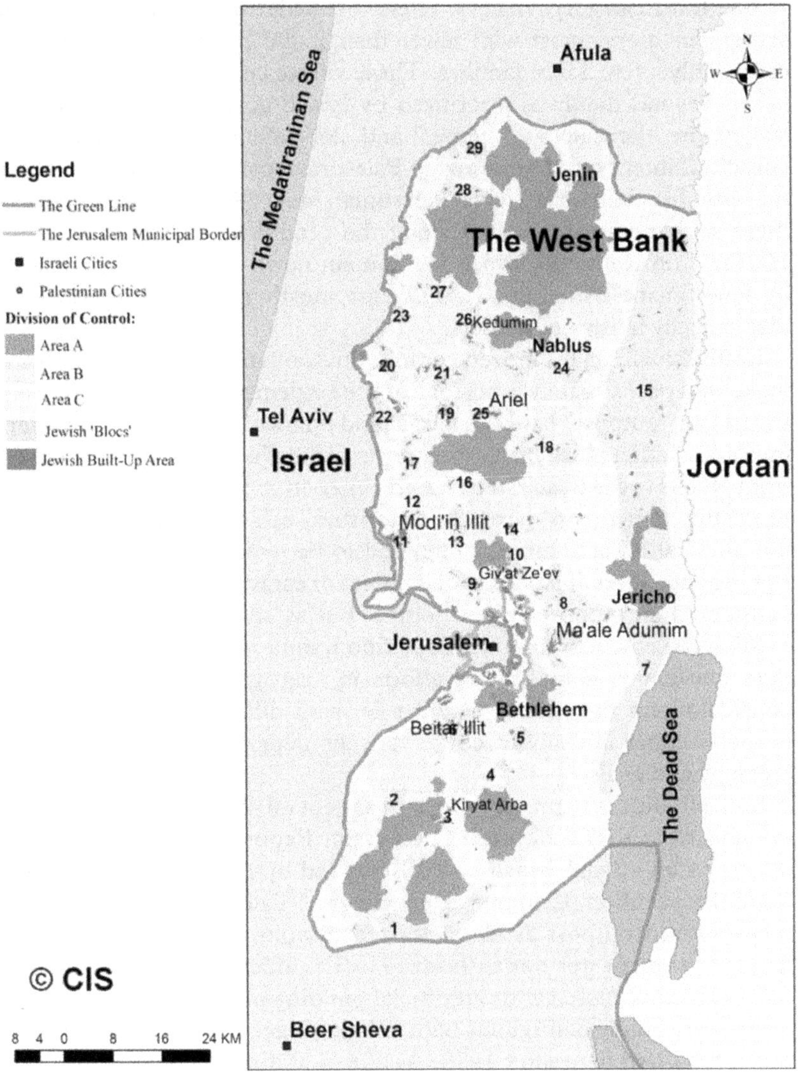

Figure 2.3 Blocs of Jewish settlements in the West Bank[13]

surrounded by clusters of smaller townships (see Figure 2.3). In the West Bank, the largest settlement blocs are the Ariel bloc and Gush Etzion (the Etzion Bloc). Currently, some 80 percent of the settlers (excluding East Jerusalem) live in settlement blocs.

The third category, villages, refers to smaller settlements outside the settlement blocs, most with fewer than 2,000 residents and, in some cases, only a few dozen families. These village communities were established beyond the areas prioritized by Israeli governments (the Jordan Valley, the "Jerusalem envelope," and along the Green Line), with the conscious intention of breaking up Palestinian contiguity and preventing the establishment of a viable Palestinian state (Arieli 2013). Many of these settlements are located along the central mountain ridge ("Gav HaHar") on Route 60, which is the main north–south traffic axis used by Palestinians (Arieli 2013). They are mostly populated by religious, ideologically motivated settlers.

Lastly, small, unauthorized communities, often described as outposts, make up approximately 1 percent of the settlements. What exactly constitutes an "outpost" has both a legal and political component. There are important differences in how outposts are defined by various sources, from NGOs to the Israeli state, based either on geography (e.g., proximity to existing settlements) or on characteristics such as finality (i.e., whether the physical infrastructure is intended to be temporary or permanent). For instance, a set of prefabricated homes or caravans on a hillside may be considered an outpost by one source, but as an extension of a nearby existing settlement by another. In addition, some outposts may have more than one name, complicating efforts to keep track of them. Political considerations also clearly play a role, with different sources defining outposts either liberally or conservatively, depending on their political ideology and goals.

Still, all sources paint a largely similar general picture of what outposts are and what they look like. The Sasson Report (2005: 92–93), produced by an official Israeli commission led by the former head of the State Prosecution Criminal Department, Talia Sasson, defines an unauthorized outpost as characterized by four defining qualities: (1) its establishment was not authorized by the official Israeli government; (2) it was constructed without official building plans and permits; (3) it is not territorially contiguous with existing legal settlements; and (4) it was established in or after 1990. As of this writing, there are more than 100 outposts (see Figure 2.4); the exact number of outposts varies between different sources, depending on the used definition.[14] Outposts are generally populated by right-wing ideologues, often stand on privately owned Palestinian land, and are considered illegal according to both Israeli and international law. The Sasson Report (2005) describes the outposts as a continuation of the settlement expansion project in the West Bank.

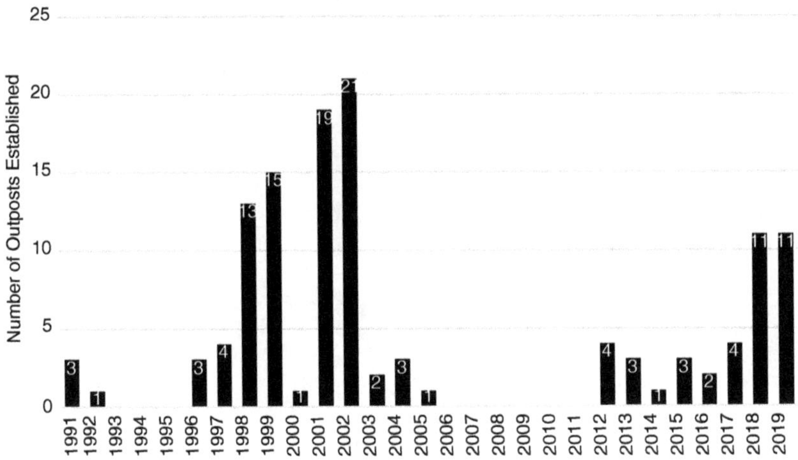

Figure 2.4 Number of unauthorized outposts per year, 1967–2019[15]

Outposts have been a point of friction between the Israeli government and the more hardline settlers. For example, in 2011, the Israeli authorities issued a declaration that all illegal settlements would be demolished by the end of the year. In response, the Chairman of the Samaria Regional Council, Gershon Mesika, said that removal of the outposts was a declaration of war on Jewish settlements. Despite the declaration, Hagit Ofran, a member of the NGO Peace Now and the head of its "Settlement Watch" project, claimed that many of the illegal outposts are actually transformed into "post-facto" legal settlements (*The Guardian*, March 8, 2011). Even the many outposts that are hastily dismantled by the Israel Defense Forces (IDF), on order from the Israeli Supreme Court and despite violent protests from settlers, are regularly quickly rebuilt too.

Collectively, all four types of settlements are largely urban and residential, though some retain a partly agricultural economy. Their infrastructure is distinct from the one that serves the Palestinian population in the West Bank. Settlers have access to a separate network of roads and to separate water and electricity infrastructures (see Figure 2.5). In addition, they are physically divided from Palestinian-populated areas by the separation barrier that Israel has constructed after the Second Intifada started, officially aimed at preventing Palestinian terrorists from penetrating into Israeli territory (Ben-Eliezer & Feinstein 2007).[16]

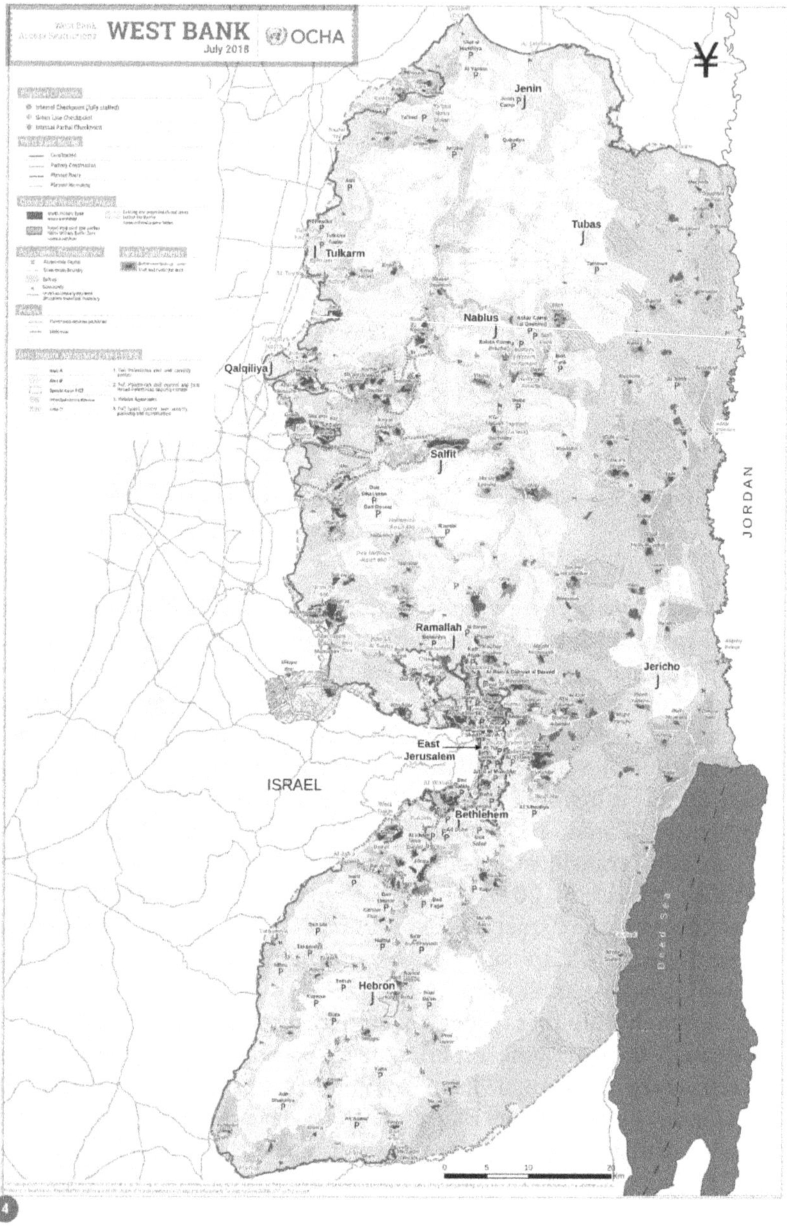

Figure 2.5 Roads and infrastructure in the West Bank[17]

2.2 The Civil Administration of the Settlements

The on-the-ground reality of dealing with the territories, immediately after the Six-Day War in 1967, had serious geopolitical implications. Israel decided that it would operate a de facto governance in the territories, as per the provisions set out by international law (Shoham 1996). As such, administrative responsibility for the territories fell to the military. The IDF was instructed to abide by international laws and regulations, particularly those demarcated in the Hague Convention III (1907), which deals with "Military Authority over the Territory of the Hostile State" (Shoham 1996: 250). Despite Israel's refusal to outright acknowledge its presence in the territories as de jure occupation, the military integrated the Hague Convention code and other regulations applicable to an occupying force, such as the Fourth Geneva Convention of 1949, into IDF regulations and rules of engagement (Shoham 1996; Israeli Defense Forces Gen. HQ Reg. 33.0133 1963).

Consistent with historical precedents and international regulations, IDF officers were appointed to administer each area under military control. The purview of each officer's sphere of responsibility was virtually unfettered, and included all aspects of the area, from security to civil issues to control over the population (Shoham 1996). Each officer had a team composed of both IDF personnel and local civilians from the regions. The Palestinian populations that fell under the administration of the newly installed military government remained largely self-governed, albeit still under the overall supervision of Israel.[18]

In the wake of the 1979 peace agreement with Egypt, Israel decided to separate civilian activities from security concerns. Hence, the administration of the territories was moved to a governing body known as the Civil Administration under the auspices of a Coordinator of Government Activities in the Territories (COGAT) in 1981. In the early 1990s, the Oslo Accords transferred responsibility for parts of the West Bank, known as Areas A and B, to the Palestinian Authority. However, control of Area C, which constitutes roughly 60 percent of the total land in the West Bank, and all the Jewish settlements, remained under the purview of COGAT (*Haaretz*, September 1, 2005).[19]

Coordinator of Government Activities in the Territories operates as a civilian operation, but sits under the command of the military authority in the West Bank (Bregman 2014). That is, it derives its authority from the IDF Central Command. According to its website,

COGAT is charged with "implementing Israel's civil policy in the territories." Among its broad responsibilities to better the life of the local population are infrastructural maintenance, water, legal, commerce, and health issues.[20] In practice, COGAT consists of twenty-two government offices located throughout the northern and southern regions, and eight district coordination and liaison centers spread throughout the West Bank. Within this framework, executive officers work to keep in continuous touch with local Palestinian residents, with Israeli settlement representatives, with international organizations, and with Palestinian security forces (in coordination with the Palestinian Authority).

On multiple occasions, COGAT has used its position to implement practices that directly affect Palestinian residents, even if this is not strictly within its outright authority. In practice, it acts as an extension of the Ministry of the Interior and functions as a liaison between the Palestinian Authority in the West Bank and the Israeli authorities, both civilian and military, in the region. However, as was the case prior to the Oslo Accords, much of COGAT's behavior is questionable – such as allowing construction on Palestinian agricultural land and fast-tracking building permits without due diligence.[21]

2.3 The International Political Context

The settlement of the West Bank (and other occupied territories) is part of the broader Israeli–Palestinian conflict and must therefore also be viewed through the wider lens of international relations in the Middle East and beyond. While Israeli politics played a substantive role in the trajectory of the settlement enterprise, international politics, including interventions by external states, have also informed the geopolitical situation of the West Bank up until now. In particular, a key Israeli concern has been shifts in US support for the development of Jewish settlements in the West Bank. For instance, former US Ambassador to Israel Daniel C. Kurtzer (2009) suggests that determining whether the expansion of the Israeli settlements is an impediment to the peace process or not has been an important question in US politics.

Since 1967, every US administration has maintained that development and expansion of Jewish settlements in the West Bank are detrimental to the peace process – a process that is particularly important to the United States because of its pivotal role as an essential third party in negotiations. Former president Jimmy Carter took a particularly hard line on settlement activity, labeling settlements illegal and in violation of the Fourth Geneva Convention (Carter 1980). In contrast, Eliott Abrams, Deputy National Security Advisor to President George W. Bush, has argued that, despite the fact that Israeli settlements beyond the Green Line have complicated the peace process, "there is no point in debating whether it was right to build them" (*The Washington Post*, April 8, 2009). Such statements reveal US support for a future peace agreement between the Israelis and the Palestinians,[22] but also show tacit endorsement of the "right" of settlers to continue living in the West Bank. The US approach seems to be to uphold its role of international policeman, while intimating continued support among the US elite for Israeli goals.

This approach is partially explained by the presence of a strong "pro-Israel" lobby[23] in Washington, which, especially since 1967, has successfully pushed the perception of common interests between Israel and the United States and the promotion of US policy toward that end (Waxman 2013). It is important to note that the US "pro-Israel" lobby does not refer to one singular entity, lacks a unified political design, and included a broad variety of opinions on Middle East policy. Keith Kiely (2017) argues that the objective of the "pro-Israel" lobby is twofold: first, to amplify existing representations of international players within the foreign policy discourse, and second, to maintain a positive relationship between Israel and the United States. He further suggests that the "pro-Israel" lobby plays a crucial role in framing US support for Israel and US representations of Israel itself.

In that vein, the "pro-Israel" lobby not only plays a direct role in influencing policy-making institutions, but also works to maintain a sympathetic narrative of Israel within US public opinion.[24] The most well-known of the "pro-Israel" lobby groups is the American Israel Public Affairs Committee (AIPAC) (Kiely 2017; Thouin 2010; Thomas 2007), which describes itself as "a bipartisan organization of US citizens committed to strengthening, protecting, and promoting the US–Israel relationship." It is important to note that AIPAC is not a political action committee, nor does it endorse candidates for elected or appointed office. In fact, its conferences have long been attended by high-ranking representatives of both parties.

The "pro-Israel" lobby deals with a whole host of issues and its relationship to the Israeli settlement enterprise and settlement expansion has been complex. American Israel Public Affairs Committee and others have framed the settlement issue as a necessity for Israel's security, rather than the fulfillment of biblical prophecy (Kiely 2017). This is probably due to the fact that the US idea of Israel is heavily related to geopolitics (both in the Cold War and in the "fight against Islamist terrorism") and self-preservation (following the Holocaust) as opposed to national-theological actualization. Leon Hadar (1992) has argued that the US's favorable policy toward Israel is predicated on "the compatibility of its policies with the dominant US foreign policy discourse and representations of the national interest" (in Kiely 2017: 143).

Despite US hegemony in the region, the EU has increasingly sought to engage in the region, highlighting its commitment to the rule of law (Santini 2010). In particular, it has demonstrated interest in playing a direct managerial role in the design and application of a solution to the Israeli–Palestinian conflict (Newman & Yacobi 2004). The EU advocates for an end to the Israeli occupation and for the dismantlement of the settlements. The EU involvement in the region follows long historical involvement in the area by key member states, in particular Britain and France, whose traditional presence in Middle Eastern affairs has given rise to a sense of responsibility to facilitate a feasible solution. Since the establishment of Israel, the EU has striven to maintain an active position as broker in country's affairs. However, over the latter half of the last century, different European countries have changed their policies and positions toward the conflict, and Jewish settlements in particular.

Initially, France was a pivotal ally of Israel, while Britain and Germany kept relatively distance. But in the run of to the 1956 Sinai campaign, Britain's position shifted, and joined France in favoring Israel over the Egyptian efforts to nationalize the Suez Canal (Newman & Yacobi 2004). Alliances and policies shifted again afterward, with Germany becoming Israel's closest European ally. By the Six-Day War, the tactics of the European states as a whole had turned to "compulsory forms of intervention," which specifically target the leadership on both sides of the conflict. This interventionist strategy has been recognized by scholars as the modus operandi for wealthy third-party nations (Newman & Yacobi 2004; Stetter et al. 2003). Since the 1970s, the EU has advocated support of the two-state solution, supporting both Israel's right to exist and the establishment of a sovereign Palestinian state, although individual member state's disagree on details.

In recent decades, the EU has been involved in a myriad of enterprises aimed at both maintaining its role as a power broker in the region and facilitating solutions to the Israeli–Palestinian conflict. Following the outbreak of the Second Intifada, the EU joined with Russia, the United States, and the UN in the "Quartet on the Middle East," which soon issued its Road Map for Peace (2002). The aims of the Road Map were to set guidelines and timelines for both sides of the conflict in "the political, security, economic, humanitarian, and institution-building fields"

(Newman & Yacobi 2004: 14–15). The initiative mandated that the Palestinians put an end to their terror attacks and promote a working democracy, and obligated Israel to take strides to ensure the establishment of a Palestinian state and end the occupation in the West Bank. But the plan fell by the wayside. The EU responded highly critically to Prime Minister Sharon's announcement of his Disengagement Plan, seeing it as a unilateral move (therefore) in contradiction to the Road Map. Eventually the EU supported it, under the condition that the process would reflect the benchmarks demarcated in the Road Map (Newman & Yacobi 2004).

Similarly, the UN has sought to play an "active role in the peace process" and "provide greater economic and technical assistance to the Palestinians" (UN 2008: 32). On the surface, there has been a consensus between the United States and other states in support of a two-state solution since the 1967 war, which was formalized in the Oslo Accords, and supported by the international community through the UN General Assembly. This is further reflected in criticism of settlement activities in the occupied territories and support for a Palestinian state (Shlay & Rosen 2010). This global consensus has persisted since the end of World War II and has been confirmed in various UN resolutions, from the decision to partition Palestine in 1947 to the passage of post-1967 War Resolution 242, which introduced the recommendation of "land for peace," whereby Israel would withdraw its troops from occupied territory in exchange for a full and lasting peace.

2.4 Conclusion

Since Israel's shock victory in the 1967 Six-Day War, settlement of the captured territories has been a contentious issue within Israel and the world. The vast majority of the world's states, as well as the UN, consider all the territories captured by Israel in 1967 and still under Israeli control to be "occupied territories." Israel has officially annexed East Jerusalem and the Golan Heights, which is not internationally recognized, but not the other territories. After decades of occupation and relatively small-scale Jewish settlement in the Gaza Strip, Israel unilaterally withdrew from that territory in 2005, dismantling its settlements but retaining military control of the Strip's external borders (except the short border between Gaza and Egypt).

The settlement of the West Bank has been slow but steady, irrespective of the political composition of the Israeli government, although it tends to increase under right-wing governments. The settlement enterprise has been advanced primarily by two camps, secular right-wing "hawks," whose main interest is strengthening the security of the Israeli state, and religious nationalists (the bulk of the leadership of the settler movement), who prioritize settlements in locations with biblical significance while seeking also to disrupt the geographical continuity of Palestinian-controlled territory (and thereby prevent the establishment of a Palestinian state in biblical lands).

As a consequence of the Oslo Accords, Israel has handed over some 40 percent of West Bank territory (Areas A and B) to the Palestinian Authority, holding on to Area C, which remains under the purview of the COGAT and is protected by the IDF. Today, more than 400,000 Jewish settlers in over 250 settlements and outposts in the West Bank (excluding Jerusalem), constituting less than 5 percent of the Israeli population. A minority of settlements started out as outposts, established by small groups of ideological settlers, which then, slowly but steadily, became linked to the official Israeli infrastructure within the West Bank, which is separate from the infrastructure for local Palestinians. Typically, once outposts are hooked up to the electricity and water systems and guaranteed IDF protection, they grow into fully legalized settlements, attracting less ideological inhabitants. The result is a maze of Jewish settlements spread across the West Bank, such that, without a significant number being dismantled, a viable Palestinian state is improbable.

This makes the settlement enterprise an essential part of the broader Israeli–Palestinian conflict, which remains one of the major international conflicts today. Given that the international community considers the Israeli presence in the West Bank in breach of international law, the settlements are an essential part of the occupation and a physical barrier to the two-state solution, which is supported by almost all major international actors (from Russia to the United States). Consequently, the issue of the settlements is not just a domestic political issue, but one with major international ramifications.

3 History of the Settler Movement

There is a tendency to describe all settlers as cut from the same cloth, with the most radical settlers tainting the entire Jewish population of the West Bank with the image of extremism. Contrary to this widespread perception, the settler population is actually quite heterogeneous. To understand the settlers' views, motivations and political impact, one must take this diversity into account. So far, few empirical studies have characterized the West Bank settler population, though several have pointed out the diverse character of settlements and their residents. This heterogeneity extends to the settler movement, even if its goals and motivations are narrower than those of the settler population.

This chapter shifts our focus from an examination of the settlement *project* to the settler *movement*. After a concise history of *the* settler movement, that is, as a unitary actor, we discuss the movement as a multifaceted "network of networks" by highlighting its main groups and actors. The aim is to characterize the *heterogeneity* of the contemporary settler movement, notably in (1) its range of sociodemographic profiles; (2) its ideological diversity; (3) its various actions and strategies; and (4) its main organizational branches.

3.1 History of the Settler Movement

To understand the settler movement one must examine it through the framework of Zionist ideology, more specifically religious Zionism. Hence, before moving on to the discussion of the contemporary settler movement, we pause to focus briefly on the most important actor in the movement for the first two decades of its existence.

The contemporary settler movement is firmly rooted in Gush Emunim, the spiritual heir of the Gahelet movement.[1] It was started by a group of largely young activists and students of Rabbi Zvi Yehudah Kook, notably Hanan Porat and Rabbi Moshe Levinger, who belonged to the youth faction of the National Religious Party (*Mafdal*, NRP). One of its earliest sparks was Rabbi Kook's infamous and impassioned speech on Israel's

Independence Day in 1967, just three weeks before the outbreak of the Six-Day War. Rather than celebrating Israel's achievements, he decried the fact that the young state's boundaries excluded key areas of biblical Israel. He admonished his listeners and the wider public for having forgotten their birthright and forsaken *Eretz Yisrael* for a modern, secular state, and tearfully called out the names of the biblical towns not included within the state's borders (Auerbach 2009; Sela 2007).

Formally, the settler movement was established only seven years later, as a reaction to the trauma of the Yom Kippur War of 1973, which rocked the foundations of Israeli society (Billig 2015). It contrasted sharply with the triumphalism experienced after the Six-Day War in 1967, when Israel annexed East Jerusalem, declaring it the unified capital of Israel, and imposed military rule on the Golan Heights (captured from Syria) and on the West Bank and Gaza Strip. The shock of the Yom Kippur War only stoked the settler project more. Religious Zionists believed that the 1973 war had confirmed the messianic process supposedly manifested in the founding of the state and the "miracle" of the Six-Day War (Aran 1986; Mendelsohn 2014). To hasten the messianic redemption of the land, they believed, it was necessary to establish a popular, all-Jewish movement, following the teachings of Rabbi Zvi Yehudah Kook, who provided its spiritual doctrine. His views on territorial maximization, whereby "each grain of soil was declared holy in a fundamental sense" (Sprinzak 1991: 45), inspired settler leaders to work actively to annex the captured land (Neidle 2013: 486). Accordingly, they established new settlements in the West Bank (e.g., Sebastia) and held street rallies and protests throughout Israel, including a march from Bet El to Jericho in the spring of 1976.

As members of the NRP youth faction, most Gush Emunim members were Israeli-born, from religious Ashkenazi families that were economically stable, and had highly religious educational backgrounds (Rubenstein 1982: 12). Together with the Land of Israel Movement (*HaT'nua L'ma-an Eretz Yisrael Hashlema*), a secular branch of the settler movement that formed around the same time, Gush Emunim was dedicated to ensuring that Israel retained the captured territories of Gaza, the West Bank, the Golan Heights and the Sinai Peninsula. Its members called for Jews from Israel and beyond to settle in these areas, to guarantee that they would remain part of Israel. However, the Land of Israel Movement did not have a young and active new membership. Therefore, despite its conflicting views of religion, it was willing to accept Gush Emunim as the leader of the cause, identifying with Rabbi Kook's yearning for redemption as its greatest goal (Billig 2015).

Gush Emunim was committed to values and principles that had been passed on from one generation to the next. In fact, the name itself was chosen with explicit attention to its religious connotations (Shafat 1995). A driving force behind the main activity of the movement was a profound connection to all, that is, Jewish, Israeli, and Zionist. Another was the belief that the past determines the present, and justifies the direction in which it develops (Feige 2002: 37). Accordingly, the essence of Zionism for Gush Emunim, which finds its expression in the act of settlement, is fulfillment of a *religious* commandment (*mitzvah*) – making the land flourish and settling it. The concept of settlement is also seen as a *national* duty, providing security for the nation's land and future (Feige 2009). In other words, Gush Emunim combined religious and nationalist aspects, both of which sanctify the past.

The nationalist aspects of the settlement project made sense to secular Zionists as well. For Yitzhak Tabenkin, a socialist and spiritual leader of the kibbutz movement, settlement activity was the primary goal of Zionism, and a necessary condition for true national independence (Zertal & Eldar 2007). But for the religious Zionists, active achievement of Israel's territorial goals was but a stage in a larger process of redemption, which lay in the hands of Heavenly Providence (Feige 2002: 63). As such, the salient premises of Gush Emunim, justifying the Jewish right to the "Land of Israel" as a whole, derived from a combination of general, historical, and existential factors, linking secular nationalism to religious Zionism (Shafat 1995; Tenenbaum & Eiran 2005). In their worldview, territorial compromise is a sin and not just an opposing political decision (Newman 2005; Weisburd 1989). In the words of Rabbi Shlomo Aviner (1990: 49), one of the most influential figures of religious Zionism and the settler movement,

> Even those who are far removed from religion, but strongly and solidly feel Jewish, understand that a people should be faithful to its land. In principle, it is simple to understand that a people without a land, is a dead people, and that a people without its entire country, are a handicapped people.

Gush Emunim perceived itself as the contemporary version of pioneering Zionism (Newman 2005), as a movement formed to continue the Zionist project, which was believed to have forsaken its original goals, ideals, and values. But its followers held views very different from the traditional assumptions of classical Zionists, for whom Israel was mainly a solution to the problem of anti-Semitism and the persecution of Jews, and for some of whom it was merely meant to be a temporary haven (Feige 2002; Shafat 1995). For Gush Emunim, a Jew does not immigrate to Israel in order to find a safe haven, but to return to the land of his ancestors. This is a crucial distinction that is worth keeping in mind as we delve deeper into the contemporary settler movement, and in particular the demographics of the settler population and the key actors involved in the movement today.

A number of factors led to Gush Emunim's reorganization into a more institutionalized form. First, the signing of the peace treaty with Egypt in 1979, which brought with it the withdrawal from the Sinai, raised questions among its members about the continued efficacy of their movement. But it was the uncovering of the terrorist organization Jewish Underground that generated a real crisis in the movement. The Jewish Underground was an organized group of Jewish Israelis that committed terrorist attacks against Palestinians from 1980 to 1984. Its members did not come from the margins of the community, but from the heart of the establishment. The organization was uncovered in April 1984, and its members were arrested.[2] These events led to the formation of two rival camps: a radical camp, headed by Moshe Levinger and Daniella Weiss, which supported the Jewish Underground, and a "moderate "camp, headed by Hanan Porat and Yoel Bin Nun, which condemned its activities and called for the creation of democratic institutions within Gush Emunim (Zertal & Eldar 2007).

In December 1980, the Yesha Council – named from the Hebrew acronym for Judea, Samaria, and Gaza – became the new formal umbrella organization for the settler movement, effectively replacing Gush Emunim. According to Gadi Taub (2010: 76), "Gush Emunim never formally ceased to exist, but it stopped being the center of political activity." In a similar vein, Rabbi Levinger, one of the founders of Gush Emunim, asserted that "what happened to Gush Emunim is exactly what happened to the Zionist Movement. It achieved its goal in principle and activity passed on to the practical activists" (*Yediot Aharonot*, December 5, 1980). In and around the Yesha Council, a loose network of networks continues to exist, which includes a plethora of smaller and bigger groups, which differ in terms of ideology and strategy, but all support the overall aims of the settler movement.

3.2 Heterogeneity of the Settlements and Settlers

To those unfamiliar or only distantly familiar with the settler movement, the conception of settlers often invokes a caricatural generalization of its more antagonistic elements. Based on the most attention-grabbing details, which make the news, the wider public's perception of the settlements and settlers often reflects only its most marginal components. In reality, the settler movement, like most larger social movements, is heterogeneous and diverse. It is crucial to understand this diversity, which is social, ideological, and tactical, to assess and explain the success of the movement.

3.2.1 Sociodemographic Diversity

Contemporary West Bank settlers are not monolithic, but differ in terms of religiosity, lifestyle, education, income, country of origin, and motives for settlement (Hirsch-Hoefler et al. 2019). In an interview with the *Jerusalem Post* (May 19, 2005), Yesha Council spokesperson Emily Amrousi described West Bank settlers as a diverse population consisting of "farmers in the Jordan Valley, Russian *olim* in Maale Adumim, secular people in Ariel, *haredim* in Beitar Illit, yeshiva students in Yitzhar and national-religious settlers in Efrat."

The settler population now includes members of the first, second, and third generations. While first-generation settlers made the decision to immigrate or relocate to the West Bank, whether from Israel or from abroad, many current settlers were born and raised in the West Bank. And, though Jewish immigration into the West Bank has dwindled since the Second Intifada, natural growth has more than offset this decline (Gordon & Cohen 2012). For example, in 1991, about 9,500 Jews migrated or relocated to the West Bank and Gaza Strip and 2,700 were born there. In contrast, only about 3,400 Jews arrived through migration or relocation in 2015, but 11,800 were born in West Bank settlements.

With respect to the places of origin of new arrivals, the main sources of immigration from abroad are France, Russia, United Kingdom, Ukraine, and the United States. Sara Hirschhorn (2017) estimates that the West Bank is currently home to 60,000 US Jewish immigrants, accounting for 15 percent of the settler population. As such, US-born settlers are strikingly overrepresented, both within the settler population itself and within the total population of Jewish US immigrants to Israel. They are mostly young, highly educated (about 10 percent of US settlers hold PhDs), and religiously traditional but not necessarily Orthodox.[3] In the past decade, on average some 12 percent of US immigrants each year cited the West Bank as their "first district of residence" in the country (Hirschhorn 2017). Additionally, at of the end of 2018, 19,144 immigrants from the former Soviet Union live in the West Bank, making up 4.5 percent of the total settler population.

Five urban settlements are their main centers of residence for the Soviet settlers: Ariel, Givat Zeev, Karne Shomron, Kiriat Arba, and Ma'ale Adumim (Berthomière 2001). In 2017, just 710 immigrants settled in the West Bank, comprising 2.7 percent of all immigrants into Israel, and only 1 percent of all immigrants from the former Soviet Union.[4] This was down from 766 in 2016 and 880 in 2015 – both equate to about 3 percent of the total number of immigrants into Israel that year (see Figure 3.1).

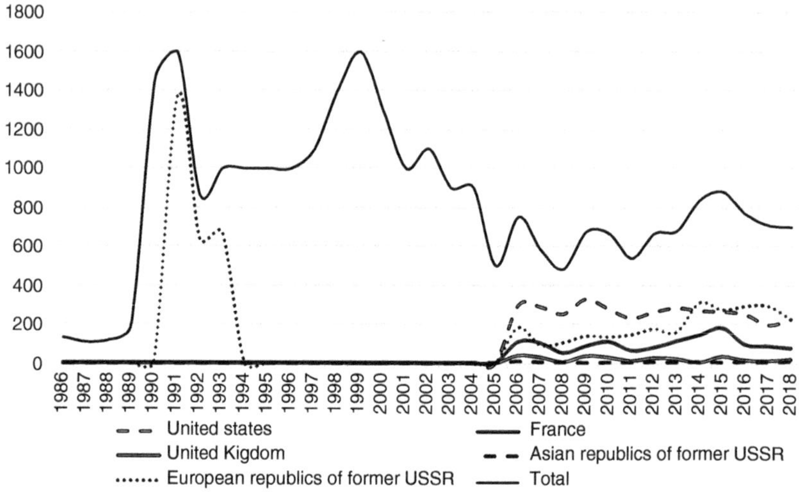

Figure 3.1 Immigrants in the West Bank by last country of residence[5]

While the settler population as a whole is heterogeneous, individual settlements tend to constitute homogenous communities, based around either a national-religious vision of "land redemption" or a desire for a better quality of life with no particular religious ideology attached (Hirsch-Hoefler et al. 2016). Hence, the prevalent distinction made among Jewish settlers is between ideological and quality-of-life settlers, the latter being not concerned with upholding the ideology of Greater Israel (Hirsch-Hoefler et al. 2016; International Crisis Group 2013). Peace Now classified each settlement as ideological, quality-of-life, mixed (i.e., quality-of-life and ideological), and ultraorthodox, using census data from the Israel Central Bureau of Statistics (see Figure 3.2). Based on this classification, there are almost as many ideological settlements as all other settlements together. Importantly, this refers to the number of settlements, not settlers. Most notably, while only 6 percent of settlements (8 out of 127 settlements in the West Bank) are ultraorthodox, more than a third of all settlers are ultraorthodox (see later).

Quality-of-life settlers have always been primarily young couples, drawn to the settlements by highly subsidized mortgages for single-family homes within driving distance of the center of the country, where most have family and friends (Haklai 2007; Sasley & Sucharov 2011). In fact, most of the quality-of-life settlers are employed inside Israel (Hirsch-Hoefler et al. 2019). Their main reason for living in the West Bank is

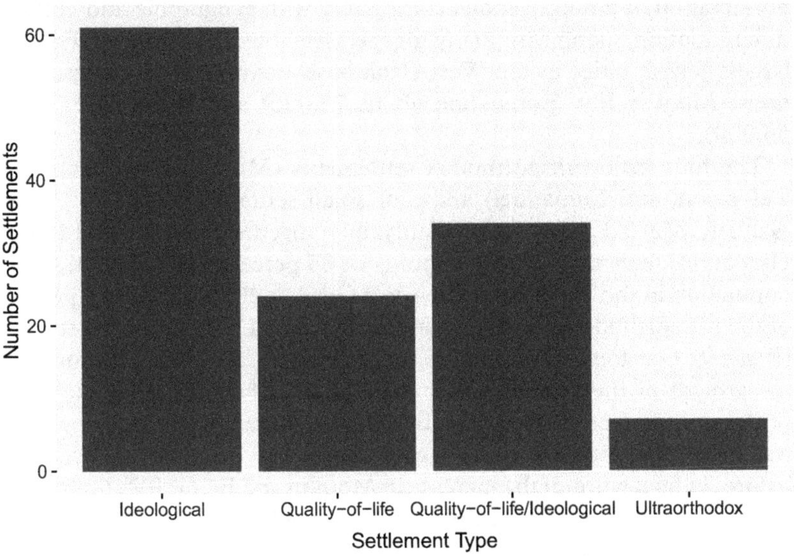

Figure 3.2 Number of settlements by type[6]

financial, since the Israeli government considers West Bank settlements to be "priority areas" eligible for mortgage subsidies. It also subsidizes construction projects and land purchases in the West Bank and provides additional benefits in spheres such as education and health.

The quality-of-life settlers include both secular and ultraorthodox (*Haredi*) groups. For the most part, residents of these settlements are urban families, which chose these settlements to be eligible for government benefits and incentives that enabled them to purchase a large home at a low price (Sheleg 2003). Nevertheless, even though they initially moved over the Green Line for purely financial reasons, many of them have since developed an ideological commitment to the settlement enterprise (Hirsch-Hoefler et al. 2019; Shamai 2002).

While ultraorthodox in their religiosity, most Haredi settlers fit more comfortably into the rubric of quality-of-life settlers as they do not share the religious-nationalist beliefs of the other religious settlers and are in fact fundamentally opposed to the Zionist idea. Lee Cahaner (2016) analyzed the factors of immigration to cities built in the West Bank by ultraorthodox families in the 1990s and 2000s and concluded that it stemmed from limited resources and low supply of apartments in Haredi cities. She argued that the ultraorthodox settlements enable the preservation of a homogenous community with geographic and cultural differentiation, along with many inexpensive housing solutions. The two largest Jewish cities in the West Bank have exclusively Haredi populations: Modi'in Illit (population about 73,000) and Beitar Illit (about 56,000).

The four major ultraorthodox settlements (Modi'in Illit, Beitar Illit, Tel-Tzion, and Immanuel) and four small settlements (Ma'ale Amos, Nahliel, Metsad/Asfar, and Matityahu) together had over 140,000 Haredi residents in 2017, accounting for 35 percent of the Jewish settler population in the West Bank (Regev & Gordon 2019). Some 13 percent of the ultraorthodox population in Greater Israel lives in the West Bank (Regev & Gordon 2019). Due to the high birth rate in this community, the growth of the Haredi settler population is far outpacing the other settler groups (see Figure 3.3). By 2015, the Haredi settler population was more than eighteen times bigger than it had been twenty-five years before. In fact, without the increase in Modi'in and Beitar Illit, the growth of the Jewish population in the territories would have been significantly reduced and the migration balance would have been negative (Shragai 2003).

As a group, ideological settlers tend to be both more religious and more politically active than quality-of-life settlers, although the growing presence of ultraorthodox settlers has changed the former. Ideological settlements were not established for the sake of material benefits, though they too received great material advantages, but rather to realize the ideal of resettling the ancient land of Israel. Ideological settlers, most of whom are deeply religious, are thus motivated by the goal of redeeming the land of their forefathers and fulfilling the biblical promise of the return of the "People of Israel" to the "Land of Israel."

For the most part, ideological settlements are generally older than quality-of-life settlements, were established by settler groups (rather than the Israeli state), and are situated in the heart of the West Bank. Locations were chosen for ideological and strategic reasons, including to prevent contiguity of Palestinian territory and (thereby) preventing the establishment of a Palestinian state. Residents of these settlements include many original Gush Emunim supporters and activists, who believed they were fulfilling an important national mission (Hirsch-Hoefler et al. 2018). The ideological settlers remain a relatively small group, however (Mendelsohn 2016). There are approximately 100,000 religious Zionist settlers, that is, less than one quarter of the whole settler population (see Figure 3.3).

Differences between settlements established for national-religious reasons and those that were not can also be seen in the names they were given.

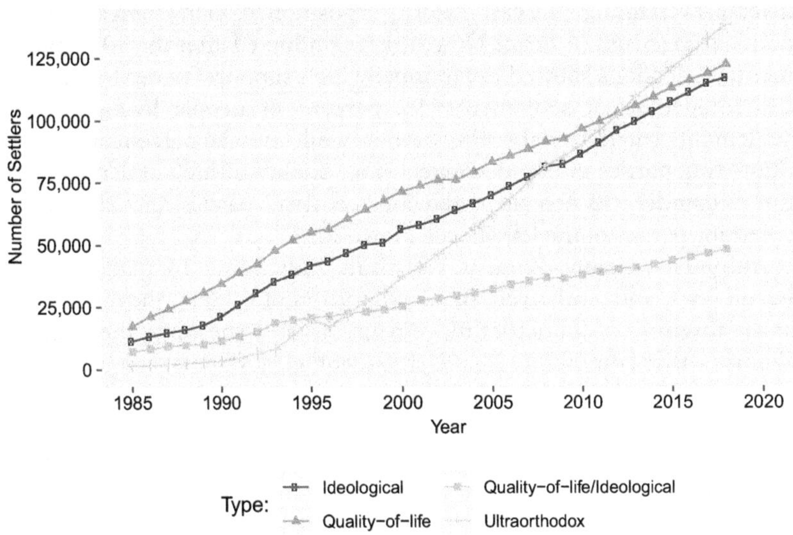

Figure 3.3 Jewish settlers by type of settlement[7]

Names of national-religious settlements generally have biblical connotations or religious-historical significance (such as *Efrat*, *Ofra*, and *Elazar*). By contrast, quality-of-life settlements typically have names taken from nature or the landscape, such as *Shaked* (almond) and *Sal'it* (ear of wheat).

Clearly, different subdivisions of the same population are possible. For instance, Hirschberger and Hirsch-Hoefler (2016) divided the secular and nationalist-religious settler population (excluding ultraorthodox settlers) into four subgroups – nationalist settlers; ultranationalist settlers; quality-of -life settlers; and a group comprising residents of Ariel, who tend to be the most secular but also more right-wing than quality-of-life settlers. Residents of Ariel, by this reckoning, constitute a unique group located between quality-of-life settlers, whose views are generally near the center of the political spectrum, and the right-wing religious-ideological settlers (see in more detail in Chapter 6). However, both Ariel residents and quality-of-life settlers cite economic and quality-of-life considerations as more important than ideological ones in their decision to live in the West Bank.

3.2.2 *Ideological Heterogeneity*

Given the difference in religiosity, between settlers and settlements, it comes as no surprise that the settler population is also ideologically diverse, even though the vast majority is positioned on the right side of the political spectrum. A Peace Now survey conducted after the 2013 parliamentary elections showed exceptionally high support for right-wing parties in ideological settlements: 92 percent of people living in such settlements voted for right-wing parties, while only 50 percent supported right-wing parties in nonideological (i.e., quality-of-life) settlements. Of the remainder, 30 percent voted for "centrist" parties and 20 percent voted for parties of the left (Peace Now, 2013).

Although religious Zionists constitute only some 15 percent of all Israeli Jews, and a relatively small proportion of settlers, they have been at the forefront of the settler movement. Broadly speaking, the religious Zionist settler community, that is, the ideological settlers, can be divided into two main camps: the national religious on the one hand, and the ultraorthodox nationalists (or *Hardal*)[8] on the other. While both belong to the Israeli right, there are significant ideological differences between them. The national religious settlers hold more moderate right-wing political positions compared to the Hardal settlers, who are characterized by a negative approach to modernity, fundamentalist religious observance and an extreme right version of religious nationalism (Mozes et al. 2014: iii).

Another, related, source of ideological division between the two religious Zionist camps is the issue of state authority (Alimi 2010: 13). In particular, the division is between *Mamlachti* (nationalist) and anti-/post-*Mamlachti* (ultranationalist) groups and individuals, where the former accept the authority of the state, while the latter value religious principles and *Halacha* over the state's authority (Mendelsohn 2014; Roth 2014). *Mamlachtiut* is a "religiously grounded loyalty to the State of Israel combined with a commitment to promoting its welfare. This is an essential element of religious Zionism, which sanctifies Jewish sovereignty" (Mozes et al. 2014: iv). It refers to a commitment to both the *authority* of the Jewish State and to national *solidarity*, that is, a desire to remain part of mainstream Jewish society. This serves as the main restraint on the religious Zionists' political behavior in cases of territorial evacuation. *Mamlachti* settlers thus support lawful protest against policies with which they disagree, but stop short of using or justifying violence against the state and its institutions.

While *Mamlachti* settlers perceive rejection of the state as a rejection of God's will, the post-*Mamlachti* settlers believe they are fulfilling a divine mandate in which power reaches beyond the democratic state. They embrace an alternative theology, which draws from the school of *Chabad*,[9] and especially the teachings of Rabbi Yitzchak Ginsburgh – a US-born graduate of the University of Chicago, who advocates for the restoration of the Israelite Kingdom and has justified the 1994 terrorist attack in the Tomb of the Patriarchs (see Mozes et al. 2014: 54). He is currently the head of the Od Yosef Hai yeshiva in the settlement of Yitzhar. Followers of the late far-right Rabbi Meir Kahane also fall within the post-*Mamlachti* camp (see later).

Post-*Mamlachti* settlers hold that government institutions have a mandate to lead Israel only in a religious-ideological direction, that is, in line with the law of the Torah as interpreted by the rabbis, and therefore refuse to accept the authority of any form of leadership, whether representing the state or mainstream religious settlers, perceived as working against a religious commandment. Consequently, there is almost no restriction on their political behavior, with some calling for aggressive, even violent, collective struggle against those charged with implementing territorial withdrawals. Others even seek to secede from Israel and establish an independent entity, a "State of Judea" or "Torah State," which would be free from Israel's secular polity. In line with this desire, their objective is to undermine the authority of the Israeli state and its ability to impose order on its citizens. The post-*Mamlachti* settlers are concentrated in northern Samaria, in the settlements and outposts centered around the biblical Shechem (contemporary Nablus).

The exact size of these subgroups is hard to assess, but the ultranationalist camp comprises probably of a few thousand people (Cherlow 2007). There is also no precise equivalence between the two sets of opposing groups, *Mamlachti* versus post-*Mamlachti*, and national-religious versus ultraorthodox. For example, the *Hardal* settlers fall into both the *Mamlachti* and post-*Mamlachti* camps. However, over time there has been a discernible weakening in these settlers' commitment to the Israeli state, due to its failure to pursue their ideological agenda (Mozes et al. 2014).

3.2.3 Strategic diversity

In terms of political and social movement action, settler groups employ a triad of strategies to attain their goals – moderate, radical, and extreme actions. The particular method chosen by different groups generally affects how they are perceived in public discourse, and also tends to reflect their willingness to work within (vs. outside or against) the established governmental system.

In general, the settler movement seeks to advance the various aspects of its agenda through a broad range of activities and strategies, most of which fall within the spectrum of a moderate (legal) approach. They range from benign Jewish history educational campaigns in regions like

Hebron, to political lobbying efforts in the Knesset, and to large-scale annual conferences and demonstrations in Jerusalem, which attract high-level public figures inside and outside the Israeli government. The more moderate settler networks employ tactics like coalition-building and lobbying, in an effort to change policies that they perceive as unfair and wrong. However, they do so within the rules of the political game, making use of their access to institutions like the Knesset.

Occasionally, settler groups will cross over into radical, that is, illegal but nonviolent, activities. Notable examples of this category include blocking roads, trespassing on private property, and encouraging civil disobedience. Groups that employ such practices often seek to amplify their effects by encouraging widespread engagement in order to paralyze law enforcement authorities. This set of actions represent direct efforts to hinder government dictates and defy standing laws, but fall short of actions in the third group, which explicitly call for violence.

For all their radicalism, actions within the second group still reflect a willingness to work within the established system. However, a small proportion of settlers does not regard itself as subject to the institutions of the state, including settler institutions like the Yesha Council, which are viewed as too cozy with the state. Over recent years, they have specialized in so-called price-tag attacks, terrorist acts of violence and intimidation that include arson, vandalism, and even murder, typically aimed at Palestinians, leftist Jewish Israeli activists, and Israeli security forces (Eiran & Krause 2018; Getmansky & Sinmazdemir 2018). The first price-tag attacks took place in 2006, in response to Israel's withdrawal from the Gaza Strip and the evacuations of Jewish outposts in the West Bank, which riled and radicalized the settler camp. Although the Yesha Council denounced price-tag attacks as immoral in 2011, fringe far-right settler groups continue to take the law into their own hands. According to Ehud Eiran and Peter Krause (2018), 185 price-tag attacks were carried out between December 2008 and August 2015.[10]

3.3 The Three Organizational Branches

Three types of actors constitute the contemporary settler movement: (1) highly centralized and bureaucratic *institutions* (notably, the Yesha Council and its executive arm, Amana); (2) informal *networks* (a segmented and polycentric body of groups, each organized around its own members, and at present without a central leading body); and (3) individual *influencers* (whose activities are not tied to any formal entity, yet who share the ideology of the general settler enterprise and create initiatives to further the settler cause). We discuss each in turn.

3.3.1 Institutions

The two main institutions of the contemporary settler movement are the Yesha Council and its executive arm, Amana. Both have their origins in Gush Emunim. Its members established the Yesha Council in the belief that interest politics could be best achieved by a formal body, a "council," as opposed to a social movement, as Gush Emunim had been (Sprinzak 1981).[11] The Yesha Council has a formal and legal structure with an elected chair, a spokesperson, and a regular budget. While sharing the same ideological vision, the Council is characterized by favoring practicality and pragmatism over the ideological fervor that was the hallmark of Gush Emunim. Accordingly, it believes that the settler movements' political goals can best be achieved by advocating for the settlements on more politically uncontentious grounds, such as security, rather than religious-ideological arguments (Neidle 2013).[12] Indeed, Dani Dayan, former Chairman of the Yesha Council (2007–13) and later its Chief International Envoy, exemplifies this, being both a secular Jew and yet ideologically committed to settlement construction (Prusher 2011).

The Yesha Council's importance lies in its capacity to represent settler interests and implement a unified strategy. Every settlement in the West Bank is represented on the Council, which is at the apex of a pyramidal structure comprising the elected mayors of the 4 large cities (Ariel, Beitar Illit, Ma'ale Adumim, and Modiin Illit), 6 counties (Binyamin, Gush Etzion, Hebron Mountains, Jordan Valley, Megilot, and Samaria), and 13 smaller municipalities, encompassing approximately 127 communities and 427,800 residents throughout the West Bank. A Board of Directors formulates its general policy, which is implemented by the Chairman and other senior figures.

The Yesha Council excels at political lobbying on settlement issues and construction (Pedahzur et al. 2014). Through its regular departments it carries out a host of functions, including territory-wide coordination (e.g., on roads, safety, security, and development); legal matters (e.g., handling applications of Israeli law to Jewish settlers); fundraising; absorption of newcomers; public relations activities (disseminating information to local and foreign media); conducting tours for politicians and public opinion makers from Israel and abroad; and coordinating security affairs with the IDF and other security forces (Shaw-Smith 1994).

While Gush Emunim supported a broad and diverse set of goals – including expansion of national and religious education, unity of the Jewish people, support for Jewish immigration to Israel, political and economic independence from foreign powers, and an activist foreign policy (Mnookin & Eiran 2005: 11) – the Yesha Council focuses on one single objective: settling the West Bank and, until the 2005 withdrawal, the Gaza Strip. According to its website, the Council aims "to establish and expand the settlement enterprise in Judea and Samaria through political, legal and media channels, to emphasize the settlement cause as the central realization of Zionism . . . .[to] emphasize our natural and moral right to the land of Israel, and oppose the transfer of land to our enemies." To achieve these goals, it seeks to strengthen its political network by building strong ties with and pursuing support from Israel's political elite (Haklai 2007). The Yesha Council works together with Israeli authorities like government ministries, the IDF, and the Jewish Agency to provide resources and amenities to the settlements, and to regulate expansion of the settlements (Lustick 1982). The Council has also been able to forge political links with large "pro-Israel" organizations in the United States, such as AIPAC and various Christian Zionist groups (Neidle 2013).

Importantly, the Yesha Council believes in the legitimacy of the Israeli state and accepts its authority, even when government policies are inconsistent with its priorities (Haklai & Loizides 2015). It not only cooperates with the government, but aims to maintain political representation within the government. For instance, Dayan was named Consul General in New York in 2016, while Naftali Bennett, another former chairman, became active in the highest echelons of Israeli politics – leading the pro-settler party Jewish Home from 2012 to 2018, and serving at various points in high-ranking ministerial positions.

The second institutional branch founded by Gush Emunim is Amana (Covenant). While the Yesha Council is responsible for existing settlements, Amana's role is to set up new settlements. It was founded as the executive arm of Gush Emunim in 1978, with the stated goal of developing communities not only in the occupied territories, but also in less-developed portions of Israel proper, mainly the Galilee in the north and the Negev in the south. Amana's rubric includes not only establishing the physical infrastructure for new communities, but also ensuring the presence of industries and services needed to support and maintain them over time. The two institutions have close organizational and personal connections (Yishai 2012: 88). However, Amana always had a distinct leadership. In the 1980s it was led by Uri Ariel, who later became an MK and Housing and Construction Minister. He was succeeded by Ze'ev Hever (known by the nickname Zambish) in 1989, one of the most influential settlers and a former member of the Jewish Underground.

As a formal institution with legal standing, Amana can compete in state tenders and has received land for construction from the WZO Settlement Division (Haklai & Loizides 2015). It plans and initiates construction projects and obtains authorization to build. Moreover, as a registered association, a cooperative land-settling agency, Amana has a well-designed institutional structure and abundant resources. It also maintains an Aliyah department, with representatives abroad, and an information department that mobilizes potential settlers (Yishai 2012: 120). According to investigations, Amana collects a small fee from each settler residing in any of its settlements. This money not only helps to finance the organization, but also supports unauthorized construction (*Haaretz*, May 28, 2013).

A third component of the institutional branch is the Yesha Rabbinical Council (*Va'ad Rabanei Yesha*), the movement's official spiritual arm, which was established by Rabbi Eliezer Melamed, a student of Rabbi Zvi Yehudah Kook, in the late 1980s. All Rabbinical Council members are rabbis who serve in West Bank settlements (and previously in the Gaza Strip). Traditionally, the Rabbinical Council provided answers to halachic questions (i.e., questions of Jewish law) related to life in the settlements. Over time, it has become for many settlers the supreme authority in terms of which forms of opposition are legitimate in the face of government decisions aimed at territorial withdrawal and settlement evacuations. The Yesha Rabbinical Council has played a major role in justifying some of the more ideologically driven actions of settlers. For example, in the past the Council has endorsed Hilltop Youth outposts on the grounds that, for modern Jews, spiritual salvation depends on physically settling the land (*Aruts Sheva*, September 27, 2007). Since the death of Rabbi Avraham Shapira in 2007,[13] the Rabbinical Council has suffered from internal division and has almost ceased to function, with its spiritual role now filled by many competing religious-spiritual networks. One major example is the network led by Rabbi Yitzchak Ginsburgh, mentioned earlier.

3.3.2 *Networks*

The settler movement also includes a number of loose, informal, decentralized network of networks, which often diverge, ideologically and strategically, from the Yesha Council. There are dozens of such networks, which include groups like Women in Green (*Nashim Beyarok* or *Ribbonut*), the Yesha Human Rights Organization, Sovereignty (*Kommemiyut*), Jewish Heart (*Halev HaYehudi*), Faithful of the Land of Israel (*Neemanei Eretz Yisrael*), Defenders of the Land (*Maginei Eretz*), Regavim,[14] Hilltop Youth, Kahane Lives (*Kahana Chai*), and The Revolt (*Hamered*). Each group has their own specific activities, focus and leadership, though they share the basic goals of the settlement movement. It is hard to discern the relative strength of these groups, as well as their cohesion as a collective movement, not least because membership is often shared (Jones & Joffé 2013).

All networks share the same ambition of safeguarding and widening the settlement enterprise. Where the networks mainly differ is in the strategies through which they try to achieve this goal. This dispute is not merely tactical. One of the most salient ideological disputes that has caused division within the decentralized settler camp is over the subject of state authority, that is, the nationalists vs. the ultranationalists. Most of the networks belong to the nationalist (*Mamlachti*) faction, which may oppose specific government decisions but accepts the legislative and executive authority of the state. Examples include the Women in Green, the Yesha Human Rights Organization, and the Professors for a Strong Israel. These groups have all come into conflict with certain actors and ministers within the Israeli state, but they do not question the legitimacy of the governmental structure itself. In contrast, the ultranationalist (post-*Mamlachti*) faction is much smaller and actually quite marginal. The most prominent examples are the Hilltop Youth and The Revolt, whose members mainly comprise second- and even third-generation settlers with extreme right ideologies (in particularly Kahanism).

Generally speaking, in terms of their action strategies, the decentralized networks fall into two main groups: those that preach and employ violence, and those that do not. Obviously, there is a positive relationship between ideology and strategy, with ideologically extreme groups being more prone to using violence; and relatedly, between strategy and the groups' position toward the Israeli state, with the post-*Mamlachti* faction being the most violent.

Nonviolent Groups Most settler networks follow the path of nonviolence. Women in Green (WiG), a registered nonprofit organization not affiliated with any political party, describes itself on its website as "a grassroots movement of women and men, young and old, secular and religious, all bound together by a shared concern ... [for] the Land of Israel." Its aim is to prevent any future withdrawals from occupied territories, and to preserve the Jewish character of the State of Israel. Founded by Ruth and Michael Matar in 1993, the group draws its name from the green hats members wore during their campaign against the Oslo Accords in the 1990s. Women in Green is committed to educational, nonviolent direct action and adheres to the classic concept of civil disobedience. Its activities include gathering at West Bank checkpoints and roadblocks in order to support the IDF soldiers serving there. In addition to weekly street theater and public demonstrations, they write weekly articles, commission posters, advertise in newspapers, and lecture to groups in order to educate the electorate on the consequences of government policies. Since November 2013, WiG has published a bi-annual journal (online and in print), called *Sovereignty*, whose aim is to carry on the ideological and practical discourse of Jewish sovereignty in the West Bank.[15] It distributed 100,000 copies of its first edition throughout Israel and to decision makers abroad (mainly the United States). Women in Green also supports the Jewish community in the city of Hebron and sponsors annual Hanukkah and Purim parties with gifts and professional entertainment for that community.

Professors for a Strong Israel (PSI), also known as the Academic Council for National Policy (ACNP), was founded by a group of Israeli academics in 1988, but stepped up its activities after the signing of the Oslo Accords in 1993. Professors for a Strong Israel describe itself as "a non-partisan organization of academics united by a shared concern for the security and the Jewish character of the State of Israel." Members include professors, researchers, and scientists from all major academic disciplines and academic institutions in Israel. It acts independently of other settler groups, with the goal of strengthening the case for a Greater Israel by influencing the educational discourse and mass media. Most of its activities are informational, such as organizing conferences, publishing articles and reports, preparing press releases, and political lobbying. However, PSI is also thought to have helped organize protests and demonstrations with other far-right settler groups of a similar mindset, specifically against the evacuations of Homesh and Amona (*NRG*, February 1, 2006). Additionally, it is deeply concerned with what its members refer to as "the leftist control over academia."

Regavim focuses on construction work in the West Bank that has been done by Israeli Arabs or Palestinians without Israeli permits.[16] Founded in 2007 by Yehuda Eliyahu and Bezalel Smotrich, the group aims to counter the monitoring and petitioning of settlement activities by left NGOs, by monitoring and petitioning Palestinian building and permitting activities. According to Dror Etkes, former Director of Settlement Watch, Regavim was not just conceived as a response to the work of anti-settlement NGOs, but it was also modeled directly on Settlement Watch and Yesh Din.[17] It utilizes the "mirror petitioning" tactic when leftist organizations petition the courts in order to gauge ideological bias (Perugini & Gordon 2015), using similar tools as state institutions and human rights organizations (e.g., aerial photos, geographic information system, and legal petitions). Using human rights language to frame their struggle, "illegal Jewish construction" becomes "illegal Palestinian construction" and "Palestinian villages" become "Palestinian outposts"

(Perugini & Gordon 2015: 116). Regavim also petitions against government removal of settler outposts. Its plan is thus to push the state to alter its policies and enforcement practices in the West Bank. By doing so, its agenda converges with those of Israeli settlers. Moreover, Regavim maintains close institutional ties with the Yesha Council (Perugini and Rabie 2012). It also focuses on lobbying Knesset members and ministries as well as the international public in order to spread its agenda.

Lastly, there are a few settler networks that focus on legal aid. Founded by Shmuel Meidad in 2001, Honenu is registered as a nonprofit legal aid organization. Its primary activities are approaching active and reserve IDF soldiers as well as citizens to offer legal services against what it perceives as "discriminatory government authorities and a court system heavily influenced and pressured by anti-Israel 'human rights' groups." It maintains a 24/7 hotline, along with a news service, and produces updates about ongoing cases in French, English, Hebrew, and Russian. Recently, Honenu was accused of funneling funds to other far-right organizations, some of which seek to overthrow the Israeli government (*Haaretz*, May 5, 2016).

The Yesha Human Rights Organization (also knows as Human Rights Organization of Judea and Samaria) was founded in 2004 by Orit Strook, a former MK for the far-right Tkuma party (now under the Jewish Home list). It aims to influence government agencies like the Border Police to fight what it describes as the co-optation of the narratives of the left. It has filed formal complaints and lawsuits, and published a large report, accusing the Israeli police of discrimination against Jews. Through its access to the Knesset, the organization has been able to have a voice in the human rights policy in Israel, primarily through the Land of Israel caucus in the Knesset.[18] The Yesha Human Rights Organization has sought to portray itself in a manner consistent with language used by its leftist counterparts, for instance by using terminology such as "demonstration organizers" to soften the intent of their activities.

The Legal Forum for Israel was established in 2004, in the wake of the Disengagement Plan, to defend the rights of Jewish residents of the Gaza Strip. After the disengagement, it continued its activities, which it describes as strengthening the country's Jewish identity, protecting human rights, and strategically influencing and balancing Israel's judicial system. The Forum's legal and administrative staff coordinates a varied range of projects in the legal arena, with the support of a 370-attorney membership. The organization drafts policy reports, prepares bill proposals and position papers, appeals Supreme Court rulings, and appears in the media. Additionally, its members cooperate with MKs from across the political spectrum with the aim of submitting and passing pro-settler legislation in the Knesset.

Violent Groups While the settler movement has always included an extremist element, the 2005 disengagement from Gaza has led to an increase in fundamental challenges to the authority of both the state and the Yesha Council. The failure of the Yesha Council to adopt more proactive measures to prevent the evacuation of the Gaza settlements provoked angry criticism from a younger generation of second- and third-generation settlers who were born and raised in the settlements (see Chapter 7). This population gave rise to the group known as the Hilltop Youth. Its members aim to redefine Zionism and the settler movement, and portray themselves as new religious pioneers settling their God-given land (International Crisis Group 2013; Neidle 2013). They do not follow long-time settler leaders and reject the formal settler leadership structure (Eiran & Krause 2018). They eschew advocating through political channels, refuse to recognize the authority of the state, and emphasize their messianic ideology (Singer 2016).

At the heart of the extremist subsection of the settler movement is the loosely organized Kahanist network. The late Rabbi Meir Kahane and his Kach party sought the annexation of all of *Eretz Yisrael* as well as the removal of all Arabs from its territory. Their overtly racist nature, coupled with the party's incitement to violence, led the Supreme Court to ban the party from running in elections in 1988 (Sprinzak 1991). Kahanism and the *Kahane Chai* (Kahane Lives) movement, which was founded after Kahane's assassination in 1990, have a rather small but highly dedicated support base (of no more than a few hundred), reaching deep into the broader Israeli far right (Pedahzur 2012). They have supported "provocations" to spur a cycle of violence that would disrupt the possibility of a peace agreement. For example, Kach's "Committee for the Safety of the Roads" formally aims to provide security for Jews traveling on West Bank roads that are out of the reach of IDF patrols (Perliger et al. 2009). But its activists have also mounted patrols on West Bank backroads, especially in Hebron, to terrorize the local Arab population (Shaw-Smith 1994: 101). After the 1994 Cave of the Patriarchs massacre, committed by a Kach member, both groups went underground. They were outlawed by the Israeli government.[19] Yet even though Kach and Kahane Chai do not exist, their legacy is alive and well in Israel. For example, there are contemporary parties (e.g., Otzma Yehudit party) that are their ideological descendants.

The Hilltop Youth take their ideological cues from the teachings of Kahane and see violence as a legitimate means of protest against the state. They are highly confrontational toward both Palestinians and representatives of the Israeli state, including the IDF. Their actions mainly aim to terrorize the Palestinian population, including through drive-by shootings and arson attacks. Among their most infamous actions were the torching of a mosque in the Palestinian village of Yasuf in December 2009, and the deadly arson attack in Duma in July 2015, which killed eighteen-month-old Ali Saad Dawabsha and his parents. In February 2010, settlers from Yitzhar attacked soldiers they believed had been sent by the government to evacuate them (*Walla*, February 17, 2010). In May 2014, settlers from the same settlement were found to be mulling the legality under Jewish law of attacking, and even killing, IDF soldiers "under certain circumstances"[20] (*Times of Israel*, May 7, 2014). If once the main goal was establishing another outpost and violence was merely a means to that end, for the Hilltop Youth, violence now seems to be an end in itself. In contrast to their parents' generation, they increasingly question the legitimacy and intentions of the Israeli government, and launch attacks, marked by threatening graffiti, to exact a "price" for the evacuation of outposts.

A somewhat different Kahanist group is *Lehava*, a Hebrew word for "Flame" as well as an acronym for "Prevention of Assimilation in the Holy Land." Founded in 2009 by Mosis Zion, Lehava includes a number of Kahanists, all of them residents of West Bank settlements. Headed by Bentzi Gopstein, a student of Rabbi Kahane, Lehava promotes the forcible removal of all Arabs from Israel. Its primary goals are to prevent any personal relationships between Jews and others and any business dealings between Jews and Arabs. It is also keen on changing the leadership of the state of Israel (*Times of Israel*, December 16, 2014). Besides distributing anti-coexistence propaganda, organizing demonstrations and the like, Lehava also engages in arson, vandalism, incitement, harassment, and violent attacks.[21]

Another extreme right network is The Revolt, which is believed to seek to overthrow the Israeli state by generating large-scale unrest between Israelis and Palestinians, eventually causing the downfall of the elected government and its replacement by a Jewish kingdom. Its leader Meir Ettinger, the twenty-four-year-old grandson of Meir Kahane, wrote:

> "The laws that commit [us] . . . are not the laws of the state . . . but far more eternal laws." As is well known, he writes, "the State of Israel does not follow the Torah and prefers assimilation to inheritance of the land. We must understand that . . . the closer we bring the conflict the better it will be for the people of Israel and the land of Israel . . . . [T]he land should be left exclusively for Jews." Ettinger continued, "We must think about how to overthrow the regime that interferes with the rebuilding of the Temple that stands in the way of the true and complete redemption" (*Times of Israel*, August 6, 2015).

There is no hierarchy among Revolt members, not even a central authorizing body or coordination between the group's various cells. It is estimated that the group's hardcore element numbers thirty to forty people, most between the ages of fifteen and twenty-four. Among their activities are arson attacks against Palestinian homes and against Christian churches, as well as the publication of manifestos on how to commit terrorist attacks. Ettinger was imprisoned for six months in 2012 for collecting intelligence about the IDF's plans to evacuate settlements.

Jewish Heart, another extremist settler group, seeks to convert the (largely secular) Israeli identity into a fully Jewish religious identity. It is concerned with perceived injustices against Jews and alleged double standards on the part of the Israeli government in its treatment of Jews versus Arabs who commit crimes. It has encouraged soldiers to refuse orders during the Gaza disengagement, and collaborates with other far-right movements to organize protests and marches. For example, Jewish Heart co-organized a march to Amona in 2006, in which nearly 300 people were injured, and marched on the demolished settlement of Homesh, which was evacuated as a part of the 2005 disengagement from the northern West Bank. Collaborators for the march on Homesh included Komemiyut, Defenders of the Land, Professors for a Strong Israel, and others (*Jerusalem Post*, March 24, 2007). Jewish Heart was very active following the 2008 incident in which a resident of Jabbel Mukhaber, an Arab neighborhood in East Jerusalem, murdered eight Jewish yeshiva students at the Mercaz HaRav Kook Yeshiva. Disappointed with the government's decision not to destroy the terrorist's family home, the activists led a march that swiftly devolved into a riot.

The group Sovereignty also wants to replace secular law with Jewish religious law (Halacha). Its leaders, including Rabbis Dov Lior, Zalman Melamed, Elyakim Lebanon, and others, are post-*Mamlachti* ideologues. The group is also concerned with raising public awareness of what they perceive as the injustices suffered by the former residents of Gush Katif, the evacuated settlement bloc in the Gaza Strip, and continued "discrimination" against Jewish residents of Judea and Samaria. Each year, they organize a day of fasting and commemoration, where they invite Gush Katif expellees to speak about their experience. Sovereignty also distributes a weekly newsletter and organizes demonstrations, marches, and rallies – sometimes with other far-right groups. It has encouraged soldiers and civilians to refuse the orders of police and soldiers (Weissbrod 2009; *Hakol Hayehudi*, August 26, 2012), and reportedly helped to keep activists apprised as to the movements of IDF troops heading to remove illegal outposts (*Hakol Hayehudi*, January 1, 2012).

3.3.3 *Influencers*

Influencers are not linked to movement organizations, whether formal or informal, but are single individuals or small groups of people, often working from their homes in the settlements to spread the message of the settler movement. Some influencers advance the goals of the movement via their supposedly apolitical relationship to the mass media infrastructure, operating via both formal channels (e.g., political institutions) and informal or civil society pathways, such as op-eds, newspaper articles, and television interviews.

An example of an influencer who advocates for the settler enterprise with a degree of intentional opacity is Emily Amrousi. Since 2003, Amrousi has been the Channel 10 News "Judea and Samaria Affairs Correspondent." In the period leading up to the disengagement, she was appointed as the "Spokesperson for the Disengagement Opposition" by the Yesha Council. After she finished her stint with Yesha, she continued as a columnist for *Israel Today*, an Israeli daily with no shortage of actors from the settler camp. In an interview with *Srugim* (September 25, 2016), an Orthodox media outlet, Amrousi elaborated on her role as a settler, woman, and journalist, arguing that these three roles do not exist independently but rather inform one another. She speaks about representing the settler interests, and about her ideological reasons for moving to the Talmon settlement in the West Bank, but the interview also stresses that "she has always accidentally or intentionally been put in the 'settler' box."

Another important influencer is journalist and radio presenter Amit Segal. Aside from being the son of Hagai Segal, a journalist and member of the Jewish Underground, Segal has a long and successful career in the Israeli media. He began in the Jerusalem-based weekly newspaper *Kol Ha'ir*, in 2000, and then worked as Knesset correspondent for *Galei Tzahal* (the IDF radio station), and as a reporter for TV *Channel 2*. As such, Segal has come to represent the media sector in the eyes of the Israeli public. His outspoken views on what he perceives as a lack of balance in the Israeli media helps normalize the movement's accusations of unfair treatment.

While space limitations preclude listing all the well-known journalists who promulgate the settler narrative in the public sphere, two more are worth mentioning. Boaz Haetzni is a regular contributor to the religious Zionist online media outlet *Arutz Sheva*, also known as Israel National News, and a writer for *Srugim*. He has also written for *NRG* and *Makor Rishon*, the latter of which is also aimed at a religious Zionist readership.[22] Haetzni writes on a wide variety of subjects, including Israeli–US relations and internal Israeli affairs.[23] Haggai Huberman is a longtime journalist for the Yesha Council newspaper *The Observer* (*HaTzofeh*), which was considered the beacon of the NRP (*Haaretz*, December 25, 2008). After its closure in December 2008, he became the military affairs correspondent for *Makor Rishon*. Beyond his journalistic work, Huberman has published several books idealizing the Israeli settlement project, including "Against All Odds" (*Keneged Kol HaSikuim*), about forty years of settlement in the West Bank, and "Roots in the Sand" (*Shorashim Becholot*), which discusses the history of Gush Katif.

Other influencers have created businesses in the region that promote the ideology of *Eretz Yisrael*. Among the most ardent influencers in Israeli settlements are Gedaliah and Elisheva Blum, US-born religious Jews, who launched the business directory Orange Pages (*Dapei Katom*) in 2009. Named for the color associated with the campaign against the 2005 disengagement, Orange Pages aims to promote small businesses in the settlements. It is a response to the Boycott, Divestment and Sanctions (BDS) movement, aimed at advocating the sale of products made in Israeli settlements. According to Gedaliah Blum, "We wanted to use that same tool everybody else is using against us, for us" (*New York Times*, January 21, 2014). They also founded Boutique Katom, an English-language online shop, which specializes in artwork made by artists living in Jewish settlements.[24]

Other influencers use tourism to promote and support the settlement enterprise. The main aims are to achieve support and legitimacy by changing attitudes and perceptions (Pizam et al. 2000). Using tourism as a business and a political tool is a familiar phenomenon in areas of political instability, conflict zones and border disputes. In fact, it has been used in a broad range of territories, including Cyprus, Hong Kong, Northern Ireland, and Spain, to name a few. The attraction for tourists may be to visit the site of a border dispute or to learn the perspectives of parties to the conflict. Tourism of this type may also be used as an educational tool to garner support (Moufakkir & Kelly 2010; Sönmez 1998; Timothy 2002).

The use of sophisticated tourist attractions enables the normalization of the Jewish settlements in the West Bank, in a way which, paradoxically, both emphasizes and minimizes their location (Handel et al. 2015). Individual influencers look to tourism as a way to help normalize the settlers' image and draw Israelis to the West Bank. They tout the region's proximity to urban centers, its biblical history and its idyllic scenery for Israelis who might frown upon the settlement enterprise. As explained by Dani Dayan, Chief Foreign Envoy of the Yesha Council, "We have a moral interest for Judea and Samaria to be toured by Israelis who for various reasons still don't see it as a place to tour" (*Haaretz*, May 6, 2011).

Settler representatives offer a plethora of sites, many of them of biblical significance. They attend tourism fairs and extol the wonders of the region to travel agents, and have launched campaigns targeting Israelis, appealing to the West Bank's Jewish history. One project, titled "Every Jew's Story," had billboards up in cities across Israel, depicting smiling children dressed as famous biblical characters, urging Israelis to return to their roots with a visit to the West Bank and offering tours to different sites (*Arutz Sheva*, December 10, 2008). Another initiative is *Mishkefet* (Binoculars), which was founded by settlers and offers tours of settlements to promote "an inside view of life in these Jewish communities" (*Arutz Sheva*, August 8, 2013). Calling itself a "national acquaintance project," the tours explore historical and national Jewish heritage sites, as well as farms and other agricultural projects. Their core target audience is secular Israelis who do not normally venture out to the West Bank settlements. Yossi Dagan, a Samaria resident and Mishkefet cofounder, put it this way: "The big enemy of settlement, and in general of Israeli society, is ignorance. No one arrives in Judea and Samaria, sees the settlements that are blossoming there, and remains indifferent" (*Haaretz*, November 14, 2015).[25]

During holiday seasons, individual settlers also promote the settlement enterprise through various festivals and events, such as Jewish music festivals, an annual cherry-picking festival in Gush Etzion, and an annual kite festival in Pnai Kedem. Various other tourist initiatives developed by individual settlers include holiday cottages (*tzimmerim*), particularly catering to religious couples; and an artisan bakery and olive pressing activities for children and families. While no records are kept as to how many Israelis visit the West Bank, settlers say the numbers are growing, spurred by an aggressive marketing campaign. According to the settlers themselves, the number of tourists rose to from 45,000 in 2008 to almost 100,000 in 2010 (*Jerusalem Post*, June 21, 2011). These include large Israeli groups that come mostly on Jewish holidays, as well as foreign tourists.

Wineries are a central feature of the tourism sector within the West Bank. Winemaking in the region can be traced back to biblical times. For the settlers, planting vineyards in the West Bank actualizes their vision and ideology of "settling the greater land of Israel." Gershon Mesika, the former head of the Shomron Regional Council, said, "We see the prophet Jeremiah's words realized with our very eyes, as he said, 'you shall yet plant vines on the mountains of Samaria'" (*Arutz Sheva*, April 5, 2015). However, boutique wineries in the area attract both religious and secular Jews. A list of boutique wineries in each region of the West Bank can be found in Table 3.1 (based on Shaked et al. 2015). The wineries offer tours and maintain restaurants, and in some cases house the region's official visitors' center. For instance, the Psagot Winery has benefited from large financial investments from the Binyamin Regional Council, for which it acts as the official visitors' center.

Table 3.1 *Wineries in the West Bank by year of opening*

Until 1990	1991–2000	2001–10	2011–18
Zion	Bustan	Bit El	Lavie
Arza	Tkoha	Acerem	Gvaot
Cormim	Anatot/Almon	Kinor David	Shilo
Hamelch Shlomo	Yatir	Ramat Hebron	Ventura
Hebron	Tura	Tania	Har Hadar
	Gush Etzion	Givhon	Givat Tkuma
		Gat Shomron	Arnon
		Ben Porat	Maele Levona
		Miller	Avner
		Psagot	Amos
		Livni	Nahala
		Neguhot	Tom
		Har Bracha	Kabir
		Hari Yerushalim	Shiran
		Parnasi	
		Drimia	
		Abrabof	

Beyond the key influencers who directly advance the goals of the Israeli settler project, individuals from arts and culture play an integral role in the settler movement too. These individuals, who are often in the public eye, can leverage their fame to reach segments of the public that would not otherwise be exposed to this discourse. They differ from the public actors discussed earlier, who come from within the movement, having gained fame for apolitical reasons but espousing a right-wing, pro-settler agenda. Through their fan bases, they provide a potential audience to which the settler movement might not otherwise have access.

Noami Shemer (1930–2004) is a classic example of an artist who used her platform to advocate for the settler movement. Shemer was one of the most famous Israeli singers and songwriters and was dubbed "the first lady of Israeli song and poetry" (*Haaretz*, June 27, 2004).[26] Over the years, she identified closely with the political right in general and Gush Emunim in particular. In the mid-1970s, Shemer voiced her support for the settler movement through her songs "Paranoid" and "Strange Man" (Mendelson 1975). Between the signing of the Israel–Egypt peace treaty in 1979 and the handover of the Sinai to Egypt in 1982, the settler movement adopted a line from one of her songs, "Do not uproot what has been planted," to protest Israel's evacuation of the settlement of Yamit.

Ariel Zilber is another artist whose fame afforded him a platform for his pro-settler political opinions. A composer, singer, songwriter, and settler, Zilber is celebrated in Israel, despite his support for the extremist policy of "transferring" Israeli Arab citizens (*Ynet,* February 13, 2002). Half of the songs on his album "The Bat and the Rooster" (*H'atalef VeHaTarnegol*) were written by Rabbi Yitzhak Ginsburg, who has publicly supported the most extreme elements of the settler movement (*Haaretz*, April 21, 2013). This notwithstanding, Zilber has used his fame to help the settlers to disseminate their ideology to a larger audience.

A final set of influencers not only spreads the settler message, but also actively influences settlement-related policies and processes. This includes influencers at the highest levels of the Israeli judiciary, such as David Mintz, who currently resides in the West Bank settlement of Dolev, after living in the Alon Shvut settlement before (*NRG*, June 13, 2017). His appointment to the Supreme Court Justice was a major event, if only symbolically, for supporters of the settler movement. For instance, Adi Mintz (no relation), the former head of the Yesha Council, said that it would bring new and more professional judgments regarding issues that "refer to the territories in Judea and Samaria as a belligerent occupation" (*Arutz Sheva*, February 23, 2017). Mintz was actually the second pro-settler judge to join the Supreme Court, after Justice Noam Solberg, a resident of Alon Shvut. Solberg has made headlines for his visibility in the pro-settlement community. In 2017, for example, Israeli media reported that Solberg attended a jubilee that marked the fifty-year anniversary of the settler enterprise, despite a warning given by the President of the Supreme Court that official representation was "inappropriate" – even though the ceremony itself, which took place in the Etzion Bloc, was funded by the Culture and Education Ministries (*Times of Israel*, October 3, 2017).

3.4 Conclusion

Most popular accounts on the settlements provide a very one-sided image of the settler population, focusing disproportionately on the most fanatic among them, the religious Zionists. Similarly, the settler movement is often portrayed on the basis of relatively small, and more marginal, groups, such as the extremist Hilltop Youth. As always, the reality is much more complex. Religious Zionists constitute a minority of the contemporary settler population, which consists mostly of (secular and ultraorthodox) "quality-of-life" settlers. While religious Zionists settle for religious-nationalist reasons, mostly in smaller settlements in the heart of the West Bank, quality-of-life settlers live in larger settlement close to the Green Line, which provide affordable communities close to Israel's major urban parts.

Religious Zionists do dominate the settler movement, however, but that does not mean that the movement is not heterogeneous either. The key institutions, the Yesha Council and Amana, are bureaucratized and centralized organizations, well funded and well integrated, working closely with Israel's political elites. The networks include a broad host of groups, catering to most subgroups of the diffuse settler population, with a broad variety of different action repertoires and strategies. Some focus exclusively on education or law, while others are more actively engaged in the creation and protection of settlements. The vast majority of networks accept the authority of the Israeli state, and reject violence against both Jews and non-Jews, but a growing group of extremists, primarily within the Kahanist subculture, reject state authority, particularly if its actions are deemed to be in violation with Torah Law (the so-called post-*Mamlachti*), and have been using violence against both Palestinian civilians and IDF soldiers. Influencers, finally, tend to aim at creating support for the settler enterprise and movement within the broader Israeli (and the US) public, mostly through the media.

4 Assessing the Settler Movement's Success

> The settlement enterprise won ... The settlement enterprise proved its power and made this process irreversible.
>
> Professor David Myers, President of the New Israel Fund
> (*Makor Rishon*, February 28, 2019)

> The liberation of Judea and Samaria and the Golan Heights, and their settlement by more than half a million people, have inscribed a new page in the annals of the Jewish people. We returned [to the land] in order to remain [on it] forever, without ceding territory or giving it up to foreign sovereignty.
>
> MK Naftali Bennett
> (*Yediot Aharonot*, September 16, 2017)

Introduction

To assess success in any context, we need to know at the very least the main goals against which success is to be measured. While this may be straightforward for organizations or individuals, it is less so with respect to social movements, which comprise networks of networks – webs of different individuals and groups with partially differing (sub)goals. This is also the case for the settler movement, which is internally heterogeneous in terms of many variables, including motivation for settlement, political ideology, and religion (see Chapter 3). That is why we begin this chapter with an analysis of the key goal of the settler movement as a whole, as well as its subgoals, mostly means to achieve the primary goal.

After identifying the overarching goal and its various subgoals, we assess the actual success of the settler movement. First, we analyze the movement's practical achievements in terms of the annexation and settlement of the "Land of Israel," in particular the West Bank, as well as bringing about the formal incorporation of particular occupied territories within the state. In the next three sections, we assess the movement's success in terms of the three separate but related aspects identified in the theoretical framework: policies, resources, and support. In the final section, we assess its success at the international level, focusing in particular on the United States, the main international actor with regard to Israel and the Israeli–Palestinian conflict, but also the main focus of the international agenda of the settler movement.

4.1 Goals

At the center of the settler movement's worldview is a belief in the holiness of Jewish law and of *Eretz Yisrael*, as formulated by Rabbi Abraham Isaac Kook, as well as the belief that the "Land of Israel" and the Jewish People constitute a single entity, as promised by God (Newman 1981; Sprinzak 1987; Weissbrod 1982). In accordance with this view, Gush Emunim viewed the establishment of the State of Israel as the beginning of the Redemption, and the Six-Day War as a divine act (Sprinzak 1985).

The settler movement wants to expand the boundaries of the state to those of the biblical Land of Israel, known as *Eretz Yisrael* – sometimes expanded to *Eretz Yisrael HaShlema* – literally "the whole or complete Land of Israel." The ultimate goal of the settler movement is the settling of *Eretz Yisrael*, which, to most within the movement, means the current State of Israel and the West Bank, or, as they call it, Judea and Samaria. Prior to the 2005 disengagement (see Chapter 7), Gaza was also considered an inseparable part of *Eretz Yisrael*, with the movement calling for Israeli sovereignty from the Jordan River to the Mediterranean Sea. Although some elements with the movement still recognize Gaza as part of the vision of a "complete Land of Israel," the settler movement has largely shifted to focus on annexation of the West Bank.[1] The settler movement believes its role is not only to settle the land, but also to instill its pioneering ideology in society and culture at large, and to lead a historic renewal of Zionism, which, it believes, has been on the wane since the 1950s (Aran 1991; Don-Yehiya 1987; Newman 1985; Sprinzak 1985).

Only a minority of settlers, notably the extremist Kahanist faction, calls for the expulsion of non-Jews, including from an annexed West Bank, primarily but not exclusively Palestinians, with the aim of making *Eretz Yisrael* exclusively Jewish. However, even among less extreme supporters of the movement, who do not call for expulsion, most oppose giving (full) citizenship to non-Jewish residents, particularly in the West Bank. Concretely, the settling of *Eretz Yisrael* is seen as a multifaceted process, which includes the defense of the current settlements, the legalization of current outposts, the expansion of both old and new settlements, and the significant growth of the settler population.

In pursuit of its ultimate goal, the settlement of *Eretz Yisrael* and annexation of those territories that fall outside the boundaries of the current state, the settler movement has two additional (sub)goals: obtaining *financial resources* and building *political support*. Like all social movements, the settler movement tries to raise resources, primarily financial, both to sustain the movement and to advance its main goal. While the state is the ultimate target for fundraising, social movements can also mobilize resources from non-state organizations and individuals. The settler movement does this both in Israel and abroad, most notably in the United States. Essential to achieving both goals is political support, which the settler movement tries to obtain from a broad range of sources, most notably the state, the military, civil society, and the broader (domestic and international) public.

4.2 Policies

In terms of the actual settlement of *Eretz Yisrael*, the settler movement has two short-term goals: (1) to settle as *extensively* as possible (in terms of numbers of both settlements and settlers); and (2) to settle *strategically*, so as to frustrate efforts to bring about Palestinian statehood and prevent a two-state solution. In the fifty years of its existence, the settler movement has been moderately successful in the first and more successful in the second.

Since establishing its first settlement in the West Bank in 1967, Kfar Etzion in the Gush Etzion Bloc (see Chapter 2), the settler movement has been creating "facts on the ground" with or without the support of government policies. Settlements that were initially created illegally, that is, as "outposts," were later legalized through government actions. In other words, while a minority of settlements were not initiated by government actions, the government has in fact supported the movement both actively, through pro-settlement policies, and passively, by failing to implement anti-settlement policies even when these were the official position of the government.

Before we empirically assess the significant achievements of the settler movement in terms of numbers, geography, and legality, it is important to stress an obvious but thus far often ignored fact: the settler movement has not achieved its ultimate goal, that is, bringing (all of) *Eretz Yisrael* under Israeli sovereignty, and more particularly, incorporating it formally within the boundaries of the State of Israel. In fact, annexation of the West Bank is supported openly only within the Israeli far right, although more recently also within Likud, but is opposed by a majority of Israeli citizens (see Section 4.4). Likewise, the movement has made few inroads in this respect within the international community (see Section 4.5). Israel's occupation of the West Bank is still considered illegal by international law, and almost the whole international community, including the United Nations, continues to denounce it. Even Israel's staunchest ally, the United States, still officially supports a two-state solution, even if President Trump seems not particularly committed to it. Moreover, the settler movement suffered several defeats in its over fifty-years existence, including the Camp David Accords (1978), the Oslo Accords (1993 and 1995), and the Disengagement Plan (2005), all of which included Israel giving up (occupied) territory. The disengagement, in particular, was evidence of the limits of its powers and of the complex relationship between the settler movement and the Israeli right wing (see Chapter 7).

That said, there is little doubt that the settlement project has advanced significantly since the settler movement emerged on the political scene in the wake of the Six-Day War. Irrespective of the party holding power in Israel (or the United States), the number of settlements has continued to grow consistently, new illegal outposts are constantly created and legalized, and the number of people residing in the West Bank is mushrooming (see also Chapter 2). More significantly, the geography of the settlement process presents a fundamental challenge to the feasibility of a future Palestinian state and two-state solution, should there ever be enough political support and will to actually push for this.

4.2.1 Numbers

The prime accomplishment of the settler movement has been to consistently and exponentially expand the number of (illegal and legal) settlements throughout the West Bank. Between 1967 and 2017, 127 official Israeli settlements were built in the West Bank. In the early period of settlement growth, from 1970 to 1980, there was rapid and steady construction of new settlements. This pace continued into the 1990s, when development and expansion of both new and existing settlements continued. In the three decades between 1991 and 2019, Jewish settlement in the West Bank has increased even further.

Since 1991, the increase in settlement building has been almost exclusively through the expansion of existing settlements rather than the construction of new ones (see Figure 4.1). However, it is important to note that the term "settlement expansion" may be misleading, as one of the tools of the settler movement is to categorize the construction of new settlements as the addition of new neighborhoods to extant settlement communities. Thus, the settlers absolve themselves from concerns about legality against the backdrop of the Israeli commitments to freeze or slow

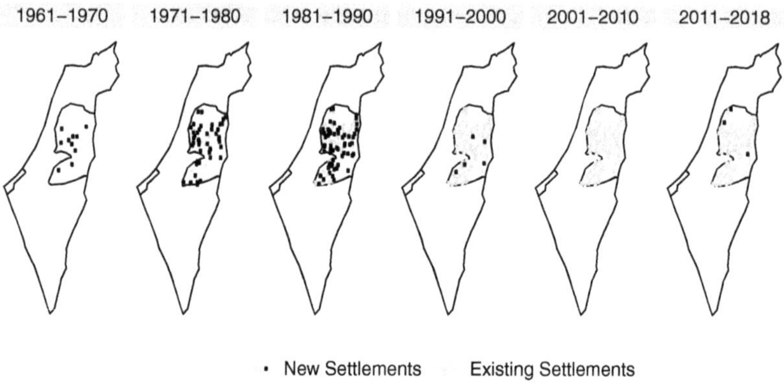

Figure 4.1 The expansion of Jewish settlements in the West Bank by decade[2]

the construction of new settlements. For example, in December 2018, the Higher Planning Committee approved plans for 2,191 housing units in the settlements, with 87 percent of the units in the so-called isolated settlements, which are farther away from the Green Line and likely to be included in a future "land for peace" deal in the context of a two-state solution.

In addition to (government-sanctioned) settlements, the settler movement has been instrumental in the explosion of Jewish outposts in the West Bank (see Figure 4.2).[3] Outposts are defined as settlements that have been established without government approval since the 1990s – or more precisely since the settlement freeze instituted by the Rabin government in late 1992 – and that are considered illegal according to Israeli law. However, they have received the support of various government ministries, the Israel Defense Forces, and the Civil Administration (under COGAT). Indeed, as noted earlier, a minority of "authorized" settlements began life as illegal outposts and were later legalized. Because of the overt or implicit support that outposts often receive from government bodies or from regional authorities in the West Bank, some researchers and scholars of the settlements do not include an absence of formal government authorization in their definition of outposts. Actually, the term "outpost," defined as an illegal settlement, is a unique Israeli construct. For the international community, all Jewish settlements in the West Bank are illegal, as evidenced by numerous United Nations Security Council (UNSC) resolutions.[4]

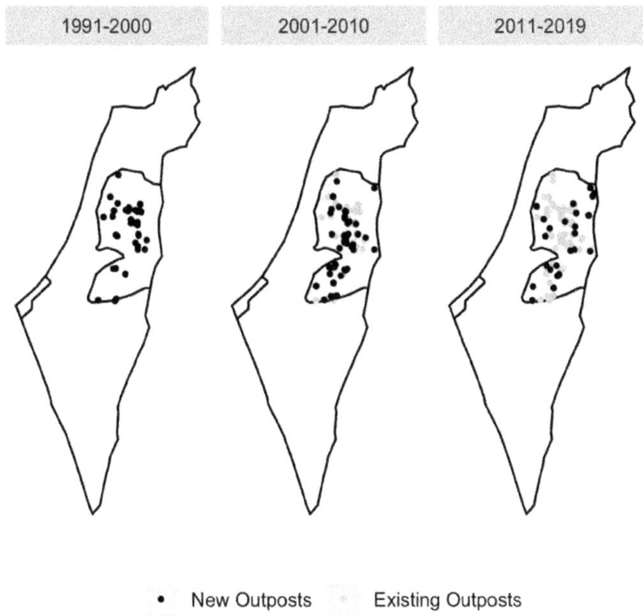

Figure 4.2 The expansion of Israeli outposts in the West Bank by decade[5]

In November 1992, the Rabin government decided to halt construction in most extant settlements and discontinue construction of new settlements (Knesset Resolution 360). But Netanyahu's first government, in 1996, loosened these restrictions, determining that no new settlements would be established except with official government authorization. In practice, more than 100 (illegal) outposts were established (see Figure 4.3). In 1998, Peace Now Secretary General Musi Raz and Meretz MK Dedi Zucker petitioned the High Court of Justice, demanding evacuation of all the outposts (HCJ 98/8287). Following the 1999 elections, Prime Minister and Minister of Defense Ehud Barak announced that an agreement had been reached with settler leaders by which most of the outposts would be evacuated and a few would receive approval. However, the court ruled that the fate of each outpost should be determined individually, and not all at once (HCJ 02/6431). Ultimately the petition was rejected.

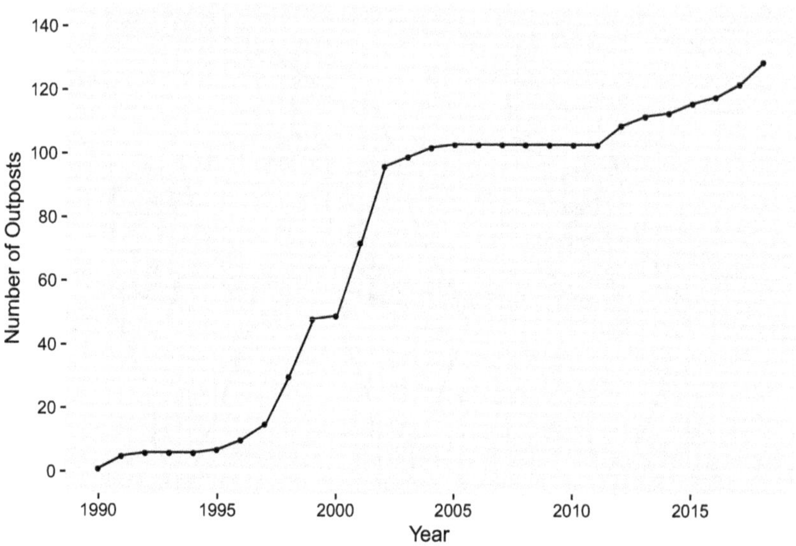

Figure 4.3 Number of Israeli outposts in the West Bank[6]

There has been a fairly steady stream of approvals for new housing units in West Bank settlements, albeit with periodic ups and downs (see Figure 4.4). Even the setback of the 2005 Gaza disengagement has barely affected the overall trend. A period of decline from 2008 to 2010 was followed by a slow then sharp uptick, with a 143 percent increase in new settlement construction in the West Bank from 2012 to 2013. The year 2016 was a particularly productive year, in which the building of 3,166 apartments began – an increase of almost 88 percent from 2015. Nonresidential construction exhibits a similar trend. For example, in 2018, a total of 147,588 m^2 of nonresidential construction was started in the West Bank, compared to 95,722 m^2 in 2017 (a 54 percent increase).[7] Construction starts for educational buildings in the West Bank saw a 3.8 percent increase in 2016, while starts for other public buildings (e.g., community centers, religious institutions, sport facilities, and welfare services) grew by 14 percent.

These statistics point to a significant and ongoing upsurge in construction in the West Bank. This becomes even clearer when they are compared to similar statistics for Israel proper. In 2018, there was a 29 percent increase in settlement construction in the West Bank. At the same time,

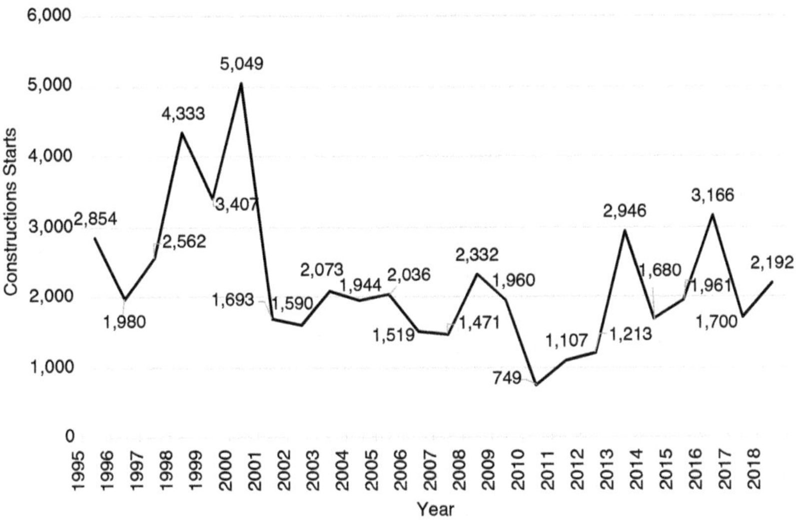

Figure 4.4 Housing unit construction starts in settlements by year[8]

there was a decrease in construction throughout almost the whole of Israel proper, with the exception of the area of Tel Aviv.[9]

The settler movement has also strongly promoted economic efforts like industrial areas in the West Bank.[10] Industrial areas are not only "facts on the ground," they also serve to show the (economic) viability of the Jewish settlement of the West Bank to international and Israeli observers. For example, the Samaria Regional Council uses the Barkan Industrial Zone to portray the West Bank as a working "ecosystem," which is said to profit both Israelis and Palestinians. According to Gershon Mesika, Head of the Samaria Regional Council (2007–15), the industrial park is an example of how Israelis and Palestinians can live and work together peacefully, and boycotts actually threaten Palestinian labor opportunities:

> It's amazing how the radical Left fails to understand that the main victims are the Palestinians themselves. Fortunately, so far these boycotts have been nothing but PR maneuvers, and we are sure that Jews and Arabs will continue to work together and strengthen our prosperous industry and live in coexistence (*Ynet*, May 20, 2012).

As Figure 4.5 shows, the approval of the construction of new housing units is not strongly related to the political makeup of the Israeli

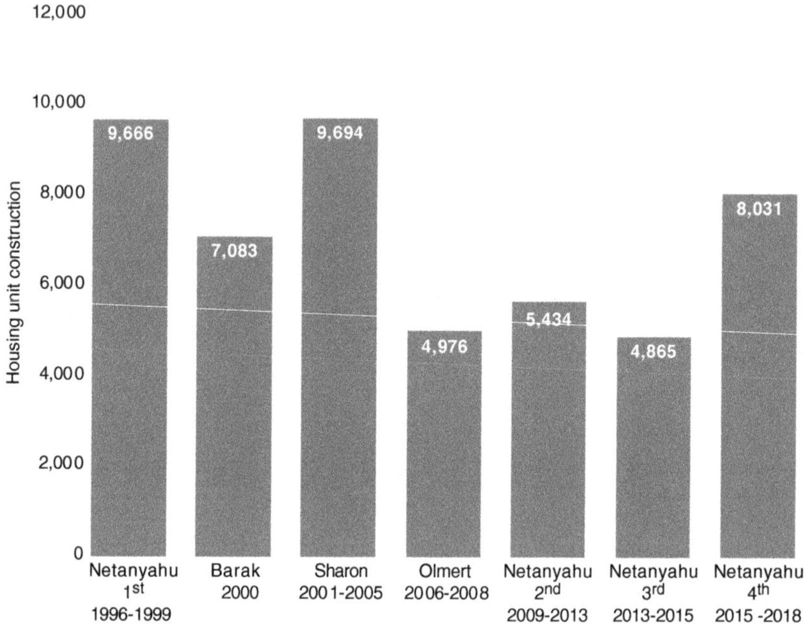

Figure 4.5 Housing unit construction in settlements starts by government[11]

government. For instance, the government of center-left Prime Minister Barak approved more units than the second and third governments of right-wing Netanyahu – and, in the case of Netanyahu's second government, in only half of the time.

Of course, increases in settlement numbers and the expansion of existing settlements – and their infrastructure, like educational facilities and industrial parks – tell only one part of the story. Another crucial part is settler numbers. All the settlement building and expansion serves a (second) purpose: to house more and more people. This, too, was by design, and reflects the political power of the settler camp. As *Haaretz* journalist Yotam Berger (2018) put it, "It was government policy to increase the number of Jews in the territories. They made five-year plans, 10-year plans, spoke about how to get to 100,000 [settlers] and 300,000 and half a million."

The number of settlements experienced a particularly steep growth spurt between 1975 and 1985, corresponding with Likud's landslide victory in the 1977 elections (Bsisu 2012: 30). Yet while the growth rate of the settlements stabilized around 1990, the growth of the settler population did not (see also Figure 2.2). Rather, the settler population began to expand in the 1980s, with numbers in the low thousands, and has increased steadily ever since. Today, the population has passed 400,000, in a trajectory that seems set to continue.[12]

This growth is also reflected in a change in the nature of the settlements, which has become increasingly urban. According to Israeli scholar Hillel Cohen, "Before Likud rose to power there was only one urban settlement – Kiryat Arba (*Haaretz*, June 15, 2017). Over the following years, to house the growing population, urban areas (towns and cities) have sprung up throughout the West Bank. However, it still remains true that half the settlements are inhabited by fewer than 1,000 individuals, and only fifteen have populations of 5,000 or more (Arieli 2017; See figure 4.6).

The annual growth of the settler population is a product of both migration and natural growth, with the relative importance of each source shifting over the years. In 1996, two-thirds of new residents in the settlements migrated from within Israel or from abroad, while a third of the increase was due to natural growth. The annual growth of the settler population is higher than that of Israel proper, which has demonstrated a steady decline over the last two decades. For example, the annual population growth stood at 10.3 percent in 1996, but was down to 3.4 percent in 2006 (Arieli 2017). In 2017, the annual population growth stood at 3.5 percent.

As of this writing, migration accounts for only about 20 percent of population growth in the settlements, and it has been even lower: it was just 14 percent in 2016 (Arieli 2017). The high rate of natural increase is a reflection of the large ultraorthodox population in the West Bank; indeed, about half the natural increase comes from only two ultraorthodox cities, Modi'in Illit and Beitar Illit, whose populations together constitute one-third of the Jewish population in the West Bank. Importantly, these populations do not identify with the ideology of Greater Israel.

4.2.2 Geography

If the growth of the settlers and settlements is taken to be an indicator of success, then the data suggest that the settler movement has been modestly successful. However, to round out the picture, we must not only look at the sheer numbers, but also at other indicators, such as the type and geographical location of settlements. Whereas the settler movement once was firmly centered around ideological tenets, such as fulfilling the biblical prophecy of *Eretz Yisrael HaShlema*, today motivations to relocate to the West Bank have diversified (see Chapter 3). Quality-of-life settlers, who move to the West Bank for the relatively lower cost of housing, availability of open space, and other advantages, have changed the composition of the settlement enterprise.

Quality-of-life settlers prefer settlements situated physically closer to the Green Line, and thus to Israel proper. The construction and expansion of settlements on state lands adjacent to the Green Line, as opposed to the heart of the West Bank, proved to be a calculated tactic in softening the settler image. These new groups of settlements attracted secular and ultraorthodox settlers and were set up in response to market demand, rather than ideological considerations (see also Figure 3.2). A prime example is Alfei Menashe, established in 1983, an urban settlement with community characteristics, populated by young families, which was initiated and funded by the Israeli government and marketed under the slogan "five minutes from Kfar Sava" (Huberman 2011). Today, almost all the larger settlements are along the Green Line or adjacent to Jerusalem (Figure 4.6). The diversification of the settler population and the geographical position of the settlements has helped the movement to close the metaphorical gap between settlers and other Israelis by reducing the physical gap between them. But it has also weakened the commitment of the average settler to the goals of the settler movement.

From the very beginning of the settlement project, settlement locations have been chosen with two superficially opposing goals in mind: maintaining a clear separation (justified on security grounds) between the Jewish settlers and their Palestinian neighbors (Handel 2009), while simultaneously choosing sites strategically so as to embed a settler presence in Palestinian-populated areas. It is often pointed out that the built-up areas of Jewish settlement in the West Bank are dwarfed by the built-up areas of Palestinian habitation: the former now totals 71 km^2, accounting for roughly 1 percent of the area of the West Bank (including 13 km^2 in East Jerusalem), while the latter totals 532 km^2, accounting for 9 percent of the area (including 17.5 km^2 in East Jerusalem) (Arieli 2017: 59). However, this picture is misleading.

From the beginning the number and density of settlers introduced into a particular location was considered less important than the size and geography of the settler footprint. As explained by Gush Emunim (1980: 15), "Our hold over a stretch of land does not depend on the size of the population inhabiting it, but on the size of the area on which this population leaves its imprint." Accordingly, many settlements have been established very close to Palestinian communities, thus by expanding the settler presence in the West Bank and

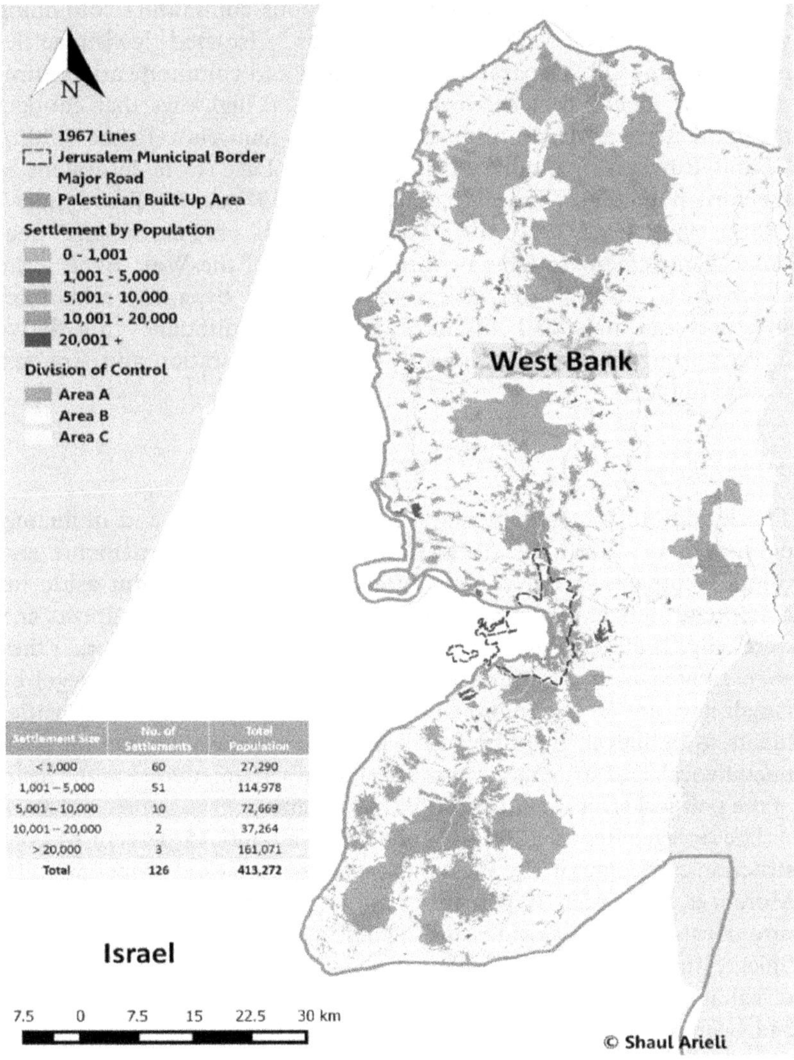

Figure 4.6 Jewish settlements in the West Bank by settlement size (2017)[13]

preventing the expansion and development of Palestinian towns and villages. Explaining the geography of settlements in the West Bank, Ariel Handel (2013) notes that they should not be seen as an aggregate of "legal" settlements and "illegal outposts," but rather as one coherent spatial system – a single, contiguous community containing various disconnected Palestinian "islands." Isolated Jewish settlements are linked by separate transportation and communication infrastructures, including a network of five lateral highways that connect the settlements to Israel proper: the "Trans-Samaria" (Route 5/505), "Trans-Binyamin" (Route 443), Route 1 – East (from Jerusalem to the Jordan Valley), "Trans-Etzion" (Route 357), and "Trans-Judea" (Route 35) (Arieli 2017: 59). The restrictions on Palestinians' freedom of movement in Israeli-controlled parts of the West Bank – the checkpoints, controls on access to roads and bypasses, and other strictures that make daily life for Palestinians so difficult – thus derive directly from the two principles of complete separation and strategic penetration.

4.2.3 Legality

The legality of the settlements is a complex, dynamic and ultimately political issue. Even the distinction between (legal) settlements and (illegal) outposts is not as straightforward as it seems. Put aside for a moment the fact that some settlements started as illegal outposts and were only "legalized" later or that even "legal" settlements, whether they were created with government authorization or not, are only legal by Israeli law, not by international law, which considers all Israeli settlements to be illegal. Even by Israeli law, the situation is often far from unequivocal, and struggles over the legality of settlements are at the heart of the political struggle of the settler movement.

The Spiegel Report (2007)[14] found that around 75 percent of construction carried out in the West Bank settlements lacked proper permits. Moreover, more than 30 percent of the settlements included infrastructure constructed on private land owned by Palestinian residents. The Spiegel Report included all settlements, not just illegal outposts, therefore revealing that the pattern of bypassing authority and ignoring procedure had been an integral part of the strategy of the settler movement for years.[15] Journalist Amos Harel has described the illegal outposts as "small money" compared to the old, established, and purportedly legal settlements that have been flagrantly ignoring the rules and procedures (*Haaretz*, November 29, 2012).

In early 2012, Netanyahu appointed former Israeli Supreme Court Justice Edmund Levy to head what has been nicknamed the "Outpost Committee" (*Haaretz*, July 9, 2012). The purpose of the Levy Report was to determine the legal status of the West Bank outposts and whether the presence of Israelis in the West Bank could be considered an occupation.

All three members of the committee – Levy, former Tel Aviv District Court, Judge Tehiya Shapira, and international lawyer Alan Baker – had clear connections to the right-wing camp.[16] Contrary to the earlier reports, the Levy Report strongly supported a Jewish presence in the West Bank and made several pro-settlement recommendations.[17] In practice, the recommendations meant that settlement construction on lands seized for military purposes should be allowed to continue. Likewise, the Report deemed the Supreme Court "bothersome use order," which grants COGAT the right to remove settlers trespassing on private lands, to be "draconian." While the Netanyahu government was hesitant to adopt the recommendations, due in large part to fear of negative responses by the international community (in particular the United States), the state did implement some, albeit it covertly (*Haaretz*, May 27, 2014).

In 2016, Netanyahu appointed another team of experts to formulate an outline for the regulation of buildings and new neighborhoods in West Bank settlements, and to address the status of structures that were legally subject to demolition because of lack of authorization.[18] The so-called Zandberg Report (2018: 116) provided a four-pronged outline for regulating Jewish settlements in the West Bank in general, and in particular for legalizing unauthorized structures, estimated by the nongovernmental organization (NGO) Yesh Din (April 1, 2019) to number more than 7,000. Unofficially, the Zandberg Report institutionalized illegal outposts by providing a legal framework under which these "neighborhoods" could receive municipal services. This was acknowledged, and celebrated, by far-right Minister of Justice Ayelet Shaked (then Jewish Home), an outspoken supporter of the settlement enterprise, who said of the Zandberg Report, "The era of uprooting settlements in Judea and Samaria has ended. The Jewish Home team has led the way in identifying legal pathways to legalize settlements in the West Bank and to halt the disgrace of settlement evacuations for no good reason" (*Calcalist*, August 1, 2018).

It remains to be seen whether the recommendations of the Zandberg Report will be adopted as official government policy. The battle over legalization continues. In February 2017, the Knesset passed legislation that allowed the government to retroactively legalize Jewish settlements built on Palestinian land. According to the legislation, the land upon which the settlements were built would remain in the hands of its legal owners, use of the land was to be expropriated by the state. This "Law for the Regulation of Settlement in Judea and Samaria" applies to land on which Israeli settlements were built "in good faith" or "with government support." The Palestinian owners, in turn, are to be compensated at a rate of 125 percent of the value of their land, as deemed by an assessment committee appointed by the Minister of Justice, the above mentioned Ayelet Shaked.[19]

However, the right's victory was short-lived, as Attorney General Avichai Mandelblitt refused to defend the law in the Israeli Supreme Court, on the grounds that it violated the rights of Palestinians.[20] Subsequently, a group of left-wing NGOs and Palestinian councils argued to the Supreme Court that the Knesset had no right to pass legislation that exercised the government's authority over the West Bank, as it has no jurisdiction there (*Times of Israel*, December 16, 2018). When the Supreme Court put a freeze on the law, MK Smotrich proposed Regulation Bill 2, which retroactively legalized settlements built on (purportedly) state land, as opposed to private Palestinian land (Regulation Bill 2, July 18, 2018). This new legislation would give Pinchas Wallerstein, former Director of the Yesha Council director and head of a special government task force responsible for legalizing the outposts, two years to legalize some sixty-six outposts, many of which were built illegally or without the required permits (*Israel Hayom*, December 14, 2018).

Under the Likud-led governments, which have ruled Israel for most of the past few decades, settler leaders have enlisted the mechanisms of the state to advance the settlement enterprise in other ways too, in an attempt to normalize the settlement enterprise. During the 1980s, for instance, the settlement enterprise was normalized through the conscious choice by the Ministry of the Interior to refer to "Judea and Samaria," and through the accompanying erasure of terms like "occupied territories" or "West Bank" from Israeli media. More recent examples include Transportation Minister Israel Katz's decision to extend rail services to the West Bank (*Haaretz*, July 9, 2012), Education Minister Gideon Sa'ar's decision to include Hebron on the list of school field trips (*Ynet*, February 15, 2011), and Culture Minister Limor Livnat's extension of governmental budget assistance to museums in the settlements (*Times of Israel*, December 22, 2012).[21] More recently, Transportation Minister Bezalel Smotrich proposed a plan that envisions another half million people in the West Bank, facilitated by a new train line, roads, and interchanges. This "sovereignty through transportation" plan includes a road that would connect Jerusalem to Gush Etzion (*Israel HaYom*, June 25, 2019).

4.3 Resources

The vast majority of funding for the settler movement comes from the Israeli government and local authorities in the territories. It is the government funding that also attests to the movement's penetration of the state. In March 2014, for instance, Labor MK Stav Shaffir revealed that the Israeli government had transferred $172 million to settlements above and beyond its regular budget during the winter parliamentary session, including $6.8 million for projects encouraging younger people to settle in the West Bank, $8 million to the settlement of Beit El to complete building projects, and $10.3 million as compensation for the settlement construction freeze (*Times of Israel*, March 23, 2014). The government also transferred more than $38 million to the WZO Settlement Division.

It is clear that this funding, which is integral to the continued expansion of the settlement project, could not have reached its current levels without the strategic facilitation and conscious effort of political figures invested in its growth (see also Chapter 5). The settler movement, and in particular the Yesha Council, employs a robust machine to perpetuate its revenue streams and secure the establishment and subsequent security and social needs of settlements (Zertal & Eldar 2007). Toward this end, it has become adept at acquiring support and assistance from state and parastatal institutions – such as government ministries, the IDF, and Jewish Agency offices – to provide resources for the settlements, and to regulate both the expansion of the settlements and municipal growth in Palestinian towns (Haklai 2007; Lustick 1982). Collaboration takes place in particular with local councils of already-established settlements, personnel in the Ministry of Construction and Housing, and actors in the IDF and the Ministry of Defense. By building alliances with authoritative elements in the state apparatus, in addition to the political echelon, the settlers have gained influence over political outcomes in significant disproportion to their relative size in the population.

Incidentally, the settlement movement's deliberate targeting of the budget serves a dual function in advancing its goals. Pragmatically, Jewish settlement of the West Bank represents an expensive undertaking (in the fiscal sense), which requires government subsidies. However, beyond the immediate practical financial necessity, the settler movement also targets the budget of the State of Israel to advance the legitimization and normalization of its enterprise. The de facto consequence of receiving financial support, especially when allocated in the national budget, is a form of normalization of the goals and achievements of the settler movement.

To encourage Israelis to move to the settlements, the government created a mechanism for providing financial benefits and incentives to settlements and settlers. For example, many of the settlements in the West Bank hold the status of "National Priority Area," making them eligible for government benefits for culture, education, housing, infrastructure, and security. The government list included dozens of new West Bank settlements in 2009 and several settlements outside the large settlement blocs, as well as illegal outposts that were legalized by the cabinet in 2013 (Government Resolution 667: Defining localities and regions as national priority, August 4, 2013). In 2018, the Housing Ministry announced its new National Priority list, which included some isolated settlements, considered to be "neighborhoods located far from a 'parent town' that do not rely on the infrastructure of said town."[22] The pattern of the National Priority list is reflective of the larger settler movement trend of legitimizing geographically distant, disconnected, or simply poorly planned settlements and outposts by using bureaucratic offices as mechanisms for normalization.

Importantly, there is disproportionate funding to the settlement project in comparison to the rest of the country. For example, according to the Central Bureau of Statistics (CBS), the settlements received around $441,787 from government revenues in 2017, including about $226,091 from the Ministry of Education, $114,809 from the Ministry of Labor, Social Affairs and Social Services, and $140,332 from government grant.[23] Under Government Resolution 1561, an additional ca. $20 million were transferred from different government offices and ministries for various purposes. In the proposed budget for 2017–18, per-capita grants to municipalities in the West Bank stood at around $425, which is $290 more than for an average Israeli not living in the West Bank. The average resident in the West Bank was expected to receive $510 in tax breaks and benefits – approximately $375 more than the average Israeli resident, and $85 more than residents of regions that are designated as peripheral for budgeting purposes, such as the Galilee and the Negev, and that are entitled to extra financial support (Nathanson & Gazala 2016: 3).

In 2014 the government also changed section 11 of the Income Tax Ordinance, which enumerates tax benefits for residents of selected localities, so as to include for the first-time settlements in the West Bank. These benefits accrue to residents of localities that meet certain criteria based on their socioeconomic status, proximity to the border, and designation as peripheral. Government Resolution 1340, a 2014 revision, introduced a new method for evaluating the criteria which for the first time included settlements in the West Bank – twenty-five in the Jordan Valley and ten in the area of Kiryat Arba and Hebron (Nathanson & Gazala 2016). Criticizing the government's priority of settlement expansion and the secretive nature of its dealings, Labor MK Stav Shaffir stated:

Instead of allocating tax money equitably and justly among all Israelis, one small group [settlers] gets more than everyone under the table ... Only thusly, when funds are transferred far from the public eye, can the government make believe it is working on behalf of the middle class or toward a framework agreement, and at the same time funnel huge budgets for developing the settlements (*Times of Israel*, March 23, 2014).

Indeed, many financial donations to the settler movement are shrouded in nebulous ambiguity. For example, a report released by the Macro Center for Political Economics revealed that funds officially designated for the Ministry of Agriculture are sometimes redirected to the regional authorities in the West Bank, with the express intent of disguising the governmental origin of the money (Nathanson & Gazala 2016). But it is not only the Ministry of Agriculture that is (ab)used in this way. According to Talia Sasson, author of the Sasson Report (2005),

The finances for the settlements do not come from one source among the government ministries, but from various ministries. Planning is in the Ministry of Construction and Housing, infrastructure work is through the local councils, with the budget apparently being channeled through the Ministry of Construction and Housing. Power comes from the Israel Electric Corporation, water from Mekorot, and the Ministry of the Interior pays the local authority monthly. The money comes from all kinds of directions in all kinds of ways. If a new road is built, or a civilian guard is set up, or a fence or a generator, the source is often the Ministry of Defense. This diffusion and the way that the money is transferred is part of the idea that there should be no single figure that anyone can point to and say "that's the budget that goes to the settlements" (*Globes*, January 1, 2017).

It is also not uncommon for pro-settler NGOs to be directly subsidized by the Israeli government. A prominent example is the WZO's Settlement Division (or *Hativa*), whose self-stated goal is to "establish and strengthen Jewish settlement in the periphery." It considers itself "an operational arm for realizing the policy of the Government of Israel in the development of settlements in areas of national priority" (Freedom of Information Cover Letter 2017). For this purpose, Hativa works under the direct guidance of the Israeli government, and is highly connected to the ministries of Construction, National Infrastructure, Absorption, Education, Agriculture, Tourism, Defense, and Labor and Social Affairs. Beyond the governmental ministries, Hativa also works within a network of established NGOs, domestic authorities, and councils, such as the Jewish National Fund, the Israel Lands, and the National Parks Authority, to name but a few. It invests its resources and efforts to bolster the settlements. For instance, in 2014 Hativa invested one-third of its annual budget in the Central region of the West Bank, a total of 122 settlements (Nathanson & Gazala 2016: 9).

While governmental support for Hativa was immortalized by the passage of the Status Law of the Zionist Organization and the Jewish Agency for Israel in 1952 (amended in 2015), which recognized the "uniqueness of the settlement division," the government's funding mechanisms are more obscure. For instance, Roby Nathanson and Itamar Gazala (2016: 6) highlight a budget bypass mechanism that has permitted the Ministry of Agriculture to exceed the Hativa subsidy limit, capped at ca. $13–18.5 million in 2010, over the course of each fiscal year. For example, the budget override oscillated between ca. $27 and $70 million, in 2010 in addition to the initial subsidy. Between 2009 and 2014, the budget override represented a 27 percent to a staggering 382 percent increase over the original grant.[24]

In trying to explain these disproportionate government and private investments in the settlements, Yigal Dilmoni, Deputy Director of the Yesha Council, declared

> There are higher values than money . . . . the settlement in Judea and Samaria is not an economic burden, but a strong and good economic support for the State of Israel . . . That doesn't mean that we are sitting on mountains of gold here. Those who live here work hard for a living . . . . It isn't settlers receiving money, but money that the state invests in Judea and Samaria. There has been a decline from 1.7 billion NIS [$480 million] in 2003 to about 1 billion NIS [$280 million], despite the fact that the population has doubled in the past twenty years. That means that the money is not going to the settlers (*Globes*, January 1, 2017).

However, in stark contrast to Dilmoni's assertion, research on the 2017–18 settlements budget suggests that support for the settlements has not diminished. A 2016 legislative decision allocated financial aid of $20 million over the course of three years (2016–18) and an additional $15 million over five years (2016–20) to communities in the West Bank, for a total of about $35 million over five years. Although the budget refers to this apportionment as "special assistance following the security situation," suggesting that it is exceptional or out of the ordinary, it represents a continuation of the trend (Nathanson & Gazala 2016: 6).

In response to domestic calls for transparency and mounting international criticism and pressure, Israeli governments have issued a series of official reports since 2005.[25] The Sasson Report, for example, revealed that millions of shekels were funneled from government agencies, including the Ministry of Construction and Housing, to support (unauthorized) settlements. It discovered that between 2000 and 2004, the Ministry of Construction and Housing provided $20.5 million toward the establishment of unauthorized outposts. According to the report, the Ministry financed the establishment of infrastructure and public buildings for unauthorized outposts by providing financial aid under the guise of building "new neighborhoods" as add-ons to old, established settlements, when in fact they were physically and spatially unrelated to the "old neighborhoods."

In 2001, the Ministry created a special budget article called "Open General Miscellaneous," which it used to finance these unauthorized outposts, with a budget of $4.8 million in 2001, which doubled to $9.7 million in 2002 (Sasson 2005: 30). No criteria were set for using these funds, and they were not subject to public transparency rules. The Sasson Report was unable to provide a precise number for how many illegal outposts had been constructed, which was attributed largely to the COGAT's unwillingness to furnish the necessary data (Sasson 2005: 21).[26] In her conclusion, Sasson recommended a list of reforms, including new legislation and enforcement of existing legislation, to reduce state support for illegal outposts and increase government transparency in funding and supporting settlements.

Finally, the settlement movement also accrues resources through more conventional means, including commerce and industry, but especially the West Bank's burgeoning tourism and wine industry. Since 2005, the West Bank, and Samaria in particular, has undergone significant development in the tourism sector (see Figure 4.7). Data from COGAT and the Israel Nature and Parks Authority show a dramatic increase in the number of visitors (from both Israel and abroad) to tourist sites in Judea and Samaria

Figure 4.7 Political tourism in the West Bank by type of attraction[27]

between 2014 and 2017. Tourist sites in the region received around 921,000 visitors in 2015, and a record 994,484 in just the first half of 2017 (*NRG*, October 11, 2017).

Although we are unable to specify exactly how much money has been invested in the development of the tourism industry in West Bank settlements, investments have poured in from private tourists as well as governmental agencies. Significant amounts of government money have been put into sites of "biblical tourism." For instance, the Tel Shiloh site, according to the Bible the location of the Ark of the Covenant, was given nearly $1.4 million in 2012 to develop the site and establish a tourist center. This then becomes a feedback loop, with greater investment leading to positive shifts in public opinion, which in turn leads to more investment.

These sources of financial resources also serve a second and, arguably, more important function, in the sphere of public opinion. Simply put, the key aim of tourism is to strengthen positive attitudes toward the residents and the disputed territory within both the domestic and international community. As Davidi Ben-Zion, Deputy Head of the Samaria Regional Council, explained

> If you want to get close to a person in Israeli society, you cannot talk to him about ideology ... You give him a good price, bulletproof transportation so they feel safe, you offer him a wine tasting that you would find in any other place, a goat cheese tasting like you might find in the Galilee. You want a natural spring? We'll build one for you, we'll build whatever you want, and that's how you get them here ... I don't want him to vote for Jewish Home ... I first want to remove the horns [i.e. the settlers' image as demons or devils] ... When a visitor sees that I am a human being who served in the army, who pays taxes, who loves his country, and a strong citizen ... after all that, we can talk politics ... When someone who has never been to Samaria comes here and experiences the scenery and the people, something in him has to change (Interview, April 2014).

4.4 Support

At the heart of the political struggle of the settler movement is its effort to increase support for its cause. While it mainly focuses on the state for policies and resources, support is approached at a broader level. At the state level, the settler movement targets all three branches of government (i.e., the executive, legislature, and judiciary) as well as the military, a particularly important institution given its crucial role in Israeli politics in general and the politics of the occupied territories in particular (see Chapter 2). But it also tries to generate support within civil society, most notably among political parties, NGOs, and the media. Finally, like all political struggles, the settler movement is involved in a battle over public opinion. This multi-arena struggle plays out at both the domestic and international level; we discuss the former in this section and the latter in the next one.

4.4.1 *The State*

The settler movement's support within the Israeli government and parliament is clearly visible. Its leaders have direct access to leading political figures up to the level of prime minister and president. At the same time, settlers have become a growing presence within both the executive and legislature over the past decades. The movement's presence in government began in 1996. Since then, every Israeli government has included at least one minister from the settlements. In the 19th Knesset, a coalition of mostly right-wing and far-right parties, five ministers from four different parties were settlers, accounting for almost one quarter of the whole cabinet (22 percent).

The settler movement has always followed a strategy of influencing and permeating many different political parties, rather than focusing on just one particular party (Newman 2005). It has a growing number of MKs in a variety of right-wing parties, including Jewish Home, Likud, and National Unity. In 1984, there was only a single MK residing in the settlements, but that number had increased to twelve by 2015 (see Figure 4.8).[28] Since the settlement enterprise began, the ratio between the proportion of MKs living in the settlements and that of MKs living within Israel proper has also grown steadily, with the result that the former are now overrepresented in the Knesset. In 1983, the West Bank was home to 0.5 percent of the Israeli population and 0.83 percent of MKs. In 1995, these ratios had leveled out, with 2.37 percent of the Israeli population and 2.50 percent of MKs residing in the West Bank. By 2008, the percentage of MKs from settlements had nearly quadrupled, to 9.16 percent, where the overall percentage of Israelis living in the West Bank was still only 3.92 percent of the population. In 2015, 10 percent of MKs hailed from West Bank settlements, while settlers still comprised less than 5 percent of the Israeli population.

In addition to building palpable connections with the official state bureaucracy and its political figures, the settler movement also pursues a strategy of permeating the state bureaucracy by inserting key figures into ostensibly apolitical offices. Indeed, a significant number of individuals who were formerly actively involved with the settler movement have since moved on to assume authoritative positions within the government bureaucracy – including positions unrelated to the settler project. For

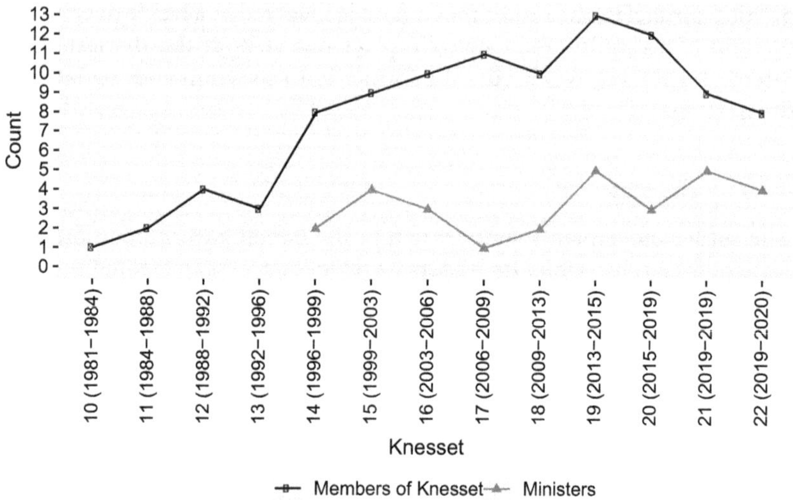

Figure 4.8 Number of ministers and parliamentarians from the settlements[29]

instance, Shaul Goldstein, a former chairman of the Gush Etzion Regional Council, was appointed CEO of the Israel Nature and Parks Authority in 2012 (and reappointed in 2017). Bentzi Lieberman, a former Yesha Council Chairman and Head of the Samaria Regional Council, served as Director of the Israel Lands Authority (2011–16), the body responsible for managing the 93 percent of Israeli land that is in the public domain. And Nissan Slomiansky, a founding member of Gush Emunim and later an active member in the Yesha Council, served on the Board of Directors of the Jewish National Fund.

Although the military is obviously part of the state, its prominence and role within Israeli politics and society, particularly with respect to the occupied territories, warrant a separate discussion.[30] The IDF's permeation of Israeli society is profound, affecting every corner of the civilian realm, from pop culture to education to immigration policy (Michael 2007). Israel's mandatory enlistment makes the IDF accessible to the Israeli public and "imbues it with special status and prestige" (Michael 2007: 523). As a result of the IDF's central place in Israeli society, it inevitably has a lasting effect on the political sphere, not only in terms of how the military-influenced public opinion informs politics, but also through the integration of military figures into the political elite. It is not uncommon for senior military officers to transition from a professional military career to the political sphere (Etzioni-Halevy 1996; Michael 2007).

The fluidity between the military and political sphere contributes to a blurring of the boundaries between the two. The openness and reciprocity between the two is also influenced by Israel's governance structure, in which the IDF is responsible for a variety of matters in the West Bank, including granting permits for the transportation of caravans and construction vehicles, as well as law enforcement. Over the past decades, the settler movement has enjoyed significant support from within the military, ranging from the top, of sympathetic generals, to the bottom, including soldiers drawn from the settlements.

Besides taking a permissive stance in granting permits and the like, the IDF has actively facilitated the construction process by providing generators, carving out access roads, and supplying building equipment and materials (Eldar & Zertal 2007; Haklai 2007). In March 2014, for example, Israeli media reported on a secret deal between Defense Minister Moshe Yaalon and settlers, who had placed four mobile homes on privately owned Palestinian land south of Jerusalem in an attempt to create a new settlement (*Haaretz*, March 10, 2014). Under the deal, the settlers agreed to move the mobile homes, but only to another nearby outpost. Such tactics force the government, most notably the IDF, to either acquiesce to the settlers' actions or challenge them outright. In fact, Amana leaders, particularly Ze'ev Hever, have regularly met with the IDF to discuss improving the relationship between the IDF and the settler community (*Haaretz*, May 13, 2013).

Evidence of the special relationship between the IDF and the settler movement can also be found in the Sasson Report, which implied that without the military's passive and active cooperation, the illegal settlements could not have been expanded. According to the report,

> The 'commander spirit' ... sees the settlers' acts [of] building outposts as Zionist deeds, although illegal, and asks them not to view such acts through the eyes of the law. This 'commander spirit' is nourished by the involvement of State authorities and public authorities in establishing unauthorized outposts (Sasson 2005: 45).

The close relationship between the IDF and the settler movement is not just a matter of opportunistic or pragmatic organic collaboration. The two are becoming more intertwined as a consequence of the national religious camp's embrace of military service and the growing number of religious Zionists and settlers within the ranks of the IDF. Some IDF officers are themselves residents of illegal settlements. As the Sasson

Report (2005: 261) stated, "When IDF officers permit themselves to live in unauthorized outposts; and to reply, when they are asked to voluntarily leave their homes, that it was the state which provided their caravans and infrastructure, the state which hooked them up to the electricity and water supply; and when nothing then happens – this sends a message."

Udi Lebel (2013: 23) maintains that this phenomenon is a product of the postmodern condition of the IDF, and notes that it is characterized by two notable shifts. First, the social elites, the group to which the large majority of military commanders belong, have begun to experience a "crisis of motivation," which has led to a paradigm shift in which the military path ceased to be regarded as the dominant way to advance their career. Second, there has been a simultaneous trend toward the integration of settlers in commanding positions in combat and elite forces. Religious Zionists are represented in these units at rates significantly higher than the general population. This is to a large extent a product of the Hesder yeshiva program, in which religious Zionist youth can combine military service with traditional yeshiva studies (see Chapter 5).

The IDF has always been considered a microcosm of Israeli society, and its top units provided Israel's future elite. Traditionally, recruits serving in the most exclusive units, and those who rose through the officer ranks, were largely secular and left-wing (Levy 2016). National-religious soldiers have increased their presence in field units and have started to appear among the ranks of senior officers since the end of the 1990s (Cohen 2004). Now, as a special report in *The Economist* (May 18, 2017) notes, "it is the boys from the yeshivas who seek to settle the land and become army officers." The percentage of religious Zionist officer cadets grew tenfold between the early 1990s and 2010. A 2010 study found that the highest overall enlistment rate came from Mount Hebron Regional Council, in the southern West Bank – an astounding 96.4 percent of which 83 percent served as combat soldiers (Billig & Lebel 2010: 202).[31] Crucially, the percentage of commanders in infantry units who live in the settlements was higher than the percentage who hail from kibbutzim and moshavim within the borders of Israel (the traditional source for Israel's military elite).

The permeation of a palpable religious Zionist presence throughout the military, and in particular in combat units in positions of rank, has affected not only the IDF's image, but also the image of the national-religious sector in Israeli society. The "revolution of the pre-military academies" has transformed the settlers into combat soldiers willing to "sacrifice for the betterment of general Israeli society" (Lebel 2015: 363–364). As the backbone of the settler movement, the growing clout of religious Zionists in the military creates broader support for the settlements within the IDF (Levy 2016). It has also led to growing internal problems, whenever the interests of the IDF and the settler movement clash.

For example, prominent rabbis, including heads of Hesder yeshivas, have issued religious decisions (*piskei Halacha*) banning religious soldiers from participating in the dismantling of settlements, or even military bases, in the occupied territories. This trend reflects the ascendance of the post-*Mamlachti* camp among religious Zionist settlers (see Chapter 3). However, other settler rabbis, like Rabbi Shlomo Aviner (2005: 3), have argued that religious soldiers should take part in the dismantling of settlements. Their logic reflects both the classic *Mamlachti* position that loyalty belongs to the state and a more pragmatic consideration: "To leave the army is to leave the nation. It is disengagement from the people! (...) If you are not inside, you have no influence. You only harm yourself while others take your place – just as with the left-wing refuseniks."

4.4.2 Civil Society

The settler movement, and in particular the Yesha Council, has engaged with all Israeli political parties in an effort to broaden its support as much as possible. These relations, however, go beyond merely talking. In the 1996 elections, for example, the settler movement called on constituents to vote for Benjamin Netanyahu, the first time it endorsed a specific candidate in its history. The call for action was explicitly meant to express voter sentiment in support of the settlement project and against the Oslo Accords (Pedahzur et al. 2000).

Israel's main political parties have held ambivalent positions toward the settler movement, at times embracing and supporting it, at times seeking to obstruct and frustrate its endeavors. Yet almost all Israeli parties have seen engagement with the settlers as unavoidable. Likewise, the settler movement understands the importance of maintaining avenues of communication with a broad variety of parties. Communication has continued even during the hardest times, such as the evacuation of Jewish settlements in the wake of the peace agreement with Egypt or the disengagement from Gaza. This awareness has helped the movement to recruit individuals within the parties to support the settlement enterprise.

In fact, individuals who are or have been formerly involved with the settler movement, and the Yesha Council in particular, have permeated almost every incarnation of the centrist and right-wing parties. The main political parties formed, and/or represented in the Knesset (and in the government), by individuals who were active in the settler movement include Revival (*Tehiya*), National Religious Party (*Mafdal*), The Faithful/Resurrection (*Emunim/T'kuma*), National Union (*Ichud Leumi*), Israel Is Our Home (*Yisrael Beitenu*), Jewish Home (*HaBayit HaYehudi*), and Likud (see Figure 4.9). Due to the volatile nature of Israeli political parties,[32] it is not uncommon to see politicians representing multiple parties over the course of their careers. For example, Uri Ariel, who served as Secretary General of both the Yesha Council and Amana, and was Minister of Agriculture and Rural Development between 2015 and 2019, served as MK for the National Union-Israel Is Our Home, the National Union-NRP, and Jewish Home.

Although Israeli policies in the West Bank have been a constant source of tension with the US administration and European allies, support for the settlement enterprise – and territorial maximization of the State of Israel (Arian 1985) – has remained a principal issue for Israeli right-wing parties. But the Israeli right-wing is not a monolithic bloc. Rather, it includes a range of different platforms and worldviews (Schwartz 2009). One key line of division is between religious (e.g., Jewish Home and NRP) and secular right-wing parties (e.g., Likud and Israel Is Our Home). Jewish Home, the main religious party, is a hardline nationalist party that not only rejects the notion of an independent Palestinian state, but also calls for the annexation of (at minimum) Area C in the West Bank, where all Jewish settlements are located, and which currently falls under Israeli military control. It has several settlers on its list (e.g., Uri Ariel, Orit Strock, Bezalel Smotrich, Hillel Horowitz, Nissan Slomiansky, and Shuli Mualem-refaeli) and is the party that is most identified with the settlement enterprise. Naftali Bennett, its former leader, has said that his conscience wouldn't allow him to ever order the evacuation of a Jew from his home (*Times of Israel*, December 21, 2012), while new leader Rafi Peretz, the Minister of Education, has declared his support for the annexation of the entire West Bank, without giving Palestinians the right to vote (*Times of Israel*, July 13, 2019).[33]

In contrast to the hardline platform of Jewish Home and other religious parties, secular right-wing parties such as Israel Is Our Home oppose unilateral annexation of the West Bank. Instead, they call for a two-state solution with land swaps, whereby Israel would annex major settlement blocs in the West Bank and in turn cede Israeli territory predominantly inhabited by Arab citizens to a future Palestine state. This is captured in the party's 2015 campaign slogan: "Ariel to Israel, Umm el-Fahm to Palestine" – Ariel is a Jewish settlement in the West Bank (see Chapter 6), while Umm el-Fahm is an Arab city in northern Israel. Party leader Avigdor Lieberman is himself a settler who lives in Nokdim, in the southern West Bank.

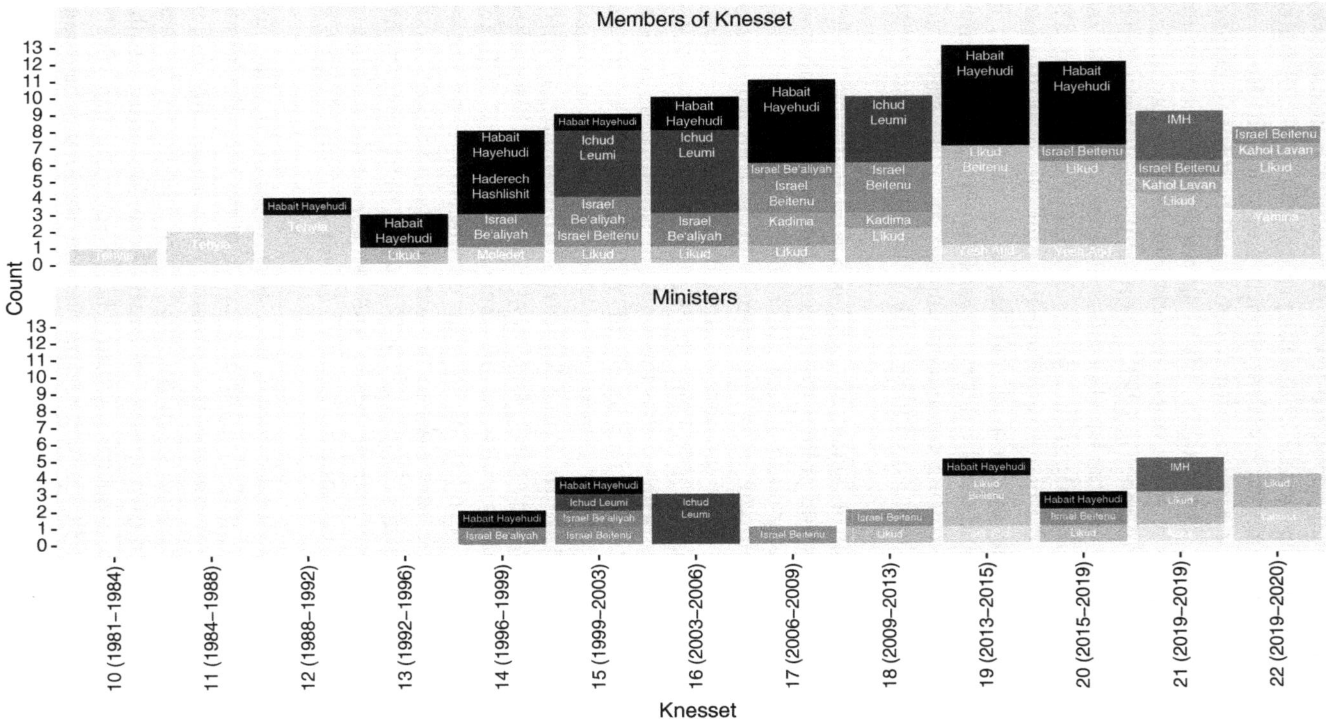

Figure 4.9 MKs and ministers residing in the settlements by political party[34]

Likud has traditionally supported Jewish settlement throughout *Eretz Yisrael*. For example, in the late 1990s, the party platforms clearly stated that Likud would strengthen Jewish settlement and cancel the freeze on settlement construction then in place. When in power, it has sometimes taken a less hard line. For instance, Likud agreed to concessions in the Camp David Accords in 1979, began negotiations with the Palestinians during the Madrid Conference in 1991, continued the implementation of the Oslo Accords, and enacted Israel's unilateral disengagement from the Gaza Strip in 2005. Under Benjamin Netanyahu, Likud has continued to tread a path between the two approaches. For example, over the years Netanyahu has frequently declared that he backed natural growth in existing settlements, and that he did not regard the settlers as "enemies of peace," while also voicing conditional support for a two-state solution to the Israeli–Palestinian conflict (with a demilitarized Palestinian state).

The massive impact of Netanyahu, and of Likud under his leadership, on Israeli society and politics over recent decades requires that we devote some more attention to it here. After absorbing the Herut party in 1973, Likud became the most important political representative of Revisionist Zionists, which had always pursued the realization of *Eretz Yisrael*. Begin, a follower of Russian Revisionist Zionist leader Ze'ev Jabotinsky, adamantly believed that the whole of Israel, "from bank to bank" (i.e., from the western bank of the Jordan River to the Mediterranean Sea), was a matter of "Jewish historical right" (Bookmiller 1997: 91).[35] As Prime Minister (1977–83), Begin introduced the "Basic Law: Jerusalem, Capital of Israel," which established the status of a united Jerusalem as the capital of the State of Israel. While Netanyahu has been less ideologically committed to *Eretz Yisrael*, he explicitly justified Israel's right to the settlements in his 1993 book *A Place Among the Nations: Israel and the World* and, more recently, has argued that "no settlement or settler will be uprooted ... That is over ... what you have done is forever" (*Times of Israel*, August 6, 2019).

Though Likud, and Herut before it, have always supported a hardline policy of expansionism, including the annexation of the West Bank (and earlier the Gaza Strip) for most of its existence, party leaders like Begin, Sharon and Netanyahu have often governed more moderately. In fact, both Begin and Sharon gave up some of Israel's occupied territories, the Sinai and Gaza Strip, respectively, and while Netanyahu has vocally disapproved of the 1993 Oslo Accords, his platform has long, if begrudgingly, included a promise to uphold them.[36] Today, however, Likud is increasingly outspoken about its support for de facto annexation of Israeli settlements.

In 2017, the Likud Central Committee unanimously encouraged legislators to approve a (failed) bill that would apply civilian law to settlements, a move that would help streamline bureaucratic procedures for settlement construction and expansion (*Reuters*, December 31, 2017). Minister of Internal Affairs Gilad Erdan said in support of the bill, "We will now promote the recognition of our sovereignty of the Jewish settlements in Judea and Samaria ... We must begin to enact this sovereignty, and we have the moral right and obligation towards our settler brothers" (*Reuters*, December 31, 2017). Since then, Likud members have proposed a number of annexation bills: during the 20th Knesset (2015–19), MK Yoav Kitsch cosponsored a bill to annex the settlement of Ma'ale Adumim, MK Miki Zohar co-introduced a bill to annex several other settlements (notably Gush Etzion, Ariel, and the Jordan Valley settlements), and MK Yisrael Katz proposed a bill to annex Givat Ze'ev (*Ynet*, January 28, 2018).

Before the Gaza disengagement in 2005, neither the national-religious nor (other) settlers were prominent within Likud, and rarely represented the party in the Knesset. The internal power of the national-religious and settlers was boosted by the introduction of primaries in the 1990s. The 2006 primaries brought Yuli Edelstein, a national-religious MK, into the small twelve-member Likud faction, while the 2009 primaries increased the number of settlers to two out of twenty-seven faction members. In September 2019, three out of thirty-two Likud faction members were settlers.

Although its natural partners are the right-wing parties, both secular and religious, the settler movement works with all parties and all governments, irrespective of political color. For example, Wallerstein, one of the leaders of Gush Emunim, believes that the settlers owe a considerable debt to the Labor Party, in the years prior to the 1977 political upheaval: "All the stages of Ariel's development were approved by Labor ... The Trans-Samaria road, Givat Zeev, Adumim, Beit Horon – it is all Labor's work" (*Haaretz*, June 15, 2017). Similarly, Shaul Goldstein, former head of Gush Etzion, points out that "the left helped a lot in rehabilitating the refugees from Gush Katif." He continues, "to stop [the government] building the [security] fence in an environmentally sensitive area, we used parties from the center and from the left" (Interview 2007).

The settler movement's cunning, determined, and ruthless approach to Israel's political parties – along with the relative openness of the party system, particularly toward the movement, the strong ties and alignment of interests between the movement and a variety of policy-makers, and the state's incapacity or lack of will to repress the movement – have undoubtedly provided support for a settlement policy that has empowered the settler movement as well as the settlement enterprise in general. But it arguably not only made the right-wing parties more pro-settler, it also helped boost the popularity of right-wing parties, which have been dominating Israeli politics since the 1990s.

In addition to political parties, the settler movement also fosters relationships with NGOs to increase its resources, most notably finances and manpower. First of all, it uses several of its own civil society organizations to raise funds for the movement and increase support for its cause (see also Chapter 5). Second, the settler movement collaborates with NGOs that have partly overlapping agendas, or which are sympathetic to its cause. For instance, *Bnei Akiva* (Children of Akiva), the largest religious Zionist youth movement, with an estimated global membership of 125,000, disburses scholarships and grants to students who wish to study and live in Israel (*Arutz Sheva*, February 7, 2016). The settler movement considers these grants as a vital tool to secure the future of the settlement enterprise (*Yesha Council Website*, March 5, 2018). It also uses its ties with Bnei Akiva to increase its nonfinancial resources, notably personnel. For example, its youths have participated in many of the settler movement's demonstrations, marches, and settlement actions (Cohen 2015; Lustick 1988; Nevo 1985). Bnei Akiva has also served as a proving ground of sorts for up-and-coming settler leaders, with the ultimate goal of achieving critical positions in the state apparatus (Aronoff 1985; Sprinzak 1985).

Finally, the settler movement draws on support from various sectors within the media. It maintains its own media, including the now-defunct newsletter *Nekuda*, the weekly *Shabbat B'Shabbato* (Each and Every Sabbath), and the news website *Arutz Sheva* (Channel 7). The latter was founded as an illegal radio station in 1988, broadcasting from a ship in the Mediterranean Sea, but transformed into an Internet radio station and website that publishes news stories in three languages (English, Hebrew, and Russian). It also publishes a weekly newspaper, *B'Sheva* (At Seven), which is distributed freely to 140,000 families each week, reaching some 6 percent of the Israeli population (*Arutz Sheva*, March 14, 2005). It is the third largest Israeli newspaper and the largest in the religious community (*Arutz Sheva*, January 24, 2018). While associated with the settler movement, *Arutz Sheva* is largely treated as a regular media outlet in Israel, with regular access to major political and state actors from across the political spectrum.

The settler movement also tries to raise support within other media, that is, those not (openly) associated with the movement, by advertising, giving interviews and writing op-eds, and through influencers. The target audience for these activities is sometimes the Israeli public, and sometimes the government, in cases where the goal is to persuade the government to adopt or change a policy (Avraham 2003). Influencers like journalists Emily Amrousi and Amit Segal have an important role in the attempted mainstreaming and normalization of the settler enterprise and movement within Israeli society (see Chapter 3). All of these efforts have started to pay off, at least somewhat.

Initially, in the early 1970s, Israeli media tended to portray the settlers as pioneers, and coverage incorporated pioneering motifs and myths related to the establishment of the State of Israel. But soon after, the image began to change radically. Up until the early 2000s, the settlements were covered as a kind of lawless "Wild West" by the Israeli media. While the settlers wanted to be called "residents" living in "Yesha" or "Judea and Samaria," the Israeli media mainly described them as "settlers" living in "the West Bank" or "in the occupied territories." Moreover, according to Eli Avraham,

> The settlers were blamed for everything bad, as negatively affecting 'all of us' in all aspects of our lives, as different from the public at large .... [T]here was no tendency among most editors and journalists to adopt the group's point of view, or even its terminology for its name, the name of the area it lives in and so on (in Tsfati & Cohen 2005: 35).

But in 2005, media coverage of the debate over the Disengagement Plan was overall evenhanded, with proponents receiving more supportive coverage in the early stages and opponents in the last week (Sheafer 2005; see also Chapter 7).

Social media, in particular, have become a battleground for the settler movement as a whole, which uses it to "blur boundaries" and appeal to the broader Israeli public. As an example, the Yesha Council has published articles on courses in New Media and explained that "Social networking is a great tool for bypassing the media. It allows us, for the first time, tell about life in Judea and Samaria without editing and filtering. It is important for [West Bank] residents to learn and recognize and be active partners throughout the new media" (Yesha Council Website).

The three branches of the settler movement have very different social media profiles. The institutions (Yesha Council and Amana) are virtually absent, the networks are mainly active on Facebook, and some influencers have significant Twitter profiles (see Figure 4.10). The lack of social media presence of the institutions is particularly striking when compared

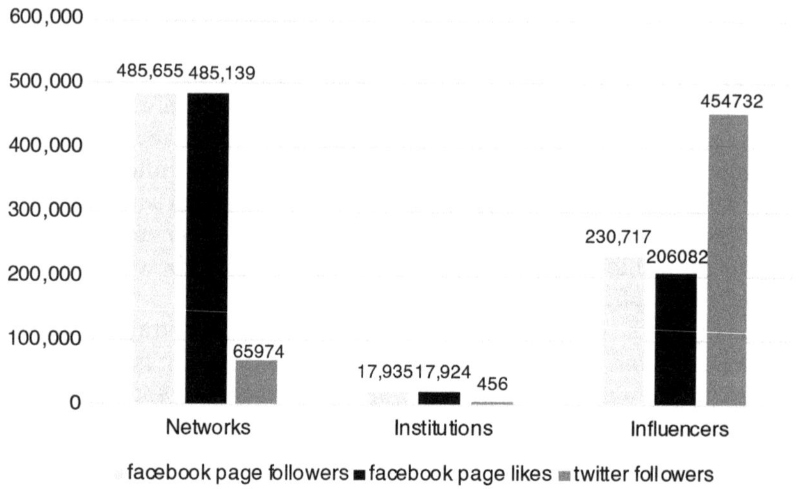

Figure 4.10 Social media profiles of the three branches[37]

to their key opponents, the anti-settlement NGOs Peace Now and B'Tselem, who have more than nine times as many followers on Facebook. Where the Yesha Council has only 14,494 Facebook followers – Amana has even fewer (3,437), Peace Now 94,103, and B'Tselem even has 83,633.

4.4.3 *Public Opinion*

While the Israeli settler movement is often portrayed as a radical minority at the margins of Israeli society, whose political power is based on their shrewd manipulation of Israel's hypercompetitive party system rather than mass support among the Israeli public, the reality is much more complex. No longer fringe radicals, supported only by the fringe right, they are now broadly embraced by the mainstream right – both ordinary people and political leaders. Indeed, many national surveys show significant public support for settlers, settlements, and the settler enterprise. While they are rarely supported by a majority of (Jewish) Israelis, in most cases they are not opposed by a majority either. Moreover, there are no clear long-term trends: Israelis are becoming more "pro-settler" on certain issues, but less so on others. In the end, the Israeli population is fundamentally divided on many key aspects related to the settler enterprise, no doubt in part because of the campaigns of the settler movement.

The Peace Index is a longitudinal research project based on a monthly survey of Israeli citizens (Jews and Arabs), which has been monitoring public sentiment on the Israeli–Palestinian conflict for over two decades now (Yaar & Hermann 1996, 1998, 2004, 2017). It has shown a (slight) decrease in the view that Jewish settlements are strengthening the national interest of Israel, from 54 percent in 2001 to 46 percent in 2017 (see Figure 4.11). Likewise, there has been an increase in public support for the statement that the settlements are *weakening* Israel's national interest, from 37 percent in 2001 to 46 percent in 2017. Consequently, the public is now fundamentally divided on this issue, with the same percentage of respondents, 46 percent, reporting that the settlements are strengthening the national interest as weakening it.[38]

Some surveys show a decline in public support for settlement construction since 2001, when 58 percent supported it, with an equal percentage of respondents (46 percent) saying it was the right and wrong decision in

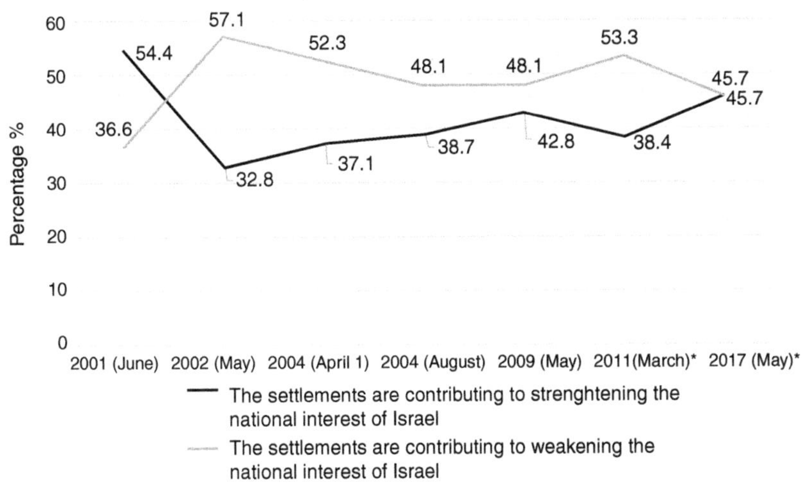

Figure 4.11 Public opinion on settlements and the national interest[39]

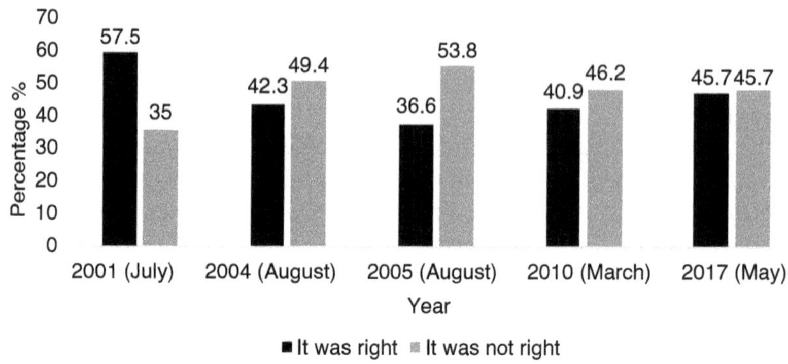

Figure 4.12 Public opinion on decision to construct settlements[40]

2017 (see Figure 4.12). However, other surveys found that more than half of Israelis (55 percent) believed that Israel should *not* cease construction in the occupied territories (Yaar & Hermann 2016). The National Security Index of 2016–17, conducted by the Institute for National Security Studies (INSS), asked Jewish Israelis about their preferred polici for settlement construction. They found that 21 percent believed that Israel should make a major effort to build in all of the West Bank, 21 percent believed it should build in all settlements in accordance with natural growth rates, 38 percent preferred only construction in settlement blocs, and a mere 20 percent wanted the state not to build at all in the West Bank.

In a longitudinal study, Miriam Billig and Udi Lebel (2009–12) found a slight increase in the number of Israeli Jews viewing the settlements as a national security resource and as "the security belt of the state," rising from 53 percent in 2009 to 57 percent in 2012.[41] This positive trend seems to continue over the years. For example, in May 2017, more than half of Israelis (including both Jews and Arabs) thought that the settlements were contributing to Israel's military security, while only 34 percent thought they were harming it (Yaar & Hermann 2017).

They further report both positive and negative trends in attitudes of Israeli Jews toward the settlements and settlers. On the positive side, their data show that more than half of Israeli Jews surveyed considered Jewish settlement in the West Bank a "true Zionist act" (56 percent in 2009 and

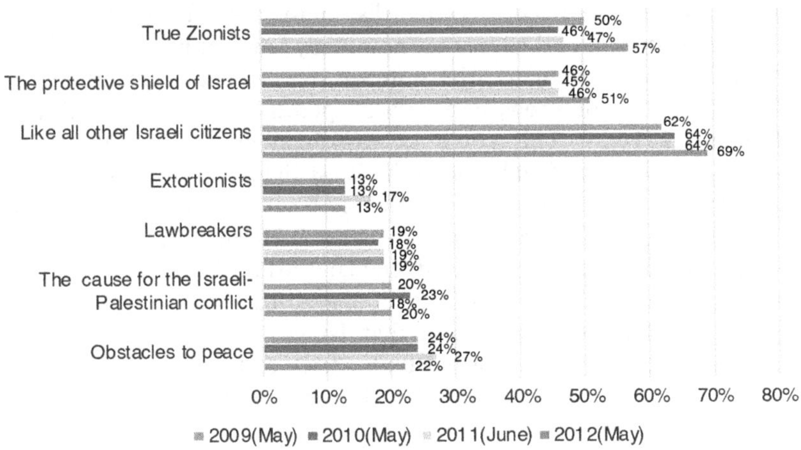

Figure 4.13 Jewish Israeli attitudes toward West Bank settlers, 2009–12[42]

64 percent in 2012) and did not view West Bank settlements as illegal (57 percent in 2009 and 62 percent in 2012). A majority even said that they did *not* consider the settlements as the source of conflict with the Palestinians (57 percent in 2009 and 56 percent in 2012).

With respect to attitudes toward the settlers, as opposed to the settlements, a majority of Israeli Jews see West Bank settlers as similar to other Israeli citizens (69 percent),[43] as true Zionists (57 percent), and as a protective shield of Israel (51 percent). Only a minority viewed the settlers as the source of the Israeli–Palestinian conflict (20 percent), as lawbreakers (19 percent), as extorting funds from the state (13 percent), or as an obstacle to peace (22 percent) (see Figure 4.13). On the other side, there has been a very small increase in Jewish Israelis who believe the settlements are a waste of state funds, from 37 percent in 2009 to 40 percent in 2014, and of those agreeing that settlers are damaging relations between the Israeli government and the United States, from 53 percent in 2009 to 59 percent in 2014. Similarly, 65 percent of (Jewish and Arab) Israelis said that the country's control over the West Bank was harming Israel diplomatically, and only 25 percent said that it was helping the country (Yaar & Hermann 2017).

Another way to assess the success of the settler movement is by examining the public's familiarity with the settlers and settlement enterprise.

Data show that the majority of Israelis, that is, 69 percent of Jews and Arabs, misestimate or do not know how many Jews live in the West Bank: 25 percent underestimated the number, 16 percent overestimated it, 27 percent did not know, and only 31 percent were correct (Yaar & Hermann 2016).[44] This could be explained by the fact that most Israelis are largely unfamiliar with the West Bank and the Jewish settlements: almost half of the Israeli public (49.5 percent) had not set foot in the West Bank over the last five years (Yaar & Hermann 2016).

Here, age also matters. Oded Haklai (2017) found that younger Israelis are much less conscious of the distinction between settlements and sovereign Israel and that Israelis born before 1967 are more likely to know the formal boundaries of the state, to perceive the settlements as being outside Israel proper, and to know that Israel has not formally declared sovereignty over Judea and Samaria. For those born after 1967, in contrast, "the boundaries of the pre-1967 war are not palpable" (Haklai 2017). Whereas 73 percent of Israelis sixty and over knew that Israel has not declared sovereignty over "Judea and Samaria," only some 40 percent of those under forty knew.

Another important question concerns Israeli public opinion regarding any possible peace agreement with the Palestinians that would include evacuation of settlements. Throughout the years, only a minority of (Jewish and Arab) Israelis supported the evacuation of all or most of the settlements as part of a peace agreement with the Palestinians, 13 percent in 1996 and 10 percent in 2017 (see Figure 4.14). There was an increase in public support for the evacuation of settlements in 2004, but that may have been associated with events like the Second Intifada, the planned disengagement from Gaza, and early Israeli government support for the Road Map framework.[45]

At present, the idea of evacuating settlements is remarkably unpopular among (nonsettler) Israelis. There has been a decline in support for signing a peace agreement that would require settlement evacuations over the years, dropping from 46 percent in 2001 to 37 percent in 2018. The National Security Index (INSS 2017) found that a majority of Israelis (53 percent) were willing to evacuate only settlements outside major settlement blocs within the framework of a final status agreement. Almost one-third (31 percent) of Israelis were unwilling to evacuate settlement under any conditions, while a mere 16 percent were willing to evacuate *all* settlements within the framework of a final status agreement (Israeli 2017).

Similarly, only one-third of Israelis believe that negotiations between Israel and the Palestinians could lead to peace in the coming years (Yaar &

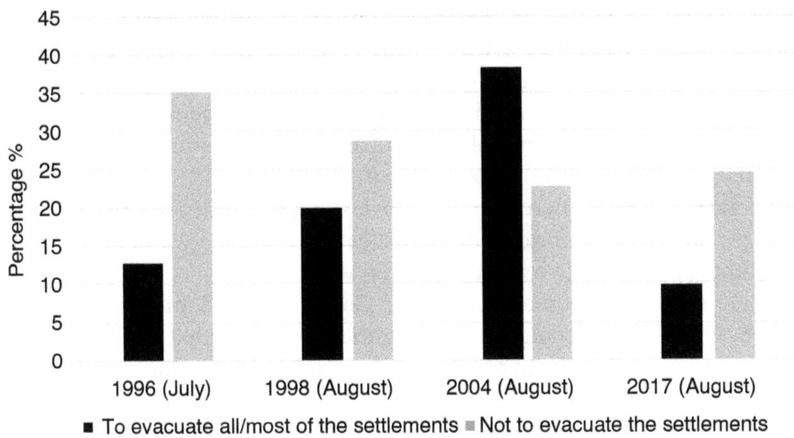

Figure 4.14 Public opinion on evacuation of settlements for peace[46]

Hermann 2018), while more than half (53 percent) disagree with the statement that Israel's control over the territories is an "occupation" (Yaar & Hermann 2017). Between 2006 and 2018, support for the two-state solution has decreased from 71 percent to 58 percent (INSS 2018; Israeli 2018). Thus, if the public believes that there is no chance for peace, and if it does not consider the settlements as occupied territories, then a peace deal with the Palestinians that relies on settlement evacuations has a small chance of obtaining public support.

Incidentally, a majority (56 percent) of Palestinians (in the Gaza Strip and the West Bank) share this gloom view about the future, believing that the settlements have made a two-state solution no longer viable (PCPSR 2018). In a 2017 Washington Institute poll, 60 percent of Palestinians in the West Bank agreed with the statement, "Regardless of what's right, the reality is that most Israeli settlers will probably stay where they are, and most Palestinian refugees will not return to the 1948 lands."

As discussed in Chapter 3, settlers constitute an increasingly diverse group and are not all cut from the same cloth. Most notably, settlers differ in their motivations for living in the West Bank. Quality-of-life settlers tend to be secular and live in the territories because of cheap housing, government subsidies, and a better quality of life than they would be able to afford in Israel proper. Ideological settlers, on the other hand, and the ultranationalist settlers in particular, cite religious-ideological considerations for settling in the territories (Ginges & Atran 2013; Hirsch-Hoefler et al. 2019; Sheleg 2004). These political and sociodemographic differences also influence their attitudes toward the settlement enterprise.

Overall, Jewish settlers hold very positive attitudes toward the settlement enterprise and the quality of life in the West Bank – a trend that has held steady or even increased over the last decade. For example, according to the Central Bureau of Statistics Social Survey (2008–18), the percentage of Jewish residents in the West Bank who said they were (very) satisfied with their lives was 92 percent in 2008 and 96 percent in 2018, while the percentage reporting they were satisfied with their economic situation rose from 65 percent to 71 percent over the same period. Moreover, West Bank settlers are the most satisfied population surveyed, relative to Jews inside the Green Line, Arab citizens, and Palestinians.

West Bank settlers' satisfaction seems to be stable over the years, albeit with 10 to 20 percent differences between the ideological groups (see Hirschberger & Hirsch-Hoefler 2016). Surveys have also found that, irrespective of ideological differences, almost all West Bank settlers have a very high degree of identification with (the state of) Israel (Hirschberger & Hirsch-Hoefler 2016). The only group to express greater identification with the settlers than with the State of Israel is, unsurprisingly, the ultranationalist settlers.

This notwithstanding, more than half of the settlers do not trust state institutions (Hirschberger & Hirsch-Hoefler 2018). Importantly, a large percentage of settlers believe that the Israeli government favor other Israeli citizens over settlers or feel victims of the political system, both between 48 and 63 percent, depending on the ideological group (Hirschberger et al. 2014). It may be that the settlers' sense of distrust and discrimination have led to the observed downward trend in their acceptance of government authority to make fateful decisions with regard to the settlements – such as decisions on state borders, control, or evacuation of the settlements (Hirsch-Hoefler et al. 2018; Schnell & Hope 2012).

Perhaps the most troubling, from the viewpoint of the settler movement, are settler attitudes toward the possibility of an Israeli withdrawal from the territories (Hirschberger & Hirsch-Hoefler 2018). As one may expect, quality-of-life settlers (and Ariel residents) show higher support for potential evacuation, at least for appropriate financial compensation, 61 and 56 percent, respectively. But even many ideological settlers do not dismiss this idea (see Figure 4.15). Furthermore, all groups of settlers agree to a surprising degree with the statement that if a decision would be made to evacuate their settlement, they would

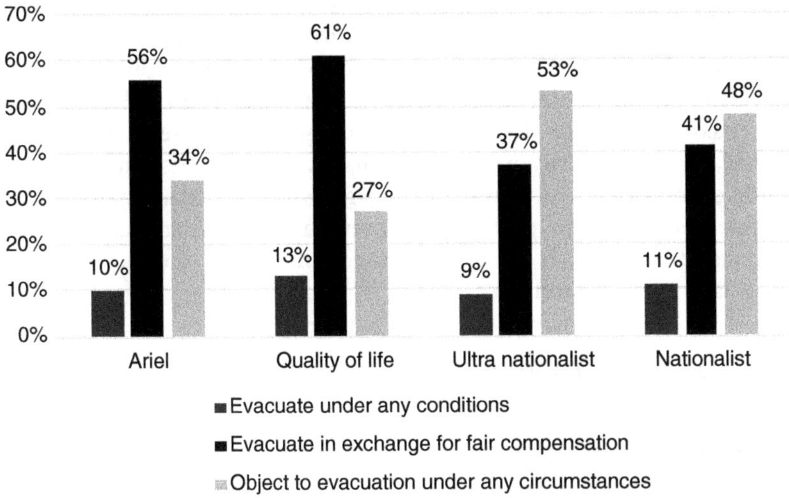

Figure 4.15 Settlers' attitudes on Israeli withdrawal from the territories[47]

relocate in exchange for fair compensation.[48] Ultranationalist settlers are the least likely to agree (29 percent), and the only group who prefers resistance to evacuation over all other options. Similarly, only a minority of nationalist settlers agrees (32 percent), but clear majorities of Ariel residents (59 percent) and quality-of-life settlers (66 percent) are willing to relocate in exchange for fair compensation (Hirschberger & Hirsch-Hoefler 2018).

In other words, while the settler movement categorically denies any suggestion of evacuation of settlements and territorial compromise, most settlers also dislike these options, but are willing to comply under the appropriate financial compensation. This indicates that the settlement movement has broad support, but that support might be quite soft, and could not hold up under pressure. While evacuation of settlements within a "land for peace" deal might not be popular, few Israelis fundamentally oppose it, not even within the settler population itself. This could also help explain the settler movement's inability to prevent the disengagement from Gaza as well as the relatively nonproblematic evacuation of the Gaza settlements.

In the end though, it is important that Israel has become increasingly polarized politically and the settlements are one of the most polarizing issues in Israel – as a key part of the broader issue of conflict/security. Within Israel, there is near-consensus support on the right for the settlements, yet near-consensus rejection on the left, with the "center" almost evenly divided.[49] This could point to the fact that the settler movement has not really been able to establish mass support for their particular cause, that is, settling of *Eretz Yisrael*, but are mainly profiting from the fact that its cause is currently seen as part and parcel of the right-wing agenda. That this can change, as it did (in part) under previous right-wing leaders (e.g., Begin and Sharon), is an important reminder that the current situation is not set in stone.

4.5 International Arena

As Sidney Tarrow (2017: 8) explains, international state actors and institutions serve as a kind of "coral reef," providing political opportunities for domestic non-state actors, encouraging their connections with others like themselves, and offering resources that can be used in intranational and transnational conflicts. Thus, international ties and networks may serve as resource providers or partners in the development of non-state activists' claims and identities. The settler movement has employed its own public affairs and diplomacy vehicles to promote the settlers' agenda by sending emissaries abroad, particularly to the United States.

4.5.1 The United States

No foreign officials or organizations have had more impact on the settler enterprise than those from the United States. The settler movement has been able to forge political ties with formidable and influential "pro-Israel" organizations in that country (Neidle 2013). This notwithstanding, officially, the United States has long supported a two-state solution and opposed Jewish settlements in the occupied territories. As the rest of the international community, it did not recognize Israel's annexation of East Jerusalem and the Golan Heights, and various US governments have called upon Israeli governments to freeze the settlement of the West Bank, leading at times to (short-lived) tensions between the two countries – particularly during the administrations of presidents George W. Bush and Barack Obama. The United States has long been a key player in the various "peace talks" in the region, in which it has often been accused of favoring the Israeli side, but never officially condoned Israel's annexations or occupation. Relations between Netanyahu and Obama were particularly tense, even though the US position toward Israel, and the occupied territories, did not change notably.

This has started to change under President Donald Trump, however, who has adopted a strongly "pro-Israel" position from the outset, and whose administration has shown a remarkable openness to the settler movement. No one more so than Trump's US Ambassador to Israel, David Friedman, whose connections to the movement run deep. For instance, Friedman has donated to a broad range of settler causes and organizations, including Ateret Cohanim, which buys Arab property in East Jerusalem. In terms of policies, Trump, by presidential proclamation, recognized Jerusalem as the capital of the State of Israel in December 2017, ordered the US embassy to move to Jerusalem, and recognized Israeli sovereignty over the Golan Heights in March 2019. Despite these policy shifts and his publicly warm overtures to the settler leadership, he also issued a request to "hold back on settlements for a little bit" during a joint press conference with Prime Minister Netanyahu (*Haaretz*, February 16, 2017).

The settler movement has long held close relationships with some of the most powerful (Christian and Jewish) "pro-Israel" organizations in the United States, including AIPAC and the Zionist Organization of America (ZOA). The "pro-Israel" lobby has provided the settler movement not only with access to high-ranking US politicians, of both parties, but also to high-profile donors, who have invested significant amounts of money into a broad variety of settler initiatives in the West Bank – including Ariel University (see Chapter 6), "biblical tourism," and pro-settler media. The "pro-Israel" camp experienced a challenge from the newly minted J Street, an organization that opposes the settlement project as well as US support for it (Saltzman 2017), which was favored by several people within the Obama administration. The increased prominence of J Street forced the settler movement to adapt to a new dynamic in the United States. Yesha Council chairman Dani Dayan, a high-tech entrepreneur and longtime member of the Council's Executive Committee, reported that just minutes after he was elected, a friend told him, "now that you're already into it, I want to tell you that it's you against the United States" – a comment which Dayan says he laughed off (*Times of Israel*, January 8, 2015).

The incoming Obama administration was set on limiting settlement expansion, confronting the new chairman with two challenges: the Obama administration effort for a settlement freeze in 2010 and a general fracturing of the settler movement over whether the Yesha Council should be at the helm of the movement (as a consequence of the Gaza Disengagement, see Chapter 7). In the summer of 2013, as

Secretary of State John Kerry attempted to restart the stalled Palestinian–Israeli peace talks, Dayan ventured into new territory by directly meeting with heads of political institutions in Washington, DC, becoming the first representative of the settler movement to officially conduct such high-profile meetings. In a remarkable coup for a representative of a social movement that had long been decried by these institutions, Dayan was invited to the State Department and the White House. As he put it to the *Times of Israel* (January 8, 2005), "I take advantage of the curiosity that arises of this exotic vision of a settler with a suit and a tie, speaking good English. I prefer to hold five secret meetings than one public meeting. But in every meeting you make inroads. Very small but important inroads."

Recognizing the shift in the "pro-Israel" lobbying landscape under the Obama administration, the settler movement, under Dayan's direction, began to focus more heavily on strengthening its relationship with the United States through AIPAC and the Republican Party. The settler movement is prominently represented at AIPAC's annual conference in Washington, DC, which boasts an attendance rate in the tens of thousands, including two-thirds of Congress, and a rotating appearance by Cabinet-level officials including the president and vice-president. It has also sent representatives to other annual conferences attended by high-level officials from the US administration, such as the 2016 Israeli–American Council (IAC) national conference. And in June 2013, Dayan attended a roundtable on the "historic and strategic significance of Judea and Samaria" hosted by the House Republican Conference, which also included several Republican Congress members.[50]

The Trump administration has presented the settler movement with an unprecedented favorable and open political context. For the first time in the history of US–Israel relations, the incoming US president has invited a settler delegation to his inaugural ceremonies. The Chief Foreign Envoy of the Yesha Council, Mayor of Efrat Oded Revivi, headed the delegation, while Ma'ale Adumim Mayor Benny Kasriel also in attendance. In explaining the settler movement's decision to accept the invitation, Revivi said

> reason number one was the fact that by receiving an invitation we actually understood that we're getting the right attention that we didn't get in the past. The fact that we are acknowledged, the fact that we're representing half a million-people living in Judea and Samaria … it was important to show that we understand, that we accept this invitation (*Arutz Sheva*, January 22, 2017).

Since the inauguration, members of the president's team have continued to meet with settler movement representatives, though in less high-profile ways. For instance, in March 2017, Jason Greenblatt, President Trump's Special Representative for International Negotiations, organized a meeting in Jerusalem with a delegation of the Yesha Council, its "highest level official meeting with a U.S. administration" (*Times of Israel*, March 16, 2017). According to Greenblatt, who claims to support a two-state solution, "Mr. Trump does not view the settlements as being an obstacle to peace" (*Jerusalem Post*, November 10, 2016).

Beyond the traditional lobbying strategies, the "pro-Israel" and pro-settler lobbies seek to reach the political elite through various other channels too. For instance, settler groups bring US policy-makers to the West Bank, to see it for themselves and to hear the settlers' point of view from close up.[51] But they also target other audiences in the United States (and around the world) with their promotional efforts. For instance, the One Israel Fund runs tours in the occupied territories, and routinely hosts events and an annual gala to bolster connections between US supporters and the settler movement. *HaYovel* brings Christian volunteers from around the world to the settlements (as agricultural workers) and trains them to be the ambassadors for the settler cause. They also run speaking tours in which settlement representatives make their case to Christian and other groups. Other groups enlist help and resources for specific efforts. The Hebron Fund, for example, runs tours and fundraises to improve the quality of life of settlers in Hebron and to reignite Jewish pilgrimage to the Cave of Machpelah (the Cave of the Patriarchs).

The settler movement, as well as "pro-Israel" groups, has invested serious resources in making their case and increasing support for Israel, and the settlements, within the US public. For example, the Israel Project hired prominent US Republican strategist Frank Luntz to help educate and train sympathizers and lobbyists on framing various "pro-Israel" topics. Their 116-page report dedicates three full pages of "do's and do not's" for terminology, framing of the discourse, and focus of the conversation. It suggests avoiding absolute stances and framing the discourse around security concerns rather than leaning on biblical arguments to justify the presence of settlements. Interestingly, the report acknowledges that the original use of the term settlement "set in motion a lexicon that was doomed from the start." The report offers its "ideal settlement argument," stating that "we cannot see why it is that peace requires that any Palestinian area would require a kind of ethnic cleansing to remove all Jews. We don't accept it. Cleansing by either side against either side is unacceptable" (The Israel Project, 2009).

As is true for most international issues, the US media coverage of Israeli politics and the issue of the settlement is extremely shallow. Marda Dunsky (2008: 64) analyzed US mainstream media coverage of Israeli settlements in the West Bank, East Jerusalem, and the Gaza Strip. She found that "the American mainstream media run a remarkable information deficit on the key issues of the Israeli–Palestinian conflict, including the role of the United States, Israeli settlements, and the Palestinian refugee question." She noted that "reporters arrive on the scene, note the details of the landscape, and collect dramatic quotes. However, rarely do they even scratch the surface to reveal the organic factors underlying the settlement issue" (Dunsky 2008: 149). These include debates about the presence or removal of illegal outposts, and the vexed question of how to distinguish between an outpost and a new neighborhood of an existing settlement, or between natural growth and unauthorized expansion. Dunsky also found that the mainstream press was poor at probing the role of international law in the status of the settlements, leading to an unquestioned acceptance of the international consensus that Israeli settlements violate the Fourth Geneva Convention and numerous UNSC resolutions (Dunsky 2008).[52]

Despite its many efforts, the long-term trend with US public opinion does not favor the settler movement, whose cause engenders little support among Americans, with the exception of the more religious Jews and Christians. For example, in a survey of US public opinion toward the settlements in 1977, a decade after the capture of the West Bank in the Six-Day War, only 35 percent of respondents thought settlement construction was wrong, while 25 percent thought it was not wrong, and a plurality of 40 percent said they were not sure (Roper Center 1977). As the settlement project expanded, this picture began to change. Throughout the 1980s, a higher percentage of Americans believed that the settlement enterprise contributed to greater instability in the region, rising from 44 percent in 1981 to 47 percent in 1988 (Penn & Schoen 1981, 1982, 1988). This trend is in line with the position of the US government at the time. For example, President Ronald Reagan (1982) called for a settlement freeze to jump-start the peace process following Israel's invasion of Lebanon: "Settlement activity is in no way necessary for the security of Israel and only diminishes the confidence of the Arabs that a final outcome can be freely and fairly negotiated."

This unsupportive position toward the settlement enterprise in US public opinion became a growing trend in the following years. A 1991 *ABC* poll found that 45 percent of Americans opposed Israel's establishment of settlements in the occupied territories in 1991, while 43 percent declared themselves in favor (see Figure 4.16). Some ten year later, 52 percent of Americans believed Israel should not be constructing settlements, while only 35 percent believed settlement construction should continue (*PIPA*, 2002). By the end of the decade, only 20 percent

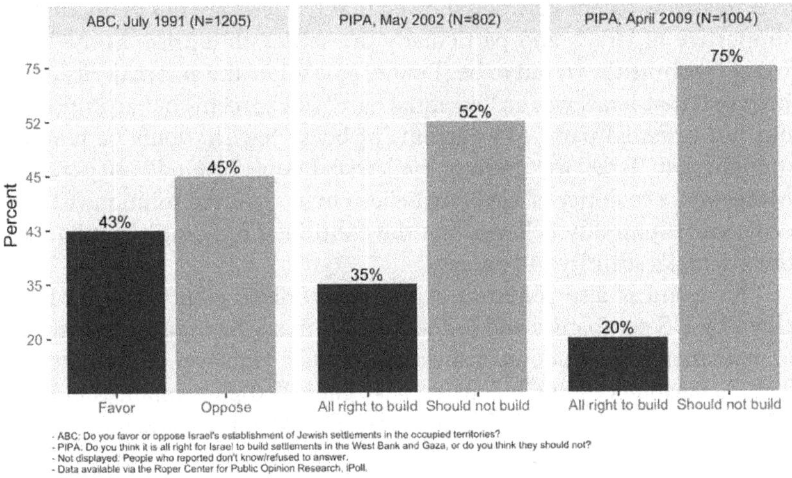

Figure 4.16 US public attitudes toward Jewish settlements in the occupied territories

supported building in the occupied territories, while a full 75 percent opposed it (*PIPA*, 2009).[53]

Under Trump's presidency, US views on Israel have become even more partisan, with Republicans becoming more supportive of the agenda of the Israeli right, including the settler movement, but Democrats becoming more critical of Israel overall. A 2018 Critical Issues Poll (Telhami & Rouse 2018) found that 57 percent of Republicans (compared to 7 percent of Democrats) believed that the United States should "lean toward Israel" in mediating the Israeli–Palestinian conflict, while 36 percent thought it should lean to neither side; the numbers were 7 percent and 82 percent for Democrats, respectively. Similarly, Democrats overwhelmingly support either a two-state solution (48 percent) or a multi-ethnic democratic one-state solution (36 percent), while significant minorities of Republicans support the current occupation (18 percent) or annexation without equal citizenship (14 percent). Finally, while two-thirds of Republicans think the US government should react to new Jewish settlements by "doing nothing" (38 percent) or by "limit[ing[opposition to words, but take no action" (30 percent), a majority of Democrats believe it should "impose some economic sanctions" (41 percent) or "take more serious action" (15 percent). While the opinions of Republicans have remained largely stable since 2014, becoming slightly more favorable toward nonaction, Democrats have increasingly embraced active opposition.

A relatively recent Pew poll showed that US Jews are not as uncritically supportive of Israel, and particularly the settler enterprise, as the "pro-Israel" lobby makes it out to be (Pew 2013). While the vast majority of US Jews said that Israel was an "essential part" (43 percent) or "an important but not essential part" (44 percent) of being Jewish, "only" a plurality thought that "Israel was given to the Jewish People by God" (40 percent). Moreover, a majority of US Jews believe in a two-state solution (61 percent) and a plurality believes that the continued building of settlements hurts Israel's security (44 percent).

This trend is also reflected in the antagonistic stance toward Israel taken by US companies and influencers, as many have come to conceive of settlement construction and expansion as a violation of international law. For instance, some US artists have cancelled performances in Israel following pressure from the Boycott, Divestment, Sanctions (BDS) movement, including the Pixies and Stevie Wonder. There has also been an increase in academic boycotts of Israel, and Israeli academic institutions, including by the Association of Asian American Studies (AAAS) and the American Studies Association (ASA). Finally, in what might have been a substantial blow to the settlements' tourism industry, Airbnb – the US-based online marketplace for hospitality services – declared in 2018 that it would remove over 200 listings in West Bank settlements that "are at the core of the dispute between Israelis and Palestinians" (*New York Times*, April 9, 2019). However, the original announcement was later subject to numerous qualifications and partial rollback, and as of this writing Airbnb continues to list homes in the settlements. The Airbnb saga shows how the settlements remain highly charged and controversial, inside and outside of Israel, with both camps putting enormous pressure on anyone wanting to do business there.

4.5.2 Other Countries

Outside of the United States, the settler movement has failed to establish significant support for its cause (Zanany 2018). The EU, in particular, has never recognized the legality of Israeli settlements in the occupied territories (Lovatt 2016). Since the Venice Declaration of June 1980, EU policy toward the settlements has been that Israel's presence in the territories qualifies as a belligerent occupation, and that the settlements are in breach of international law and constitute an obstacle to peace. In March 1999, the EU reinforced this position by calling upon Israel and Palestine to forge a two-state peace agreement predicated on international law (the EU's Berlin Declaration). Since 2002, it has asserted that the solution should be based on the 1949 Green Line (Harpaz 2017).

Statements by individual European leaders have supported the EU position. Already in the 1980s, British Prime Minister Margaret Thatcher said, "All our efforts to convince Mr. Begin that his West Bank policy was absurd, and that there should not be Israeli settlements on the West Bank, had failed to move him" (*The Jewish Chronicle*, December 30, 2010). Decades later, her fellow Conservative Prime Minister David Cameron was equally firm: "Settlements are illegal under international law and will do nothing to create the kind of peace process we all want" (*Daily Mail*, September 1, 2014). Similarly, Italian premier Silvio Berlusconi has called Israel's "settlement policy "a mistake" (*Haaretz*, January 31, 2010), while German Chancellor Angela Merkel, normally quite cautious in her remarks and supportive of the State of Israel, has said that it is "sabotaging the peace process" (*Walla*, March 24, 2017).

In December 2012, the EU Foreign Affairs Council declared that "all agreements between the State of Israel and the European Union must unequivocally and explicitly indicate their inapplicability to the territories occupied by Israel in 1967, namely the Golan Heights, the West Bank including East Jerusalem, and the Gaza Strip." Since then, the EU has attempted to cement this policy via its trade and trade-related agreements with Israel, by withholding the benefits of EU–Israel cooperation from companies and research institutions based or operating in the territories, as well as from products produced there (Harpaz 2017). In 2013, the EU published guidelines declaring that only Israeli entities within Israel's pre-1967 borders are eligible for EU grants, prizes, and financial instruments, and only with respect to their activities pursued west of the Green Line. In November 2015, the European Commission approved a document calling on EU countries to enforce the labeling of products originating from Jewish settlements beyond the Green Line. In November 2019, the European Court of Justice ruled that "Foodstuffs originating in the territories occupied by the State of Israel must bear the indication of their territory of origin" (*Guardian*, November 12, 2019).

It has been suggested that these official measures not only express the EU's perception of the settlements as lacking legitimacy, but in turn generate unofficial, and even official, secondary boycotts of Israeli companies linked in one way or another to activity in the West Bank (Eran et al. 2015). In 2014, the Spanish and Italian governments warned their citizens against doing business with settlements in the West Bank (*Haaretz*, June 27, 2014). The Luxembourg state pension fund voted to boycott the five largest banks in Israel, as well as Israel-based investment company Africa Israel Investments Ltd., for "illegal activity in settlements in Palestine" (*Walla*, February 25, 2014). Deutsche Bank, the largest bank in Germany, added Bank Hapoalim to its blacklist of 16 "immoral targets for investment" (*Walla,* February 14, 2014). The largest pension fund in the Netherlands, PGGM, also voted to boycott Israeli banks for financing projects in the settlements (*Haaretz,* January 8, 2014). And, more recently, the Danish parliament adopted a resolution calling for the exclusion of the settlements from any bilateral agreement with Israel (*Haaretz,* January 26, 2018).

Interestingly, a national online survey of 2,385 Israeli adults, which examined the political effects of the EU's 2015 decision to label goods produced in the West Bank, showed that this decision produced a backlash effect. Individuals exposed to the labeled information were less supportive of a settlement freeze, and less likely to support renewal of statehood negotiations with the Palestinians. They also showed an increase in solidarity with Israeli settlers, support for hardline policies, and hostility toward Europe (Grossman et al. 2018).

The perceptions of ordinary European citizens with respect to the Israel–Palestinian conflict seem to be similar to those of their governments, though somewhat less strong. In general, public opinion polls among European respondents show negative attitudes toward Israel,[54] and in particular toward the settlements. For example, a European survey in six main West European states (France, Italy, Germany, the Netherlands, Spain, and the United Kingdom) found that 40 percent of respondents agreed with the statement "Israeli settlements are the biggest obstacles to peace in the Middle East" and 44 percent agreed with the statement "The settlements are illegal" – 17 percent said legal and 38 percent said they did not know (Abdullah & Chehata 2011).

Lastly, Eulalia Han and Halim Rane (2011) analyzed almost 10,000 articles on the Israel–Palestine conflict published in *The Australian* and the *Sydney Morning Herald* between 2000 and 2010. They found that almost a quarter addressed the issue of Israeli settlements on Palestinian land. Of the three final-status issues in the Israel–Palestine conflict – namely the Palestinian refugees, Israeli settlements, and the status of Jerusalem – the issue of settlements received by far the most coverage. As for Australian public opinion on the issue of Israeli settlements, over three-quarters (78 percent) expressed opposition (Han & Rane 2011).

4.6 Conclusion

From the left to the right, in Israel and beyond, it is received wisdom that the Israeli settler movement is highly successful. In some accounts the movement is considered all-powerful, untouchable, playing Israeli and US governments alike. An empirical assessment of the success of the settler movement shows a much more complex picture. While the movement has definitely been successful in obtaining resources and support from the Israeli state, including the bureaucracy and military, public support within the Israeli and particularly international public arenas is more limited. In terms of policies, the Israeli state mainly follows the settler movement, rather than leading it – at times reluctantly, at times more enthusiastically, legalizing and funding settlements that the movement illegally created. Neither Israel, nor the international community, has officially adopted their key agenda, although it is becoming increasingly popular within the right-wing in both Israel and the United States (as well as within some far-right parties in Europe).

Let us not forget that the main goal of the settler movement is the annexation and settling of the whole "Land of Israel" (*Eretz Yisrael*), including East Jerusalem, the Gaza Strip, the Golan Heights, and the West Bank (or, as the settlers prefer to call it, Judea and Samaria). It is clear that this is something the settlers have not achieved; and in fact, they are not even really close. East Jerusalem and the Golan Heights have been officially annexed, but this has not been recognized by the international community (until recently, not even by Israel's most ardent supporter, the United States), which considers all the territories to be under "illegal occupation."[55] A majority of the populations around the world, from the European Union to the United States, also see the West Bank as "occupied territories," while the Israeli population is divided on the issue. Moreover, Gaza and the Sinai, while of less (religious) significance to the movement, have even been evacuated and are now controlled by the Palestinians and Egyptians. And even a significant part of the West Bank (Areas A and B) are now under the rule of the Palestinian Authority, although both Palestinian areas are far from free of Israeli oversight.[56]

The settler movement's main successes are in Area C, roughly 60 percent of the West Bank, which includes all the major religious-nationalist sites. It is here that the settler movement has created its "facts on the ground," often starting with an illegal outpost, getting it connected to the Israeli infrastructure within the West Bank, after which it is legalized (post factum) by the Israeli government, which will then allow or even stimulate its growth. The settler movement has been particularly successful in mobilizing resources for the settlement enterprise, primarily from the Israeli state, but also from private donations, primarily from the United States. There are currently 127 (legal) settlements, and more than 100 (illegal) outposts, in the West Bank (excluding East Jerusalem), which together are home to almost 427,800 settlers. Yet while these are significant numbers, settlers still account for fewer than 5 percent of the total Israeli population.

The settler movement has been most successful in its second subgoal – using settlements to frustrate the peace process with the Palestinians, and particularly to undermine the viability of a Palestinian state. While most of the largest settlements, in terms of population, are close to the Green Line (the border of Israel proper) and mainly cater to pragmatic "quality-of-life" settlers, smaller groups of mostly religious-nationalist settlers have settled in areas with nationalist and religious significance. As a consequence, the settlements are spread throughout Area C of the West Bank, and the specific Israeli infrastructure, which cannot be used by Palestinian residents of the West Bank, divides the whole territory. As a consequence, no viable Palestinian state is possible without the dismantling of a substantial number of settlements.

This seems highly unlikely, however, because the settler movement has also been very successful in gaining protection and support for its project from Israel's main parties. All major right-wing parties, from the secular (like Likud and Israel Is Our Home) to the religious (like Jewish Home and New Right), support the settlement enterprise, and key leaders like Naftali Bennett and even Benjamin Netanyahu have promised that they would not dismantle any of the settlements. Given that right-wing parties have been dominating Israeli politics since the turn of the century, this is all that matters in Israel today.

Still, most opposition parties either tacitly or openly support the existing settlements too: for example, the 2019 challenger (and winner of the September 2019 election) Blue and White's platform calls for strengthening the large settlement blocs and making the Jordan Valley a "security border," while insisting there will be no further "disengagements." And, importantly, there is also support within the Israeli population for a large-scale dismantling program. While Israelis are divided over the pros and cons of the settlement enterprise, and reluctant to support significant expansion, they have by and large accepted the existing settlements and oppose their dismantling.

5 The Action Repertoires of the Branches

In its more than fifty years of existence, the settler movement has had a significant impact upon a broad range of interrelated political actors: the state, the military, civil society, and the wider domestic and international publics. This was achieved by a variety of actions and tactics, employed by the different branches of the movement. This chapter delves deeper into the different action repertoires of the various movement branches and shows how they work in concert to advance the settler cause.

The settler movement as a whole employs all types of actions: moderate, radical, and extreme. Moderate actions are by far the most common, and are used by all three branches, while radical actions are used primarily by networks, and extreme actions exclusively by a small subgroup of networks. Moreover, individual branches play specific roles in the different political arenas. Institutions mainly employ moderate actions aimed, first and foremost, at collaboration *with* and capture *of* the state. Networks employ all three repertoires, but their unique role within the social movement is to use radical, and occasionally extreme, actions to exert pressure on the state. Influencers, finally, almost exclusively use moderate actions aimed at gaining public support for the movement and its goals. Before we analyze the different actions, we first describe the political opportunity structure (POS) that influences the mobilization of the settler movement and its repertoire of actions.

5.1 The Political Opportunity Structure

Social movement scholars often discuss the political structure in terms of opportunities and constraints on collective action (McAdam 1982; Tarrow 1989). Opportunities represent moments when cracks appear in institutional or situational conditions, opening the door to changes that advance the movement's agenda. From the perspective of resources, opportunities lead social movements to embrace tactics and techniques that increase their access to resources, in terms of finances and personnel, which were not previously available. Constraints lead movements to embrace tactics and techniques that best maximize their existing resources (Haklai 2003). The actions chosen by social movements are thus affected by the wider political context within which social movements exist (Koopmans & Statham 1999).

Political opportunity structure theory emphasizes the role played by (institutional or situational) shifts in the political system (Kriesi et al. 1995; McAdam 1982; Tarrow 1994). These shifts can produce cracks or vulnerabilities in the existing political environment, rendering it susceptible to challenges. The notion of the POS suggests that

> exogenous factors enhance or inhibit a social movement's prospects for (a) mobilizing, (b) advancing particular claims rather than others, (c) cultivating some alliances rather than others, (d) employing particular political strategies and tactics rather than others, and (e) affecting mainstream institutional politics and policy (Meyer 2004: 126).

Broadly speaking, there are four analytical dimensions of the POS: (1) the relative openness or closure of the institutionalized political system; (2) the stability or instability of that broad set of elite alignments that typically undergird a polity; (3) the presence or absence of elite allies; and (4) the state's capacity and propensity for repression (McAdam 1996). The greater the opportunities of *access* to the institutionalized political system, the more movements tend to use moderate strategies, while *closure* of the institutionalized political system and repression tends to lead to radicalization (Della-Porta & Diani 1999).

This theoretical framework can be used to understand the tactics the settler movement, and its branches, have employed over the years to garner both popular and political support. First, it is helpful to consider the structure of the Israeli political system itself. Israel is a consolidated parliamentary democracy. The Knesset is a single-chamber parliament, whose members are elected on the basis of a proportional electoral system with one district (the whole country) and party-lists (Rosenthal 2016). The proportional electoral system, combined with a fairly low electoral threshold, inherently leads to party fragmentation or the penetration of minor parties into the Knesset (Coleman 1990; Norris 1997).[1]

Before the mid 1970s, the Labor Party was so dominant that it controlled much of the political action. As Labor's power waned, the high number of minor political parties in the Knesset started to breed extreme party competition, which provides a natural opportunity for mobilized minorities and social movements. The power of well-organized and mobilized minorities, such as the settlers, was further strengthened by primaries, which exist in some Israeli parties, most notably Likud. Finally, social movements like the settler movement profit from another legacy of Labor Zionism, that is, a historically and institutionally close collaboration between the state, political parties, social movements, and nongovernmental organizations (NGOs).

Since the inception of the settler movement, the Israeli state has been actively involved in the settlement enterprise (see Chapter 2). Although Israeli governments have held ambivalent positions toward the settler movement, at a minimum, all governments have seen the settlers as an unavoidable presence since the 1970s. For the most part, the Israeli political system has systematically favored the settler movement. Given the structure and historical development of the Israeli political system, we can point to three interrelated factors as most responsible for this. First, irrespective of changes in Israeli policies and coalitions, there has been a steady rise in both the number of settlements and their population. These rising settler numbers mean rising numbers of settler votes. Second, the proportional representation feature of the Israeli political system grants disproportionate political influence to relatively small parties (Herzog 1987), including small nationalist-religious parties that adhere to the settler cause. Third, over the years movement leaders have increasingly penetrated the state, becoming parliamentarians and ministers, as well as judges on the Supreme Court and (combat) officers in the IDF, especially combat units. This has created an alignment at the elite level between the settler movement and various branches of government, policy-makers and state apparatus.

Given these structural factors, the settler movement's main strategy, during most of its existence, has involved maintaining a direct line of communication to the institutionalized political system. Indeed, even during the hardest times, such as those centered around peace agreements and evacuations of Jewish settlements, discussions between the settler movement and the Israeli government never stopped completely. Likewise, even if the government's door was not always wide open to the settlers, the importance of maintaining close, routine communication with the institutionalized political system was well understood by the movement's leaders.

Naturally, the settler movement feels greater affinity to parties and governments of the right. For instance, on average, settlements have been allowed to expand more under right-wing governments compared to left-wing governments – at the same time, there have been more right-wing governments and most left-wing ("centrist") governments have not been particularly anti-settler either. However, neither its institutional nor its informal branches appear to change their tactics based on whether right-wing or left-wing coalitions are in power. The institutional branch tends to use moderate actions regardless of the political color of the government. For their part, networks use both moderate and radical tactics even under right-wing governments, which are ideologically closer to the settlers, and thus permit greater access to the decision-making system. The key issue for the networks is not whether the government is on the right or the left, but whether the circumstances at the time are threatening to the movement – in which case the use of radical and extreme tactics will increase (in fact, two of the major setbacks of the settler movement, the withdrawal from the Sinai and the Gaza Strip, happened under a right-wing government).

While drawing our attention to political–institutional opportunities for successful movement mobilization, POS theory tends to neglect *cultural dynamics* that also play a pivotal role in movement outcomes. Ruud Koopmans and Paul Statham (1999: 228) have introduced the term "discursive opportunity structure" (DOS) to identify ideas in the broader political culture whose presence would facilitate or constrain specific forms of collective action framing.[2] In other words, DOS theory provides a more nuanced understanding of what kinds of framings are likely to have the greatest capacity to mobilize existing and new recruits, to convince the public of the rightness of a social movement's demands, and to persuade authorities to alter policies and practices in line with its agenda (McCammon 2013). Discursive opportunity structure theory's main focus is on the ability to diffuse movement messages into the public sphere (Molaei 2015).

Applying this theory to the settler movement offers an understanding of the cultural mythology and nationalistic legacy that made the Israeli environment ripe for the settler enterprise. The founding narrative of religious Zionism is based upon the (messianic) notion that it is the Jewish responsibility and right to settle the entirety of the "Land of Israel" (Samson & Fishman 1991). This narrative, coupled with the nostalgia and romanticism of an Israeli transcendentalism that focused on rebirth, growth, and prosperity in a land perceived as having been barren and infertile, set the stage for the modern settler enterprise. Although modern Zionism has distanced itself from religious and radical Zionism, they come from glaringly similar origins. Not unlike religious Zionism, Labor Zionism embraced motifs of an agrarianized society via "redemption of the soil," pioneerism, and romantic nationalism (Segev 1999). These narratives have been ingrained in the whole of Israeli society and are an integral part of the Israeli cultural fabric and national identity.

The link between religious Zionism, which tends to see its apotheosis in the settlement of all of *Eretz Yisrael* (the land of Israel), and its secular counterpart, which sees it in establishing and securing the future of *Medinat Yisrael* (the State of Israel), helps the settler movement to reach out to the kibbutz movement. Benny Katzover, former head of the Gush Emunim movement, has spoken of a surprising connection forged between the settlers and the Youth Guard (*HaShomer HaTzair*), which emanated from the left-wing kibbutz movement.[3] Noting the contradictory nature of these visits, he said

> Sometimes I ask them, "Why did you come?" I ask this kindly, as they are my guests and my intention is not to insult them. They answer, "We want to see the wonder of what is taking place, we hear that the settlements are getting stronger despite the terrorism and its victims. And in spite of the hardships, your youths continue to be one of the leading populations in the IDF. How does this happen?"

Katzover continued, "Every kibbutz that comes here does so after arguing about whether to come at all, but those who do come are more open to hearing what we have to say" (*Globes*, January 3, 2017).

What Katzover tapped into is in fact the meeting point of two antipodal ideologies – the knowledge that a successful movement is one that continues to retain its youth. This is an area in which, to a certain degree, the (right-leaning) settler movement has flourished where the (left-wing) kibbutz movement has failed. But by hosting the Youth Guard, and exposing them to the ideational and conceptual links between the two movements, the settler movement has been able to influence public opinion, particularly that of an otherwise completely oppositional sector of Israeli society.

In the end, the national-religious ideology of the settler movement is not a "normal pathology" (Scheuch & Klingemann 1967), unconnected to Israel's mainstream values, but rather a "pathological normalcy" (Mudde 2010), a radicalization of mainstream values. It builds upon key elements of (Labor) Zionism and the foundation myths of the State of Israel, but takes them a step further, mostly by extending the borders of the State of Israel to include the (whole) "Land of Israel." This means that its key assumptions, claims, and themes are closely connected to those of the Israeli mainstream, and the differences are more in terms of degree than kind.

5.2 The Action Repertoires of the Settler Movement

The settler movement is a diverse network of networks whose components differ in terms of structure as well as beliefs and ideologies. These different components employ different types of actions, some confrontational and others cooperative, to advance different aspects of the settler cause. For instance, institutional actors may use bargaining and persuasion to influence state representatives, while networks choose more radical, and sometimes even extreme actions, to mobilize the domestic and international public to oppose state actions. Ami Pedahzur and Holly McCarthy (2015: 450) call this combination of insider–outsider tactics a "dual hybrid strategy." For example, the settler movement's repeated attempts to settle in Sebastia, in 1973, involved both violent clashes with the IDF and fierce negotiations with the Labor Party. In the case of the 2005 disengagement from Gaza, street protests took place alongside legislative attempts to block the plan in the Knesset (see Chapter 7).

Unlawful actions such as barricading public buildings, locking roads, and physical confrontations with security forces have a long history within the settler movement (Lustick 1988; Pedahzur et al. 2009; Sprinzak 1999). Evidence of violent settler behavior became public in the 1980s, when the Jewish Underground came onto the scene. Although Israeli security forces were able to quash its terrorist plan to blow up the Al Aqsa Mosque, and arrested the perpetrators, the legacy of settler extremism persisted. The apex of the extremist trend in the settler movement was the assassination of Israeli Prime Minister Yitzhak Rabin, in 1995, over his signing of the Oslo Accords. While not a settler himself, but a law student from Herzliya, the killer had organized rallies in the occupied territories to denounce the Oslo Accords (Filkins 2015).[4]

5.3 The Institutional Branch

To understand the Yesha Council's action repertoire and strategy, and how they depart from those of its precursor Gush Emunim, it is important to look at the rhetoric of the Council's founding literature. Its founding charter avoided Gush Emunim's fervent religious language and instead appropriated secular rhetoric reminiscent of early political Zionism. Whereas the rhetoric of Gush Emunim was built on messianic conceptions of *Eretz Yisrael*, the Yesha Council aimed to appeal to a wider audience, in recognition that the rhetoric of redemption used by the earlier movement had proved to be ineffective, if not detrimental to the cause, outside of a small circle of ideologues. It was recognized that the religious settlers needed to project a realistic and rational image in order to engage the wider public (Taub 2007). The shift in language set the precedent for the Yesha Council's larger shift in modus operandi to further the settler enterprise. It would not only act within the Israeli political apparatus but also "create the 'tools' for widespread settlement activity inside and outside the existing system by combining political lobbies with extra-legal 'facts on the ground'" (Taub 2007: 294).

The new institution chose its language intentionally and meticulously to carve out its future space as the broker between the settler movement and formal Israeli political institutions as well as the Israeli public. Consequently, its main strategy is one of collaboration with the state, including the bureaucracy and military. In addition, (former) Council members play an important role within the settler movement's attempts to capture the state, by taking up high-ranking state positions. Opposition to state actions and plans is almost exclusively expressed through moderate actions, such as lobbying and sometimes organizing (lawful) demonstrations. As far as the Yesha Council is involved in radical actions, it mainly facilitates the networks. The organization categorically rejects the use of violence and has never been involved in, or linked to, extreme actions.

The paradigm shift from messianic to secular, which came with the ascension of the Yesha Council as the authority on political and civil matters in the West Bank and Gaza, also signaled a shift in the settlers' attitudes and behaviors to an increasing acceptance of state authority. Yet the Yesha Council has at times found itself at odds with the Yesha Rabbinical Council, the spiritual authority that presides over issues concerning the religious legitimacy of different modes of action and responses to government decisions which affect the settlement enterprise (Newman 2005). For example, in some cases, its rabbis made public appeals to rebel against the state and warned soldiers to disobey orders to evacuate settlements.

Since the Yesha Council's main concern is the welfare of the settlers who elected the Council's members, it is constantly engaged in a bargaining process with the government to provide services for its constituency (Haklai 2003). Accordingly, it employs more cooperative political bargaining strategies, such as lobbying, persuasion, representation by parties, and especially fusion with the apparatus of the state (Pedahzur & McCarthy 2015). This has taken place through "a diverse network of political parties, splinter factions, settlement movements, planning agencies, and local governmental and municipal positions, from which it has been possible to advance the political objectives of settlement with the use of public sector resources" (Newman 2005: 195).

The Yesha Council has at times been a powerful negotiator between the settler community and the state (Alimi & Demetriou 2018). For example, Ehud Barak insisted that the evacuation of several outposts was done with the direct involvement of the Yesha Council in the late 1990s. Ultimately, it was the Council itself, as opposed to formal security institutions, such as the police, which dismantled the ten outposts in 1999 (Haklai 2003). In the last decade, the Yesha Council has used the resumption of settlement construction in the face of a settlement-freeze policy as leverage to move the government more toward its agenda, primarily over issues like planning and construction of settlements on state lands (*Ynet*, August 31, 2016). Amana has contributed significantly to this effort by constructing access roads, and routinely petitioning the courts to not demolish illegal structures conducted with its financial or logistic support – for example, in cases where Amana has organized the paving of access roads to settler outposts.

In terms of its structure and activities, the Yesha Council occupies a middle ground between public-sector institution and NGO. As an umbrella organization for the municipal councils of Jewish settlements, its members are both activists and public sector employees receiving government salaries. For example, Hananel Dori, who was elected chairman in 2017, serves as chairman of the Kedumim Local Council (*Arutz Sheva*, February 11, 2017). As such, members of the Yesha Council leadership use their positions in the public sector, and the state funding that accompanies these positions, to leverage the political aims of their movement. Simultaneously, these civil servants, whose resources and salaries come from the public coffers, promote oppositional activities, encouraging settlers (and the Israeli public in general) to engage in large-scale public protest, as was the case during the run-up to the 2005 Gaza disengagement.

Many leaders, who have made their mark in the Yesha Council, continue to serve the settler movement's goals through political positions within the state apparatus. For example, Naftali Bennett has significantly contributed to advancing the settlement enterprise as both an MK and a minister. In 2013, Bennett pushed for the passage of a Basic Law, which would require a referendum to be held before any territories are handed over to the Palestinians in either a political agreement or unilateral diplomatic plan. At the passing of the law, he declared: "Tonight we make history – it must be clear to everyone: The Land of Israel belongs to the people of Israel" (*Haaretz*, August 1, 2013). After the 2015 elections, through a coalition agreement between his Jewish Home party and Likud, he succeeded in obtaining budgets of tens of millions of US dollars for the settlement enterprise.[5]

Uri Ariel, another former Yesha Council Chairman, continued to support the settlement enterprise as leader and MK of Jewish Home and as Minister of Agriculture. Ariel was one of the most prominent opponents of the Gaza disengagement and even moved to the Gaza settlement of Kfar Darom to lead protests there. He also founded the Orange Front (*Hahazit Haktuma*), a forum of MKs and public figures that supports the evacuees of Gush Katif and northern Samaria and lobbies for them in the Knesset (*Kipa News*, November 19, 2012). As MK, Ariel submitted several bills and resolutions aimed at improving support for the evacuees and mediating between the evacuees and the various committees of the Knesset and government ministries. As Minister of Construction and Housing, he promoted settlement construction in the West Bank, including a transfer of $7.7 million from the agriculture budget to the budget for strengthening the security of settlements in 2018 (*Kipa News*, August 29, 2018).

Similarly, Dani Dayan, Yesha Council Chairman (2007–2013) and the Council's unofficial "Foreign Minister" (2013–2016), has been the settler movement's major international player. He maintains close ties with the foreign diplomatic corps in Israel, as well as with foreign journalists and high-ranking guests, and held meetings in foreign offices in many countries, including the White House. He also sought to influence international public opinion through a concerted media campaign.[6] In March 2016, Prime Minister Netanyahu appointed Dayan as Consul General in New York City, following a failed attempt to install him as ambassador in Brasilia.[7] The appointment allowed Dayan to continue advocating the settler movement's goals by using it as a platform to spread the message, by connecting to high-power figures, and by normalizing the representations of settlers to the American people and the western world.

Understanding that elected politicians hold their positions only for limited periods of time, the Yesha Council also directly influences the bureaucracy. It mobilizes supporters from within the public administration and has gradually placed its own members in key bureaucratic positions (Pedahzur 2012). Scholars have described this action strategy as *state penetration*, that is, "the ability of organized societal forces to infiltrate into arms of the civil and military bureaucracies and build alliances with elements in the state apparatus such that the latter's loyalty to state rules becomes eclipsed by sympathy to the societal group's objectives" (Haklai 2007: 715); or *fusion*, "a bear hug, virtually fusing with the state apparatus to such a degree that the boundaries between the state and the group become indistinct" (Pedahzur & McCarthy 2015: 447). Jewish Home MK Bezalel Smotrich, a former Sovereignty board member and one of the founders of *Regavim* (see Chapter 3), explained the strategy as follows: "I think that our art was in engaging the State of Israel at all system levels, and not sneakily in the middle of the night. Rather, everything was done in broad daylight so that it would be the state that manages the settlement [of the land]" (Interview 2007).

However, the Yesha Council also promotes protest activities and campaigns, mostly against decisions to freeze settlement construction or to dismantle outposts. Over the years, it has specialized in organizing large demonstrations. When an issue arises around which the settler movement wants to mobilize, "battle headquarters" are set up by the different regional councils in the occupied territories. These are an effective source of activist recruitment and a way to mobilize support for particular struggles (see also Chapter 7). These headquarters make effective use of traditional media channels, like newspaper advertisements, as well as the Internet, to get the word out about upcoming protests and to mobilize supporters. As explained by Bentzi Lieberman, former Head of the Samaria Regional Council and Chairman of the Yesha Council (2002–2006):

> When we are in a process of struggle, in every regional council there is a 'battle headquarters' ... Within a quarter of an hour the settlements know exactly what was happening ... If I want to transmit an announcement, within 24 hours my newspaper has appeared in all mailboxes.

The Yesha Council's systems for organizing protests, rallies, and demonstrations are well oiled. According to Pinchas Wallerstein, another former Yesha Council head, "We have certain rules for events ... ... Let's say, we say that after three Zion [Jerusalem] Squares you can do Rabin [Tel Aviv] Square" (Interview 2007). Importantly, protest activities also provide a good opportunity for political lobbying, as clarified by Shaul Goldstein, a former head of the Gush Etzion Regional Council: "When you come to a Knesset member you say, I'm going to have a demonstration, and if you vote for me I'll let you make a speech in prime time in front of the cameras" (Interview 2007).

The Yesha Council does not call upon soldiers to disobey orders, not even orders to evacuate settlements. However, its leaders make a clear distinction between a personal decision to disobey and a public call. They accept the former but reject the latter. For instance, Wallerstein has said,

> "I believe that if a private person receives orders to do something that he considers immoral, it is more than legitimate for him to refuse to obey the order. This is different from the case where I as an institution [the Yesha Council] call on the public not to do military service – something that would threaten the state. In my view, that crosses a line ... The essential thing is, as a soldier do you serve the state or the Prime Minister?" Indeed, the position of the Yesha Council seems to be that to publicly call upon people to disobey orders would be the beginning of the end for the State of Israel (Interview 2007).

The Yesha Council's line between undermining the state and collaborating with it is very fine. The example of not making public calls for disobeying IDF orders but supporting private decisions to do so is a great example of this. It underscores the Council's existence at the edge of accepting the state's legitimacy: playing by the rules of the game when it's helpful, ignoring them when it's not.

One of the best-known settler actions is "creating facts on the ground," that is, establishing new settlements or reestablishing settlements that were evacuated by the Israeli government. This tactic has been central to the settler movement since the early days of Gush Emunim, which in turn adopted the tactic from the early Zionist movement. The Yesha Council plays a central role in the settlement-building endeavor. However, herein lies an important difference between the institutional and network branch of the settler movement: the former works within the law, only establishing new settlements or neighborhoods with formal government authorization, whereas the latter is not concerned with niceties such as official permission.

The Yesha Council's settlement-building activities are also public. This was not always the case. At first, when settlement building was not necessarily organized in any formal way, it was a public endeavor. However, at some point the public direct-action strategy was exchanged for one that involved building in secret. Daniella Weiss, former head of the local council of Kedumim, explains: "[At first, we] did not ask for an architect, an urban planner, an organizational adviser. Nothing. We said, what should we do? ... we will plant trees here [in Samaria]. We will organize all of the families, and then more families will come ... and we'll let the newspapers and television know" (Interview 2007).

Beyond settlement-building activities, lobbying, and demonstrations, the Yesha Council invests heavily in educational or explanatory activities: writing pamphlets and editorials, visiting educational institutions, giving speeches, and so on. The underlying idea is that in order to have influence, you must have public awareness. Hence, educational activity takes place on a routine basis and in different forms and settings. As Shaul Goldstein, former Head of the Gush Etzion Regional Council, noted, "The main role of the Yesha Council is to represent the image of the residents of Judea and Samaria in the eyes of the citizens of the rest of Israel. The main task of the Yesha Council is to prevent the possibility that people will want to uproot our communities" (Interview 2007).

Although its prime role within the broader movement is to collaborate with the state, the Yesha Council also tries to increase support for the movement and its goals within both the (domestic and international) elites and masses. With regard to the former, the institution uses awards and honors for public officials who show a strong commitment to the settler goals and ideology. For instance, the Yesha Council bestowed its prestigious "Yehuda and Shomron Faithful" award on Interior Minister Silvan Shalom in 2015. In an accompanying letter, signed by all West Bank local council leaders and mayors, it thanked him for his "brave support in ensuring the wholeness of the Land of Israel and the encouragement of settlement throughout Judea, Samaria, and the Jordan Valley" (*Arutz Sheva*, September 10, 2015). It has also tried to seduce politicians through less savory means. For example, the Yesha Council used its resources to allegedly rig public tenders so that funds could be funneled to the Jewish Home party (*Times of Israel*, November 21, 2017).[8]

Persuasion and explanation take place through traditional channels – flyers, pamphlets, newsletters, newspaper advertisements, speeches – and through technological resources, such as email, instant messaging, and the Internet. The Yesha Council publishes a free weekly bulletin entitled *Yesha Shelanu* (Our Yesha), which is distributed throughout the country and includes information about public events in various settlements as well as general news updates. Through these channels, the movement simultaneously transmits information, mobilizes existing supporters, and recruits new activists. As Weiss puts it, "You put a notice in the newspaper, saying that there will be a march, and suddenly 20,000 people come. So they are members. No, they are recruits. They have received a call-up notice" (Interview 2007).

The Yesha Council further actively supports West Bank business and entrepreneurs, who seek to make a living through tourism and help shape public opinion around the settler cause. For example, it launched a campaign titled "Every Jew's Story" in 2008, to counter Prime Minister Ehud Olmert's proposal for a unilateral withdrawal from most of the occupied territories (*Ynet*, October 5, 2008). In the campaign, the Yesha Council plastered cities across Israel with billboards urging Israelis to return to their roots by visiting West Bank sites and settlements (*Haaretz*, May 6, 2011). This campaign was its first large-scale effort to promote Israel's occupation of the West Bank to the broader society in a positive way, as valuable in itself, rather than as simply a security imperative. As such, it marked a milestone in the Yesha Council's development as a sophisticated lobbying, marketing, and promotional machine (*Ynet*, October 5, 2008).

To sum up, the history of the Yesha Council offers a case study in how social movements can become institutionalized, and how energies that are messy, spontaneous, uncontrolled, and potentially violent can be harnessed to serve the cause while working within the structures and mechanisms of the state. While it was created as a more institutionalized and moderate replacement for Gush Emunim, one that would work within the Israeli political apparatus, the Yesha Council has nonetheless facilitated numerous radical actions during its early years. The Council went through a period of de-radicalization during the mid-1990s, removing its more radical and extreme leadership and giving pragmatic considerations precedence over ideology (Haklai 2003).

Today, education and legal protest are favored over confrontation and illegal protest, and the Yesha Council denounces in strong language extremist actions like the recent "price-tag" attacks, although it often does so more for strategic than principled reasons. The Council has at times publicly called out the Hilltop Youth and "price-taggers" for their actions. For instance, Dayan has said that "price-tagging" constitutes "the gravest danger to our camp" (*Haaretz*, June 24, 2012), while Bennett has called it "the number one threat to the nature of [the settlement project in] Judea and Samaria" (Eiran & Krause 2018: 638). This is an attempt to show respect for the law – to counter the image of settlers as Wild-West lawbreakers – and to try to bolster the legitimacy of the state, so that as the state supports the settlement enterprise, it becomes more legitimate.

But while the Yesha Council officially rejects violence and disobedience, it has heralded one of the most violent confrontations, during the Amona evacuation in 2006, "a success."[9] As Shaul Goldshtein, Head of the Gush Etzion Regional Council, explained, "After Amona they stopped destroying houses and uprooting outposts, because the government understood that it couldn't have another Amona" (Interview 2007). Similarly, Amana had no problem with making Ze'ev Hever Secretary General, despite the fact that Hever had served time in prison for his participation in the Jewish Underground.

As the executive arm of the settler movement, Amana has the formal and legal status to allow the government to funnel money through it to establish (new) settlements in the West Bank and Gaza (Newman 2005: 222). Consequently, it has become the main donor of settlement activities and has employed a number of Gush Emunim leaders (Aronoff 1989). Amana is only involved in moderate actions, such as establishing communities and securing the necessary political and bureaucratic approval; organizing groups to found communities; supervising all aspects of community life (until independent capabilities have been firmly established); and building homes and public structures through its associate company, Binyanei Bar Amana. It operates a lobby group that pressures the government to retroactively legalize illegal outposts and obtain funds for its activities (Peace Now 2017). It also raises funds to build and assist illegal outposts through a subsidiary organization, the Foundation for the Development of the Zionist Vision, which has been recognized as a nonprofit by the Israeli state and is therefore exempt from taxes.

Amana also runs marketing and public relations campaigns to create (domestic and international) public support for its core activities. For example, together with the Yesha Council, Amana launched a joint public campaign calling upon US Jews to purchase a second home in a settlement in 2009. Yesha Council leader Wallerstein even met with US Jewish community leaders to pitch the idea of organizing groups of individual investors interested in the West Bank (*Ynet*, June 15, 2009). In 2017, Amana launched a public campaign with the explicit aim of increasing the number of settlers to one million. As stated in the campaign banner: "Now, it's time to get stronger. Come and join us. Together we will move on to the next vision: to settle a million Jews in Judea and Samaria." In its public appeal, Amana explained the actions needed to reach this number as follows: "Convince friends, talk to the family, organize Shabbat and community evenings, tag them on social networks, tell everyone and help them understand in every possible way – Judea and Samaria is your home. That way we can all, together, settle a million and much more" (Amana 2017).

5.4 Networks

The network branch is generally loosely organized around the goals and desires of its members and, at present, does not consider itself subordinate to any central leading body. While it is, in general, more radical than the formal institutions, networks employ a wide array of activities, and individual groups tend to specialize in one or a few specific ones. There also seems to be a certain division of labor within the broader settler movement, including within the network branch. For instance, Women in Green and the Academic Council for National Policy promote educational activities; the Yesha Human Rights Organization focuses on legal and state policies; Regavim monitors, documents, and records the status of land and petitions against illegal Palestinian construction work; the Hilltop Youth builds (illegal) outposts; and *Arutz Sheva* reports on the activities and issues of the settler movement. Thus, the network branch of the settler movement reflects an organizational ecology in which different groups develop distinctive action repertoires, utilizing a diverse spectrum of means and modes to promote distinct sets of goals and visions.

While radical actions are the networks' prime contribution to the broader struggle of the settler movement, their groups also engage in many moderate activities. Several groups focus on legal activism, often adopting methods from anti-settlement groups, which include monitoring of activities by both the Israeli state and Israeli Arabs and Palestinians. For example, Regavim monitors construction work by Israeli Arabs or Palestinians without Israeli permits in the West Bank and the Yesha Human Rights Organization files lawsuits and formal complaints of alleged discrimination against settler activists by the Israeli police (Perugini & Gordon 2015). And *Honenu* provides legal aid to settlers suspected or convicted of violent, nationalist-motivated crimes, which usually target Palestinian civilians.[10]

These organizations also use their political ties to influence policy-making, in particular on human rights policy in the West Bank, primarily through the Knesset Land of Israel Lobby (*Shedulat Eretz Yisrael*). This is perfectly illustrated by Orit Strook, who served as the chairperson of the Yesha Human Rights Organization as well as the director of the Land of Israel Lobby in the Knesset. The expressed goal of the latter is to "strengthen the State of Israel's hold on all of the Land of Israel, particularly in Judaea, Samaria and the Jordan Valley" (Knesset 2018). MK Smotrich, another Lobby leader, has used his role as deputy speaker of the Knesset to lobby against settlement evacuations and to resolve legal issues concerning settlers in the West Bank. This demonstrates the settler movements' ability to co-opt conventional avenues of the Israeli judicial system to further their own goals.

Other networks are primarily aimed at influencing the military. Most importantly, the national-religious Yeshivat Hesder system provides an institutional infrastructure that aims to integrate national-religious Israelis into the army by imbuing them with values pertinent for reaching IDF command positions (Lebel 2013). The current program follows early Gush Emunim efforts to establish a religious education system that prepares young people for positions in the government and army later in life (Aronoff 1985).[11] Under the program, young men first study in a Hesder yeshiva for about eighteen months, then serve in the army for a similar period, after which they return to the yeshiva for another two years of study. In the 1980s, pre-military Torah colleges (*mechinot*) were set up to provide young people with "spiritual fortification" before enlisting, as a means of balancing out the military's secular influences (Cohen 1999). In 2019, 25 percent of the pre-military Torah academies and 30 percent of the Hesder yeshivas in Israel were located in the settlements (Association of Hesder Yeshivas 2019; Ministry of Education 2019).

Educational campaigns are another staple activity of the networks. Through educational work (or propaganda), these groups seek to engineer a new dynamic within Israeli and global Jewish society by informing various audiences, from foreign governments to the broader Israeli society, about their ideological worldview and goals. Some settler groups organize school and tourist trips to promote the settler movement and its goals. Women in Green, for example, organizes camps for young people in a nature preserve in Gush Etzion. The camps, which run during school breaks and in the summer, give participants the opportunity to strengthen their bond with the land (of Israel) by doing agricultural work. It also runs educational lectures and tours covering various topics that concern the settlers, such as the biblical history of various West Bank sites. Their target audience include students from high schools, yeshivas and seminaries, and IDF preparatory schools as well as various organizations from Israel and abroad.

Educational campaigns may be directed inward as well as outward. *Mattot Arim* produces a bi-annual report that ranks MKs and cabinet members on their level of support for the settlements and the "national camp."[12] The reports award marks for pro-settler legislative, lobbying, and media activity by all MKs – from bills prohibiting boycotts of products made in the settlements to media interviews.[13] These reports are intended for internal use by settler activists and are not distributed to the general media (*Haaretz*, November 24, 2011). In that context they serve an important purpose, guiding settlers to political figures they should support and vote for as well as spreading the word in the settler community about unpublicized activities to advance West Bank settlements.

Some networks follow in the well-established footsteps of the traditional Zionist movement by bringing (young) people to work in the settlements. *HaYovel* is an NGO that is run by Tommy Waller, a Christian fundamentalist from Missouri, US. Its stated aim is to bring "Christian volunteers from all over the world to serve Jewish farmers in Israel." In August 2019, its website boasted to have brought 2,613 people from 22 countries – the equivalent of 190,505 volunteer hours – to "Israel," where they mostly worked in olive groves and vineyards owned by settlers. Its activities are aimed at improving both the resources and support for the settler movement. In addition to bringing volunteers to work in the settlements, the organization also organizes visiting tours for journalists, collects online donations and sends spokespersons to various countries to spread "the positive voice from Judea and Samaria into the nations." HaYovel had allegedly raised over $50 million for the settler movement by 2018 (*Haaretz*, December 9, 2018).

Many networks define activism in a more militant way than the institutional actors, however, and are also involved in both moderate and radical actions. While radical actions constitute a minority of their overall activity, and extreme actions are particularly rare, they are more naturally allied with the broader outlook of the networks. While most acknowledge the authority of the Israeli state, they are more suspicious toward the state than the institutions, and favor struggle over collaboration. As such, they use more radical rhetoric and protest slogans to distance themselves from the Yesha Council, which they perceive as engaged in a constant effort to normalize its semantics so as to ingratiate itself with the political elites (Newman 2005). Their confrontational strategies include protest, illegal settlement operations, political violence, and in some cases even terrorism (Aran & Fiege 1987; Lustick 1988; Pedahzur et al. 2009; Sprinzak 1999).

One strategy used by the networks is to raise awareness of their cause among the masses by engaging in social protest. For example, Sovereignty has organized demonstrations, marches, protests, and rallies, particularly in and around the Amona outpost, sometimes with other groups within the far-right political family. Other settler networks blend oppositional and symbolic strategies in order to gain attention from the public. Orange Cell held a number of demonstrations in Tel Aviv, around a street performance called "On Blindness," in which activists dressed in orange capes and crowns followed a blindfolded "king" who bumped into poles and obstructions (*Haaretz*, June 14, 2005). They also held a ten-day hunger strike to protest the Gaza Disengagement Plan, which was ultimately broken after the personal intervention of President Moshe Katsav (*Haaretz*, August 17, 2005). Similarly, The Revolt has staged demonstrations in the heart of Tel Aviv to expose and protest administrative detention and the alleged denial of access to lawyers to Jewish militants.[14] These demonstrations are designed to pressure the Israeli public into feeling ashamed of how their government treats their compatriots, and to generate bottom-up disaffection with perceived state repression of Jews.

A special position in the repertoire of symbolic actions is reserved for Holocaust imagery. Settler networks that opposed Begin's peace negotiations with Egypt, in the second half of the 1970s, already evoked the horrors of the Holocaust in an attempt to shame Begin into abandoning the talks (Naor 2003). Decades later, Holocaust imagery is still a central factor in the public relations of the movement. During the disengagement from Gaza, some settlers wore orange Stars of David, reminiscent of the yellow stars that Jews were forced to wear under the Nazis. Women in Green also employed Holocaust imagery during the prelude to the disengagement, sending the head of the disengagement administration a copy of a 1942 document in which the Berlin *Judenrat* (Jewish Council) informed the city's Jews of their impending deportation (Nadia Matar, Interview 2007). These symbolic gestures were meant to turn public opinion against the government by framing the latter as continuing or repeating the work of the Nazis.

Occasionally, settler groups also engage in more radical activities, such as blocking roads, trespassing on private property, encouraging civil disobedience and calling for widespread illegal action to paralyze law enforcement authorities. As this set of actions transgresses legal norms but does not involve violence (i.e., against persons), it is classified as radical action. Some organizations call openly for civil disobedience.

Interestingly, the network branch recognizes that civil disobedience and refusal to obey orders are in and of themselves wrong, because they distinguish between such acts when performed by settlers, which are permitted and even regarded as obligatory, and those performed in other contexts, which they regard as rightly forbidden. The logic here, of course, is that in the settlers' view, the law of God, by which Judea and Samaria are inalienable parts of *Eretz Yisrael*, supersedes the law of the state.

Civil disobedience was prominent during the Gaza evacuation, when settler groups gathered in crowds and barricaded communities to prevent soldiers from approaching to evict residents (see Chapter 7). Some settlers threatened with evacuation held out until the last minute, in some cases forcing soldiers to carry them physically from their homes. Organizations like Sovereignty and Jewish Heart actively encouraged civilians to defy police officers and soldiers seeking to remove them and called upon them to refuse to obey the orders (*Haaretz*, May 1, 2006). These groups reportedly used text messages to keep protesters and residents informed on the movements of Israeli troops assigned to remove illegal outposts.

Other radical activities include building farms and outposts as a form of creating "facts on the ground," aimed at nullifying the reality of the Oslo Accords. A prototypical example of this activism is the Hilltop Youth's central mission of fulfilling Sharon's famous injunction to "grab every hilltop" (Eldar & Zertal 2007). Direct action aimed at countering evacuation orders or political concessions has become a key part of the settler repertoire too (Alimi & Demetriou 2018). This may involve establishing new outposts and settlements, sometimes by converting prime locations abandoned by the military, sometimes by reestablishing settlements that were evacuated earlier. One organization known for such actions is Homesh First, which has labored to reestablish the settlement of Homesh, evacuated as part of the Disengagement Plan. For example, on Israel's Independence Day in 2007, 12,000 demonstrators marched to the destroyed settlement (Weiss 2007).[15] The Hilltop Youth also sends its activists to reinforce settlements slated for evacuation, to make evictions more difficult (Pedahzur & Perliger 2009).[16] In 1995, the group "This is Our Land" (*Zu Artzeinu*) engaged in an extensive campaign of demonstrations and civil disobedience within the Green Line, which devolved into outright violence, leading to a public rebuke by the Yesha Council (Eldar & Zertal 2007; Pedahzur & McCarthy 2015).

The great majority of networks consider the use of violence against other Jews, especially potentially lethal violence, a red line that cannot be crossed. As Shulamit Melamed, founder of *Arutz Sheva*, stated, "I am ready to face them, but I won't be the one to kill" (Interview 2007). However, it is unclear whether, for the networks, refraining from violence against Jewish targets is based on a moral stance or a pragmatic one, that is, the perception that using weapons will lose them public sympathy and support.

Recent years have seen an increase in violence and, indeed, terrorism by settlers (OCHA 2018). Extreme activism has gained prominence in particular within the Kahane network, like Lehava, whose modus operandi includes arson, vandalism, incitement, intimidation, and harassment (Alimi & Demetriou 2018; Engelberg 2017). The Hilltop Youth and The Revolt have taken the polarized "us versus them" perspective a step further by targeting Palestinians and left-wing Israeli activists alike (*Jerusalem Post*, June 20, 2017). Ami Pedahzur and Arie Perlinger (2009: 116) have described the attitude of this loose network as one of "extreme alienation" to the laws of the State of Israel.[17]

The Hilltop Youth's actions and threats are so removed from acceptable political behavior that any groups employing the term "price tag" is officially declared an "unauthorized association" by the Ministry of Defense since 2013. Over the years, Hilltop Youth activists, sometimes operating under different names (such as Gilad-Shallhevet Brigade, Sword of Gideon, Tears of the Widows, and the Orphans), have devastated the lives of their Palestinian neighbors through intimidation and terrorism (Pedahzur & Perliger 2011). In particular, the period of the Al Aqsa Intifada saw the emergence of various clandestine and semi-clandestine settler groups that were prepared to use violence, including a cell of the Hilltop Youth, the Bat Ayin Underground, which was accused, and subsequently found guilty, of planning a terrorist attack against East Jerusalem schoolgirls.[18] Hilltop Youth members have even used intimidation tactics (such as slashing tires and other forms of vandalism) against the settler elite, to express their disillusionment with the Yesha Council (Pedahzur 2012).

The Revolt, an offshoot of the Hilltop Youth, uses a very similar action repertoire, including arson, bodily harm, property destruction, and vandalism. Notably, its activists were responsible for the deadly Duma arson attack in July 2015. In Spring 2015 the group launched a public anti-Christian campaign, which has led to several desecrations of churches and mosques since (*The New Yorker*, August 4, 2015). These violent actions are part of a concerted program of so-called price-tag attacks, committed in revenge for Palestinian attacks on Jewish settlers or the demolition of settlement housing. To ensure that their purpose is clear, they leave graffiti reading "price tag," "revenge," or "you will pay the price" sprayed at the scene (Alimi & Demetriou 2018; *Ynet*, March 1, 2016).

No organization better reflects the extremist nature of some settler opposition groups than Kahane Lives (*Kahane Chai*), a vigilante organization that aims to halt further evacuations, and that has used terrorist acts like arson, stabbings, shootings, and grenade attacks to target West Bank Arabs. It condones violence as a legitimate method for establishing a Halachic State, which would uphold Torah law and remove Israel's secular democratic practices. A cell of the Kahane Chai network, God of Vengeance (*Elnakam*), carried out a terrorist attack in November 1992, dropping a fragmentation grenade (stolen from the IDF) into an Arab market in Jerusalem's Old City. A Palestinian worker was killed in the explosion and seven other Palestinians were wounded (Pedahzur & Perliger 2011: 97).[19]

Some scholars have noted that, in many respects, the Hilltop Youth represent a continuation and even extension of the Kahanist ideology. Both seek a religious alternative to secular Israeli culture and wish to replace the existing democratic regime with a theocratic one. However, whereas the Kahanist movement operated from within the heart of Israeli society, the Hilltop Youth locates itself in isolated communities that are completely detached from the state and its authorities (Pedahzur & Perliger 2011).[20]

5.5 Influencers

Individual influencers are not linked to movement organizations, whether formal or informal, but are single individuals or small groups of people working directly or indirectly to spread the message of the settler movement. Individual actors further the goals of the movement using a plethora of channels, including both formal (political institutions) and informal (civil society) pathways as well as media outlets. Influencers primarily play a role in mobilizing public support for the settler enterprise and movement, at the domestic but also international level, in particular through activities in the media and tourism. In addition, some influencers mobilize resources for the movement, through businesses, or influence policy, through high-rank positions within the state apparatus.

The key role of influencers in social movements is to boost public support beyond traditional circles by using their personal platforms and reputations. Individuals from the arts, business, media, and sports have all played an integral role in the advancement of the pro-settlement agenda. One of the most high-profile examples was Naomi Shemer, once dubbed "the first lady of Israeli song and poetry" (*Haaretz*, June 28, 2004), who leveraged her fame one Israel's most famous Israeli singers and songwriters to increase support for the settlement enterprise.[21] In a 1995 *Maariv* interview, Shemer appeared jaded by her (early) political engagement, arguing that it had not been very successful.

> There were times when I thought that if I shouted, 'Do not uproot the rooted' then they would not be relocated. Since then I have sobered up and I know that this was tremendously naïve on my part. On political matters, I have remained silent for 15 years. I learned my lesson, I saw that my power is limited, if I have any at all (*NRG, May* 6, 2012).

This seems too modest, however. For instance, some of her very popular apolitical songs were reappropriated for the settler cause, such as her song "On All These," which has become a settler anthem, despite the fact that the song was written for her sister who had been widowed.

Singer–songwriter Ariel Zilber serves as another example of an artist who used his fame as a platform for his right-wing political opinions. Despite being shunned by parts of the artistic community after openly supporting the extremist policy of "transferring" Israeli Arab citizens (see Chapter 3), Zilber has received several high-profile awards over the years, including the 2016 lifetime achievement prize by the Israeli Union of Performing Artists (*Arutz Sheva*, January 20, 2016).[22] In 2018, Zilber released the song "Route 5," written by West Bank resident Naama Zanbar, which calls upon the people of Israel to return to Samaria. The song is a symbolic response to calls by other Israeli artists to boycott the settlements. Yossi Dagan, the Head of the Samaria Council, said about it,

> I call this the silent boycott. It's a protest that is not spoken about but I am sure that it is felt by the residents of Shomron and many others in the country. Artists are afraid to broach the subject for fear that they will face retribution in the guild. We set a goal for ourselves to combat this boycott? (*Ynet*, November 22, 2018).

Zilber himself stated about the song, "Seventy years for Israel and thousands of years for Samaria, it is time. It is always time. Stop the quiet Cultural Boycott on Samaria, it is a shame that it took so long to bring out a song about Samaria . . . . We have the right to be here" (*0404 News*, November 22, 2018).[23]

There are also important pro-settler voices within the scholarly community. One of the most important is Professor Israel Aumann, a Nobel Prize winner in economics, who has often spoken in favor of the movement in the media. For example, he attacked the decision to remove a soldier from his unit after refusing to shake the hand of IDF Chief of Staff Dan Halutz, in protest against the evacuation of Gush Katif. Aumann called the expulsion "Bolshevik behavior" in an interview (*Ynet*, June 14, 2006). He also boycotted a conference at Hebrew University in Jerusalem in 2013, because he did not want to sit next to

Professor Moshe Zimmerman, who had likened the settlers to the Nazis (*Haaretz*, January 13, 2013).

Another important influencer in the intellectual arena is Yoaz Hendel, a historian, publicist, radio presenter, and head of the Institute for Zionist Strategies think tank. Raised in the Elkana settlement, Hendel has written and spoken in support of the gradual annexation of the settlement blocs and the Jordan Valley and has argued that "most of the price tag people are not terrorists" (Hendel 2013, 2014). In 2019, Hendel joined the Blue and White party, which became the second largest party in the April elections.

The settler movement has many influencers who advocate for the settler enterprise in the media sphere, using both traditional and virtual media outlets (see Chapter 3). First and foremost, these influencers have advanced pro-settler positions in mainstream media outlets. For example, Yifat Erlich – an Israeli writer, journalist, and publicist – has supported the Law for the Regulation of Settlement in Judea and Samaria (see Chapter 4) and has regularly criticized the Amona evacuation, which affected her personally. Amit Segal, a Channel 12 political analyst and *Yedioth Ahronoth* political columnist, also criticized the Supreme Court decision to evacuate Amona, arguing that "Instead of decent compensation for the Arab owners and building a new home for the Jewish settler, the first remains without compensation, and the second without a home" (Segal 2018). And Haggai Huberman, who has been writing for nationalist-religious media for decades, has frequently criticized government policy toward the settlement enterprise. In 2016, he wrote

> Israeli public relations must focus on the historic rights of the Jewish people in Judea and Samaria – and focus on this in the next 50 years. Any political discussion in the next fifty years must focus on the question of who was here before – the Jews or the Arabs? To whom does the land belong in the first place – to Jews or Arabs? Only after this discussion is over will it be possible to begin discussing the fundamental questions of one political solution or another (Arutz Sheva, December 26, 2016).

Influencers have also written articles and books that popularize the settlements and settlers. For instance, Emily Amrousi (2009), a former Yesha Council spokeswoman who now writes for various Israeli media, including the popular free newspaper *Israel HaYom* (Israel Today), published a novel about a young female settler, which tells the story of the daily lives and collective traumas (as a consequence of evacuations and terrorist attacks) of the settlers.[24] And Huberman wrote several books that idealize the Israeli settler movement, including "Against All Odds" (*Keneged kol Hasikuyim*, 2008), which tells the story of forty years of settlement in the West Bank, and "Roots in the Sand" (*Shorashim B'acholot*, 2005), which discusses the history of Gush Katif.

Pro-settler individuals have created and utilized social media platforms like blogs, virtual communities, private websites, and online businesses to support and promote the movement and the ideology of *Eretz Yisrael.* As virtual media allow for fast, easy, and cheap transnational action, not limited by time, space, or distance (Castells 2002; Juris 2005; Selander & Jarvenpaa 2016), they are the perfect medium for oppositional actors like the settler movement. For instance, during the disengagement from Gaza, many informal websites supported the Gush Katif struggle, including Katif.net, the leading communication website for residents of Gush Katif and their supporters before and right after the disengagement (Roth 2005).[25]

The settler movement also has a broad range of influencers who promote the settler enterprise via their businesses, most notably tourism and wineries. This includes Gedaliah and Elisheva Blum, who launched the online business directory Orange Pages (*Dapei Katom*) in 2009, which promotes small businesses in the settlements and currently lists more than 2,500 local businesses (including caterers, mechanics, and real estate brokers). The political aim of these businesses is twofold: to bring resources to the settlements, and thus the movement, and to improve the image and thereby boost support for the settlers and settlements. Elisheva Blum has explained this position very clearly: "our dream is to bring the settlements investments of millions, to change the consciousness to independence, and through this to influence the status of Judea and Samaria. Our dream is to deepen the roots, to lead a change in the public consciousness and economics" (*The Digital Magazine of Mateh Binyamin,* August 2, 2017).

Perhaps the most important entrepreneurial initiatives of individual settlers and their supporters are the promotion of tourism and wineries in the West Bank. Groups and individuals step forward to protect particular historical sites, many of which have biblical significance, and set up businesses based around sightseeing and tourism (from Israel and abroad) and field trips for schoolchildren. In doing so they create a greater Jewish presence in the area, and also encourage Israelis from within the Green Line, as well as Jews from the diaspora, to visit the settlements and see that they are well-run towns with good facilities. Promotional adverts and videos make no reference to political tensions in the area, but rather stress the idea that the land is ancient, belongs to the Jewish people, and offers spectacular views of nature. By promoting attractions and encouraging tourism to the area, these influencers aim to normalize the lives of the settlers and garner more support for the settler enterprise. As one influencer explained to tourists on a tour through the West Bank, "All we want is to sit on our land, and we want you to be our ambassadors" (*Jerusalem Post,* June 21, 2011).

Private tour guides also promote the Israeli settlement agenda, sometimes with support from settler organizations. The tours are neatly tailored to suit the specific character of each visiting group, and the settlers have managed to bring many government ministers, opinion makers, and media personalities on visits to the area. Following his visit, for instance, columnist and poet Menachem Benn moved to the Nofim settlement, while media personality Avri Gilad told Army radio,

> I went on a tour that revolutionized my awareness of settlements in Samaria. I visited places I was raised to detest. I returned in a state of confusion: confused about the injustice done to citizens who were called on by the state to settle, given building permits and then frozen out. I was surprised to meet people with whom I had a lot to talk about, with great warmth and intimacy. Most of the discussion [about settlers] on the left is hatred. What really surprised me was the proximity – 23 minutes and you are deep into the area (*Haaretz*, September 12, 2010).

During holiday seasons, influencers promote Jewish music festivals, fruit-picking festivals, and an annual kite festival. Other tourist initiatives include holiday cottages (*tzimmerim*), mainly catering to religious couples; adventure activities; and an artisanal bakery and olive pressing activities for children and families. Another area that has flourished is artists' colonies. As Yochai Damari, head of the Mount Hebron Regional Council, stated in an interview with *Kipa News* (August 29, 2018):

> In the past five years, we have brought the first line of Israel's artists to Mount Hebron . . . The cultural flourishing in the area is an expression of the normalcy of the region, while in the media the region is tied to security and political coverage issues – these are only small percentages of cases which do not indicate what is really happening here.

Similarly, wineries, organic foods, and artisanal cheeses have become a new frontier for the settlements' public image, along with a range of tourism-oriented offerings. Adventure parks featuring all-terrain vehicle tours of the Judean desert, mountain biking, and zip lines; "New Age" massages, craft-beer breweries, spiritual retreats, and petting zoos have sprouted across the territories to attract religious or secular Israelis, as well as foreign tourists. Many businesses have been partially funded by the Yesha Council and regional councils. Bed-and-breakfasts serving the tourist population are a new form of "facts on the ground" as well as a new marketing strategy.[26] Most of these tourist offerings are not explicitly political, but are aimed at burnishing the settlers' image and normalizing the presence of the settlements as well as providing the settlers and settlements with a source of income.

This new way of appealing to the Israeli public is most apparent in the burgeoning of settlement wineries. Wine tourism in the West Bank has been a significant phenomenon since 2005 (Handel et al. 2015).[27] This phenomenon is related to the development of a wine culture and wine tourism in both Israel and the world in the last twenty years (Shor & Mansfeld 2012). However, there is a special narrative about the development of vineyards in the Samaria area. The biblical prophecy, "Again you shall plant vineyards in the mountains of Samaria" (Jeremiah 31:4), is associated with the redemption of the "People of Israel" and its return to its land following the exile of the Israelites to Babylonia in 586 BCE.[28] For the settlers, this prophecy is now being realized.

The wine industry in Samaria serves as a good benchmark for the change and development of tourism in the region, because it is aimed at an audience that is new and unique to the area and appeals to a sector of tourism that was previously unmet by the religious–historical tourist archetype. For influencers like Yaakov Berg, CEO of Psagot Winery, winemaking in the West Bank is a blend of commerce and ideology: "Wine is the best thing to happen to Judea and Samaria. It's a very good tool. When people come here to drink, they get to know us and they see how we live. It makes a huge difference" (*Jerusalem Post*, July 2, 2017).

The last group of influencers works from within the state, influencing policies and resources for the settlers and settlements. While they are much rarer, they can be much more consequential. Among the most influential pro-settler individuals are those within the Israeli legal system, and none more so than two Supreme Court judges, David Mintz and Noam Solberg (see Chapter 3). For example, Mintz petitioned the High Court of Justice in 1994, against the Education Ministry, in order to disqualify a curriculum dealing with the peace process and the Oslo Accords. Both judges are indicative of the "entrism" strategy the settler movement has adopted, where key individuals occupy select positions in the state and society, which allow them to advance its political agenda. Ultimately, by placing settlers or their vocal supporters in respected public positions, the movement is increasing its impact and visibility in mainstream Israeli discourse and normalizing its image and opinions in the eyes of the broader public.

5.6 Discussion

To understand the success of the settler movement and the role different branches play in achieving it, we first have to acknowledge that the movement operates in a very favorable political context. Israel's POS is extremely open, providing settler leaders with ready access to the institutionalized political system. Because of its strongly proportional electoral system, the party system is very fragmented, which provides small parties with outsized power in politics, and highly mobilized and organized groups like the settlers with disproportionate power within parties. This plays out even more within political parties that organize primaries, like Likud.

In addition to the (extreme) openness of the formal structure of the Israeli political system, the settler movement also profits from a very favorable DOS (Koopmans & Statham 1999). Although there seems to be a great gap between the national-religious ideology of the settlers and secular Zionism, the two are actually quite closely connected, which further helps explain why the settler movement has been relatively successful in mobilizing support in the Israeli cultural context. As mentioned, the national-religious ideology of the settler movement is not a "normal pathology," unconnected to Israel's mainstream values, but rather a "pathological normalcy," a radicalization of mainstream values. Particularly in its approach to (older) Labor Zionists, within kibbutzim and the Labor Party, the settler movement portrays itself as the modern-day incarnation of the original settlers of the *Yishuv*, which, unlike the Labor Party, has not given up on the original goals of settling the "Land of Israel."

This favorable discursive and political opportunity structure explains the substantial state support for the key institutions of the settler movement, the Yesha Council and Amana, which are both hybrids of the Israeli state and the settler movement. It also helps explain why the settler movement in general, and the institutions in particular, prioritize moderate actions and feel less need for radical, let alone extreme, actions. Moreover, it enables the institutions to advance many of the movement's goals through collaboration *with* the state, rather than opposition *to* the state. While this support tends to be ideological among religious and right-wing nationalists, it is more nostalgic within the left, most notably (older) Labor politicians, which has its origins in the pre-state settler movement.

The specific political structure of the Israeli occupation of the West Bank offers additional opportunities for collaboration with the state as well as capture *of* the state. Area C, the part of the West Bank governed by Israel, is under civilian and military rule, both formally under the central authority of the national government, but with significant autonomy. These authorities have chosen to actively collaborate with the settlers to meet their infrastructural and security needs, which include employing settlers for the implementation of these tasks (such as state-financed security guards in settlements). In addition, the local administrative structure of the West Bank settlements is completely controlled by leading members of the settler movement, which provides them with resources not just for their communities but also for the movement. Finally, activists and sympathizers from the settler movement have entered COGAT and the IDF to advance the goals of the movement from within the system, including in leading capacities such as high-level COGAT staff and local IDF commanders.

Although the networks overall accept the authority of the State of Israel, with some exceptions (notably the post-*Malachti* groups), they are much more cautious toward collaboration with the state. The favorable POS allows them to advance their goals mainly through moderate actions and ensures that network activists and members can function at the heart of Israeli society (think, for example, of the Professors for a Strong Israel). That said, the specific role of the networks within the broader settler movement is to pressure the state, and increasingly the institutional branch, into taking bolder actions to advance the settler agenda – or, more often, to prevent planned actions that go against that agenda – particularly, countering external pressure on the Israeli government to freeze settlement building, evacuate existing settlements, and give up land for peace. While most oppositional activities still fall within the moderate repertoire of actions, networks also participate in radical actions, that is, those that are illegal but nonviolent, such as creating (illegal) outposts, organizing disruptive protests, and physically opposing evacuations of existing outposts and settlements.

Although the networks may appear to constitute a cohesive subset of the broader settler movement, sharing the same values, goals, and beliefs, they actually exemplify the movement's diversity. Cooperation between networks does exist, but it is nonbinding. The different groups recognize the utility of collaboration, especially in recruiting activists from different segments of the population and even linking different segments together, but in practice, each network maintains organizational independence and a right to act autonomously. It appears that decisions to cooperate stem from a calculation of *quality* vs. *quantity*. As explained by Menashe Levinger, son of one of the founders of the Jewish settlement in Hebron and a key activist of the Land of Israel Faithful Movement, "When we want breadth, when we want scope, we put all of the networks together. If, at a certain event, it is important to have many people, I give up on nuance. I have to find a compromising formula among the networks" (Interview 2007).

However, while cooperation does exist among the networks, it appears that, since the disengagement from the Gaza Strip (see Chapter 7), there has been little cooperation between the institutional branch and the networks. The networks feel that the institutional branch, specifically the Yesha Council, treats them as outcasts, and that the cooperation is unidirectional; the networks come when the Yesha Council asks them to, but this is not reciprocated by the Council. As MK Smotrich asserts, the Yesha Council "is used to being the authority, used to being in super control, it is difficult for it to accept there are new forces that have to be given room and whose opinions have to be considered" (Interview 2007).

The networks have always included a small extremist faction, which rejects the authority of the State of Israel, at least when it opposes (their interpretation of) religious law, and considers violence against the state and its representatives acceptable under such conditions. At the heart of the extremist faction is the loose subnetwork of Kahanists, that is, followers of the murdered Rabbi Meir Kahane and his nationalist-theocratic ideology, which include groups like the Hilltop Youth, Lehava, and The Revolt. Their activists have been involved in a broad variety of radical and extreme activities, including deadly terrorist attacks against Palestinians. The 2005 disengagement from Gaza has further soured their relationship with the State of Israel, which a growing number of activists within this subculture now consider an enemy rather than a friend.

Finally, influencers mainly address the broader public, through their (moderate) actions within the economy, media, and tourism. Through their various activities, these influencers have helped mainstream, normalize, and even popularize the goals and image of the settler movement. Through business they have brought (products from) the settlements to Israelis within the Green Line, and even non-Israelis abroad, while tourism has brought nonsettlers to the settlements for seemingly nonpolitical reasons. In both cases, the influencers also use their products to mainstream and normalize the settlements as well as improve the public image of the settlers.

Influencers have been particularly successful in promoting settler positions in the mainstream media, which also helped diversify the image of the movement and its supporters. For instance, Nobel Prize winners or think tank directors give its positions more intellectual gravitas and help counter the negative stereotype of settlers as a group of irrational religious zealots. Similarly, being represented by professional women like Amrousi and Erlich has helped "soften" the image of the settler movement, at least in some circles, given that well-established sexist media tropes present females as well as femininity as less ideological and less threatening (e.g., Snipes & Mudde 2019). This can be seen in particular in the coverage of Amrousi, a young and ambitious settler woman, who has been described as "fashionable" and even "the Israeli settler movement's Girl" (Ghert-Zand 2011).

6 A Case of Success
Ariel

> Ariel is a modern city with a high quality of life, which aspires to develop globally in the fields of industry and science and to accomplish the Jewish vision of Greater Israel.
>
> Ron Nachman, Mayor of Ariel (1985–2013)

Ariel is the fourth largest Israeli settlement in the West Bank. As the best example of a mainstreamed and normalized settlement in the West Bank, it constitutes an "extreme case study" for the success of the settler movement (Gerring 2008). Although the city is legally a settlement, and falls under the bureaucratic jurisdiction of the Civil Administration of the West Bank (part of COGAT), it is in many ways, and to many Israelis, an Israeli city. Ron Nachman, the longtime mayor of Ariel, noted already in 2004, "There has been consensus on the Right and on the Left over the course of the years regarding Ariel. As a result, it is natural that the city's development and construction would remain consistent, especially considering the policy of the prime minister, the minister of defense and the housing minister" (*NRG*, August 8, 2004). But even left-wing politicians, like Labor Party MK Sheli Yachimovich, agree that "Ariel is not an illegal outpost, it is a city in Israel that was established by successive Israeli governments, including periods when the Labor Party was in power" (*Ynet*, December 8, 2009).

Ariel is now home to 20,456 Israeli residents. It was officially designated a city by the State of Israel in 1998. Ariel is one of the four West Bank settlements that have received municipal status. However, unlike the other three, Ariel is geographically deep in the West Bank. Its location plays an important role in the settler movement's strategy. The recognition of Ariel as a city contributes to its perception in the public mind as a permanent and indisputable part of Israel, which will never be evacuated, despite its location. Ariel offers not only a range of housing options but also mainstream community services such as community centers, healthcare facilities, shopping centers, and a theater. It has a soccer team, Beitar

Ironi Ariel, which plays in the lower tiers of the Israeli league system, and, surprisingly, includes both Arab and Jewish players (*Haaretz*, February 9, 2017). Perhaps most significantly, it has a university, Ariel University, which serves thousands of students from across the West Bank and Israel.

The settler movement implemented a diverse repertoire of strategies in order to transform the perception of Ariel from a West Bank settlement into an Israeli city, recognized by both the Israeli public and the Israeli state. Its success is owed in large part to its variegated approach to legitimizing and normalizing Ariel, using official government channels as well as grassroots, popular avenues. As will be shown in this chapter, Israeli governments have funded the construction of thousands of residence units, established an array of public institutions, and set up the infrastructure for an advanced road system designed to connect Ariel to the centers of activity within the Green Line. Along with the state, and particularly through the Judea and Samaria Administrative Authority, the network and influencer branches of the settler movement have been instrumental in making Ariel the movement's crowning success. Networks and influencers have contributed financial and infrastructural support, which played an integral role in providing the stability necessary for building and expanding the city.

6.1 The Establishment of Ariel

Ariel is one of the largest settlements in the northern West Bank, and is known colloquially as "the capital of Samaria." It is located just off Highway 5, which connects Ariel to large Israeli cities like Petah Tikva to the south, Ramat Hasharon to the west, and Kfar Saba to the north. However, even as its infrastructure conveys a sense of proximity to Israel proper, Ariel is actually located in the heart of the West Bank, both literally and figuratively. Ariel – which is approximately 5 km long and 700 m wide – is at its closest only some 16 km from the Green Line. It is closer to the western border of Jordan (28 km) than to Tel Aviv (40 km).

The physical location of Ariel is not insignificant, of course. Its location reflects the settlers' strategy of "divide and conquer," that is, breaking up the physical contiguity of the Palestinian territories and serving as a physical obstruction to Arab expansion in the West Bank (Arieli 2017). Most of the Jewish settlements constructed in the first decade of occupation were remote and rural, promoted as security assets or as opportunities to imitate the pioneering ethos of Israel's early days (Weiss 2011). The physical location of Ariel was meant as a signal to the Israeli government that it could not compromise or negotiate its permanent status as part of the State of Israel. Prime

Minister Benjamin Netanyahu has stressed the strategic advantage of the city's location as well as its historical, cultural, and psychological importance: "Ariel, the capital of Samaria, is a major component of the security belt of the State of Israel. Its name is synonymous with Jerusalem and the Temple, and not for nothing. Just as Jerusalem will remain our united capital for all eternity, Ariel will always remain part of Israel" (*Ynet*, January 20, 2013).[1]

The tactical and strategic advantage of Ariel is clear: It creates the illusion of connectedness between the settlements and Israel proper. The term "Ariel bloc" is often used to refer to the area of the West Bank demarcated by Ariel in the east, Kedumim in the north, Karnei Shomron in the northwest and Beit Aryeh–Ofarim in the south. The Ariel bloc includes a multitude of smaller settlements, which are in fact the practical outcome of the largely uninterrupted development of the West Bank in conjunction with government-subsidized infrastructural enterprises. Not all of the settlements of the Ariel bloc enjoy the same status as Ariel itself. In fact, seven of the other settlements were designated illegal outposts in 2005. Yet, when we look at the *physical* arrangement of the Ariel bloc today, we clearly see that what was once a scattering of illegal outposts is now an organized collection of settlements and cities that links Ariel with key reference points in various directions. This arrangement guarantees continuity between Ariel and the Green Line via an assortment of roads, industrial zones, and residential areas (Maggor 2015).

The settler movement has worked assiduously to link Ariel with settlements that are more distant from the Green Line, and in particular the so-called Gav HaHar settlements located along the central mountain ridge on Route 60, to the east of Ariel – an area which was initially viewed as falling outside the greater Ariel area. This arrangement was meant to ensure that the Gav HaHar settlements can never be dismantled either, as Pinchas Wallerstein boasted in an interview with the Israeli daily *Yediot Aharonot* in May 2003.

Ariel was founded in 1978, when a large group of families set up tents at what was then known as the Tel Haris settlement. The group was part of a larger network established by Labor Party Minister of Defense Moshe Dayan, called the Tel Aviv Group, which sought to settle territories that Israel had captured in the Six-Day War. Following the war, Dayan had said the country needed young Israelis to be more involved in settlement, which was viewed as the true expression of Zionism and a source of security for the new state. This call to action was initially answered by a small group of employees in the Israeli Military Industries (now IMI Systems), who sought a higher quality of life and a suburban experience for their families. Josef Bar-Ilan, Ron Nachman, Gyora Shachar, and

David Hasman led a group of forty families, which together formed the nuclear founding party of Ariel.

It is important to remember the political context in which the initial settlement of Ariel took place. Between July 1974 and December 1975, the Rabin government had prevented the establishment of seven settlements by Gush Emunim (Lein & Weizman 2002). Rabin opposed Jewish settlement in highly populated Arab regions, and especially Gush Emunim's strategy of creating "facts on the ground" without official permits or recognition. Ultimately, he did approve the establishment of the Jewish settlement of Kedumim (Leon 2004). Begin, who came to power in 1977, introduced a new policy that rejected partition of the land and sought to establish Jewish settlements in the entire West Bank (Arieli 2012).

The Gush Emunim movement, which had previously faced pushback and hesitation from Rabin's Labor government, now seized the opportunity to exploit the new right-wing momentum, which they (rightly) viewed as more favorable toward their cause. A delegation of six Gush Emunim members arrived at Begin's apartment in July 1977 and submitted a detailed plan for settlement to him, which included twelve new settlements in various locations in the West Bank. Interestingly, Begin claimed that he was already prepared to receive this plan from them, highlighting his willingness to help facilitate the settlement expansion and signaling a watershed moment for the nascent settler movement (Zertal & Eldar 2009).

Although the efforts of the Tel Aviv Group to settle the freshly conquered territories started as a nongovernmental, grassroots social movement, several important MKs played a key role in greasing the wheels for the settler movement (Maggor 2015). Ariel Sharon, who served as Minister of Agriculture and head of the Ministerial Committee on Settlement Affairs in 1978, approved the Tel Aviv Group's expansion into what would become modern-day Ariel (Ministerial Committee for Settlement, August 17, 1978). This decision appears to have stemmed from a plan to expand the Jewish settlement of "Judea and Samaria," which he had presented to the Foreign Affairs and Defense Committee in 1977. In his view, the plan addressed the central problems facing Israel on its eastern border, including the rapidly expanding Palestinian population, which was perceived as a threat to the state's Jewish majority (Arieli 2008, 2017).

The plan was met with objections, however. For example, Rabin, then an MK, claimed that "building new settlement in the heart of Samaria could endanger the negotiations with Egypt," which followed President Sadat's 1977 visit to Israel (*Davar,* January 10, 1978). Furthermore, left-wing MKs on the Foreign Affairs and Defense Committee opposed the plan to establish settlements in the midst of highly populated Arab cities or villages (including the Tel Haris settlement). In response, Sharon reported back to the committee that the settlements were intended to be built in arid and undeveloped areas, and that there was no need to expropriate land for them (*Davar,* January 10, 1978).

Despite objections raised by members of the Labor Party in April 1978, the Ministerial Committee for Settlement and the World Zionist Organization decided to establish settlements in the West Bank and authorized the Tel Aviv Group to build in Tel Haris (Decision No. 414, Ministerial Committee for Settlement 1978). In the first stage, 120 housing units were built under the auspices of the Ministry of Housing (Ministerial Committee for Settlement, Decision No. 414, 1978). Like other contemporary Jewish settlements in the West Bank, Ariel was, and continues to be, considered illegal and occupied territory by most international organizations and agencies. However, unlike other settlements, Ariel was planned to be a metropolitan hub from the outset. Official documents of Ariel's first planning team clearly demonstrate that the process of establishing Ariel was organized and executed with the assistance and institutional support of the Israeli government and government ministries (Ariel planning team documents, Ariel Local Council 1982).

In fact, the active involvement of the official Israeli political and governmental infrastructure was integral to the establishment of Ariel. And this was not merely a right-wing endeavor. Although Ariel received its political backing largely from the political right, the Labor Party was also fundamental in bolstering the settlement enterprise by announcing support for the establishment of Ariel and another West Bank metropolitan center, Ma'ale Adumim (Benvenisti 1986). Among the prominent Labor Party supporters was Minister of Defense Shimon Peres. An initial meeting of Ariel's planning committee was also attended by architects, city planners, building inspectors, engineers, representatives of the Ministry of Defense, and representatives of the Jewish Agency. The planning documents indicate that the city was designed to be home to 120,000 settlers and to provide services to 300,000 people from the surrounding region (Planning team documents, Ariel Local Council 1982).

Interestingly, in contrast to other settlements, whose founding was driven by religious and ideological motives, Ariel's founders sought to establish the city on more secular grounds. Instead of citing religious goals, such as a yearning to build *Eretz Yisrael,* its founders sought to provide a solution to infrastructural inadequacies faced by all Israelis, such as the rising cost of living and exorbitant housing costs. Additionally, one of the goals of the city was to create more professional opportunities by developing industrial zones (such as Barkan), and granting tax breaks and other amenities to new industries (Maggor 2015; Weiss 2011).

According to Asher Weiner, former Director General of the Housing and Construction Ministry, Ariel and Ma'ale Adumim, along with Emmanuel and Kiryat Arba, were conceived of as large centers that would draw upon state resources for their overall development, in part for the purpose of reducing pressure on housing and economic opportunities in overcrowded Tel Aviv (Israel State Archives/109/Gal/14616/8). Parallel with the establishment of these centers, a "national and regional infrastructure system was set up [to ensure] a high level of service for these communities and to connect them to the centers of Israeli activity" in Tel Aviv and Jerusalem (Weiner in Magor 2015: 148). The large construction companies that operated in Israel during those years emphasized the involvement of the Ministry of Housing and Construction in marketing the housing projects. For example, a 1983 advertisement for the Rassco housing project in Ariel noted that "thanks to increased assistance [by the Housing Ministry], a young couple can purchase a three-bedroom apartment (72 m^2) with a balcony, valued at IS 1,750,000, for only IS 750,000" [equivalent to $57,100 in 2019] (in *Yediot Aharonot*, May 3, 1983).

The Ministry of Housing and Construction indeed promoted an aggressive development policy beyond the Green Line. Many millions of shekels were allocated to educational institutions and other public buildings, as well as housing. For instance, in 1983–1984, the ministry financed the construction of swimming pools and sports halls in the settlements of Ariel, Ma'ale Adumim, and Kiryat Arba (Maggor 2015). In addition to financial support from the Ministry of Housing, the settlement project also received funding from semi-governmental organizations, such as the Jewish Agency, which helped finance the absorption of 150,000 immigrants in the settlements (including Ariel) in 1990.

Although Ariel was established in cooperation with Gush Emunim, at the time of its foundation Ariel's primary support base came from secular individuals who were hawkish on security, on the grounds that its topography would give Israel a strategic advantage (Arieli 2017). The Tel Aviv Group's planning and tools also differed drastically from Gush Emunim's modus operandi, which ultimately played a central role in cementing Ariel's success. Pre-Ariel, Gush Emunim's strategy for establishing settlements mostly involved disorganized or decentralized religious groups, which settled land without government approval, without much planning, and almost without any thought to the quality of their future life (Lein & Weizman 2002: 1).

Ariel was planned to attract a secular population interested in high-quality housing and a lower cost of living. It was also meant to facilitate the absorption of many different populations. The formal change in status, from West Bank settlement to Israeli city, was a moment to celebrate for the settler movement. Perhaps most important, Ariel's new status definitively distinguished it from the other West Bank settlements and outposts in the eyes of ordinary (nonsettler) Israelis, making it seem both ordinary (and therefore not worth special attention) and immune to any potential evacuation in the event of successful negotiations with the Palestinians.

Ariel's focus on creating an infrastructure that could support large-scale immigration also highlights the forethought apparent in its planning stages, which contributed to the settlement's success. By making it a hub for immigration into Israel and providing a network that could cushion immigrants' otherwise harsh acclimation into Israeli society, Ariel appealed to citizens who did not necessarily share the religious-nationalist fervor of the proponents of the settler movement. Turning the city into a beacon for new immigrants played a pivotal role in fostering diversity in its population too, another key component in ensuring the city's success. The diversification of the population has lent a continued sense of moderation and legitimacy to Ariel, as opposed to other settlements, which tend to be rather homogenous. Most crucially, Nachman's vision for Ariel as a "city of the future" embraced the modern and urban incarnation of the settlement (*Ma'ariv*, December 27, 1985).

6.2 The Struggle over Growth and Expansion

Ariel has grown exponentially since its inception. However, from the outset it has faced the challenge of attracting a large enough population to fulfill its founders' dream. In order to develop from a local council to a full-fledged municipality, Ariel needed a dramatic uptick in population. In the 1990s, this need was met with a large influx of immigrants from the Soviet Union. These immigrants (and others) bolstered the population by 8,000 residents between 1989 and 1999, ultimately allowing its designation as a city (Weiss 2011). In 2014, they made up 35 percent of Ariel population.

The new residents of Ariel did not cite ideological or religious motives for moving to the West Bank. This was so even though the city's name – a symbolic name from the Bible used to describe Jerusalem and the Temple – itself conveyed religious ardor (Meisels 2015). Rather, settling in Ariel was an attractive option because "unlike [in] Israel, the apartments were plentiful and cheap" (*The Spokesman-Review*, April 9, 1990).

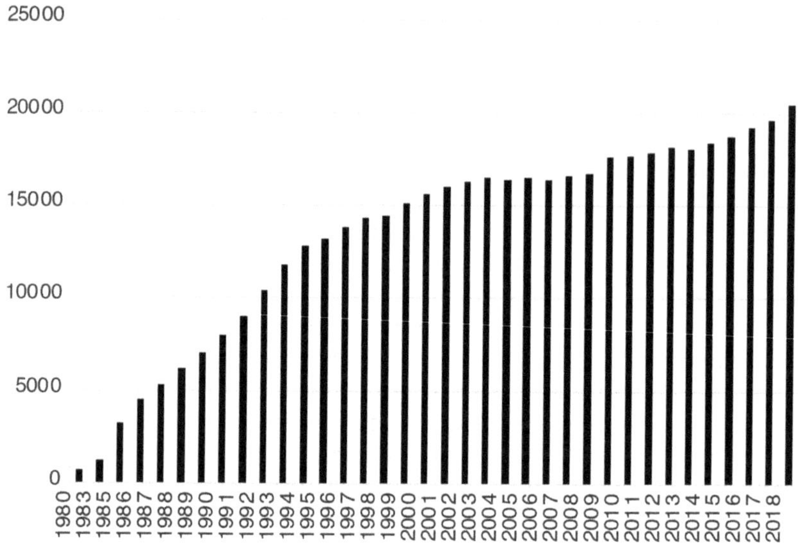

Figure 6.1 Population of Ariel, 1980–2018[2]

The appeal for new immigrants and residents lay in the city's affordable housing, relaxed and comfortable lifestyle, and positive attitude toward newcomers (Sharlin & Moin 2002). Ariel was eager to attract productive, highly educated people. Additionally, Ariel residents were very welcoming to the new immigrants, donating furniture and even helping them navigate the complexities of the bureaucracy (Weiss 2011). The local council offered Hebrew classes and schools absorbed the immigrant children. Furthermore, the newly established Barkan Industrial Park provided convenient professional opportunities, and the trans-Samaria highway provided accessibility to the Tel Aviv area.

Some experts have even suggested that the immigrants who moved to Ariel were unaware of its status as a settlement prior to arrival, and were uninterested in the implications when they did find out (Keinon 1990). Immigrants settled in Ariel mainly for economic motives, not ideological or security concerns (Moin & Sharlin 2005). Nachman, who was in the middle of his second term as mayor in 1990, reported that Russian immigration multiplied quickly: "The recent arrivals had been calling relatives in Moscow and Leningrad urging them to come and settle in Ariel" (*The Spokesman-Review,* April 9, 1990). Recent surveys confirm that Ariel residents prioritized quality-of-life considerations over ideological ones in their decision to live in the West Bank (Hirschberger & Hirsch-Hoefler 2018). By far the most attractive aspect of Ariel, for its residents, is the generous Israeli government economic incentives and subsidies. For example, in 2005 the government offered to subsidize as much as 90 percent of mortgages for people who wanted to purchase new apartments in Ariel – a practice unmatched for Israeli citizens living within the Green Line (Peace Now 2005).

The importance of a quality-of-life settlement like Ariel for the broader strategy for normalization of the settler enterprise is acknowledged by Daniella Weiss, a settler from the founders' generation and a former mayor of the settlement Kedumim:

> If we take Ariel as an example – people understand . . . that in a climate where there is little sense of a pioneering atmosphere, a blossoming into new spaces, where a Zionist spirit blows – the education will be better, and the atmosphere will be better. Quality of life is not just a green lawn, it is education, a good environment for the children, and good company (Interview 2007).

Hanan More, a real-estate agent in Ariel, suggested that the settlement's growing legitimacy may emanate from financial considerations: "From my real-estate perspective, Ariel is not part of Judea and Samaria. Ariel today is an Israeli city in every way. It's not like the small [West Bank] settlements . . . where, due to government decisions, they invested a lot of money in infrastructure and roads that lead to small communities" (*Haaretz*, July 25, 2014).

Despite the secular motivations that drove Ariel's initial growth, not all immigration to Ariel has been based entirely on secular considerations or quality of life. In 2005, Ariel saw an additional population spurt when a number of families, who were relocated after the disengagement from Gaza, decided to make Ariel their permanent home. For example, the Netzer Ariel neighborhood in Ariel contains twenty families who were evacuated from the settlement Netzarim in Gush Katif. More recently, the settler movement has also sent a group of nationalist-religious settlers to make their homes in Ariel, in order to strengthen the ideological basis of the city (Peace Now 2011).

Ariel has also begun to market itself as a resettlement point for the Anglo-Saxon community – the umbrella term popularly used in Israel for Jews immigrating from English-speaking countries, mainly the United Kingdom and the United States (Hirschhorn 2014). Pro-settler NGOs have facilitated campaigns aimed at strengthening the connection of the Anglo-Saxon community to the West Bank. For example, between 1980 and 1985 the Jewish Agency for Israel, the World Zionist Organization, Gush Emunim, Hadassah, and US–Jewish religious groups carried out a cooperative campaign, entitled Operation 1000, encouraging American Jews to move to the West Bank and the Gaza Strip (Hirschborn 2014). Currently, less than 5 percent of Ariel residents are US immigrants. Yet *Nefesh b'Nefesh* (Jewish Souls United), an NGO that supports new immigrants to Israel, refers to the English-speaking community of Ariel as "a close-knit one" and "warm and welcoming to new Olim who make Aliyah to Ariel."

Ariel residents constitute a unique group. They are similar to the broad category of quality-of-life settlers in their secular lifestyle (see Chapter 3). In 2018, 77.9 percent of Ariel's residents defined themselves as secular, 15.7 percent as religious, 3.4 percent as ultraorthodox, 1.8 percent as ultraorthodox-nationalist (*Hardal*), and 1.2 percent as some combination of secular and religious (Regev 2019). Most Ariel residents hold right-wing political views, as is typical for religious ideological settlers. For instance, in the September 2019 elections, some 80 percent of Ariel voters cast their ballots for right-wing parties: 44 percent voted for Likud, 22 percent for Israel Is Our Home, 11 percent for Yamina, and most of those remaining for smaller right-wing parties (Israeli Central Elections Committee 2019).[3] Somewhat surprisingly, recent surveys suggest that a large proportion of Ariel residents (72 percent) believe that retaining *Eretz Yisrael* is more important than keeping Israel democratic (Hirschberger & Hirsch-Hoefler 2016). However, surveys also show that more than half of Ariel residents (58 percent) would consider relocating to Israel in exchange for fair compensation, if the Israeli government were to evacuate the Jewish settlements (Hirschberger & Hirsch-Hoefler 2016).

Ariel's immigrant population helped not only to influence its personality internally, but also contributed to the external perception of Ariel as a typical metropolitan hub, untouched by the extreme ideologies of other settlements. By successfully portraying the city as a secular city with a high quality of life, the settler movement kept Ariel unblemished by the controversy that tinged the other settlements (Tal 1985).

Ariel's success has also been enabled by its consistent expansion, which has provided a solution to the shortage of living space in other Israeli cities in the center of Israel. Besides providing homes for the steady influx of new immigrants, the increase in construction projects has been integral to Ariel's growth, even if it flies in the face of international criticism of Israeli expansion in the West Bank. Despite harsh international and domestic criticism, there was a sharp uptick in the initiation of new construction projects in 2013, from less than 100 new projects the previous year to almost 500 (see Figure 6.2).

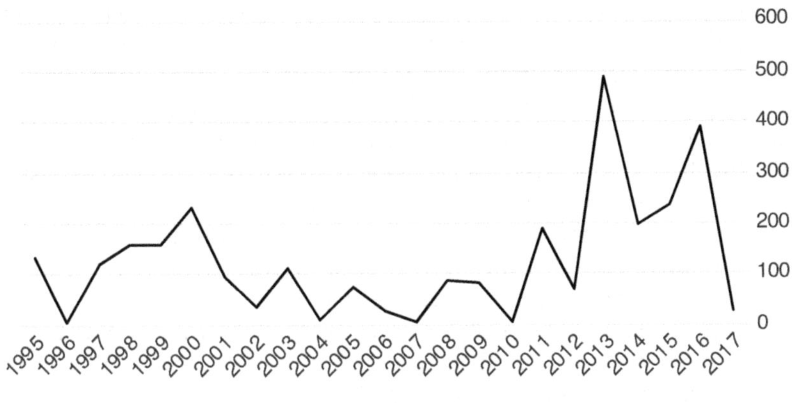

Figure 6.2 Construction starts in Ariel, 1995–2017[4]

This sharp rise in construction was justified by what appeared to be a population explosion linked to immigration over a twenty-year period. Ariel more than doubled in size, from 8,000 residents in 1990 to 20,000 today (see Figure 6.1). It is not entirely clear whether this is a convincing justification though. While the overall population did increase between 2001 and 2005, most of this was due to natural growth, that is, more births than deaths in each of those years except for 2002. During the same period, population growth due to immigration was negative, meaning that from 2003 to 2005 more people left Ariel than moved to live there.

In addition to government support, Ariel has also received a vast amount of support from domestic and foreign private citizens (influencers) for construction initiatives (*Haaretz*, November 21, 2017). For example, Zeev (Vladimir) Epshtein, a West Bank real estate baron with the rights to build 2,500 to 3,000 units in ten different settlements, started a vast building project in 2017 that spreads over 2 to 3 km (1.2 to 1.8 miles) in the northern West Bank area between Ariel and the Green Line (*Haaretz*, November 21, 2017). And US billionaire Sheldon Adelson has played a major role in Ariel's successful transformation into a metropolitan hub, including massive support for Ariel University (see below).

But informal networks, including foreign NGOs like American Friends of Ariel (AFA), have also helped to develop resources. Established in 1991, AFA has three central points of focus: (1) to develop resources for the community's infrastructure by bolstering programs in education, social welfare, immigrant absorption, culture, health, and religion; (2)

to provide educational materials about Ariel to the public and the domestic and foreign press; and (3) to strengthen the international support network of Ariel. American Friends of Ariel also claims responsibility for several of the central facilities and programs that have become emblematic of Ariel, such as Ariel University, the Ariel Regional Center for the Performing Arts, and the Field Center for Entrepreneurship. Although providing services and support exclusively for the city of Ariel and its residents, the organization is registered in Boca Raton, Florida, and is recognized by the US Internal Revenue Service (IRS) as a charitable organization. Its support has touched all sectors of life in Ariel, from externally facing programs, such as tourism, to public relations initiatives, such as *Talk17*, AFA's own media outlet that offers media content (in both English and Hebrew) promulgating a pro-Ariel narrative for viewers in Ariel, Israel, and abroad.

American Friends of Ariel also provides information on, and support for, a myriad of internally oriented programs in the areas of education and health and wellness. The organization runs educational programs that help non-Hebrew-speaking Israelis adapt and integrate, and fosters and maintains international connections and relationships. In 2017, AFA organized a two-week-long US tour in honor of Ariel's 40th anniversary, and AFA's "dedicated friends and supporters," which included events in locations such as Birmingham (Alabama), Dallas, Miami, and New York City. The organization's website emphasized that the tour served to "showcase decades of excellence and ingenuity in the capital of Samaria and the heart of Biblical Israel." Although the content of the tour was set against the biblical narrative of the settler movement, the choice to showcase Ariel's varied arts programs is characteristic of AFA's strategy of bolstering the settlement through community programs, as opposed to specifically religious programs.

The Ariel Development Fund (ADF) has also played a central role in the mainstreaming and normalization of Ariel as effectively a regular Israeli city. The ADF is an Israeli NGO that offers a host of programs and services aimed at strengthening Ariel's infrastructure. It also helps to bolster Ariel internationally, through partnerships and relationships with the pro-Ariel network abroad. Unlike AFA, which utilizes nongovernmental channels to strengthen Ariel across a range of sectors, ADF is a direct beneficiary of the Ariel Municipality. Although it is an NGO, its proximity to the municipal government indicates that it has exploited governmental avenues to advance its goal of entrenching Ariel in Israel.[5]

Support for Ariel also comes from the political sphere in Israel. Although Ariel's future was dubious at points, Israel's right-wing has remained steadfast in its commitment to the settlement. For example, in 2010, Prime Minister Netanyahu planted a tree in the settlement and declared Ariel "the capital of Samaria" and an "indisputable part of Israel" (*Jerusalem Post*, January 24, 2010). Other rightist politicians, most notably Uri Ariel, a Jewish Home MK and Minister of Agriculture and Rural Development, were particularly instrumental in facilitating the continuation and expansion of building in the West Bank, and specifically in Ariel. In 2013, amid heightened tensions surrounding the continued construction projects east of the Green Line, Uri Ariel announced that 1,200 tenders for residential complexes had been secured, 400 of which in Ariel (*Calcalist*, August 11, 2013). He was also vocal about his plans to expand the settlements in the West Bank, promising in 2013 to erect an additional 10,000 housing units.

Despite a building freeze, due to ongoing negotiations with the Palestinians, COGAT approved a Housing Ministry plan to build 839 new housing units in Ariel in 2014 (*Haaretz*, March 20, 2014). Uri Ariel faced backlash for his persistent support of construction in Ariel (and the area around Ma'ale Adumim) when Peace Now (2017) published a report indicating that he had transferred millions of shekels to building projects in the West Bank without PM Netanyahu's approval or knowledge. Israeli media relayed that he had contracted a city planner to advise on the construction of 3,200 new residential complexes in 2014, a year after Netanyahu had rejected a similar plan (*Ynet*, December 29, 2015). A further economic boost came in 2018, when, after some deliberation, it was announced that Ariel would be included in Israel's latest list of "national priority" areas, allowing it to benefit from land-development subsidies (*Haaretz*, November 26, 2018).

Politicians from Ariel have also played a pivotal role in the success, and normalization, of the settlement. Nachman, who led Ariel – first as local council head and then as mayor – from its inception until his death in 2013, was pivotal to Ariel's success. In addition to tirelessly advocating for Ariel in political and apolitical spaces, Nachman cultivated a framing narrative for Ariel that was based upon secular themes. Ian Lustick (1988) writes that Nachman accentuated the secular allure of Ariel, and thus placed particular emphasis on presenting Ariel as a high-end "yuppie" city that could offer a stylish, high-quality lifestyle for young, secular, and upwardly mobile individuals, who he himself seemed to epitomize. Nachman was also an ardent advocate for Ariel during times of crisis. He publicly voiced his outrage over the building freeze imposed in 2009, which he portrayed as an injustice against Ariel residents,[6] stating, "If they were to freeze the building of the Arabs within the Green Line, an unprecedented intifada would break out. We will do everything to protect ourselves and our children – this is not the Hilltop Youth, but ordinary people" (*Ynet*, January 15, 2008).

Political support continued to come not only from the right. Ariel's local paper, *Mabat L'Ariel* (November 20, 1993), reported that representatives from across the political spectrum had voiced support for Ariel. For instance, in 1993, Labor Party MK Yuli Tamir visited Ariel to oversee the absorption of immigrants, and even Meretz MK Shulamit Aloni visited the settlement to show her support for the Russian-speaking members of Ariel's active choir. Upon Aloni's visit, she was greeted by Nachman, who declared, "Arts and sciences have no borders, and that is why we are here."

Political elites have also pushed their pro-settlement agenda via government-backed infrastructural developments. Expansion of roads bypassing Palestinian towns shortened commute times to places like Ariel, which helped the settler population grow by over 40 percent from 1992 to 1996 (Shafir & Peled 2002: 181). Route 5, as it is sometimes colloquially known, is actually called Kvish Hotze-Shomron, or the Trans-Samaria Highway. The religious and cultural–historical symbolism of the name should not be overlooked; in calling the road the "Trans-Samaria" Highway, the state deliberately emphasized that the land it crosses is the heartland of biblical Israel (Enav-Weintrab 2009). The highway offers transportation from the heart of modern-day Israel (the Tel Aviv region) into the West Bank.[7] One checkpoint at the entrance to Ariel and another one on your way back to Israel are the only reminders for visitors that they have just been in the occupied territories.

In March 2018, Likud Transportation Minister Israel Katz announced that he planned to push forward with plans to construct a light rail system through the northern West Bank. The project, set to be completed by 2025, will connect Ariel to Israeli cities within the Green Line. Although Katz listed "reduction of traffic congestion" as the impetus for the project, this was not the first time he has attempted to develop the transportation infrastructure in the West Bank. In the past, Katz had announced a similar project that would connect the settlements of Etz Efraim, Elkana, and Oranit. The completion of such a railway system would mark a huge success for the settler project and is consistent with the movement's strategy of using the Israeli administration to benefit its enterprise.

Katz, in his announcement, sought to present the line from Ariel to central Israel as a necessity for West Bank residents, the majority of whom work in the Barkan Industrial Park, 25 km east of Tel Aviv. However, although the Transportation Minister may have tried to portray his project as a pragmatic solution to traffic flashpoints, settler movement representatives have lauded the light rail as a positive development toward their goal of establishing permanent and immutable settlements, notably Ariel. The new mayor of Ariel, Eli Shaviro, heralded the plan as "an important message regarding the importance of the continued development of the city." Even more blatantly, Samaria Regional Council Chairman Yossi Dagan pointed out that it would "make Samaria not only geographically, but also practically, the center of the country" (*Times of Israel*, March 15, 2018).

Another interesting component of the Ariel enterprise is the popular resistance it faces, both domestically and abroad. Although public criticism has consistently accompanied settler efforts at expansion, one must ask whether the pushback in this case did more to bolster the settlers' goals than to impede them. As the adage goes, "all press is good press" and it is interesting to observe the somewhat symbiotic relationship between pro-settlement activists and anti-settlement boycotts, which may well be mutually sustaining.

Ariel has faced widespread calls for boycotts during various stages of its development and expansion. For instance, in 2010, an Israeli group by the name of Courage to Refuse, along with a coalition of Israeli actors, directors, and producers, called for a boycott of the Ariel Regional Center for the Performing Arts (*Haaretz*, November 22, 2010; Peled 2013). They issued a statement to the Cameri, HaBima, Beit Lessin, Khan, Haifa, and Beer Sheva theaters, expressing their abhorrence of plans by the theaters to perform in Ariel (*Ynet*, August 27, 2010). The letter appealed to the boards to restrict their performances to theaters within the sovereign borders of the State of Israel and the Green Line. As the playwright Anat Gov, one of the signatories, stated:

> Just as a player who says I do not perform on Friday nights because I keep Shabbat will be respected and not fired, we should be respected too. The state must understand that for me it is like desecrating the Sabbath. Can you understand that this is the same pain that desecration of Shabbat causes you? (*Walla*, September 2, 2010).

The boycott led to an escalating dispute that drew in other Israeli and international artists and public figures on both sides. One hundred and fifty international actors, directors, and playwrights signed a letter supporting the boycott, including the prominent Israeli writer A.B. Yehoshua. However, dozens of artists from the Israeli Union of Performing Artists (IUPA/EMI) signed a petition against the boycott, claiming that "wherever an Israeli Jew sits under the laws of the State of Israel, and in Ariel in particular, he is entitled to enjoy performances of art and entertainment" (Nevo 2010). Political figures also weighed in. For instance, Israel Is Our Home MK Alex Miller argued,

> You can't have innocent, law-abiding, taxpaying citizens suffer from ugly political discrimination that prevents them from having access to arts and culture. This is collective punishment and a dangerous precedent that calls for discrimination under the guise of ideology (*Ynet*, August 28, 2010).

Nachman and Culture Minister Limor Livnat also argued vociferously against the boycott (*Haaretz*, November 14, 2010), while National Union MK Michael Ben Ari and Kahanist activist Itamar Ben-Gvir even interrupted a performance at the Cameri Theater in Tel Aviv, heckling actors who had supported the boycott (*Ynet*, August 27, 2010).

The Yesha Council responded swiftly and harshly to the boycott, stating that settlers represent "the best of the state's sons" whose activity protects "anti-Zionist leftist and refusenik actors." It called upon the country's theater boards to issue a clear response to the call for a boycott (*Ynet*, August 27, 2010). Its demand was met by public statements from the heads of theaters across the country. Dror Gerber of the Haifa Theater said, "The way to express protest and objection to the occupation is not via boycotting the residents of Ariel. The Haifa Theater was founded in order to bring the art of theater to all the citizens of the State of Israel." Tzipi Pines of the Beit Lessin theater responded, "I personally object to the occupation and support peace, but there are people living in Ariel who I respect, and I respect their desire to consume culture." And the board of the Cameri Theater stated, "We are against boycotts and will perform anywhere where there are people who desire culture and wish to see Israeli theater" (*Ynet,* August 27, 2010).[8]

These responses were a significant victory for the Yesha Council and for proponents of Ariel. Although they were born out of an effort to stifle the occupation, ultimately, by calling upon theaters to choose between boycotting the settler movement and supporting the individual rights of settlers (to have access to entertainment), they forced theater boards – many of whose members personally oppose the occupation – to publicly express their effective support for the Ariel cultural center, and by extension, for Ariel.

The settler movement has employed this strategy to capitalize on widespread public protest over the years. The interplay between the settler movement and anti-occupation advocates is mutually reinforcing, and supporters of the settlements have often managed to exploit the latter's efforts to their own benefit. Aside from their external effects, as in the case of the failed theater boycott, external criticism also serves to strengthen internal allegiances and efforts within the settler movement. In fact, this "us versus the world" mentality has served as the lifeblood of the settler enterprise and has time and time again reinvigorated and reified settler in-group loyalties. Protest against the settler movement thus has been instrumental in shaping its successes.

Indeed, there have been other cases where anti-settlement actions resulted ultimately in public reassertions of Ariel's legitimacy. In June 2019, disabled IDF veterans protested a decision by the McDonald's fast-food chain to not open branches in Israeli settlements, comparing its policy to the BDS movement. They erected large red signs at the entrances to McDonald's restaurants, stating in Hebrew, English, and Arabic: "Israelis please note! 'Area M' is ahead of you, which is controlled by a company that boycotts parts of Israel. By entering this area, you become a supporter of the boycott." In the same vein, Yossi Dagan, head of the Samaria Regional Council, wrote to Finance Minister Moshe Kahlon, Transportation Minister Israel Katz, and Airports Authority Director-General Yaakov Ganot that

> a company that boycotts part of the state must not be allowed to compete in government tenders. The State of Israel recently passed the 'Boycott Law' whose purpose is to impose sanctions that will help deal with internal and external elements that seek to harm and confiscate parts of the State of Israel and its citizens.

Dagan argued that

> McDonald's Israel, headed by Omri Padan, blatantly boycotts the citizens and territories of the State of Israel beyond the Green Line. This blatant boycott was not created casually, but officially and openly, as Omri Padan emphasized in 2013 when he vehemently refused to open a branch of the chain in [the West Bank settlement of] Ariel (*Ynet*, March 6, 2019).

An example of the subtle normalization of Ariel is its inclusion in the daily weather forecast maps used by most Israeli news outlets. The nation's weather maps rarely attract attention, but the decision to omit or include cities in daily weather maps can reveal popular political sentiments. Although Ariel is not inside Israel proper, and has not been annexed by Israel, all of Israel's largest daily newspapers as well as TV Channels 12 and 13 include it in their daily weather forecasts. Interestingly, these maps also do not show the Green Line, which delineates the border between Israel and the occupied West Bank.

One could argue that decisions over which cities to include in weather maps may be based on many considerations, none of them necessarily political (e.g., population size, regional centrality, popularity as destinations, etc.). However, maps are tools by which nations narrate their histories and ideologies (Wallach 2011). For instance, Christine Leuenberger and Izhak Schnell (2010: 833) have noted that

> the national religious camp produces maps that function to help Israeli drivers and tourists navigate the West Bank. On these maps, Israeli spaces extend into the West Bank through settlements, roads, and territorial control. These areas are superimposed on Palestinian territories that are frequently eliminated or transformed into danger zones. The maps' purposes dictate the selection and omission of data, which inevitably becomes tied to politics.

In short, the inclusion of Ariel in the daily weather maps, combined with the absence of the Green Line, is reflective of the public's figurative-political perception of Ariel with respect to its status. And indeed, Nachman openly admitted that he had for years applied pressure on editors and senior executives at all of Israel's main media outlets to include Ariel in their forecast maps (*Walla*, July 22, 2012). That this has not remained without consequences, can be seen in polls, where a staggering 56 percent of Israelis say they think Ariel is located inside the territory of the State of Israel and only 42 percent outside of it (Haklai 2017).

6.3 The Struggle over Ariel University: The Ultimate Legitimization

The transformation of the small College of Judea and Samaria into Ariel University, one of the newest Israeli universities, despite its location in the West Bank, is another testament to the settler movement's success in Ariel. Several actors from the institutional branch have noted the importance of building a university in Ariel as part of the strategy to normalize the settlements. For example, then Yesha Council Chairman Bentzi Lieberman noted, "It was decided to change the language and go toward Israelization of the Samaria area. The College of Judea and Samaria is a factor that blurs the Green Line in light of the fact that about 9,000 students study there and no one asks them what their political views are" (*Arutz Sheva*, October 15, 2006).

For Ron Nachman, the development of Ariel as a university town was a crucial part of his plan for the city from the beginning:

> In May 1979 I wrote a memo to [Former Prime Minister Menachem] Begin, laying out my vision to establish a city in Samaria. The city, I said at the time, should have a road accessing the highway, a connection to the sea or an airport, and a university. This does huge things for the branding of the city. The university

contributes to the city, increases demand for housing and encourages people to come and visit and see what Ariel is. A person who comes to study here becomes our fan. And then, instead of Ariel being a sleepy city, coffee shops and restaurants open up and it becomes a university city. Success brings more success (*Haaretz*, August 1, 2012).

Ariel University started as an extension of Bar Ilan University in Kedumim, about 12 km north of Ariel, and was referred to as the College of Judea and Samaria. According to the Ministry of Justice, it was founded in order to "provide academic education, whether in or outside the Land of Israel, based on developing and enhancing the spiritual connection to the Land of Israel, its history and its culture" (in Davidovitch & Iram 2014: 211). Ariel University's expansion and normalization, in many ways, mirror that of the settlement itself. In fact, the institution arguably has played the most important role in legitimizing the city in the mind of the broader Israeli public.

In 1982, the College of Judea and Samaria was moved to Ariel, just as the settlement was transitioning from prefabricated concrete buildings to permanent infrastructure. From the outset, the College set out to develop an academic experience by fostering a "spiritual connection to the Land of Israel" (Ministry of Justice 1982). In 1990, the College relocated to Ariel's Science Park and quickly became a cornerstone of the developing settlement. The relocation itself was emblematic of a shift in both branding and strategy. In terms of branding, the physical move was accompanied by a curriculum shift to focus on science and applied research, as well as an ambition to host scientific conferences (Davidovitch & Ram 2014). In terms of strategy, it changed from cultivating a spiritual connection to Israel to seeking expansion by catering to secular Jewish and Arab students in the West Bank. The college was granted university status in 2012.

Today, Ariel University is recognized as Israel's eighth publicly funded university and one of the largest employers in the West Bank. The university website claims a student population of 15,000 and 450 faculty members. Media reported that the university's student body also included several hundred Muslim Arab and Druze students in 2010 and 2011 (*Ynet*, October 17, 2010; *Arutz Sheva*, October 23, 2011). More recent data from the Council for Higher Education in Israel show that in 2018, only forty-four Arab students were enrolled in Ariel University, none of whom were pursuing a doctoral degree.

The story of the transformation of the College of Judea and Samaria into Ariel University bears deeper scrutiny. The college had set its eye on the goal of upgrading to university status as early as the late 1990s. In 1999, Minister of Education, Culture and Sport Yitzhak Levy (NRP) announced the government's decision to convert the college into a university at a meeting of the Council for Higher Education, based on its rapid development and growth (Davidovitch & Iram 2014). Levy stated that he would be heading a committee that would outline the suggested transformation process by the end of that year. His initiative was met with opposition, however. Critics from the Council for Higher Education felt that the move was antipodal to its policy of developing the capacity and quality of extant universities in Israel, as opposed to creating new ones. In any event, the 1999 Labor Party's victory interrupted these plans.

A more hospitable political environment came in 2005, when Likud's Limor Livnat became both Minister of Education and Chair of the Council for Higher Education. In April 2005, the Ministry of Education released a proposal stressing the value of converting the College of Judea and Samaria into a university. According to government documents from the time, "the government sees national importance in turning the College of Judea and Samaria in Ariel into a university, as a lever to strengthen the higher education system in the region" (Government Decision No. 3579, 2005). In May 2005, the proposal was approved and Livnat was placed in charge of pursuing the matter (*Ynet*, May 2, 2005).

The government's decision to convert the college into a university was met with criticism and pushback from within the bureaucracy as well as the public. The Council for Higher Education conveyed disappointment over the government's decision. Additionally, when Ariel first filed its application to transition its college into a university, opposition arose from the other universities in Israel on academic grounds (*Ynet*, April 26, 2005). The leaders of other Israeli academic institutions, such as the Technion and the Weizmann Institute, maintained that their opposition to Ariel's new status was staunchly apolitical (*Haaretz*, June 27, 2012). But while the initial opposition was ostensibly rooted in academic and pragmatic concerns, there was also huge pushback on ideological grounds. For example, more than 1,000 academic scholars signed a petition calling for the rejection of the college's upgraded status, on the basis that entangling the Israeli academic sphere with the "ideology of conquest" threatened the entire Israeli academic endeavor (*Haaretz*, March 25, 2012).

In 2007, in an effort to facilitate the change in status, the institution changed its name to "Ariel University Center of Samaria." But the Ministry of Justice issued a ruling rejecting that change the next year. The name change was only recognized officially in 2010, and two years later Ariel University received accreditation as a research university.

Although the decision to recognize Ariel University Center as a full-fledged university came against the recommendation of the Council for Higher Education, right-wing politicians, including Finance Minister Yuval Steinitz and Education Minister Gideon Sa'ar (who was also head of the Council for Higher Education at the time), heralded the move and expressed public support (*Haaretz*, July 17, 2012). Sa'ar even sent a letter to the chairman of the Judea and Samaria Higher Education Council commending the move.

The relationship between Israel's Council for Higher Education and the Judea and Samaria Education Council is a unique one. The latter was established in 1997, after the Council for Higher Education refused to discuss academic issues in the territories. Members of the Judea and Samaria Education Council are appointed by the IDF's Central Command and must be either current or previous members of Israel's Council for Higher Education (*Knesset Announcement,* February 12, 2018). The relationship between the two bodies was a major source of tension during the decision process with respect to Ariel University. The committee chairman for the planning and budget of the state's Council for Higher Education, Professor Manuel Trajtenberg, composed a letter to Professor Amos Altshuler, the chairman of the Judea and Samaria Education Council, calling the legitimacy of the panel to grant university status into question, alleging that the panel was subject to a conflict of interest, and had relied only on "narrow academic standards" to make their decision (*Haaretz*, July 17, 2012). Members of the Judea and Samaria Education Council conveyed their dismay at Trajtenberg's allegations.

Senior officials in the settlers' institutional branch also put pressure on the government during the dispute. As Yesha Council Chairman Danny Dayan said:

> It is clear that this decision is a cocktail that combines political bias . . . despite all this, with all due respect to this body [the Planning and Budgeting Committee of the Council for Higher Education], it is the government that needs to decide, and this is the test of Gideon Sa'ar and Netanyahu . . . The report, which was presented by serious professors, among them a Nobel Prize laureate, examined compliance with the conditions. The question is whether there is a government in Jerusalem (*Ynet,* July 5, 2012).

In 2018, the Knesset passed legislation placing Ariel University under the purview of the Council for Higher Education in Israel. Right-wing politicians celebrated the annexation of the university as one step closer to "applying Israeli sovereignty on Israeli communities in Judea and Samaria" (*Jerusalem Post,* February 12, 2018).[9] The legislation authorized not only the addition of Ariel University to the Council for Higher Education but also the inclusion of other academic colleges in the settlements, such as those in the Elkana and Alon Shvut settlements. The bill was put forward by Jewish Home MK Shuli Moalem-Rafaeli, and received the support of his party leader, Education Minister Naftali Bennet (*Haaretz*, February 12, 2018). But MKs from other parties, including the "centrist" Yesh Atid, supported the legislation too. In April 2019, the Council for Higher Education also approved the establishment of a medical school at Ariel University. The decision came just two months after the Council had voted against the establishment of the school. Education Minister Bennett celebrated the decision by stating that "a two-year battle ended with a great victory" (*Jerusalem Post*, April 11, 2019).

Finally, Ariel University's relationship to a support network in the international arena, most notably US donors, has also been vital to the success of the university, and thus of Ariel itself. The settler movement and its US supporters have taken advantage of particularities of the US tax system, which allows donors to contribute money to the settlements despite the fact that the US federal government considers them illegal. As such, various US donors support the university through the Friends of Ariel University, a nonprofit registered in the United States. In 2014, Sheldon Adelson announced a $25 million donation to Ariel University (*Haaretz*, June 24, 2014). When interviewed about his donation, the US billionaire commented, "the contribution to Ariel University is to build a Zionist wall instead of a crack, and I hope that the city of Ariel, the capital of Samaria, will grow and flourish in the wake of the expansion of the university" (*Haaretz*, June 24, 2014). Today, the new medical school is called the Dr. Miriam and Sheldon G. Adelson School of Medicine.

6.4 Conclusion

The successful establishment and (exponential) growth of Ariel was fostered by a network of interlocking organizations and individuals in Israel and the United States. Moreover, even popular opposition to the settler movement has played a role in Ariel's success. It is important to remember that Ariel worked in large part because it was never considered a political project in the traditional (ideological or expansionist) sense of the notion, by the state or the settlers (Weiss 2011). Indeed, to a great extent the government's support for Ariel derived from a need to resolve socioeconomic problems within the sovereign borders of Israel, such as the high cost of housing (and cost of living generally) in the Tel Aviv area. Ultimately, this approach to the Ariel project, which differentiated it from earlier settler projects, is what made it uniquely successful. As such, it was also used as a model for later government-initiated settlement, located close to the Green Line, and emphasizing quality of life.

If we take Ariel as a case study for what constitutes success for the settler movement, it becomes evident that active cooperation is required from all the following: key individuals, bureaucratic representatives, the Israeli government, political figures and parties, and NGOs and informal networks at the national and international level. There is no doubt that the secular-pragmatic composition of Ariel has helped it to garner political and public support as well. Different branches of the settler movement have performed different functions, often in close collaboration, and taken the lead at different stages of the settlement process.

The initiative comes from the networks, which create an illegal presence, a so-called fact on the ground, and defend it against eventual eviction attempts by the state – or return for a new attempt when evicted. As soon as the nucleus of the settlement is created, the networks try to mobilize support from the broader settler movement. The institutions and influencers within the state apparatus are expected to help institutionalize the new settlement, by getting it recognized de facto by the West Bank Civil Administration and, eventually, de jure by the Israeli state. In the meantime, the various branches fundraise within both national and international (mostly US) audiences, with the aim of making the settlement bigger and of normalizing it, so that it becomes harder for the state to deny it legalization, let alone dismantle it. Whenever there is public pushback, or lack of political support, the different branches play their separate, but coordinated roles: the institutions lobby parties and the government, as well as key state officials; the networks bring pressure in the streets; and influencers try to create broader public support through interventions in the media and other channels.

Over four decades after its founding, Ariel is quite dissimilar from other settlements. Both in its aesthetic and in its population, Ariel resembles any medium-sized city in Israel. However, as we see from our Ariel case study, success is not just defined as economic support and resources for infrastructural development or government incentives, but also as normalization in the eyes of the general Israeli public. Despite being located in the heart of the West Bank, Ariel has managed to achieve a status of exceptionalism in the collective consciousness. It is viewed simultaneously as a beacon of the settlements and an assimilated Israeli city. As explained by Bentzi Lieberman,

> We have one loss over the course of 30 years, but you need to remember that we are here. I am sitting and talking to you in the center of Samaria, in the Barkan

industrial zone. Where to the east of me is Ariel University, where there are 10,000 students – these are numbers that no one, even [then Meretz leader] Yossi Beilin, can deny. (Interview 2007).

Political leaders from across the political spectrum regard Ariel as an undeniable part of Israel. Where Israel Is Our Home has campaigned with the slogan "Ariel to Israel, Umm el-Fahm to Palestine" (see Chapter 4), Labor Party MK Eitan Cabel has said, "Show me the Israeli leader who will evacuate Ma'ale Adumim! Show me the leader who will get rid of Ariel! He doesn't exist!" (*Times of Israel*, May 29, 2018).

Still, even if Ariel constitutes a clear example of settler movement success in terms of the realization and normalization of a larger West Bank settlement, it falls well short of its original ambition. After all, it was planned as a city of 120,000 more than thirty-five years ago, but less than 20 percent of that target number lives in Ariel today.

7 A Case of Failure

The Gaza Disengagement

> We are confident that we will remain in our homes for many years, but there is no doubt that the willingness of the Prime Minister to even talk in this manner sounds an alarm for us and encourages the enemy. We have therefore embarked on this campaign today, which can succeed only if we are determined, strong, and believe in the justness of our cause. It would be appropriate for this verse to echo in our ears: "Let us arise and inherit the Land, for we are well able to overcome it."
>
> Avner Shimoni, Mayor of Gush Katif
> (*Arutz Sheva*, February 15, 2004)

In 2005, Israeli society was riven by the unilateral disengagement from Gaza, which involved the withdrawal of Israel's military presence in Gaza and the dissolution of the Israeli settlements in the region known as Gush Katif, along with four settlements in the northern West Bank. The evacuation of some 9,000 Jewish settlers from the twenty-five settlements, and in particular the complete removal of an Israel's presence from the Gaza Strip, was a watershed moment in Israeli history, both because it represented a response to domestic and international calls for a peaceful solution to the Israeli–Palestinian conflict, and because it flew in the face of the belief that settlement expansion was the fulfillment of a messianic prophecy – a belief that had driven the settler movement for decades (Eiran 2009; Shechory & Laufer 2011; Zertal & Eldar 2007).

The motivations of the settlers in the Gaza settlements were more than just strategic or tactical. Rather, their connection to the land was faith-based and deeply interwoven with expressions of a spiritual connection to *Eretz Yisrael*. Their ideology framed their mission as one of divine providence and their entire political platform was therefore negotiated through a discourse of "total sacralization" (Weisburd & Lernau 2006: 37). The withdrawal was thus not only significant for its historical political implications for Israel proper, but also for the settlers themselves, most notably the religious Zionist camp.

Indeed, Yaacov Bar-Siman-Tov (1994, 2009) points out that, from June 1967 onward, any attempt to sever Israel's connection to any occupied territories, whether through agreement or unilateral withdrawal, has triggered not only discussion about Israel's national or security interests, but soul-searching with respect to the country's national identity. This can be seen even in the withdrawal from the Sinai Peninsula, to which Israel agreed as part of its peace agreement with Egypt in 1979. The Sinai does not lie within the borders of *Eretz Yisrael*, as delineated in the Bible, and was never considered part of the ancestral homeland of the Jewish people. The violent opposition to evacuation of the Sinai settlements, which culminated with the traumatic handover of the settlement of Yamit in April 1982, can therefore be seen as an attempt to create a crisis that would preempt any future withdrawals.

Israel's 2005 disengagement from Gaza is the clearest, and most painful, case of failure for the settler movement to date. Even if Gaza is less central to its core ideology, and holds much less religious-nationalist significance than "Judea and Samaria," the settler movement was vehemently opposed to the disengagement and fought it tooth and nail. As such, it offers a case study in how the three branches of the movement, alone and in interaction, contributed to the failure to prevent it.

7.1 The Disengagement Plan

Although the disengagement was carried out under the auspices of Prime Minister Ariel Sharon, its inception can be traced to Prime Minister Yitzhak Rabin. According to Neill Lochery (2007), much of Rabin and the Labor Party's election success as far back as 1992 was grounded in a fledgling version of the disengagement policy. Following the murder of a young Israeli girl by a Palestinian man from Gaza in May 1992, Rabin asserted that Likud wanted to "bring Gaza to Tel Aviv," and that to avoid this it was necessary to "take Gaza out of Tel Aviv by creating two distinct entities so the populations could avoid points of friction" (Lochery 2007: 2). Ultimately, this position was instrumental in solidifying Labor's ascendancy, and contributed to the ratification of the Oslo Accords in 1993.

The proposal was revived by Prime Minister Sharon in December 2003, when he endorsed the plan at the Fourth Herzliya Conference.[1] Sharon, who had become known as the father of the settler movement, establishing dozens of settlements with the aim of preventing Palestinians from maintaining territorial contiguity, had seemingly experienced an extreme change of heart. Yet his support for unilateral disengagement did not arise in a vacuum, but rather within the context of the Second Intifada (also known as the Al-Aqsa Intifada). Although diplomatic efforts had been made to mitigate tensions, such as the Quartet on the Middle East's Road Map for Peace (see Chapter 2), they did little to alleviate the friction. The Road Map was put forth by the EU, Russia, the UN, and the United States as "a starting point toward achieving the vision of two states, a secure State of Israel and a viable, peaceful, democratic Palestine ... It is the framework for progress towards lasting peace and security in the Middle East" (US State Department, July 16, 2003). Contrary to these optimistic objectives, the publication of the proposal was met with hostility. Hamas rejected the plan outright and hardline Palestinians responded with a series of terrorist attacks against Israeli targets. Israel then responded, as per its longstanding policy, by demolishing the family homes of those believed to have been involved (*Aljazeera*, April 30, 2003).

There has been much analysis and speculation as to Sharon's motivations (Shragai 2015). The disengagement was completed in September 2005, and only a few months later in January 2006, Sharon suffered a stroke, which left him in a permanent vegetative state until his death eight years later. He was therefore never able to publicly discuss or reflect on his motivations and intentions from a retrospective standpoint, with an eye toward either filling in the historical record or shaping his legacy for the future. However, while Sharon's inner thoughts remain unknown, his intentions were likely neither to end the occupation nor to usher in an era of peace (Zertal & Eldar 2009). Rather, scholars point to his desire to shift the power dynamic between Israel and the Palestinian Authority, which had been relatively static since the start of the Al-Aqsa Intifada in 2000 (Levy 2007). Bernard Avishai (2014) noted that, although Sharon's statement at the Fourth Herzliya Conference was "moving," his seemingly extreme change of heart, coupled with his newfound and unprecedented use of the word "occupation" to describe the Israeli presence in the West Bank and Gaza, came out of a desire to preclude any future peace deal, rather than set the framework for one, as Sharon had claimed.

Other scholars have noted that Sharon's interest in disengagement from Gaza paralleled the interests of the IDF (Bar-Siman-Tov 2009). That is, removing the settler population from heavily Palestinian-populated areas and designating a defined border between Israel and the Palestinian Authority would inherently reduce confrontations between IDF soldiers and Palestinian civilians. As such, the proposed withdrawal from Gaza and the four settlements in the northern West Bank was part of a broader plan that also included the construction of a separation barrier or security fence, which would divide heavily

Palestinian and Jewish-populated areas of the West Bank. Discussing his support for the separation barrier, Sharon said:

> The demographic consideration played an important role in determining the route of the separation barrier, due to concern about annexing hundreds of thousands of Palestinians who might link up with the Israeli Arabs. It is impossible to control densely populated areas for extended periods without ultimately granting their residents rights (*Haaretz*, April 22, 2005).

In a letter to US President George W. Bush in April 2004, Sharon wrote that the Israelis had no negotiating partner for the peace process on the Palestinian side, and argued that the Palestinian leadership had taken no steps to further the goals delineated by the Road Map (Israel Ministry of Foreign Affairs 2004). The letter also highlighted various security measures that Sharon asserted would bolster the economic situation of both the Israelis and the Palestinians. Finally, in both his 2004 letter to Bush and his 2013 conference speech, he emphasized that the continuation of Palestinian terrorism was a major catalyst for his decision to disengage from Gaza. At the Fourth Herzliya Conference, Sharon stated

> The purpose of the Disengagement Plan is to reduce terror as much as possible, and grant Israeli citizens the maximum level of security ... These steps will increase security for the residents of Israel and relieve the pressure on the IDF and security forces in fulfilling the difficult tasks they are faced with. The Disengagement Plan is meant to grant maximum security and minimize friction between Israelis and Palestinians (Herzliya Conference, December 18, 2003).

Sharon also emphasized that the planned disengagement, along with the construction of the separation barrier, would not only reduce terrorist attacks on Israel but would also bolster Israel's control over areas that would "constitute an inseparable part of the State of Israel in any future agreement" (Israel Ministry of Foreign Affairs 2003). Although Sharon did not specify which blocs he meant, it is evident from this remark that strengthening certain settlements in the West Bank, even while abandoning others, was part and parcel of his larger plan.

Nonetheless, Sharon's call for disengagement was unforeseen and came as a shock to the settler movement, the Israeli public and his own party. Likud ministers questioned his loyalty to his mandate, particularly given that he won the 2003 elections on "his reputation and Likud's defense and security platform" (Klein & Ansell-Brauner 2005). Political opponents of his plan, such as Netanyahu and Natan Sharansky, pressured Sharon to hold a national referendum to prove he still had a mandate. Fearful that the Disengagement Plan would fail in a national referendum, Sharon opted to seek a majority vote in a party referendum (among 193,000 registered Likud Party members) in May 2004 instead.

The Yesha Council was thrown off guard by Sharon's announcement of the Likud party referendum. Shaul Goldstein, Chair of the Gush Etzion Regional Council, expressed concern that the movement was unprepared to argue its case with Likud functionaries, with whom the settlers had little in common – he likened it to being thrown onto an unfamiliar playing field with no training (Roth 2005: 174). Nonetheless, the Yesha Council and its supporters vigorously campaigned against the referendum, canvassing door-to-door, protesting and calling on Likud members to vote against the plan, which they named "the expulsion plan" (Tsfati & Cohen 2005). They divided the country into regions and mobilized activists in each one. On the day of the referendum itself, businesses and schools were closed, and schoolchildren were dispatched to rally support at intersections, offices, and synagogues. Further aid came from the ultraorthodox population. For instance, several days before the referendum, the renowned rabbi and kabbalist Yitzhak Kaduri threw his weight behind the settlers. Followers of the Lubavitcher rabbi distributed thousands of leaflets to Likud members, declaring that the rabbi had ordered followers to vote "no" (Roth 2005). Despite poll results showing that a majority of Likud members, and the broader Israeli public, supported the plan (Tsfati & Cohen 2005), Likud members rejected the plan by a majority of 56 percent.

Bent on seeing his plan come to fruition, Sharon reformulated it into legislation that included civilian and military provisions as well as compensation for the settler communities affected by the withdrawal. Furthermore, he took a strong-arm approach by warning ministers that they would be fired from their government positions if they did not vote in favor of the disengagement (*Haaretz*, July 8, 2005). Sharon's technique ultimately culminated in the dismissal of two National Union ministers (Avigdor Liberman and Benny Alon) and the resignation of two NRP ministers (Effi Eitam[2] and Yitzhak Levy), leaving Sharon with a minority government.

In June 2004, the plan was approved by the government (Government Decision no. 1996), but with the footnote that each settlement to be evacuated would be voted upon individually. The preliminary Knesset vote passed in October 2004, with sixty-seven in favor, forty-five against, seven abstentions, and one absentee (Knesset Meeting no. 173). In February 2005, the Knesset approved the "Implementation of the Disengagement Plan Bill," also referred to as the "Compensation–Evacuation Bill," the purpose of which was to regulate the following matters in order to implement the Disengagement Plan:

(1) The evacuation of Israelis and their assets from the Gaza Strip and the northern Samaria area, in accordance with government decisions; (2) The

granting of fair and appropriate compensation, under the special circumstances of the case, from the State Treasury, to those entitled thereto under this Law; (3) Assistance to persons entitled to do so under this Law in the evacuation process and in the transition to new places of residence and employment; (4) Relocation of groups of settlers and relocation of cooperative settlement societies to alternative places, in accordance with the provisions of this Law (Implementation of the Disengagement Plan Bill 2005; Knesset Meeting no. 223).

The Knesset deliberations on the Compensation–Evacuation bill took many hours and aroused many reservations. Ultimately, the version of the law that was passed differed fundamentally from the bill prepared by the Ministry of Justice and submitted by the government, to the benefit of the settlers. MKs Michael Eitan (Likud), Yitzhak Levy (NRP), Avraham Shochat (Labor), and Haim Oron (Meretz–Yahad), in particular, succeeded in amending many sections of the law.[3] Interestingly, even left-wing politicians and parties went out of their way to help Gush Katif evacuees. At the government level, instability within Sharon's center-right base and the constant calls for a national referendum by Netanyahu led to the formation of a coalition with the Labor Party in January 2005. Israel's Supreme Court also became involved, increasing the compensation offered from its original base.

On the day of the government vote, demonstrations took place in front of the Prime Minister's Office. Among the demonstrators were settlers from Gush Katif as well as from groups like Women in Green, calling upon Likud ministers to vote against the Disengagement Plan. At the same time, members of the Likud Central Committee plotted to convene the Likud Convention, with the aim of ousting Sharon from his post as Likud chairman (*The Marker*, June 6, 2004). In a final stop-gap measure, a small group of Likud ministers even introduced a bill to delay the disengagement plan, but it failed by a wide margin (seventy-two votes to thirty-nine).

There was a widespread expectation among the general Israeli public that the withdrawal would be met with violent responses from the evacuees. A survey conducted around a year before the withdrawal found that 60 percent of the Israeli public believed there was a very high chance of violence against public figures and political leaders who supported the disengagement.[4]

7.2 The Actual Disengagement

The Disengagement Plan mandated the military-facilitated evacuation of twenty-one Israeli settlements in Gush Katif and four Israeli settlements in the West Bank (see Figure 7.1).[5] Sharon informed the directly affected Israeli citizens that they had to leave their settlements by Monday,

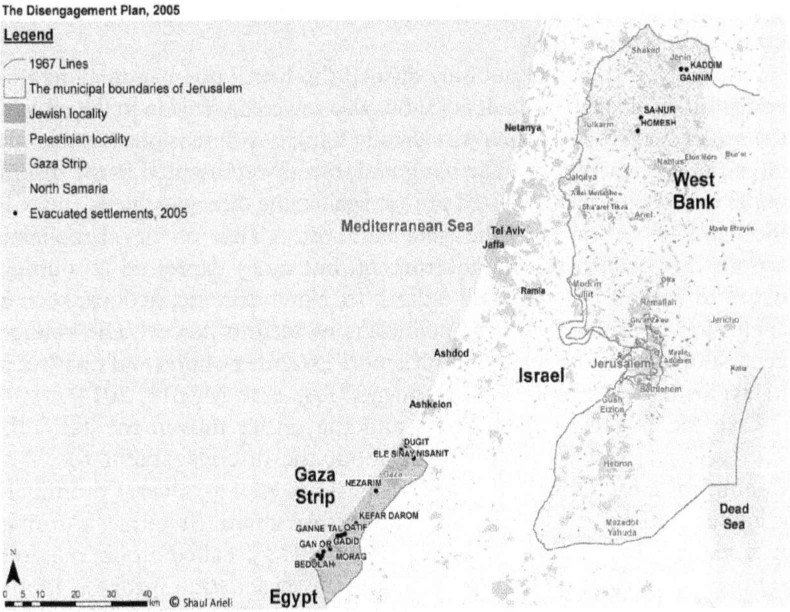

Figure 7.1 The disengagement plan, 2005[6]

August 15, 2005, or they would be forcibly evicted.[7] On July 13, 2005, Sharon officially designated Gush Katif a closed military zone. Israelis with documented residency in Gush Katif were permitted to enter the area for the next forty-eight hours. Leading up to August 15, many Gush Katif leaders attempted last-ditch attempts to stave off the imminent forced evacuation, such as appealing to international bodies for sovereign recognition. All measures failed and the IDF-led evacuations began that morning.

As the withdrawal had drawn closer, illegal protests of thousands of people – and two incidents of self-immolation – reaffirmed the media doomsday predictions of disorder (*Haaretz*, September 1, 2005; *Ynet*, August 18, 2005). However, despite the brimstone reporting and the terrifying images proliferated by the media, the withdrawal itself was relatively peaceful. While the vast majority of the settlers did not leave voluntarily, but were forcibly evacuated, images from the scenes portrayed them as "offering little more than passive resistance to the Israeli security forces" (Weinburd & Lernau 2006: 40). With the exception of a few buildings, mainly agricultural, Israel demolished all infrastructure that was left behind from the former residents immediately after the evacuation (Eiran 2009)

The Gaza withdrawal not only divided the Israeli population along pro- and anti-disengagement fault lines, but also sowed dissension in the ranks of the settler movement, which was already fraught with tensions between the old and new generations. The old guard, mostly represented in the institutional branch, avidly supported protest against the disengagement, but toed the line when it came to the state's authority. They endorsed moderate actions that challenged the government, but rarely expressed an outright desire to engage in large-scale radical, let alone extreme, actions, such as aggression or violence against politicians or security forces. The younger generation, on the other hand, took a more extreme position and was "ready to lay down their lives for the settlements" (*Haaretz*, May 13, 2013).

Like the Israeli political arena and the settler movement itself, the IDF was plagued by factionalism about the disengagement too. The Rabbinical Council of Judea and Samaria as well as several prominent religious-nationalist rabbis, like Rabbi Avraham Shapira, a former Ashkenazi Chief Rabbi of Israel (1983–1993), called upon religious soldiers to refuse orders to facilitate the evacuation process in the settlements (*Haaretz*, June 27, 2004). The reverberations of these declarations rippled throughout intersections of the religious and military worlds, most notably the Yeshivot Hesder. However, while many religious military officials publicly expressed their dismay at the withdrawal, few went as far as to encourage soldiers to refuse orders. Ultimately, the number of soldiers who actually refused to serve in the evacuation was small. An IDF report, issued almost a year and a half after the withdrawal, listed just 163 cases of insubordination (among conscripts, officers, and reservists) before and during the disengagement (*Haaretz*, December 19, 2006).[8]

Of the sixty-five soldiers who faced trial in disciplinary court, forty-six received a punishment that included incarceration (*Haaretz*, December 19, 2006). Many of the sentences meted out were relatively light, as in the case of Captain Moshe Botivia of the combat engineering brigade, who had refused orders to block an access road leading to the settlements of Homesh and Sa Nur in North Samaria. It turned out that Botivia was a resident of the Kiryat Arba settlement, a fact that the presiding military judges took into account when they sentenced him to a reprimand on his record and suspended jail time (*Haaretz*, December 19, 2006). This case highlights the complexity of the broader relationship between the IDF, as a people's army, and the settler movement, particularly given the growing relevance of religious-nationalists and settlers within the IDF.

A somewhat different perspective suggests that the relatively smooth operation of the withdrawal derived from the IDF's ability to leverage the large religious-nationalist population within its ranks.[9] For instance, Yagil Levy (2007) argues that the IDF was able to convince settlers who might otherwise have led violent resistance to the evacuations that doing so would undermine their cause by politicizing the IDF. This was also apparent in the reactions of the Jewish international public. As explained by Shulamit Melamed, the founding head of *Arutz Sheva*, "For Jews who live abroad, the Gush Katif crisis was very difficult and confusing. For them, we represented those people who go *against the army*, and it was really hard and confusing for them to go against the army . . . it made them less likely to donate to us" (Interview 2007, our emphasis).

7.3 The Disengagement and the Three Branches

All three branches of the settler movement vehemently opposed and resisted the Disengagement Plan and the actual disengagement from Gaza. However, they exhibited very different approaches and specific responses. We examine first the institutions, then the networks, and finally the influencers. As will become clear, the disengagement laid bare simmering divisions within the broader settler movement, particularly, but not exclusively, between the institutions and the networks.

The institutional branch, most notably Amana, had a particularly complex relationship with the Disengagement Plan. One of Amana's principal leaders, Ze'ev (Zambish) Hever, had established an intimate relationship with Ariel Sharon during Yitzhak Shamir's second government (1986–1992), which was predicated on building developments and outposts in the settlements (*Haaretz*, July 11, 2002). Under Sharon's guidance, the settlements benefitted from an immense construction boost. Amana thus found it hard to confront the reality of imminent evacuation under a Sharon government.

Initially, the institutions based their opposition primarily upon security considerations, including the dangers inherent in a unilateral withdrawal and an evacuation of settlements under fire. Their message drew on remarks by prominent figures within the Israeli security establishment, such as Moshe Ya'alon, the head of the IDF General Staff, who had claimed that a unilateral withdrawal would give "a tailwind to terror" (*NRG*, February 11, 2004). Other naysayers included the head of the General Security Service, Avi Dichter, and the head of the Intelligence Directorate, Major General Aharon Ze'evi-Farkash. The latter expressed concerns similar to those of Ya'alon: "The Palestinians view Sharon's plan [for disengagement] from the Gaza Strip as a victory for terror, and this could be a catalyst for an increase in terrorist activity in Judea and Samaria" (*NRG*, February 11, 2004).

After Sharon's formal announcement of the Disengagement Plan, the Yesha Council embarked on a different framing, introducing a new slogan, "Uprooting Settlements – Ripping Our People Apart." Similarly, in the run-up to the Likud referendum of May 2004, it ran a door-to-door campaign under the heading "Brothers Do Not Break Up," which aimed to reach the homes of all Likud members to convince them personally to oppose the plan. Volunteers in the campaign were also asked to proactively approach members of their extended families who might be Likud members. To ensure consistent and effective messaging, the Council provided volunteers with a booklet detailing the mission as well as operational guidance and talking points (Roth 2005).

In addition to promoting primarily moderate actions, the institutional branch continued to forthrightly articulate its support for the state (Newman 2005). Generally speaking, the Yesha Council's activities operated on two levels, one more collaborative, one more confrontative. Regarding the former, the Yesha Council participated actively in the formal political arena, primarily targeting the right-wing political parties, which naturally supported the expansion of the settlements. The NRP, for example, vehemently opposed the disengagement on both nationalist and security grounds, seeing it as a potential step toward the establishment of a Palestinian state, and calling upon Israel to annul its commitments to the Oslo Accords.

There were also attempts to persuade members of the Likud Party Central Committee to support the struggle. A few settlers were sent to the Knesset to drum up support. Gush Katif Mayor Avner Shimoni, among others, spent many hours laboring in the Knesset, but he had little success. In October 2004 only seventeen of the forty Likud MKs opposed the disengagement (Knesset Meeting no. 173). The settler movement worked in conjunction with lobbies and special interest groups that were in direct contact with the political parties. For instance, Jewish Leadership (*Manhigut Yehudit*), a faction and lobby within Likud, argued that Sharon's position represented a defection from Likud policy and that the disengagement would advance the establishment of a Palestinian state, an outcome that the group maintained was antithetical to Jewish values.

The Yesha Council even sought to enlist elite support for its more confrontative protest activities, in particular within Likud. For example, it recruited no less than twenty MKs from the governing coalition, four of them active ministers, to appear at a large demonstration in Rabin Square in January 2004. Yesha Council leaders also met with MKs and ministers and organized tours of Gush Katif for influential politicians, with the aim of expanding the circle of opposition to the planned disengagement among the political elite (Roth 2005, 2014).

The second level of its protest activity was more confrontational. In this respect, the Yesha Council did what it was used to doing, organizing large-scale civil protests. The idea was to mobilize support at the mass level, by means of demonstrations and mass rallies, to put pressure on the government and its supporting parties. It quickly set in motion an extensive and well-organized campaign, blanketing the country with billboards and flyers and planning marches and rallies that drew up to 200,000 people.[10] The size of the demonstrations, as well as the regular presence of prominent Likud politicians among the protesters, was meant to show Sharon the magnitude of the opposition within both the Israeli public and his own Likud party (*Ynet*, January 11, 2004). The nationwide campaign featured Sharon's own past statements condemning proposed settlement evacuations. For example, just two years earlier, Sharon had argued that the evacuation of Netzarim would "only encourage terrorism and increase the pressure on us" (*Arutz Sheva*, November 30, 2003).

At the ground level, the Yesha Council's activities were run from an operational headquarters in Gush Katif. According to Bentzi Liberman, head of the Yesha Council at the time, "These battle headquarters are the most well-oiled organization in the world." The "battle headquarters" were formally established in February 2004, just two months after Sharon's announcement of the plan at the Fourth Herzliya Conference, when a hundred youngsters embarked on a four-day march to Jerusalem from Gush Katif. According to one of the march organizers, "Everyone will do his part – and together we will continue to march forward!" (*NRG*, January 16, 2005). Wallerstein described the headquarters as follows: "There were group leaders, and there were teams of volunteers, and coordinators who were paid for the period of work and then went home, it was usually guys in their twenties, not yet in their thirties, and they were the skeleton of the struggle" (Interview 2007).

Overall, the "battle tactics" employed mainly moderate actions, including grassroots campaigns and demonstrations. Activists hung banners, protested at intersections, held demonstrations in front of the prime minister's house, set up information booths, held conferences and solidarity rallies, and distributed Gush Katif produce. In July 2004, they also organized an unprecedented human chain, in which approximately 13,000 protesters linked hands to form an unbroken chain that stretched over 90 km (ca. 56 miles) from the northern part of the Gaza Strip to the Western Wall in Jerusalem (Lev-On 2010). The Gush Katif headquarters further organized operation "One Million on the Map," which brought visitors to Gush Katif under the guidance of dozens of settler volunteers. The settler movement embraced a strategy, dubbed "settle in the people's hearts" (with the goal to be indistinguishable from Israel), that included a "face-to-face campaign" in which thousands of yeshiva students traveled to metropolitan centers and explained the alleged dangers of the plan (Roth 2005).

However, Dror Vanunu, then-director of the Gush Katif Development Fund, the fundraising arm of the opposition movement set up by the Yesha Council, described the fundraising difficulties of the movement,

> We're still mostly a story that's just beginning. Relatively speaking, we have very marginal promises. It won't be easy to raise money. We don't have an infrastructure here, we don't have a database of friends and names [of potential donors]. All told, we were caught at a pretty early stage. Our infrastructure is in its infancy, both here and abroad (*Haaretz*, February 16, 2004).

The disengagement also marked the first instance in which the institutional branch supported more radical actions, such as civil disobedience, although it did not endorse violence. For example, Wallerstein, in what became known as the "Wallerstein letter," encouraged the public to "violate the transfer law en masse and be ready to pay the price of mass imprisonment." He stated that he "was not afraid to go to jail . . . and that we are obligated to pay this price in order to oppose, in a *nonviolent* manner, the immoral crime of forcibly uprooting Jews from their homes" (*The Marker*, December 19, 2004, our emphasis). The use of nonviolent civil disobedience marked a convergence in terms of tactics between the institutional and network branch, while the tactical decision to refrain from violence served to ingratiate the mainstream settler organizations with right-wing parties.

However, this kind of moderate and even radical political action, while completely in line with the settler movement's ideology, proved to be too cooperative for some of the networks. While the institutional branch explicitly rejected violence, the impulse by some network groups to take up arms in the face of the evacuation contributed to the further factionalization of the settler movement. The newer and younger settler networks placed more discursive space between themselves and the rest of society, by positioning themselves as antipodal to their predecessors. This "internal disengagement" marked the starting point of their rejection of the older generation's respect for the constraints and boundaries of the legal system (see below).

For example, the Yesha Council engaged in peaceful protests like the "orange protest," adopting the color of the flag of the Gaza Regional

Council. Orange ribbons were tied to cars and houses and opponents of the Disengagement Plan wore orange clothes, carried orange bags, and used the color at demonstrations and on billboards (Newman 2005).[11] However, some networks ventured beyond what was perceived as acceptable framing, borrowing imagery and symbols from the Holocaust. They donned orange stars, wrote identity numbers on their arms, and referred to the withdrawal as "forced expulsions," "transfer of Jews," and "ethnic cleansing" (Newman 2005).

In addition to the emergence of these younger and more volatile networks, which undermined potential national and international support, the settler movement continued to fragment in other ways too. Grassroots networks sprang up with the express intent of challenging the mainstream leadership of the Yesha Council, which consistently embraced approaches aimed at appealing to the widest possible base while working with (as opposed to against) the Israeli government. Among these informal networks, Women in Green, This Is Our Land (*Zo Artzeinu*), and Professors for a Strong Israel deliberately and visibly countered the leadership in the institutional branch, often with the financial support of European and US patrons (Newman 2005).

One of the defining attributes of the networks is their lack of a rigid bureaucratic management structure, which means that their actions often lack organizational cohesiveness. As Women in Green leader Nadia Matar explained, "I feel that there was not enough organization and that we could have achieved much more" (Interview 2007). This also means that much of what we know about their activities during the period leading up to the disengagement comes from secondary sources, rather than official group statements or positions. Reports of their behavior come mainly from media outlets, in particular those working with the settler movement, such as *Arutz Sheva*. These reports make no effort to maintain standards of journalistic objectivity.[12]

The willingness of the networks to act in opposition to the state reflects the overall good cop/bad cop relationship between the formal and informal branches of the settler movement. While the institutional branch largely tried to collaborate with the Israeli government, the networks took a confrontational stance. They thereby acted also like a kind of watchdog of the Yesha Council, in an effort to safeguard the ideological-territorial principles of the settler movement. As Jewish Heart Chair Rabbi Gadi Ben-Zimra put it, "I see myself as responsible for the fact that the fire is always burning on the alter and never goes out, that there is always agitation" (Interview 2007).

Different networks challenged the government at differing degrees of intensity, mostly corresponding to their different ideologies. For example, the Hilltop Youth categorically framed its actions in *defiance* of the state. It deliberately infiltrated Gush Katif once it was declared to be closed military territory in order to resist the evacuation. Because of the group's refusal to cooperate or compromise, and frequent outright animosity toward official Israeli institutions, it has often faced hostility, even from within more moderate groups of the movement. Hilltop Youth leader Avri Ran revealed this dynamic in a rare statement in a Jerusalem court in 2005, where he explained that his group's tactics faced censure and reproach from the Yesha Council:

> The phenomenon was difficult for the members of the Yesha Council. After years of no communities being founded in the State of Israel through private initiative and means, it was unacceptable to them. They said to me, "Avri, because of you we are not receiving budget allocations – get down quickly!" I answered them, "I am not your emissary. I am from the Land of Israel, and me and my sweet nation are doing things." (*Arutz Sheva*, September 23, 2005).

Ran and his followers viewed the institutional branch, and anybody willing to compromise with the state, as puppets of the government.

But despite the fact that more extreme networks of the settler movement were often the recipients of harsh criticism from both Israeli government officials and the mainstream leadership of the settler movement, holistically, their role in the disengagement discourse should not be considered as purely antagonistic or even entirely detrimental to their overall goals. Indeed, they contributed to the fight against the disengagement by facilitating actions that the Yesha Council and many of the networks could not have endorsed without losing face with the Israeli political elites.

Although extremist settler groups have been active since the mid-1980s (see Chapter 3), the broader settler movement has consciously positioned them as pariahs and radical outliers. This became much harder to do during the disengagement, as extreme acts were no longer limited to small groups of activists but were adopted by a growing part of the activists too. According to Meir Elran (2005: 2), during the week of the disengagement, forty-seven incidents were defined as "extremism cases" (forty in the Gaza Strip and seven in Samaria). Some settler networks felt that it was not their responsibility to outline the limits or boundaries of the struggle against the disengagement. Smotrich said about this: "I don't want to waste one minute of energy discussing what the limits are. That is not my responsibility. That's the responsibility of the government" (Interview 2007).

Still, settler support for violent action before and during the disengagement was low – contradicting grim predictions by the media. In one study on the levels of support for violence in Gaza, 97 percent of respondents maintained that violent revolt (use of firearms) is "absolutely not legitimate," and 78 percent defined any physical response against those "participating in uprooting Jews" as illegitimate (Weisburd & Lernau 2006). In fact, for the great majority of settlers, the use of violence remained a red line. Ami Shaked, the security officer of Gush Katif, told the crowds at a mass protest against the disengagement at Kfar Maimon, "We will continue to light up the orange color around the world, and this gives strength to the residents of Gush Katif in maintaining their daily lives. 'Not by military might or force, but by My spirit, G-d said' – keep smiling, keep lighting up, and that's how we will win" (*Arutz Sheva*, July 21, 2005). More explicitly, Rabbanit Shulamit Melamed, founding head of *Arutz Sheva*, said in an interview, "I am ready to face them [the military], but I won't be the one to kill" (Interview 2007).

This avoidance of violence derived from both moral and pragmatic considerations. The settlers assumed that using weapons would lead them to lose the battle for public sympathy. At the same time, and for the same reasons, they relied on the authorities to also not use violence during the evictions either. Hence, the shape of their struggle depended largely on the actions of the authorities. As explained by Elyakim Haetzni, former Yesha Council member and one of the leaders of The Country's Defenders (*Meginei Aretz*), "They come with clubs, he [his son] will come out with a club" (Interview 2007).

A 2006 survey reveals the range – as well as the limits – of settlers' activism during the disengagement (Hirsch-Hoefler 2008).[13] More than half of the settlers had participated in some kind of political activity. The survey revealed a mixed strategy of both legal and illegal tactics to halt the disengagement efforts, most of them moderate (such as letter-writing campaigns, lobbying, petitions, and demonstrations), some radical (such as blockades and establishing settlements), and a few extreme (including physical violence) (see Figure 7.2). As expected, the more radical the action, the fewer people participated in them. For example, while almost a majority had signed a petition (48 percent) or had taken part in a demonstration (47 percent), a modest minority (15 percent) had moved deliberately to areas that were under threat of being evacuated, and very small numbers (2 percent) admitted to participating in more radical or extreme actions, such as damaging property or physically harming an elected representative or member of the security forces.

By and large, the activists tended to be religious, from ideological settlements, and right-wing. Quality-of-life settlers, whether secular or ultraorthodox, took little part in anti-disengagement activism. This holds true for both moderate and radical modes of action. For example, only

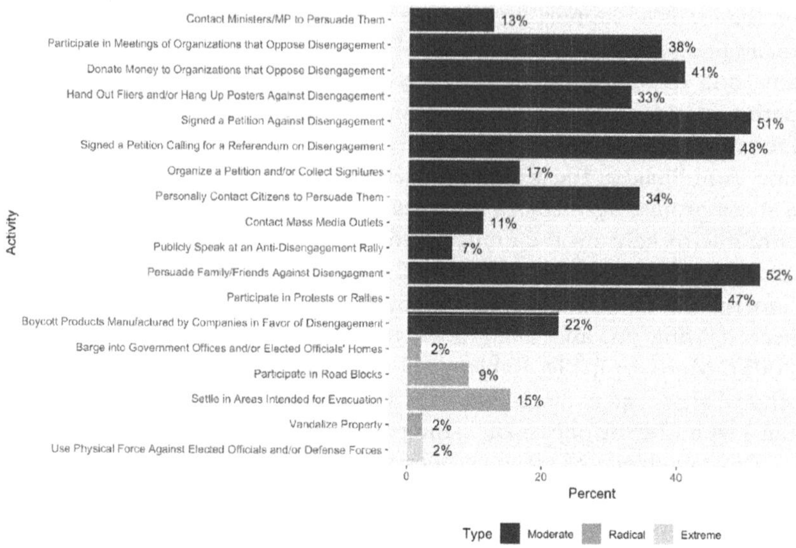

Figure 7.2 The repertoire of action of settlers during the disengagement

8 percent of the radical activists were secular. Participation rates within the religious-nationalist vs. secular settler populations show that, for instance, 79 percent of religious settlers took part in demonstrations, but only 17 percent of secular settlers (Hirsch-Hoefler 2008).[14] Moderate activists were diverse in terms of age, education, gender, and income. The radical activists tended to be young, from ideological settlements, and with ties to various networks and religious groups.[15]

Differences in behavior between secular and religious settlers even played out within the evacuated settlements themselves. Residents of the evacuated settlements were of a diverse nature, including both ideologically driven religious families and secular families seeking a better quality of life (Sheleg 2004). They shared concerns about security (such as rocket and terrorist attacks) and about the imminent evacuation. However, their attitudes, feelings, and behavioral responses regarding the evacuation varied sharply (Tsfati & Cohen 2005). While most secular residents willingly evacuated their homes without confrontation, many religious ones had to be forcibly dragged out by the security forces.

Surveys showed that approximately one-third of all Jewish settlers (32%) took part in organizational meetings or events dealing with the disengagement issue (Hirsch-Hoefler et al. 2016). A similar number considered themselves active members of a settler organization

(31 percent). Thus, roughly one in every three settlers was affiliated with a settler network or organization during the disengagement period. This figure is not striking, especially considering the wide range of formal and informal organizations that emerged out of the settler population, some of them exclusively for the purpose of dealing with the disengagement issue. The most frequently reported organizations were the Yesha Council, the Gush Katif "battle headquarters," and Orange Cell, a right-wing student organization that helped to lead anti-disengagement protest activities. Some respondents reported being active in two or more organizations.

Organizational affiliation increased political activism by individual settlers. More specifically, settlers who defined themselves as members of an organization, whether active or not, participated in activities to a much greater extent than nonmembers (Hirsch-Hoefler 2008). Furthermore, organizational affiliation was found to be especially prevalent among those aged eighteen to thirty, but active membership was found to be slightly higher between the ages of thirty-one and fifty. Finally, religious settlers were more likely to join organizational activities.

As for gender, men participated more than women in organized political activities. Yet, of those who were affiliated with an organization, women were slightly more likely to be active members of these organizations. In most of the political activities regarding the disengagement, be it moderate or not, gender played no significant role in decisions to engage in political activity over the disengagement.[16] Men were slightly more likely to engage in high-risk illegal political activity, but the difference was statistically insignificant. Female Israeli settlers, some still teenagers, protested against the disengagement throughout the country. Women seeking to block their eviction were involved in actions such as burning rubbish to barricade their homes, fighting with police officers, and throwing eggs and water bottles at the police and soldiers.[17]

Finally, influencers played a major role in the settler movement's efforts to mobilize the public by swaying public opinion, in particular through the mass media. Because the settler movement was determined to stop the decree by appealing to the "hearts of the nation," the public discourse became one of its central battle grounds. The Israeli media certainly offered room for settlers to press their case. Many influencers voiced the positions of the settler movement under the pretext of their supposedly apolitical relationship to the mass media infrastructure. For example, the journalist Boaz Haetzni wrote, "Widespread and overt refusal to obey this clearly illegal order will cause it to fail ... Such refusal, however difficult, may be what saves the IDF, along with 'trifles' like Gush Katif, the Land of Israel and democracy" (*News1*, January 2, 2005). Likewise, the journalist Haggai Hoberman justified violent resistance to the withdrawal:

"Blood will be spilled, and justly … If Sharon acts like a dictator, the reaction will be as befits a totalitarian state" (*The Seventh Eye*, November 1, 2005). In 2004, the singer, Ariel Zilber moved to the settlement of Eli in the north Gaza Strip, and became actively involved in the struggle against the disengagement.

The efforts of the settler movement, including its influencers, were not without success. The disengagement was covered exhaustively in the media. Special correspondents from mainstream media channels reported daily from the Gaza Strip, bringing commentary and stories to Israeli audiences. Prominent Israeli media ran special programs on the issue, such as "On the Road to Disengagement" (*Yedioth Ahronoth*) and "The Disengagement Diary" (*Channel 1*) (First 2009). Aside from the discourse created by the pro-settler media (such as *Arutz Sheva*), which was inherently anti-disengagement, coverage in the mainstream press was on the whole unbiased. A content analysis of 534 news and editorial items on the Disengagement Plan, published in three leading Israeli newspapers in the run-up to the Likud referendum, showed relatively balanced treatment (Sheafer 2005). Sharon and his plan enjoyed slightly more positive coverage in the earlier stages of the campaign, while his opponents received more supportive coverage in the week prior to the referendum. However, Anat First (2009) found that the disengagement was portrayed as a legitimate and necessary process in the television news channels, while opponents were presented as dangerous and violent.

7.4 The Aftermath

The disengagement was obviously detrimental to the livelihood of the former residents of the Gaza Strip, but the emotional and psychological trauma was also profound (Hirsch-Hoefler et al. 2019). The Gaza settlers had transformed their settlements into the physical and spatial anchors of their self-identification as the messianic vanguard of Israeli society (Schnell & Mishal 2008). As a result, the evacuation not only contradicted their religious-nationalistic mission, but also challenged their collective identities at a deeply fundamental level. Self-reported statistics revealed that 41 percent of evacuated settlers visited a mental health professional in the period after the relocation (*Haaretz*, July 10, 2007). In 2008, Ronit Shoham, the welfare service coordinator for evacuees from the disengagement, indicated a 77.5 percent increase in the number of families that needed welfare services in comparison to the period prior to the evacuation (*Haaretz*, January 7, 2008). His report cites a host of problems originating from the relocation, including weakened financial stability, family tensions, and depression.

But the trauma of the disengagement extended far beyond the relatively small Gaza settler population. All settlers were affected in one way or another and the settler movement was rocked to its core. First and foremost, the failure of the settler movement to prevent the disengagement caused a lot of settler activists to lose faith in the state authorities as well as in their own leadership. The undermining of authoritative figures in the settler community affected the institutional branch the most. Many settlers held the Yesha Council responsible for the disengagement and were harsh in their criticism of their leaders. For example, Yoel Elitzur, a resident of the Ofra settlement, stated, "Had we not had the Yesha Council in 2005, the results certainly would not have been worse, [and] perhaps, better" (Elitzur 2006: 18–19). Similarly, Smotrich argued, "The anger was not towards how it ended, because we could all fail ... the anger was that they [the Yesha Council] failed along the way, and while we said guys, you are bound to this from the start. They tried to deny those facts" (Interview 2007).

Criticism also came from within the Yesha Council. Wallerstein had this to say:

> People did not understand the purpose of the struggle, not in Gush Katif nor in Kfar Maimon. The goal for me was not to overcome the army or the police, my goal was to topple the government, and we failed because the only one who resigned was Bibi. It is not that we failed or not in demonstrations, but we failed in the test of parliamentary pressure (Interview 2007).

He further claimed that "if we had started the struggle over Gush Katif a week earlier we would have won the struggle."

While Wallerstein argued that the Yesha Council failed because they did not focus sufficiently on the political arena, others saw the outcome as reflecting a failure to look beyond the political arena. For instance, NRP MK Slomiansky, who had previously served as the Operations Officer of the Yesha Council, claimed that the Yesha Council's key problem was that it focused primarily on the political arena, rather than working in several parallel spheres (Roth 2005: 312). A third view held that the Yesha Council's main failure was its absolute opposition to any sort of territorial concessions or evacuations.

After the failure to prevent the disengagement, settler movement leaders engaged in a period of internal reflection and soul-searching. This was not an easy process, and for some, it did not go far enough. Shaul Goldstein, former Chair of the Gush Etzion Regional Council and Deputy Head of the Yesha Council, summarized the Council's internal discussions after the withdrawal from Gaza as follows:

There was one discussion in which I participated, where we tried to summarize what happened with the withdrawal, the disengagement. We tried to gauge where we succeeded and where we failed. We did not say "we failed," but rather we talked about when we were more successful and when we were less successful. In my opinion, we did not get to the bottom of things. I think, if we had gone into it in a deep way, some of our conclusions would have been painful and some positive. However, we did not do this (Interview 2007).

As if it were not enough that the settlers were calling into question the legitimacy of their movement's leadership, they also experienced dwindling faith in the spiritual-religious leadership of the movement. This was in part a self-inflicted wound, as the Yesha Rabbinical Council had offered the prophetic promise that the disengagement would not come to pass. When it did pass, the Council and its rabbis lost much of their constituent support.

During the disengagement there were confrontations among two religious camps regarding what constituted legitimate behavior. Some rabbis opposed violent opposition but advocated for a passive civil disobedience (for example, Rabbi Avraham Shapira's support of refusal to obey orders). Other rabbis (such as Rabbi Shlomo Aviner and Rabbi Zvi Tau) argued that the struggle against the disengagement must take place through public information, education and persuasion (i.e., to settle in the hearts), and not through physical struggle or disobedience. This cleavage within the Yesha Rabbinical Council became stronger after the disengagement. For example, of all the rabbis in the Gush Katif settlements, only two continued in their positions after the Gaza withdrawal as a result of the tension that had surfaced over legitimate protest action (Sheleg 2015). Moreover, the status of the rabbis who opposed disobedience has declined since the disengagement. Rabbi Tau has distanced himself from mainstream religious Zionism and actively opposed the Jewish Home party, while Rabbi Shlomo Aviner became a much more controversial figure (Sheleg 2015: 55–56).

The issue of state authority, and in particular, the settler movement's relation to the state, led to a rearrangement of the settler branches in the post-disengagement era. Prior to the disengagement, the state and established parties saw the institutional branch, particularly the Yesha Council, as the authentic representative of the settler movement (not without reason). The old guard in the Yesha Council valued the authority of the state and felt that the best way to achieve its goal, that is, preventing the disengagement, was to operate within the structure of the state, that is, through parliamentary pressure. Following the disengagement, the settlers' feeling of betrayal and shock was incredibly divisive for the settler movement. Factions within the movement, particularly its younger members, were steadfast in their assertion that the state did not possess the authority to evacuate Jewish settlements, and that it was interfering with God's will.

The schism birthed by the disengagement continues to divide the settler movement today and has arguably been more damaging than any external influences. While all the branches still share the same goal, a contiguous Israeli state mirroring that of biblical times, the divisions between them, in terms of their positions and tactics, have become more and more fundamental. Some of the sources of contention that arose during the disengagement period remain unresolved to this day. For example, several radical groups continue to dispute the legitimacy of the state and its laws, suggesting that disobeying these laws qualifies as a justified form of protest. Rabbi Gadi Ben-Zimra has referred to this internal fragmentation as "the post-trauma of the disengagement" (Hirsch-Hoefler 2008: 120).

Two years after the implementation of the Disengagement Plan, the Yesha Council changed its structure in an effort to renew itself and broaden its reach. Its new membership included community leaders, educators, rabbis, and young activists as well as elected heads of municipalities and community officials. As the Council noted on its website at the time:

> Two years ago we were faced with one of the bigger challenges in our history – the uprooting of Jewish families from Gush Katif and communities in Northern Shomron [Samaria] .... [Knowing that] the divisions between us could well paralyze us in the face of new challenges, the leadership set about to repair ruptures in the general Israel public and, specifically, in Yesha ... .The Yesha Council began a slow, lengthy process to unify all those committed to Jewish settlement in Yesha .....The general board .... chose 124 members, including 64 public officials, 23 rabbis, educators and community leaders, 28 public leaders ... and [there were also] young activists.

But was there a real shift in the actions, objectives, and roles of the "renewed" Yesha Council? Interestingly, when faced with this question, members of both the institutional and network branch gave the same answer: the "renewed" Yesha Council was the same organization as before, with the same actions and objectives, only structured differently. For example, Bentzi Lieberman said, "There is a new approach, broadening the council, but actually, the general line is the same" (Interview 2007). And according to Weiss, the Council "brought in some people but didn't give them anything ... He [the new chair] is subject to the system that existed before and to the same people as before" (Interview 2007). The restructured Yesha Council did widen its organization, so that it represents more varied branches in the settler camp. At the same time, it retained its original content and goals, which determine not only the process but also the form of the chosen actions and their outcomes. Interestingly, some of its leaders see the post-disengagement Council as a weaker institution. For both sides, it is not clear if the glue will hold. Moreover, not all networks agreed to be part of the new Yesha Council.

It further appears that since the disengagement, the network branch has felt subordinated. Some network activists expressed fears that if their groups cooperated with the institutional branch, the Yesha Council would devour them. As Smotrich put it, the Council was "used to being the authority, used to being in super control. It is difficult for it to accept there are new forces that have to be given room and whose opinions have to be considered" (Interview 2007). Nadia Matar from Women in Green even described the Council's role as being "the sleeping pill" of the settler camp (Interview 2007). The networks feel that the Yesha Council treats them as outcasts, and that the cooperation is unidirectional; they are asked to work with the Council, but the Council is only willing to work with those posing no challenge state authority.

Finally, Israeli public opinion about the Gaza withdrawal has shifted over time. In the direct aftermath of the disengagement, in August 2005, the majority of the Israeli public viewed it as justified and as likely to improve prospects for peace. For example, one survey found that 38 percent of the Israeli public, and 41 percent of Jewish Israelis, remained opposed to the disengagement. And another survey found that 54 percent thought that the peace process should be restarted and that Israel should display willingness to withdraw from additional territories in Judea and Samaria. But by 2018 this had changed. According to the Peace Index, the percentage of Israeli's that saw the disengagement as "the right step" had dropped from 59 percent in 2005 to just 42 percent in 2008. In fact, in 2008 a near-majority of 48.5 percent thought it was "the wrong step." The shift in public opinion might be a result of ongoing terrorism and rocket attacks from Gaza, which generated a threatening context for the Israeli public. In fact, 70 percent of the Israeli population became exposed to the threat of rockets. Since the disengagement, 11,600 shells and rockets have been fired at Israel and eight military operations were followed (Shragai 2015: 34).

7.5 Conclusion

Israel has experienced two large-scale evacuations of populations resulting from political decisions: the 1982 evacuation of the Sinai Peninsula, in the framework of the peace treaty between Israel and Egypt, and the 2005 evacuation of the Gaza Strip and a portion of the northern West Bank, as part of Israel's unilateral disengagement from those areas. This chapter analyzed the action repertoire employed by the settler movement in its ultimately unsuccessful struggle against the disengagement from Gaza. That struggle was not only between (settler) challengers and (state) authorities, but also among the challengers themselves, primarily (most of) the networks against the institutions of the settler movement.

The settler movement was extremely active both before and during the disengagement. More than half of the settlers engaged in some kind of political action against the disengagement and their activism was multidimensional (Hirsch-Hoefler 2008). But while the settler population is pretty diverse, including in terms of motivations for settling, the settlers who were active in the fight against the disengagement were primarily motivated by ideological and religious beliefs. As such, they were not representative of the settler population as a whole. Secular and ultraorthodox settlers, which constitute the vast majority of the settler population, barely participated in the struggle against the disengagement.

The active settlers did not follow precise scripts, but engaged in different forms of activism, from standard moderate actions, like contacting elected officials, face-to-face persuasion, and demonstrations, to more radical actions, such as blocking roads, and, at times, even acts of violence. It was typically so-called splitters, individuals who split off from the institutional branch, who offered radical alternatives, implicitly challenging the authority of the settler movement's institutions (i.e., the Yesha Council) and even of the Israeli state.

Despite its wide range of activities and organizations, the settler movement failed to prevent the Gaza withdrawal. Indeed, the evacuation proceeded far easier and smoother than was expected. What explains this failure? It is true that the disengagement laid bare the internal divisions of the settler movement, which is generally treated as an extremely well-organized unitary actor. But factionalized social movements are not doomed to failure. They can actually benefit from this structural division (Meyer & Whittier 1994). So, why did the settler movement lose this battle? Paradoxically, at least part of the reason may be found in the key to its previous success, that is, its close relationship to Israeli authorities.

For decades, the settler movement, and particularly its institutions (both the Yesha Council and Amana), had worked hand in glove with various Israeli governments and ministers, and with no one more closely and profitably than with "the godfather of the settlers," Ariel Sharon. Consequently, the settler movement's institutional leaders were caught off guard by Sharon's seemingly radical departure from his previously held positions, and from the official party position up to that point. In fact, it seems Sharon himself acknowledged his reluctant change of mind. On August 15, 2005, the day the withdrawal began, Sharon said, "It is no secret that I, like many others, believed and hoped that we could hold on to Netzarim and Kfar Darom forever. But the changing reality in Israel, the region, and the world has forced me to make a reassessment and alter positions."

Second, and related, the close relations between the state and the settler movement affected the structure of the movement and its repertoire of actions. Since 1967, the state had always supported the settlement enterprise in one way or another. This had led to a transformation of the internal power structure of the settler movement, illustrated by the demise of Gush Emunim and the rise of the Yesha Council. Facing a mostly supportive state, which provided massive resources to the movement through its institutions, the Yesha Council became the main player within the settler movement. Consequently, a collaborative (and even trusting) attitude and an almost exclusive use of moderate actions came to define the movement's position toward the Israeli state.

Third, the settler movement found itself with restricted access to the institutionalized political system. While this had happened before under some Labor governments (e.g., Rabin's government), it had never happened under a right-wing government. Events like the NRP's withdrawal from the governing coalition in November 2004, instability and infighting within Sharon's center-right base, and the formation of a coalition with the Labor Party in January 2005, cut off some of the movement's traditional paths of access to the corridors of power. With the institutions politically sidelined, factions appeared within the settler movement, and the longstanding divisions between institutions and networks gave way to a growth of the radical alternative, the so-called radical flank effect.[18]

Fourth, and final, the settlers failed to mobilize elite and particularly mass support for their cause within the Israeli public. In fact, as indicated by its shift in framing of its opposition, it appears that the Yesha Council did not recognize the extent to which the Israeli elite and public were not on its side. According to Yaacov Bar-Siman-Tov (2009), the Israeli public accepted Sharon's fundamental assumption that the demographics of an increasing Palestinian population represented an existential threat to the State of Israel as both a Jewish and democratic state. Even security hawks, who consider an Israeli presence in the West Bank as crucial for defending the state from future attacks, did not see eye-to-eye with the settler movement on the significance of the Gaza Strip. Shifting frames midway the campaign, the Yesha Council had failed to instill its security message in the public, merely opposing the proposed plan while failing to present an alternative that would improve the security situation (Roth 2005).

Consequently, what had long been considered unthinkable in the Israeli mindset, became thinkable (Elran 2005).

In the end, the settler movement relied too heavily on its institutions (notably the Yesha Council) and their connections to its natural allies within the political establishment. By the time other elements within the movement realized this would not be enough, it was too late. Moreover, although the networks eventually took a more confrontative stand toward the state, which the institutions were clearly failing to accomplish, they themselves failed to grasp the need for broader mobilization of the population, including secular and ultraorthodox Israelis outside and (especially) within the settlements. Ultimately, the religious-nationalist subculture lacked the organizational muscle and public support to prevent the disengagement.

8 Conclusion

> Despite the failure to establish the territories and the settlements as a legitimate part of the State of Israel, it appears that the settlement enterprise has nevertheless been successful. With the encouragement or acquiescence of all Israeli governments, it has succeeded in blurring the Green Line – which is the only clear line likely to be accepted by both sides, Israeli and Palestinian, and also to gain international recognition. This is the surprising and worrying success of the settlement enterprise: undermining the Green Line as a mutually agreed foundation for peace between the State of Israel and her Palestinian neighbor. It is not by accident that all Ministers of Education from right-wing parties have erased the Green Line from the maps used in Israeli schools.
>
> Former Meretz MK Ran Cohen
> (*Haaretz*, July 11, 2005)

The success of the Israeli settler movement is often simply assumed, or proclaimed, rather than explained or proven. Most accounts both exaggerate the triumphs of the movement and simply ignore the defeats. Few offer such a subtle assessment as Ran Cohen, which goes beyond mere numbers of settlements and settlers and also includes cultural elements. Still, while we agree with much of his statement, our comprehensive and systematic assessment warrants a more complex and qualified conclusion.

In this final chapter we first summarize the key findings of the book, that is, the theoretical framework (Section 8.1), the assessment of the success of the settler movement (Section 8.2), and the explanations for its success (Section 8.3). We then discuss our contributions to the broader academic literature, focusing specifically on the literature on social movements (Section 8.4) and on Israeli politics (Section 8.5). We contend that, while the Israeli settler movement is particular, but not necessarily unique, in several aspects, its success follows more general patterns. Moreover, while it is true that the settler movement belongs to the more successful social movements in history, its success is often (strongly) overstated, by both its opponents and supporters. We end the book with the most delicate task, a look into the future, just at a time that the unsaid is openly said (annexation) and the longest-serving Prime Minister (Netanyahu) in Israeli history is facing both a political exit and a prison sentence.

8.1 Theoretical Framework

The issue of "success" is crucial to the study of social movements, yet it is still fairly underdeveloped in the scholarly literature. Building upon the limited, but insightful, scholarship on the issue, we have developed a comprehensive and original theoretical framework for the study of social movement success. This framework allows for a more fine-grained analysis of both the *assessment* and the *explanation* of success, distinguishing between different dimensions of success, branches of social movements, action repertoires, and political arenas in which the social movement (and its branches) operate (see Table 8.1; also Table 1.1).

In the context of social movement, *success* has three separate but related dimensions: policies, resources, and support. The primary indicator of political success is whether the social movement manages to attain its stated goals, in whole or in part, which is first and foremost measured by change(s) in *policies*. While bigger and smaller policy changes are the ultimate measure of success, *resources* are a crucial means to achieve the policy ends, as they help sustain the movement and (potentially) strengthen its policy effects. Finally, (elite and mass) *support* for both the movement and its goals is crucial for a social movement to both acquire resources and affect policy change. Importantly, all of these dimensions of social movement success can play out at various levels – subnational, national, or supranational – depending, in part, on the actions and goals of the social movement.

While social movements can be treated as unity actors in the *assessment* of their success, *explanations* should also take into consideration their internal diversity. Every social movement is diverse in terms of many

Table 8.1 *Theoretical framework of social movement success*

Success	Movement branches	Repertoire of actions	Political arenas
Policies	Institutions	Moderate	State
Resources	Networks	Radical	Civil society
Support	Influencers	Extreme	Society

different aspects – for instance, sociodemographics of supporters – but we focus here specifically on organizational heterogeneity. Within social movements, individuals and organizations can be categorized into three *branches*, according to their organizational structure: the centralized branch (*institutions*), the decentralized branch (*networks*), and the individual branch (*influencers*). These different branches tend to prioritize different action repertoires and target different political arenas.

The *action repertoires* of social movements are exceptionally broad, ranging from online petitions to street protests and from lobbying to terrorism. All different actions can be divided into three different types, depending on two factors, legality and violence. *Moderate* actions are legal and nonviolent, *radical* actions are illegal but nonviolent, and *extreme* actions are both illegal and violent. Institutions and influencers employ almost exclusively moderate actions, while networks also engage in radical actions, and even in some extreme actions. In general, the more extreme the action, the fewer activists and organizations engage in them.

Finally, social movements try to achieve their success in a number of different and diverse *political arenas*: the state, civil society, and society – all have a national and an international dimension. *The state* includes a broad range of sub-arenas, most notably the institutions of the *Trias Politica* (executive, legislature, judiciary), but also the bureaucracy and military. *Civil society* is even more diverse, with three sectors being particularly important for social movements: political parties, nongovernmental organizations (NGOs), and the media (traditional and social). *Society*, finally, mainly involves public opinion. Given the interconnectedness of the globalized world, many social movements address issues that transcend one national context and, while many are national movements, they often operate, at least in part, internationally.

The four dimensions are obviously closely interrelated. Each branch has a specific role to fulfill within the broader social movement, which shapes its primary actions and political arenas. The institutional branch mainly plays a *collaborative* role, working with(in) the state to further the social movement's goals. In contrast, the network branch plays a more *confrontative* role, using also radical, and sometimes extreme, actions to pressure the state into either advancing pro-movement actions or into abolishing anti-movement actions. Finally, the individual branch (influencers) plays a more *transformative* role, using moderate actions, primarily through the media, to make both elite and mass opinion more supportive of the social movement and its goals. It should be clear that these branches are fluid and dynamic; the categories are neither mutually exclusive nor collectively exhaustive. The relationships between the different branches can vary. Influencers, networks and institutions may coordinate and collaborate, either on an ad hoc basis or in a more structured way.

It is important to stress that our theoretical framework is complimentary, rather than contrary, to the main theories in the field, most notably political opportunity structure (POS) theory and resource mobilization theory (RMT). In fact, it allows for a more thorough analysis *within* these theoretical frameworks, identifying how they affect the different branches of the heterogeneous social movement and how that affects the overall success (and failure) of the social movement as a whole. For instance, a favorable political opportunity structure, in which political structures are open to social movements in general and political elites are sympathetic to a particular social movement, strengthens the power of the institutions *within* the broader social movement and thereby the predominance of a collaborative strategy that prioritizes moderate actions (like lobbying) and a primary focus on the state. An unfavorable political structure, in contrast, reinforces the internal power of the networks and the use of more radical actions (like legal and illegal protests) to pressure the state and win support of (civil) society.

8.2 Assessing the Movement's Success

The success of the Israeli settler movement is almost universally accepted as an established fact, rather than posed as a still to be researched question.[1] In fact, there are very few systemic analyses of the actual activities of the settler movement – even the number of (legal and illegal) settlements is unclear and varies between different sources. Our comprehensive analysis of the different dimensions of success (i.e., policies, resources, and support) shows a much more nuanced picture. While the settler movement has been very successful in certain aspects (e.g., resources), it has been at best moderately successful (e.g., domestic support and policies) and largely unsuccessful in others (e.g., international support).

The settler movement is not primarily an interest group for the settler population, even if it also tries to be that. First and foremost, it is a social movement with an ambitious, ideologically and religiously inspired, goal: the annexation and settlement of *Eretz Yisrael* (Greater Israel). While there are differences of opinions within the settler movement – most notably, over its exact *borders* (e.g., with or without the Gaza Strip) and its exact *population* (e.g., exclusively Jewish or inclusive of some Arabs, albeit with more limited rights) – all activists and groups agree that the West Bank (Judea and Samaria, in their terminology) is an essential part of *Eretz Yisrael*.

Clearly, the settler movement has not (yet) succeeded in achieving its overall goal, if that is taken to be the annexation of all occupied territories. The settler movement has its origins in the Six-Day War of 1967, which gave the young Israeli state control over most of *Eretz Yisrael*, in what many religious Zionists considered a messianic process. The movement, though its original organization Gush Emunim, became truly active in the wake of the traumatic Yom Kippur War of 1973, which saw Israeli forces taken by surprise, and the future of the messianic process questioned. Since 1973, Israel has held on to most of its occupied territories. However, the Sinai was returned to Egypt as part of the Camp David Accords of 1978; roughly 40 percent of the West Bank (Areas A and B) was handed over to the new Palestinian Authority as part of the Oslo Accords of 1993 and 1995 (though with the caveat, as explained in earlier chapters, that Israel retains ultimate control over security-related issues there); and Israel withdrew unilaterally from the Gaza Strip in 2005. Of the remaining territories, Israel annexed East Jerusalem de facto (through government administrative orders) in 1967 and the Golan Heights de facto in 1967 and de jure in 1981 (Golan law).

While the bulk of the West Bank (Area C) remains under Israeli control (about 60 percent of the territory), it is governed outside of the regular framework of the Israeli state – notably, through the Israeli military (IDF) and its civil arm, the Coordinator of Government Activities in the Territories (COGAT). The roughly 220 Jewish settlements constitute less than 2 percent of the territory of the West Bank, and about 100 of them, the so-called outposts, are not officially recognized by the Israeli state (though this may change if the "Law for the Regulation of Settlement in Judea and Samaria" is ever implemented; see Chapter 4). Moreover, for the vast majority of the international community, *all* the territories that Israel conquered in 1967 are illegal and considered "occupied," including East Jerusalem and the Golan Heights. Only very recently, the United States shifted its position on the annexation of the Golan Heights and the question of Jerusalem as the capital city of Israel, but only by presidential decree (by President Trump). However, the glass is not just half empty.

There are currently 127 Jewish settlements that are officially recognized by the Israeli state. They are home to the vast majority of the more than 400,000 Jewish settlers in the West Bank (excluding East Jerusalem). Most importantly, these settlements (and outposts) are spread out across almost the whole territory of Area C and are (mostly) connected by an extensive and exclusive Israeli-built and -controlled infrastructure. This broader settlement infrastructure, which includes roads that are off-limits to the local Palestinians, strategically cuts up the territory of the current Palestinian Authority, making a future Palestinian state impossible without the dismantlement of significant parts of the infrastructure and settlements. So, in terms of *policies* (and settlement), the settler movement has been, at best, moderately successful. That said, the settlement of the West Bank is much more complex and elaborate than it ever was in the Gaza Strip or the Sinai Peninsula, which makes its reversibility far more challenging and far less obvious.

The settler movement has been much more successful in terms of *resources*, most notably through its two main institutions, Amana and the Yesha Council, which are both complex hybrids of state and non-state organizations. Over the past decades the Israeli state has invested billions of US dollars in the settlements, through a complex and opaque network of state and para-state organizations. There is virtually no ministry that is not involved in the financial support of the settlement enterprise, although ministries like Defense and Housing are particularly important. Significant amounts of money go directly to the settlements, in terms of construction of buildings (both residential and commercial) and supportive infrastructure, or to the settlers, in terms of housing subsidies, but significant parts go to the settler movement, notably the institutions, but also various (less radical) networks. In fact, several movement leaders are at least partly paid by the state, either as leaders of their settlement community or as employees of the Yesha Council.

Finally, in terms of *support*, the settler movement has been mainly successful within the Israeli and US right. Settlers have been disproportionately represented in the Israeli government and legislature (but not only the legislature – executive, judiciary, army as well) since the 1980s, and the trend is clearly up. Almost all right-wing Israeli parties have settlers within their leadership and openly support (most of) the movement's goals. Similarly, the US Republican Party has become very supportive of the settler movement, with the so-called pro-Israel lobby doing much of its bidding. The settler movement also enjoys support from various other sectors of Israeli and US civil society, such as NGOs and the media, particularly among Jewish (and in the US also Christian) conservatives. However, public support is less forthcoming. While a majority of Israelis are sympathetic to the existing settlements, only (growing) minorities support for either significant expansion of the settlements or, particularly, the annexation of the West Bank. International public opinion is largely hostile to the whole settler enterprise, including in the United States, where, like everything else, it has become largely a partisan issue.

8.3 Explaining the Success

The settler movement is an ideologically related but disorganized hodgepodge that includes more moderate groups all the way to extreme fringe groups, all of which interact with one another to produce a complete social movement. While the umbrella settler institution (the Yesha Council) focuses on building capacity, strategically sequencing its actions to gain elite and mass support, the more radical groups advance the cause on the margins, gradually shifting the locus of the discourse. The institutions have been instrumental to the overall success, particularly in terms of resources, but the settler movement could never have been so successful had it chosen to operate only within the framework of a well-defined and static organization (see also McCarthy & Pedahzur 2015).

In terms of its action repertoire, the settler movement engages in a wide variety of actions, some conventional and more explanatory (or propagandistic) in nature, others more radical and violent (extreme). The form and structure of the organization (institutional or noninstitutional, centralized or decentralized) appear to play a central role in shaping the preferred action repertoire and strategies. Some scholars have presented this structural–tactical division as a struggle between two types of Zionism: political Zionism, which places the State of Israel at its center, and redemptive Zionism, which prioritizes the Land of Israel (e.g., Taub 2007).

Organizations within the institutional branch tend to work *with and within* the state, either through the lobbying for and implementing of policies or by engaging in lawful protest. Several networks prefer a more radical action repertoire, calling for disobedience, denouncing the institutions, presenting themselves as an alternative leadership for the movement, and employing militant tactics, from intimidation through vandalism to the worst forms of violence. The various organizations, especially within the network branch, overlap and intertwine in a complex manner, so that many activists are members of several organizations at the same time. As a result, different organizations not only work together, but also benefit from their segmented structure. That is, they are frequently embedded in various coalitions and networks that collaborate on different issues. Overall, the structure of the settler movement – with its organizational specialization, coalitions between multiple organizations, and individual overlapping memberships – enables it to offer something to everyone interested in furthering the movement's goals.

At the same time, different organizations and action repertoires also help attract not just different individuals, but the same individuals at different times. In this, age matters. Many moderate actions, such as participation in (legal) demonstrations, appeal to all ages. Activities that involve working within the state apparatus, like lobbying and deal-making, require the contacts, experience, and positions that are generally acquired with age. And the more radical and extreme acts are primarily attractive to the young(er), who have less to lose. In fact, the settler movement depends more and more heavily on young settlers (i.e., between seventeen and twenty-two years old) to "create facts on the ground" and to set up outposts. However, these young settlers are not only more willing to engage in radical actions, they are also more prone to extreme actions, including against the state and its representatives as well as the settler movement leadership.

The presence of multiple settler organizations with structural specialization generates the phenomenon of a "radical flank effect." A moderate branch allows the movement to advance particular solutions, mobilize large numbers of activists, access adequate financial resources, and achieve stated goals such as educating large audiences, enacting legislation, influencing social behavior, or recruiting members. The Yesha Council is the main organization within the institutional branch, with official ties to the Israeli government, which has intentionally fostered a frame that portrays it as the only legitimate organization within the settler movement, which *collaborates* with the state. In sharp contrast, extremist groups within the movement, such as the Hilltop Youth, have framed themselves as fundamentally opposed to the leadership of both the settler movement and the Israeli state. Unsurprisingly, the broader Israeli public perceives them as political extremists, engaged in illegal and violent activities. The radicalism (and increasing extremism) of the Hilltop Youth has had a normalizing effect on more moderate groups like the Yesha Council. When the two are viewed side by side, the Yesha Council is seen as the legitimate flank, through which the Israeli political establishment can enter a constructive dialogue with the settler movement and, at the same time, keep its more radical (and extreme) flank at bay.

However, the radical flank effect also has had quelling effects on the "legitimate" flank of a social movement. This can happen when the more radical flank questions the mandate, and by extension the internal legitimacy, of the moderate flank. This reversal was evident during the disengagement from Gaza, when more radical networks like the Sovereignty and Women in Green openly challenged and criticized the mainstream leadership of the movement (i.e., the Yesha Council), while extremist groups, like the Hilltop Youth, outright rejected its leadership. While the radical, and even extreme, forms of protest saw a dramatic uptick in collective participation from a much broader base, the combative behavior and discourse also has (unintended) negative consequences for the broader movement, including the distancing of potential supporters and the reduction of fundraising abilities by the more established groups, in particular from US donors (Newman 2005).

The lack of complete uniformity is both the strength and the weakness of social movements. The main disadvantage, of course, is the inherent disorganization and inability to engage in strategic planning for the long run, which raises the question as to whether a social movement can actually succeed without a cohesive structure. On the other hand, the lack of an organized, bureaucratic structure affords the movement a high degree of activism and dynamism. Its dynamism is highlighted by the tendency to adapt to the ever-evolving political arena and the ambitions of its own members. This adaptability is also evident in the galvanizing of "preexisting networks and organizations into vehicles of collective struggle" (McAdam & Tarrow 2000: 17). It also helps both the raising and distribution of funds. The fundraising juggernauts can leave radical actions to the networks, ensuring that the moderate image of their institutions is not tainted by controversial actions and positions. At the same time, funds can be distributed to different parts of the broader movement, depending on their particular expertise.

The settler movement is the quintessential exemplification of this tactic. The institutional branch (notably the Yesha Council) aims to represent the collective political and social needs of a honeycomb of smaller political factions, whose agendas are not always synchronous. Likewise, the networks, which would normally have little or no impact, are afforded the opportunity to piggyback on the successes of the institutions, thereby mobilizing support from the elites and the masses. Essentially, the success of the institutions may act as a source of vicarious success for the smaller networks, ultimately leading to an increased perception of success by its various leaders and members. As explained by Elyakim Haetzni, a prominent figure from the early core of Gush Emunim, "that's a very good way to mix up the enemy ... from this perspective, a firm organizational structure creates atrophy. The system quenches the burning" (Interview 2007).

In the end, social movements are most successful when the different branches complement each other, working separately together, achieving partly different aspects of the common goals. Institutions are best suited to collaborate with the state and ideally even capture part of the state. Both happened in the case of the Israeli settler movement, where the Yesha Council was founded as a hybrid state/non-state organization, which made the settler movement part of the Israeli state. As the Israeli state tried to co-opt the settler movement, mostly through subsidizing its institutions and settlements, the settler movement also tried to capture the state, particularly the organizations in charge of administrating the West Bank – that is, COGAT and the IDF. State capture was not exclusively the domain of (former) leaders of the institutions, however. So-called influencers, individual supporters of the settler movement, have also captured key positions in the state apparatus, primarily but not exclusively in the West Bank administration.

But institutions (and influencers) are primarily successful within a supportive political opportunity structure. They are much less effective within an unsympathetic political context. This was highlighted in our two case studies, Ariel and the Gaza disengagement. The case of Ariel shows how successful the settler movement can be through continued and coordinated campaigns of the branches, which work together by using their particular strength within an overall sympathetic political context. Although established before the institutions were around, most of the story of Ariel is similar to that of the other most successful settlements. A small group of settlers seizes upon a favorable political opportunity, most notably sympathetic individuals in the Israeli government, to create a new settlement and integrate it into the Civil Administration in the West Bank. Once that is achieved, institutions and influencers push for growth through "extensions" (which are often planned to maximize territorial gains) and for normalization as an Israeli city, whose status as settlement in occupied territory is slowly but steadily erased from the city's narrative.

In addition to the settlements that are initiated through a collaboration between the state and the settler movement, which are often larger quality-of-life settlements situated close to the Green Line, there are also successful cases in which the settler movement takes the initiative and pressures the state into cooperation. These mostly smaller and more ideological settlements originated as (illegal) outposts deeper inside the West Bank. A small group within the network branch creates the "fact on the ground," prominent members of the networks as well as influencers (and now also institutions) lobby COGAT for electricity and water and IDF for protection, before targeting the government and legislature to get the settlement officially recognized by the Israeli state. During this process, networks play a key role in protecting every achievement, by physically and politically mobilizing against any attempt to roll back the process. When a settlement is threatened with dismantlement, networks bring more people to the settlement, temporarily to protect and structurally to settle, or physically obstruct state efforts to limit or reverse the settlement process. But they also keep pressure on the institutions to not give into political and state pressure and to remain loyal to the movement rather than the state.

However, the disengagement of Gaza showed the limits of the power of the settler movement, when faced with an (unexpectedly) hostile political context. Although Gaza was never as central to its goals as the West Bank, the settler movement bitterly opposed the Disengagement Plan. But the movement, and particularly the institutions, were blindsided by the fact that the initiative came from Prime Minister Ariel Sharon, unofficially known as "the Godfather of the Settlers," with whom many institutional leaders had a decades-old close and cooperative relationship. When they had finally come to terms with Sharon's "betrayal," their moderate actions (lobbying and propaganda) and framing (national security) proved wholly ineffective – as Sharon's hawkish credentials proved more convincing to the Israeli elites and masses. Its last-minute shift to a more religious-ideological framing isolated the settler movement not just from the vast majority of the Israeli population, but also from a large part of the settler population (notably the secular and religious quality-of-life settlers).

The settler movement had long believed that the institutions, the Yesha Council in particular, could succeed in changing the opinions of either Sharon or the right-wing parties holding up his government. They gave in to pressure from the Yesha Council to respect the state authority and to only use moderate actions. Many activists within the networks openly rejected extreme actions, particularly violence directed at Jewish Israelis (notably IDF soldiers), but even brazen radical actions were only truly embraced when it was already too late. On the day of the disengagement, the settler movement was divided and ineffective, barely putting up a fight to the dismantling of the various settlements. They were demoralized by the lack of support by the Israeli elites and masses and internally divided over the blame question. The disengagement opened up wounds within the settler movement that continue to exist today. Many activists drew a similar lesson as us, namely that the settler movement can only be successful when the different branches operate collectively but separately and that it had relied too much on the moderate actions of the institutional branch.

Moreover, the Ariel and Gaza cases also teach us an important lesson about the mobilization challenges of the settler movement, whose national-religious leadership (and core membership) is unrepresentative of the Israeli public and even increasingly of the settler population. The majority of the settlers are led mainly by practical (quality-of-life) and not ideological motivations. This also applies to the ultraorthodox, who will soon constitute the majority of the settler population – they are the only source of growth within the settler population – but remain largely ignored by the leadership of the settler movement. As Rabbi Yaakov

Meidan, head of the Har Etzion Hesder yeshiva, noted in reflecting upon the Gaza failure, "In order to forge an alliance with the secular elites, we neglected our more natural union with the Haredi [ultraorthodox] public. Today I think that was a mistake. In the future, we will behave differently" (*Haaretz*, July 19, 2005). And indeed, they have done so. The Haredi population is now strongly right-wing throughout Israel, and Haredi parties consistently regard right-wing governments as their natural partners. Eli Yishai's nationalist Yachad party was able to reach out equally to far-right politicians and to ultraorthodox Likud voters (Malach 2019).

In sharp contrast, Ariel shows the level of success the settler movement can achieve by adopting a less ideological and religious frame, which speaks to the whole settler population. From the outset, the Ariel leadership emphasized more broadly shared national security and quality-of-life arguments, which created political goodwill well beyond the traditional support base of the settler movement (i.e., the national-religious and the right-wing). However, it has mostly done so within a broadly sympathetic political context and it remains to be seen whether this approach will also work under intense pressure, as was the case during the Gaza disengagement.

8.4 Contributions to the Literature on Social Movements

Our study is the first in-depth examination of the modern Israeli settler movement from a social scientific (rather than purely historical or political) perspective and one of the few studies that focuses on a longstanding, (radical) right-wing social movement in a "non-Western" political context. To study the impact of the Israeli settler movement, we developed a comprehensive and original theoretical framework that can be used to assess and explain the success of social movements in general. The theoretical model is based on two popular theories in the field: RMT and POS theory. When applied to the Israeli settler movement, this multifaceted approach showed how the organizational structure of that particular social movement, together with constraints and opportunities in the political system, have contributed to both its successes (e.g., Ariel) and failures (e.g., Gaza disengagement). In other words, our theoretical model suggests that individual and structural factors, both internal and external, shape social movement success *in combination.*

We believe our study makes at least two major contributions to the broader literature on social movements. First, our theoretical framework presents an important and original corrective to the conventional view of the social movement as a homogenous unitary actor. It particularly highlights the importance of examining and comparing various organizations *within* the social movement, rather than studying them exclusively as unified entities. Movement structure is a multifaceted phenomenon. Our goal was to capture the entire mosaic of the movement, so that each component – whether formal or informal, large or small, familiar or unfamiliar to the public – would be represented.

The settler movement is hardly alone in its heterogeneous structure. All social movements contain the seeds of fragmentation and internal division within themselves. The structure of the movement not only shapes its growth, but also its tactical choices and sociopolitical outcomes. Like other studies (e.g., Zald & Ash 1966), we found that formal, bureaucratic structures are likely to develop internal splits. Furthermore, where Gamson (1975) found factionalism to be merely a manifestation, and not a cause, of failure, this study found structural division to be, in a paradoxical way, highly useful from a tactical point of view of the social movement. Due to the presence of multiple organizations, working together and with overlapping memberships (Meyer & Whittier 1994), a social movement can cover a plurality of actions and topics. This may eventually strengthen the social movement, making it more visible to both the state and (civil) society.

The choice of a certain organizational structure can constrain the use of particular modes of collective action and facilitate the use of others. For example, a large number of activists can be mobilized for moderate activities (such as demonstrations) by both institutions and networks, but activists can only be mobilized for radical (riskier) actions by networks. Hence, we argue that we cannot fully understand social movements without acknowledging and studying their internal worlds – that is, its members, intra-movement splits, and organizational structure. This should lead social movement scholars to not just rethink and reformulate the structure of social movements but also their influence on public policy.

Second, we show that the political opportunity structure does not only affect the social movement as a whole, but also its internal dynamics, which again affects the social movement as a whole. Political opportunity structure theory explains how legal and political arrangements facilitate or repress the development of social movements, shaping their action repertoires and (lack of) political success. In line with other studies (e.g., Kriesi 2004; Tilly 1978), we found that the action repertoires and mobilization levels of the settler movement are profoundly influenced by political opportunities and constraints. But we also found that the political opportunity context influenced different parts of the settler movement differently, affecting the internal power dynamics of the broader movement.

More specifically, the greater the *discursive and political* opportunities for access to the institutionalized political system and the presence of stable elite alignments, the more the social movement will prioritize its institutions and their moderate action repertoire. In contrast, closure of the institutionalized political system and political repression tend to lead to intra-movement divisions, which leads to radicalization (Caiani & Graziano 2018) and to more antagonistic relations between the institutions and the networks branches. Moreover, changes in state–movement relations eventually affect the internal structure of social movements as well as their ability to advance their goals. This is particularly true during traumatic political events, as, for example, the disengagement from Gaza. During the disengagement period, the institutions lost their direct access to the political system, and alignments became unstable, which led to the appearance of factions within the settler movement, a clear distinction between formal and informal branches, and the growth of the radical flank.

In sum, not only do the paths of action and mobilization of social movements vary from one type of actor (branch) to another, they are also influenced by the interplay between the discursive and political opportunities and, consequently, the resources available at both the domestic and international levels.

8.5 Contributions to Understanding Israeli Politics

The settler movement evolved in the wake of the 1967 and 1973 wars, and quickly developed into a major political force on the Israeli scene. As Ian Lustick stated already more than three decades ago: "The settler movement has become, and will unquestionably remain, a major player in the elemental struggle now under way to determine the shape and purpose of Israeli society" (1988: 16). Yet while almost everyone has heard of the settlers or the settlement enterprise, many key questions regarding the character of the settler movement, and particularly its impact on Israeli politics throughout fifty years of occupation, have remained unanswered. We have tried to fill this theoretical and empirical gap.

Our book is one of the first academic studies to systematically assess the role of the settler movement in Israeli politics in general, and in relation to Israel's policy toward the West Bank in particular. Indeed, despite the extensive (national and international) public attention paid to the settler movement, and the general consensus that it is politically important in both domestic Israeli and (because of its impact on the Israeli–Palestinian conflict) broader international affairs, very few *empirical* studies of the movement exist. The settler movement is mainly discussed within the framework of examinations of Israeli politics (e.g., Ben-Porat et al. 2008;

Karsh 1997; Marteu 2009; Newman 2005; Weissbrod 2002; Yishai 1987), the Israeli radical right (e.g., Pedahzur 2012; Sprinzak 1991, 1999), the Israeli media (e.g., Tsfati & Cohen 2005; Wolfsfeld 1984, 1997); Jewish fundamentalism (e.g., Aran 2013; Feige 2009; Inbari 2009; Shahak & Mezvinsky 1999); political violence and radicalization in Israel (e.g., Alimi 2016; Alimi & Hirsch-Hoefler 2012; Hirsch-Hoefler, Canetti & Eiran 2016; Pedahzur & Perliger 2009; Sprinzak 1985), or the Israeli occupation (e.g., Weizman 2007; Yiftachel 2006). Moreover, most of the few existing studies are highly normative and primarily descriptive. In addition, an impressive body of scholarly research has drawn attention to the origins, cultural, psychological, and religious aspects of religious settlers, most notably of the Gush Emunim movement (e.g., Aran 1986; Aronoff 1985; Don-Yehiya 1987; Lustick 1988; Newman 1985, 2005; Sprinzak 1986; Weissbrod 1982).

However, in contrast to Gush Emunim, the contemporary movement is heterogeneous. Its members vary in ideology (ideological versus quality-of-life settlers), socioeconomic variables (e.g., secular versus religious, women vs. men, young vs. old), and tactics (moderate vs. radical actions). These differences have produced internal structural divisions, which in turn have influenced the mobilization of the settler movement and its political outcomes. We finish this book by highlighting our contribution to three questions surrounding the settler movement: (1) who belongs to it?; (2) what is its role in the settler enterprise?; and, more speculatively, (3) what is its future?

8.5.1 *Who Belongs to the Settler Movement?*

While this might sound obvious, it is nevertheless often forgotten or ignored: the settler movement is not the same as the settler population. Moreover, the settler movement never succeeded in turning itself into a mass movement. Already more than three decades ago, Danny Rubenstein (1985) noted that

> very striking and instructive is the fact that thousands of other Israelis living in the Occupied Territories have nothing to do with the Yesha Council, because they do not consider themselves as political partners of Gush Emunim. The Yesha Council [...] has almost no representation [of] Israelis in the West Bank, who are residents of Ma'ale Adumim and the neighborhoods known as "Five Minutes from Kfar Saba" (*Davar*, February 11, 1985).

This situation has not changed. In fact, it has become more profound and much more visible. The majority of contemporary settlers (more than two-thirds) have *no* ideological zeal and do not truly *believe* in the idea of

Eretz Yisrael. Simply put, a substantial portion of the settler population, although formally represented in the settler movement (i.e., Yesha Council) through their regional and local councils, is not ideologically represented. Residents who moved to the settlements to improve their quality of life, including the sizable ultraorthodox community in the settlements, are geographical rather than ideological settlers.

Why is this important? One may argue that the settler movement has been successful in terms of numbers – more than 400,000 Jews have settled in the West Bank since the Six-Day War – but this large number does not reflect the settler movement's small ideological base. The settler movement emerged from an ideological core (Gush Emunim) but, in part because of its own success, the number and weight of ideologues within the settler population, and slowly but steadily the settler movement, has dwindled. As rightfully suggested by Motti Inbari (2012: 187), scholars must not treat contemporary settlers as simply a modern-day extension of Gush Emunim – as a modern "Bloc of the Faithful." Our book supports this call, and especially the need to take distinctions between different settler groups and organizations more seriously.

8.5.2 *What Is the Role of Settler Movement in the Settlement Enterprise?*

One of the significant questions in debates on the settlements is: who is leading the settlement enterprise? Some scholars argue that the settler movement is the motivating factor, while the state, however important, provides mainly passive support – for example, by failing to honor commitments to freeze settlement construction. The late Ehud Sprinzak, one of the leading scholars on the topic, has argued that "the government does not have the political muscle to act decisively [against the settlers]" (in Shaw-Smith 1994: 108). However, as we have witnessed on several occasions (most recently in the Gaza disengagement; see Chapter 7), the Israeli government does have the means to act, but it generally lacks the will.

On the other hand, many scholars have argued that the settlement enterprise is entirely dependent on continuous government support and funding. The settlements are seen as part of a "state project" (Rosen-Zvi 2007), in which the state serves as a guiding hand in both the establishment and expansion of the settlement enterprise. Should the government choose to "pull the plug," dry up the flow of funds, and destroy the supportive infrastructure (electricity, protection, roads, water), the settlement enterprise would wither rapidly. As the journalists Akiva Eldar and Idith Zertal (2004: iii) have stated, "Take them [these infrastructure elements] out of the equation, and this tower has become a card tower."

Moreover, without their state-issued budgets and grants, the settlements would be unable to survive and would quickly be emptied of their residents.

Some have argued that the whole settlement enterprise is a "state project" (Weizman 2007: 35), that is, that the Israeli state not just tolerates and supports the settlements, it is the main initiator of the settlements, not the settler movement (Rosen-Zvi 2007; Schnall 1984). Oren Yiftachel (2006) even sees state support for the settlement enterprise as a continuation of the Zionist project writ large, that is, the reestablishment of Jewish sovereignty in "their ancient land." Similarly, Yoav Peled and Gershon Shafir (2005) argue that the original settlement project, which laid the foundations for the new Israeli state during the period of the *Yishuv*, was never truly abandoned or completed. Instead, it has remained perhaps the only constant in the ever-changing history of the Israeli state.

Finally, several scholars argue that the settlement enterprise is primarily state-driven, but that ideological and even security motives are secondary. According to Peled and Shapir (2005), "economic incentives" and "material interests" have to a great extent controlled the settlement process and determined not only the number of settlements in the territories but also their locations – that is, the choice of sites close to the Green Line, which are attractive to members of the lower and middle classes priced out of homes in Israel's expensive main cities. More specifically, socioeconomic processes that occurred within Israel, most notably the liberalization and privatization of the Israeli welfare state, had a significant impact on the growth of settlements. Danny Gutwein (2004: 205) has argued that, because these privatization processes mainly affected the lower classes, the settlements – which benefited from subsidies and incentives in the realms of housing, education, health, taxation, and infrastructure – became a kind of "compensatory mechanism protecting the lower classes."

Given the close connections between the Israeli right and the settler movement, in terms of both ideology and personnel, and the right-wing dominance of Israeli politics in most of the period of the settler movement's existence, it is very hard to empirically disentangle the state and the settler movement. This is even more problematic given the status of the institutions of the settler movement, which are almost parastatal entities, and given the particular way in which the Israeli state governs the West Bank, that is, through the IDF and COGAT.

Still, if we engage in counterfactual reasoning, that is, theorize how the situation would look in the case of an absence of the settler movement, we believe that much would look the same, but there would be a significant difference. In terms of number of settlers, the vast majority would still be there, as they are quality-of-life settlers in the larger settlements. But in terms of number of settlements, and particularly their *geography*, we would have a very different situation. The state has always been primarily driven by pragmatic and security concerns. Consequently, they primarily initiated and supported settlements that are either close to the Green Line or at specific locations deemed to strengthen Israel's security. Yet, because of the pressure of the settler movement, the state has built a much more elaborate Israeli infrastructure, which physically disrupts the territorial integrity of the Palestinian Authority and seriously complicates the future of a viable, independent Palestinian state.

8.5.3 *What Will the Future Bring?*

Our analysis found that the settler movement has so far been moderately successful in achieving its overall goal, that is, the annexation and settling of *Eretz Yisrael*, but it has been particularly successful in raising resources for its goal and movement. The settler movement is undoubtedly one of the best-financed social movements in history. Moreover, given the ever-closer ties to the Israeli and US right, and the right's dominance of Israeli and US politics, the future should look very promising. Netanyahu has promised the annexation of all Jewish settlements and to never dismantle them and will undoubtedly find little pushback from the Trump administration, which has open supporters of the settler movement at various key places (including the US Ambassador to Israel, David Friedman). Still, there is a reason to be cautious proclaiming an imminent victory for the settler movement.

The settler movement's mantra – namely that the construction and expansion of the isolated settlements is vital to the security of the state, and that only a permanent Israeli presence throughout the West Bank will enable Israel to defend itself in the event of attack – is far from universally accepted. For instance, former Prime Minister Ehud Barak just recently argued that they actually damage Israel's security interests by putting an unnecessary burden on the IDF, and by complicating the necessary process of separating Israelis from Palestinians (*Haaretz*, August 22, 2019). Similarly, almost all high-ranking US Democrats support a two-state solution and see (most of) the settlements as an important and illegal obstacle. In short, although the settler movement enjoys significant elite support, it has become more and more reliant upon the (Israeli and US) right, as the Israeli, and particularly US, center-left is hardening its stand toward the settler movement.

Perhaps more crucially, the settler movement has failed to settle in the hearts of the Israeli public. As Vered Noam, a sister of Gush Emunim leader Uri Elizur, already noted in the early 1990s,

> In the psychological sense, the Green Line was not erased, it deepened. The "settlements" did not become "communities," and the "settlers" did not become "people." Ariel did not become Carmiel, and Nablus did not become Jaffa. As in Rabbi Yoel Ben-Noon's beautiful wording: "We couldn't settle in their hearts." (*Nekuda*, 1992)

Despite the growth in settlers and settlements, the situation does not seem to have changed much since. As Michael Feige (2009: 274) noted about ten years ago,

> The settlers failed to settle in people's hearts because they proposed a vision that ran counter to dominant trends in the society ... They offered collectivism in the age of individualism, traditional commitment in times of personal self fulfillment, sanctification of place in an age of cyberspace and easy territorial mobility, and memory in an era of forgetting.

This lack of national and international public support, and the one-sided elite support, makes most of the achievements of the settler movement rather vulnerable. As the geographer Elisha Efrat (2010: 91) wrote in his book *Two States for Two Peoples*,

> The density of settlements in the Occupied Territories is not very high, and the distribution of settlements is unbalanced. From a geographical standpoint, the settlement system that has been established through vast investment over the years is flimsy. It is not well aligned with the logic of spatial planning, and is therefore unlikely to be self-sustaining. The collapse and disintegration of this system is only a matter of time.

This could be seen in the disengagement from Gaza. Once the settler movement lost its support from the state, it was virtually powerless in its defense of the settlements. Not only did many settlers not show up to defend the settlements, but few of those that did were willing to go beyond ineffective radical actions, categorically rejecting the use of violence (against the IDF). And the public was in vast majority on the side of the state, not the settler movement.

For the settler movement, the trauma of the disengagement extends far beyond the mere failure to retain Israeli control over the Gaza Strip (and four small settlements in Samaria). What Gadi Ben-Zimra (Interview 2007) has called "the post-trauma of the disengagement" has reverberated deeply within the settler movement, and the effects are still felt today. Prior to the disengagement period, the settler movement had one clear leadership, the Yesha Council. Even though there were internal disputes, the Yesha Council could come to the Israeli state and reach an agreement in name of the (whole) settler movement. This is no longer the case. Today, a much broader leadership is required in order to reach agreements as well as decisions regarding actions and strategies. Moreover, a small, but increasingly significant, part of the settler movement openly rejects the authority of both the settler institutions and the Israeli state, alienating both the Israeli elites and masses.

Ironically, perhaps the biggest failure of the settler movement lies in the transformation of the settler public. It has become received wisdom that (all) West Bank settlers fundamentally oppose any decision that would require Israeli withdrawal from any part of the West Bank. But empirical research on settlement evacuations reveals that most settlers, despite their desire to remain in their homes and communities, hold much more nuanced views on a possible relocation (Hirschberger & Hirsch-Hoefler 2016; Hirsch-Hoefler et al., 2019). Most West Bank settlers understand that the future of settlement in the occupied territories is uncertain and are open to an evacuation as part of a "land-for-peace" deal with the right financial compensation. This applies to the vast majority of quality-of-life settlers, the bulk of the settler population, but also to large minorities of the more ideological settlers.

Whether the withdrawal from the occupied territories will ever become a serious political possibility depends on (changes in) both the Israeli and international political contexts (notably Palestinian and US). The current political environment, most notably the Netanyahu and Trump governments, clearly favors the settler movement. But with an increasingly polarized Israeli and US political context, and the settler movement's open choice for the right-wing, government change can have profound consequences for the settler enterprise. Moreover, the settler movement knows it cannot fully trust Netanyahu, having been "betrayed" by much more pro-settler right-wing politicians before (notably Begin and Sharon).

However, time is working in the settler's favor. The longer the current situation continues, let alone (some) settlements are officially annexed, the harder it will become for future governments to fundamentally dismantle the settlements. First of all, more Jewish settlers will have to be resettled in Israel, which will be even more problematic if they are to be compensated "fairly" – that is, receive similar homes at similar rates as in the settlements. Second, more and more settlers have been born in the settlements, thereby considering it their "natural home" (irrespective of ideological or religious meanings). Third, as polls show, Israelis born after 1967 are much less aware of the significance of the Green Line and tend to perceive both the settlements and the whole West Bank as part of Israel proper. Moreover, several generations of Israelis have been socialized primarily under right-wing governments, which have actively defended the rights of the settlers and minimized the relevance of the Green Line and illegality of Israel's presence in the West Bank.

Still, the disengagement and its aftermath have laid bare a paradox of the settler movement, which until then had been hidden from both the broader public and the settlers themselves. The more institutionalized and legitimate the movement became, the more limited its real power was. And the more radical and vigorous the settlers' resistance, the greater the general public's alienation toward them and their enterprise. So far, it has not been able to overcome this paradox.

Notes

Introduction

1. Rabbi Abraham Isaac Kook developed a unique political theology blending universalism and Jewish particularism (for an introduction to his thought, see Agus 1946). His son and successor, Rabbi Zvi Yehudah Kook provided the spiritual foundation of the settler movement (Hellinger 2008; see also Chapter 2).
2. All data on the Israeli and settler populations are taken from the various reports and website of the Israeli Central Bureau of Statistics (CBS), unless explicitly stated otherwise.
3. Although the State of Israel was long dominated by Ashkenazi Jews, with roots in (Eastern) Europe, who shaped Israeli political culture and institutions in line with (West) European ones, Israel has always had a significant non-European Jewish population (so-called Mizrahi), as well as a sizeable Arab minority, and is situated in a non-Western region, the Middle East. In short, while having "Western" features, Israel is not part of the classic "Western context" of North America and Western Europe.

1 Theoretical Framework

1. Scholars have proposed various terms for policy gains, such as "structural gains" (Kitschelt 1986; Burstein et al. 1995), "reactive and proactive effects" (Kriesi et al. 1995), and "power orientations" (Killian & Turner 1993). Paul Burstein, Rachel Einwohner, and Jocelyn Hollander (1995) have also distinguished between "policy responsiveness" and "outcome responsiveness."
2. Within the three broad spheres of action, further refinements are also possible. For instance, some scholars divide the moderate, conventional tactical repertoire into four categories: persuasion, facilitation, bargaining, and coercion (Taylor & Van Dyke 2004: 267).

2 History of the Settlements

1. The West Bank is also called Judea and Samaria, ancient names for the territories overlapping parts of the biblical kingdoms of Judah (in the south) and Israel (in the north), which together comprise most of the West Bank. Between Judea and Samaria lies a territory known as the "Land of Benjamin."

2. The army itself used to refer to it as "belligerent occupation." For the far-right it is not disputed at all, they only use Judea and Samaria. Much public discourse (e.g., media) refers to it as "occupied territories" (or just "territories" for short).
3. While the settler movement is also active and relevant within East Jerusalem, we exclude it from our analysis because the de facto annexation, and consequent settlement, of East Jerusalem was initiated and formalized by the Israel government directly after its occupation in 1967, before the settler movement had emerged. Today, some 215,000 Israelis live in the annexed areas of the Jerusalem municipality (The Jerusalem Institute of Policy Research 2019).
4. The term "Aliyah" is used to describe Jewish immigration to (the Land of) Israel, both as a collective and an individual process.
5. Zionist socialism was in general also ethnically exclusive. The Yishuv was operated by and, for the most part, for Ashkenazi Jews who had migrated from European nations. Jews from Arab lands, known as Mizrahim, were a minority in pre-state Israel.
6. Israel also captured the Sinai Peninsula from Egypt, but the Sinai plays a smaller role in the settlement story.
7. Figure 2.1 is from the Israel Ministry of Foreign Affairs.
8. The WZO's involvement was solidified further with the establishment of the Ministerial Committee for Settlement (also known as the "Inter-institutional Committee for Settlement") in 1970. The Committee comprised an equal number of ministers from the relevant government ministries and members of the WZO Executive (Benvenisti 1987; Rokach 1978).
9. It should be noted that Labor's Shimon Peres thought along the same lines, arguing that "settlement in the western slopes of the Judean and Samarian mountains liberates us of the curse of Israel's narrow middle ... " (Peres 1978: 8).
10. The end of the Rabin administration in 1995, following his assassination, meant the discontinuation of the Committee. It was reinstated by Ehud Barak's government in 1999, only to be dismantled again by PM Sharon in 2001. In 2012, Prime Minister Benjamin Netanyahu reestablished the Committee under his own leadership. Since then, the Committee has been an important tool in the pro-settlement kit in Israel. Its existence also illustrates the degree to which pro-settlement advocates have infiltrated the highest echelons of the Israeli executive branch (see Chapter 4).
11. We do not mention the terrorists by name, because this only feeds into their myth-making and potentially inspires other terrorists.
12. The number of settlers and settlements come from Israel's Central Bureau of Statistics, while the settler figures for 1968–1975 and settlements figures for 1968–1981 are taken from Peace Now. The data exclude East Jerusalem.
13. Source: Arieli Shaul, 2019.
14. Thus, for example, the number of outposts existing in 2005 was 105 according to the Sasson report, but 87 according to the Ministry of Defense.
15. As Israel's Central Bureau of Statistics does not track outposts, we took our data from Peace Now (October 2019) and the Sasson Report. The total

number of outposts shown is 125, which excludes two now-dismantled outposts (Migron and Amona) and some 15 that have been legalized (3 as independent settlements and 12 as "neighborhoods").

16. The construction of the barrier, while claimed to have successfully reduced terrorism in Israel, has raised objections, based on the argument that the barrier was not built on the Green Line and that it both expropriated Palestinian agricultural lands and de facto annexed settlements that had been built in the occupied territories (Ben-Eliezer & Feinstein 2007: 171).
17. Source: United Nations Office for the Coordination of Humanitarian Affairs Occupied Palestinian Territories.
18. The lives of the Palestinian residents of the territories are ruled by an array of agencies, including the Civil Administration, the Border Police, the Coordinator of Activities in the Territories, and the General Security Service. For elaborate discussion on the bureaucracy of the occupation in the West Bank (see Berda 2012).
19. More precisely, the Oslo Accords made the Palestinian Authority responsible for civil and security affairs in Area A and for civil affairs only in Area B, with the IDF retaining responsibility for security there. However, the IDF also retained ultimate authority over security throughout the West Bank, including the right to conduct security operations in Area A (which it does regularly).
20. The COGAT website also details its legal duties in the region, which include registration of companies and commercial licensing, as well as more politically charged matters such as granting licenses and permits for land transactions and realizing the Israeli government's policy on issues of real estate in Area C.
21. For example, Yoav Stern (2005) cites a case where, upon inquiry from the State Comptroller about an access road that impinged upon Palestinian land, COGAT implemented an "abbreviated protocol" instead of the necessary extensive probes to determine collateral damage from the road construction. Although in this case the State Comptroller reported that the Civil Administration officials did their best to locate private Palestinian landowners to allow them the chance to claim their land or receive some degree of financial compensation, Dror Etkes, member of the Peace Now settlement-tracking project, suggested that their intentions are far more nefarious. He stated that the majority of land appropriation incidences in the West Bank by the Civil Administration go unnoticed and unchallenged.
22. This support has been expressed most notably in US-sponsored talks between the two sides at Wye Valley (1998), Camp David (2000), Annapolis (2007), and Washington, DC (2010).
23. The term "pro-Israel" has become part of a broader political struggle, in Israel and particularly the United States, which is why we use the term in quotation marks. While groups like AIPAC are certainly "pro-Israel," so are groups like J Street, in the sense that both support the State of Israel. However, right-wing Jewish and Israeli groups tend to reserve the term "pro-Israel" for groups that are uncritical toward right-wing Israeli governments, as well as toward the occupation of the West Bank (and other territories), implying that groups that criticize the Israeli government (or state) on these issues are anti-Israel.

24. The "pro-Israel" lobby is a complex and heterogeneous complex of political actors, mainly, but not exclusively, consisting of (evangelical) Christian and (conservative) Jewish Americans. While some scholars have asserted that the "pro-Israel" lobby has overwhelming influence on the US Congress and policy-makers and employs coercive methods to secure its goals (e.g., Mearsheimer & Walt 2007), others have rejected these claims (Chomsky 2006; Kiely 2017; Massad 2006; Zunes 2006).

3 History of the Settler Movement

1. Gahelet began in the high school yeshiva of Kfar Haroeh, a religious *moshav* in central Israel named after Rabbi Abraham Isaac HaKohen Kook. The yeshiva was founded and headed by Rabbi Moshe-Zvi Neria, a former student of Rabbi Kook. Many of Neria's pupils in the 1950s became spiritual leaders of the settler movement later (Neusner & Goldscheider 1990).
2. While many members of the Jewish Underground were convicted and sentenced to prison, most were handed short terms or were granted pardons by Haim Herzog, Israel's president at the time. The last three were released in December 1990.
3. Many of the first US settlers had been politically active in leftist social movements in the United States in the 1960s and 1970s, prior to immigrating to Israel (Hirschhorn 2017).
4. Of the 710 immigrants in 2017, 293 were from Russia, 194 from the United States, 87 from France, 14 from the United Kingdom, and 7 from Asian republics of the former USSR.
5. Figure 3.1 is based on data from the Central Bureau of Statistics (1986–18). Data until 2005 include Gaza Strip.
6. Type of settlement is based on data from Peace Now.
7. Type of settlement is based on data from peace now.
8. *Hardal* is a Hebrew acronym for Haredi-Leumi, or ultraorthodox nationalists. In sharp contrast to the Hardal population living in the West Bank, most ultraorthodox Jews, both in Israel and abroad, embrace a non-, and even anti-Zionist ideology.
9. Chabad is an alternative name for the Lubavitch Hasidic movement.
10. Though this number may represent an underestimate, as Eiran and Krause (2018) only counted those reported in a collection of Israeli, Palestinian, and US newspapers.
11. The leading figure behind the founding of the Yesha Council was Israel Harel, an Ofra resident who took part in establishing many settlements in the territories. Harel was also the founder of the Yesha Council's monthly magazine, *Nekuda*. He currently serves as a columnist for *Haaretz* newspaper, one of Israel's premier daily newspapers.
12. This is a familiar strategy. Other states which have maintained communities of settlers (such as France in Algeria, or England in Ireland) have relied on a similar logic of security to justify their positions (Kimmerling 1993).

13. Rabbi Avraham Shapira was considered one of religious Zionism's spiritual leaders and was Chief Rabbi of Israel from 1983 until 1993. In 1982 Shapira was appointed head of the religious Zionist flagship, Mercaz HaRav Yeshiva, after the death of Rabbi Zvi Yehudah Kook. Known principally for his uncompromising opposition to any territorial compromises, Shapira called on soldiers to refuse orders to aid in the dismantling of Jewish settlements in the Gaza Strip during the 2005 disengagement.
14. Regavim is a Hebrew word meaning clods or patches of earth.
15. The group distributed 100,000 copies of its first edition throughout Israel and to decision makers abroad (mainly the United States).
16. It should be noted that the military government applies almost a blanket rejection of Palestinian requests for building permits. According to Israeli Civil Administration data, only 33 of the 2,020 applications for building permits in Area C submitted by Palestinians between 2010 and 2014 were approved (see also OCHA 2015).
17. Yesh Din is an Israeli NGO that aims to protect the human rights of Palestinians living in the occupied territories. It collects, documents, and disseminates information regarding Israeli human rights violations in the territories.
18. The Land of Israel (*Eretz Israel*) Caucus operates as a lobby group within the Knesset with the aim of strengthening Israel's hold on all of the Land of Israel, particularly in the West Bank, and safeguarding the settlement enterprise. As an example, in January 2014, a delegation of fifteen MKs and Ministers representing all the parties of the coalition visited the Jordan Valley in protest against then US Secretary of State John Kerry's plans for removal of civilians from the Jordan Valley, and in solidarity with the people there. This visit was organized by Orit Strook (*Jewish Home*), chair of the Land of Israel caucus in the Knesset (*Jerusalem Post* 2, January 2014).
19. Kach ran in the elections for the Eighth (1973), Ninth (1977), and Tenth (1981) Knessets, but did not pass the electoral threshold. Prior to the 1984 elections for the 11th Knesset, the Central Elections Board disqualified the party from running. The Supreme Court overruled the decision, and the party went on to win a seat for the first time. The Knesset soon passed an amendment to the "Basic Law: The Knesset," which stipulated that no party may participate in Knesset elections if one of its objectives is incitement to racism (section 7a of the law). In the 1988 elections for the 12th Knesset, Kach was indeed disqualified from running (Israel Democracy Institute 2019).
20. A Hebrew University poll of 2010 found that 21 percent of settlers believed that "all means must be employed to resist the [future] evacuation of settlements, including the use of arms [if necessary]." Note, though, that the extreme views of this group date to before the 2005 disengagement from Gaza. A 2003 survey found that 73.5 percent of Hilltop Youth members saw "deportation, revenge, and war" as the solution to the conflict ("The Hilltop Youth of Yesha," http://www.bhol.co.il/forums/topic.asp?topic_id=931581&forum_id=8888; in Hebrew).

21. In 2014, three activists from the group were charged in an arson attack against a Jewish–Arab bilingual school in Jerusalem (*Haaretz*, December 11, 2014).
22. Both NRG and Makor Rishon were bought out by media conglomerate *Israel Today* in 2014 (*Arutz Sheva,* April 30, 2014).
23. In a 2013 *Arutz Sheva* op-ed, Haetzni describes the political left's attempt to villainize right-wing leaders by dramatizing acts of destruction of property and "price tag" attacks in Fureidis, an Arab town near Haifa. He claims that the attacks, which should be considered "no more than minor harassment," were labeled "a sin" by left-wing leaders to advance their own political agenda by waging "a media war and field trials" against the right (Haetzni 2013).
24. Boutique Katom bills itself as the "first online international boutique showcasing handmade products created exclusively in Judea and Samaria," and aims to instill in buyers a sense that the West Bank is an integral part of Israel. Revenues from the boutique are channeled back into Dapei Katom.
25. Multiple other private tour guide initiatives promoting the Israeli settlement agenda and ideology work through individual networks or are supported by other settler organizations (one example is Bet El Tours, run in conjunction with *Arutz Sheva*). The tours are neatly tailored to suit the character of each group, and the settlers have managed to bring many government ministers, as well as media personalities, on visits to the area.
26. Shemer's presence in Israel, both artistically and as an icon, was so prolific that her songs have been said to have "formed the very bedrock of Israeli culture" (Ibid).

4 Assessing the Settler Movement's Success

1. For part of the settler movement, this overarching goal includes a desire to build a Third Temple, which would serve as the national and religious center for the Jewish people (Aran 1991; Inbari 2009).
2. Figure 4.1 is based on data from the Central Bureau of Statistics and the Israel Statistical Yearbook (1967–2018).
3. No Israeli government office or department systematically collects or maintains data on outposts. Data are scattered between the Ministry of Defense, the IDF, the Civil Administration, the Ministry of Housing and Construction, the Ministry of the Interior, the Settlement Division of the World Zionist Organization, and other government offices and regional authorities in the West Bank. In assessing the actual number, growth and expansion of Israeli outposts and settlements, we relied on official state documents, including the Sasson Report (2005), the Spiegel Report (2007), the Levy Report (2012), and the Zandberg Report (2018). We also drew on independently collected data from the Settlement Watch project of Peace Now.
4. The UNSC considers Israeli settlements on land occupied since 1967 illegal under the Fourth Geneva Convention, and a serious obstruction to achieving a "comprehensive, just and lasting peace" (wording frequently employed in UN General Assembly resolutions on the Israel–Palestinian conflict; e.g., resolution A/RES/73/89). As such, the UNSC considers Israel's claims on all

existing settlements to be null and void, and calls for them to be dismantled (see, for example, UNSC resolutions 446, 452, 465, 471, and 2334).

5. Figure 4.2 is based on data from the Peace Now dataset (2019).
6. Figure 4.3 is based on data from the Peace Now dataset (2019). The number of outposts shown includes dismantled outposts and outposts that have been legalized.
7. Construction starts for previous years were 91,922 m^2 in 2016, 75,009 m^2 in 2014, and 45,540 m^2 in 2012.
8. The data for the years before 2005 include settlements in the West Bank and Gaza Strip (Israel Central Bureau of Statistics 2019).
9. It is important to stress that, in contrast with other areas in Israel, building and construction in the West Bank is influenced not only by market and economic considerations, but also by ideological and political ones. In fact, an active presence of pro-settlement individuals in the Knesset has long served to bolster the settler movement's standing in the political sphere.
10. There are eleven district industrial zones in the West Zone as well as eighteen local zones. These zones include a total of 773 factories and 325 additional businesses (Arieli 2017).
11. The data for the years before 2005 include settlements in the West Bank and Gaza Strip. Source: Israel Central Bureau of Statistics.
12. Reminder: all numbers are from the Israel Central Bureau of Statistics and exclude East Jerusalem.
13. source: Arieli Shaul, 2017.
14. In 2006, the Israeli government, in cooperation with the defense establishment, commissioned a report aimed at examining the degree to which Israeli settlements were built on private Palestinian land. The so-called Spiegel Report was to create an exhaustive dataset of the settlements based on data from COGAT. However, upon completion, the report was deemed potentially harmful to state security and was therefore kept under wraps by Prime Minister Barak.
15. The Spiegel Report included a section on every Jewish settlement in the West Bank, highlighting in red which construction projects had taken place without the necessary authorization.
16. Levy publicly opposed the Gaza Disengagement (*Walla*, March 12, 2014); Schapira is related to the right-wing activist Israel Harel, and Baker, a resident of the settlement Har Adar, is a prominent voice in the call for the legalization of outposts (*Globes*, July 19, 2012; *Haaretz*, July 9, 2012).
17. The Levy Report (2012), officially titled the Report on the Legal Status of Building in Judea and Samaria, sought to redefine the appropriation of private lands for military purposes by asserting that "such lands can be used for settlements, subject to a professional security opinion on the needs of the adjacent community." Only one of its recommendations favored the Palestinians – namely, the suggestion that in matters of land claims, judges should be instructed to wear civilian clothes so as to not to prejudice the case in the eyes of the Israeli.
18. The committee was established as part of the government coalition agreements between Likud and Jewish Home, and headed by Haya

Zandberg, former head of the Civil Law Division in the State Prosecutor's office, who was appointed to the Jerusalem District Court in 2018.

19. The notion of "good faith" is based on the fact that settler groups, often unknowingly or unintentionally, settled on private land owned by Palestinians, as a result of an extremely convoluted land registry system in the West Bank. However, many critics have noted that the stipulation allowing for expropriation "with government approval" will legitimize the seizing of Palestinian land without the preexisting claim of "good faith" (*Times of Israel*, December 16, 2018).
20. The law, which effectively legalized some 4,000 settler residences, was criticized by the left as the first step towards annexation of the West Bank territories. For its part, the right was vocal about its support. Jewish Home MK Smotrich, who cosponsored the legislation with Likud MK Yoav Kisch, said that the Regulation Law was a momentous step towards their goal of applying Israeli sovereignty to the Jewish settlements in the West Bank (*Jerusalem Post,* February 6, 2017).
21. In particular, Livnat established the "Judea and Samaria Museum Council" for the purpose of providing government subsidies to such institutions.
22. Thus, beneficiaries of national subsidies include the West Bank settlements of Migron, Kerem Re'im, and Shvut Rachel – all of which are defined as neighborhoods of larger towns (such as Kochav Yaakov, Talmon and Shiloh, respectively (Government Resolution 3738: Defining localities and regions as national priority, April 15, 2018).
23. All amounts were recalculated in US dollars at rate of 0.26 cents per 1 New Israeli Shekel (rate of July 2019).
24. In March 2018, the Accountant General and the Ministry of Finance announced a new measure that grants serious relief for debt and loan repayments for settlers. Reviewing the work of the Appeals Committee and the Debt Settlement Committee, the Hativa website lauds the discount of 50 percent for settlers attempting to repay loans (*Operation Debt Settlement,* 2018).
25. These reports – the Sasson Report (2005), Spiegel Report (2007), Levy Report (2012), and Zandberg Report (2018) – all touched on the continued extrajudicial expansion of the settlements.
26. Based on the data provided to her, Sasson estimated the number of unauthorized outposts as 105. However, she noted that the true number of outposts is probably higher.
27. Based on data from Shaked et al. (2015).
28. The 2015 Knesset had twelve MKs from the settlements: five each from Likud and Jewish Home, one from Yesh Atid (There is a Future), and one from Yisrael Beitenu (Israel Is Our Home).
29. The figure 4.8 refers to ministers and MKs who served partial or full terms and who resided within settlements either during their time in office or previously. Residents of the Golan Heights were not included. Source: The Knesset website.
30. Because Israel has had compulsory enlistment at age eighteen since the establishment of the State, the IDF experience has played a particularly

crucial part in crystallizing public opinions on a huge range of issues, but especially on security. Moreover, the IDF's almost ubiquitous assimilation into Israeli culture has made it an incredibly formative entity in society.

31. In the same year, 61 percent of recruits from the Samaria region opted to serve in combat units, compared with only 36 percent of their counterparts from Tel Aviv – a stark contrast (Heller 2000; Lebel 2010).
32. Israeli political parties are notoriously fluid. For example, the Jewish Home party was formed as a union of the National Religious Party (NRP), Homeland, and Resurrection in November 2008. The latter two then left that union, leaving Jewish Home as the successor to the NRP. For the 2013 and 2015 elections, Jewish Home and Resurrection ran together under a joint list headed by the chairman of Jewish Home, Naftali Bennett. In April 2019, Jewish Home ran on a joint list with Resurrection and Jewish Power (*Otzma Yehudit*) under the name Union of Right-Wing Parties (*Ichud Miflagot HaYamin*). For the September 2019 elections, the Union of Right-Wing Parties joined with the New Right, a party established in December 2018 by Naftali Bennett, who had left Jewish Home, and Ayelet Shaked, to form a new alliance known as Rightwards (*Yamima*).
33. Peretz used to head a yeshiva in Atzmona, a settlement in the Gaza Strip that was destroyed as part of the disengagement in 2005 (see Chapter 7).
34. Source: The Knesset website.
35. Historian Joseph Heller (2000) even referred to Begin's Herut party as a one-issue party, dedicated to broadening Israel's borders.
36. Another key moment occurred during the Arab summit of June 1996, which was crucial to cementing the increasingly positive relationship between Israel and Jordan, as King Hussein helped guide the Arab nations toward a less antagonistic stand on Israel (Bookmiller 1997). Jordan played a key diplomatic role during Netanyahu's first year in office as the mediator between the Palestinian Authority and Israel. In this role, King Hussein succeeded in convincing Netanyahu to withdraw from 85 percent of Hebron, in what became known as the Hebron Agreement, marking the first accord signed between the Palestinians and the Likud (*The Baltimore Sun*, January 19, 1997).
37. Data gathered on October 29, 2019. Yesha followers included three Facebook pages, my Yesha, Yesha, and For Yesha.
38. It is generally assumed that interpersonal differences about a political agreement with the Palestinians involving a significant Israeli withdrawal from the West Bank reflect ideological and religious inclinations; the more right-wing and religious a person is, the more he or she will oppose such an agreement. While there is a great deal of validity in this argument, recent evidence suggests that differences in how threats (namely existential and symbolic threats) are perceived underlie ideological differences. While symbolic threats increase support for political compromise, physical threats reduce support for compromise (Hirschberger & Hirch-Hoefler 2016).
39. In 2011 the question was: "In your opinion, in terms of Israel's national interest, are the settlements located in the heart of the Palestinian population

in the West Bank an asset or a burden?" In 2017, the phrasing was: "In your opinion, in terms of Israel's national interest and from today's perspective, has the policy of various Israeli governments to establish settlements in Judea and Samaria been correct or incorrect?"

40. The question between 2001 and 2010 was: "Looking back, has the Israeli government made the right decision by permitting and encouraging construction of settlements in the territories?". In 2017, the phrasing was: "In your opinion, in terms of Israel's national interest and from today's perspective, has the policy of various Israeli governments to establish settlements in Judea and Samaria been correct or incorrect?"
41. Some shifts in Israeli public opinion can be associated with current events. For example, the decline in support for the settlements between 2001 and 2004 may be related to the Second Intifada, and to optimism in light of the Disengagement Plan, announced in December 2003, as well as early Israeli government support for the Middle East Quartet's Road Map plan. Similarly, between 2009 and 2012 Israel launched two military operations against Hamas in Gaza (Operation Cast Lead and Operation Pillar of Defense), which may have led Israeli Jews to experience disappointment with the 2005 Gaza Disengagement.
42. Figure 4.13 is based on Billig and Lebel (2009–12).
43. Focusing on the commonalities among settlers [in the Gaza Strip] and liberal Israelis across the Green Line, Dalsheim find that the conflict among Israelis on both sides of the Green Line arises from the suppression of sameness, rather than difference (for elaborate discussion see Dalsheim 2011).
44. It is interesting to note that this is similar to knowledge of the number of Palestinians in the West Bank: 21 percent underestimated the number, 16 percent overestimated it, 25 percent did not know, and 35 percent was correct.
45. It is well established that events like terrorist attacks tend to increase support for government authorities and policies (e.g., Chanley 2002; Huddy et al. 2002; Jost & Banjai 1994; Moskalenko et al. 2006; Pyszczynski et al. 2003).
46. The question was: "What do you think should be Israel's policy regarding the future of the Jewish settlements in Judea and Samaria as a part of the peace agreement with the Palestinians." Source: The Peace Index, a monthly survey done by the Israel Democracy Institute and Tel Aviv University (1996–2017).
47. The question was: "If the government decided to evacuate Jewish settlements and the decision were confirmed in a referendum, would you (1) Evacuate under any conditions; (2) Evacuate in exchange for fair compensation; (3) Object to evacuation under any circumstances." Source: Hirschberger and Hirsch-Hoefler, 2016.
48. The wording of this question was: "If the government of Israel enacts, in the near future, an 'evacuation–compensation' law that would allow you to receive fair compensation in return for evacuating your home, to what degree would you be prepared to accept? (1) Not at all; (2) With low probability; (3) With moderate probability; (4) With high probability; or (5) With very high probability."

49. Surveys found that any kind of question with the word "settlement" in it gets the same result: near-identical division by ideology (i.e., left/center/right), about half who support settlements (including when phrased as "expansion") and just under half who oppose them (e.g., Shikaki & Scheindlin 2019). However, if the question is about building new "isolated" settlements in the heart of Palestinian cities, most Israelis oppose it (on both sides of the political specter).
50. At the roundtable, Dayan reportedly criticized the State Department's prevention of "US funding for any Jewish activity in Judea and Samaria ... such as denying research grants to Ariel University" (Zionist Organization of America, July 8, 2013). This tenacity was representative for the settler movement's approach to the Obama administration (2008–16).
51. J Street also organizes such trips, such as its first Congressional delegation in 2010, when it brought five Congress members to Israel, Jordan, and the Palestinian Authority. Its delegations include visits to Jewish settlements, such as those in Hebron and Kiryat Arba, but balance meetings with settlers with those with the Hebron-based Palestinian NGO Youth Against Settlements as well as walking tours of the city of Hebron, to see the market and checkpoints that affect Palestinian residents of the town.
52. Other studies have also found the "point-and-shoot" pattern of reporting, which gives primacy to superficial description over analysis, to be pervasive in coverage of the settlements (e.g., Friel & Falk 2004). The *Columbia Journalism Review* noted that the Israeli–Palestinian conflict generates more complaints of biased media reporting than any other news topic, with both parties often perceiving the same media representation as biased toward the opposition.
53. Another survey that year found that opposition to the settlements increased when the question was framed in the context of international law (World Public Opinion 2009).
54. A 2016–17 Country Ratings Poll in nineteen European countries found that perceptions of Israel remained largely negative in Europe – half of respondents had a negative opinion, only 25 percent a positive – although this had softened since 2014 (Globscan 2017).
55. As noted earlier, US President Trump recognized Israeli sovereignty over the Golan Heights in March 2019. Some observers also see the relocation of the US embassy from Tel Aviv to Jerusalem in May 2018 as implicit recognition of Israel's annexation of East Jerusalem. However, as the embassy's new location is in West Jerusalem, this interpretation is open to debate.
56. As noted earlier, the Palestinian Authority formally has civil and security control over Area A, and civil control over Area B. However, Israel retains ultimate security control over all of the West Bank. With respect to Gaza, that area is under Palestinian governance, but Israel remains firmly in control over many aspects of life in Gaza (including access to some goods, fishing waters, the electro-magnetic sphere, the population registry, and all perimeters except Rafah).

5 The Action Repertoires of the Branches

1. In Israel, the threshold, that is, the minimum share of the vote required for a party to obtain representation, is 3.25 percent. The threshold has been raised several times over time though, from the initial 0.83 percent in 1951 to 3.25 percent in 2014 (Rahat & Hazan 2005). By way of comparison, the electoral threshold is usually (4 or) 5 percent in most European countries.
2. According to Koopmans and Olzak (2004), DOS bridges the gap between POS and framing theories. Framing theory only explains the nature of successful movement frames, and POS focuses only on the link between political and institutional opportunities and movement failures and/or successes.
3. According to Katzover, the settlements had hosted seven or eight groups from the Youth Guard in 2016–2017.
4. Another Jewish terrorist network, known as the Bat Ayin Underground, emerged after the outbreak of the Al-Aqsa Intifada in late 2000. Members of the Bat Ayin Underground, a network of activists living in several West Bank settlements, began to carry out violent attacks against Palestinians in the West Bank, such as shooting at passing vehicles and planting explosive devices in public buildings. The network recruited young people from the Hilltop Youth and from the Jewish settlement in Hebron (Pedahzur & Perliger 2009).
5. These included an annual amount of ca. $13.8 million over six years for bulletproof public transportation and student transportation in Judea and Samaria, as well as ca. $4.1 million for the construction of a permanent building for the Gush Katif and Northern Samaria Heritage Center (*Walla*, May 10, 2015).
6. In an interview on his international activities, Dayan proudly claimed: "We published opinion articles and interviews in the *New York Times* and the *Guardian*, the *Los Angeles Times*, the *Boston Globe*, *USA Today* and many others. Against all the odds and with almost no money, we have turned the 'settlers' into a sought-after interlocutor in the strategic, diplomatic, academic and international media. We have questioned our interlocutors about positions that have been adopted for decades" (*Kipa News*, March 26, 2015).
7. The Brazilians opposed the appointment of a settler as ambassador. Dayan later taunted his Brazilian opponents by saying, "Those who did not want a settler leader in Brasilia received a settler leader in the capital of the world, in the beating heart of the United States" (*Times of Israel*, March 28, 2016).
8. In another case, the State Comptroller accused Yesha Council Chairman Avi Roeh of tailoring the criteria for public funding awards so that only two NGOs would be eligible. MK Smotrich founded one of the NGOs in 2006, and served as its chairman until his Knesset campaign in 2015, while Roeh sits on the board of the second. The Comptroller's report was published two days after Smotrich introduced a Knesset bill that would reduce the authority of that office (*Times of Israel*, November 19, 2017).
9. Amona is a Jewish outpost in the West Bank where an attempted evacuation in 2006 degenerated into a violent confrontation between thousands of settlers and thousands of soldiers and police officers. Two hundred people were reported to have sustained injuries, including eighty members of the security forces, most of them police officers (*Ynet*, January 2, 2006). The legal status of

Amona remained unresolved until it was finally evacuated by government order in 2017.

10. Its cases have included high-profile defenses of individuals like Meir Ettinger and Amiram Ben-Uliel, the main suspect in the notorious Duma terrorist attack, in which eighteen-month-old Ali Dawabsheh and his parents were burned to death in the Palestinian village of Duma (*New York Times*, January 11, 2016).
11. The origins of these military-prep yeshivas go back to the 1950s, when they were introduced to enable religious youth to combine religious studies with combat service in homogeneous religious frameworks.
12. The ranking is similar to those produced by the National Rifle Association (NRA) and AIPAC in the United States, which rank representatives on the basis of their support for gun owners and Israel, respectively.
13. For example, the 2018 Mattot Arim Report noted that "about 10% of the National Camp's elected leaders were found to be 'top achievers.' However, the achievers were the exception rather than the rule. In sharp contrast, almost 70% of the National Camp's elected leaders earned 10 or fewer marks. Moreover, 20% of Knesset members managed to earn only a single mark – or none." Justice Minister Ayelet Shaked, who was ranked first in the 2018 report, responded on her Facebook page: "It is a great honor for me to be in first place . . . in the Mattot Arim report . . . . It's good someone is keeping tabs on what elected officials are actually doing." Tourism Minister Yariv Levin, who came in second, declared on his Facebook page that he would "continue to work with all my power for the Land of Israel – and for our right to build throughout the Land."
14. One of the Revolt demonstrations used props like metal bed frames to highlight what they claim is "inhumane treatment" of settler activists (*Haaretz*, December 24, 2015).
15. Prominent sympathizers have used their platforms in support of their campaigns. For example, in an interview with *Algemeiner* (May 24, 2017), MK Smotrich said, "The burning of the yeshiva in Homesh is a reminder for us to continue working for the return of the Jewish people to all areas that were destroyed during the [2005] expulsion."
16. As they did, for example, in the cases of Gush Katif and Sa Nur in 2005, Amona in 2006, and Amona and Migron more recently.
17. In one brazen example the Hilltop Youth issued fliers promising a reward of $300,000 to anyone willing to murder a member of the left-wing organization Peace Now (*Walla*, September 25, 2008).
18. It is important to note that while the Jewish Underground came from the mainstream settler movement, the Bat Ayin underground was drawn from young people, second- and third-generation settlers, who were raised on the hills. None were associated with the settler elite (*Haaretz*, October 1, 2003).
19. In 2003, Kahane Chai is thought to have called for the assassination of former Prime Minister Ariel Sharon, who had spearheaded the disengagement.
20. Some organizations have gone one step further, calling for secessionism, that is, full disengagement from the State of Israel and the establishment of the

settlements as an independent state. For example, in 2005, *Ynet* reported that a group of residents from the Gaza settlement Kfar Yam had declared a plan to establish a "Gaza Region Jewish Authority," which was slated to have a sovereign government, parliament, and military (*Ynet*, November 8, 2005). It should be stressed that this group constitutes only a minuscule part of the networks.

21. At the height of the struggle against the Sebastia eviction, Shemer came to the Knesset accompanied by two Elon Moreh settler leaders (*Channel 10*, March 25, 2018).
22. Two years earlier, he had been slated to receive a similar award of the Union of Composers, Writers, and Publishers in Israeli Music (ACUM), but this was changed to a "contribution to music" award after fierce protest against Zilber's political views by other artists and left-wing activists.
23. Zilber's actions were not limited to his songs and words. He became a settler himself in 2004, taking up residence in the Eli settlement in the northern Gaza Strip and becoming actively involved in the struggle against the disengagement. Prior to the disengagement, during an improvised tour for IDF soldiers on bases in the Gaza Strip, he had implored soldiers not to participate in the disengagement (*Walla*, July 12, 2005).
24. Amrousi explained her motivation to write the novel as follows: "I thought it was my sign from the Torah ... to write about settlers, to show their humanity ... over the years I wrote about the disengagement, about that pain, in a lot of different words ... I wrote about the beauty of the pioneers of this land, giving them faces. I wrote so this [disengagement] would not happen again" (*Israel HaYom*, August 2, 2018).
25. The Katif.net website is managed by the Sender family, primarily Motti Sender, a former resident of Gush Katif. It was first established as a public relations tool to document daily life in the settlements and to bolster sales of local produce from Gush Katif, thus creating an online community for the settlers and their supporters. During the disengagement, the website dealt primarily with the struggle against it, serving as a hub for information on nationwide protests. Once the disengagement was over, the site morphed into a memorial to both the struggle and the homes that made up Gush Katif and offered services to former residents (Lev-On 2010).
26. In 2011 Karni Eldad and Shlomo Bashan published a book, "YESHA is Fun," which reviews every tourist attraction in West Bank. For example, they describe "Award-winning wines in Binyamin, single-strain olive oil in Samaria, bed and breakfast with a Jacuzzi underneath the open skies in the Judean desert, an excellent restaurant in a Gush Etzion farm, and superb cheeses in the Hebron Mountains."
27. West Bank settlements are home to 29 of the 150 Israeli wineries and can be found in even the most extreme ideological settlements (*Jerusalem Post*, July 2, 2017). Most of the wineries are included in tourist maps, and quite a few have active visitor centers (such as the Gush Etzion, Har Bracha, Psagot, and Shilo wineries). Many wineries offer the option of combining the visit with a tour of the vineyards from which they produce the wine.

28. Although the biblical Hebrew word for "vineyard" can also refer to olives, the discovery of ancient winepresses in the area helped legitimize the recent development of wineries as an economic and cultural enterprise.

6 A Case of Success

1. Ariel (literally, "Lion of God") is one of the names for Jerusalem and the Temple in the Hebrew Bible.
2. Source: Israel Central Bureau of Statistics.
3. In addition, 13 percent voted for Blue and White, a right-wing party that self-identifies as "centrist" (which seems to mainly indicate the party's opposition to Netanyahu).
4. Source: Israel Central Bureau of Statistics.
5. According to Guidestar, the Israeli government's official registrar for nonprofit organizations, ADF is most active in Jerusalem and Tel Aviv. Its annual income stood at $1,006,934 in 2017. The annual financial reports of the organization, which are public information, reveal that ADF devotes considerable effort to enlisting foreign donations. Its 2017 report indicated that it spent $36,223 on fundraising trips to the United States and succeeded in raising $970,244. The foreign fundraising efforts in 2017 significantly dwarfed those of 2016, which totaled only $16,916. According to the annual reports, ADF's fundraising efforts are restricted to the United States.
6. The "freeze" was actually a short-term moratorium on settlement construction, IDF Order 1653, which was in place for only ten months, from November 26, 2009 through September 26, 2010.
7. In recent years there has been ongoing development of new settlement "neighborhoods" in the "finger" zone along route 5, part of an attempt to fill the territory between Ariel and the Green Line with a continuous line of settlements.
8. A.B. Yehoshua disputed that the boycott was directed against the residents of Ariel. In a letter, he stressed that his intention was not to boycott the settlers, but to protest the government's settlement policy: "The boycott was not of the residents of Ariel, but of the city, located in the heart of Palestinian territory. If they'd invite me to lecture there, I wouldn't have come. It's been a while since I went there except for political discussions. I wouldn't go there to entertain people" (*Haaretz*, August 31, 2010).
9. Yigal Cohen-Orgad, who served as Likud MK and Finance Minister, has been a longtime supporter of the settler movement. He is the current Chancellor of Ariel University and sits on the board of the Ariel University R&D Company. According to ADF and AFA, Cohen-Orgad was also instrumental in turning the vision for an academic center in Ariel into a reality.

7 A Case of Failure

1. The annual Herzliya Conferences are hosted by the Institute for Policy and Strategy at the Interdisciplinary Center in Herzliya. The conferences have been the setting for the articulation of national policy by a number of Israeli leaders. Ariel Sharon used the third Herzliya Conference to announce his support for the Road Map and the fourth to introduce his unilateral disengagement plan.
2. In April 2005, Eitam even moved to Netzer Hazani in order to reinforce the settlers and help prevent their eviction.
3. MK Avraham Shochat of the Labor Party, who chaired the Finance Committee subcommittee responsible for compensation to evacuees, argued that the original law had been unfair to the residents. Under his leadership, the Finance Committee increased the total sum available for compensation from approximately $810 million to $1.1 billion (Knesset meeting no. 223).
4. The degree of concern even reached the point where a conference was held to discuss the potential for civil war (*Ynet,* September 5, 2004). The conference was organized by The People's Voice, an Israeli–Palestinian civil initiative launched in 2003 with the aim of using civic pressure (such as petitions) to force political leaders on both sides of the conflict to reach a peace agreement.
5. The settlements in the Gaza Strip were Bedolah, Bnei Atzmon, Dugit, Elei Sinai, Gadid, Gan Or, Ganei Tal, Katif, Kfar Darom, Kfar Yam, Kerem Atzmona, Morag, Neve Dekalim, Netzarim, Netzer Hazani, Nisanit, Pe'at Sadeh, Rafiah Yam, Slav, Shirat Hayam, and Tel Katifa. The settlements in the West Bank were Kadim, Ganim, Homesh, and Sa-Nur
6. Source: Arieli Shaul, 2019.
7. Under the Revised Disengagement Plan, which was passed on June 6, 2004, Israel would continue to supply Gaza with infrastructural fundamentals, such as water, communications, electricity, and sewerage (Israel Ministry of Foreign Affairs, June 6, 2004). Israel would continue to maintain a military presence along the border between the Gaza Strip and Egypt (the so-called Philadelphia Route), though responsibility for this was eventually shifted to Egypt. Israel would further retain the right to guard and monitor the external land perimeter of the Gaza Strip, would continue to maintain exclusive authority in Gazan air space, and would continue to exercise security activity in the sea off the coast of the Gaza Strip. The Palestinians would have the right to govern the territory, and stipulation was made for transportation between Gaza and the West Bank as well as a seaport (Ibid).
8. According to another source, fifty-three soldiers registered their intent to refuse orders before the forced evacuations began, and another ten did so during the operation. Of these sixty-three soldiers, just twenty-four were members of Hesder yeshivas (*Maariv,* September 7, 2005).
9. In fact, a survey by the Tami Steimetz Center in August 2005 found that 77 percent of respondents believed the security forces displayed a large or very large degree of consideration during the evacuation, whereas 9 percent felt that the security forces' degree of consideration was negligible or very negligible.

10. Interestingly, the Yesha Council's struggle against the evacuation of the Gaza settlement of Netzarim began more than a month before Sharon announced the Disengagement Plan, suggesting that they had inside information provided by supporters within government circles.
11. In response, supporters of the disengagement sported blue ribbons, taking the color from the Israeli flag.
12. Two examples will suffice here, both relating to the prosecution of Nadia Matar on charges of insulting a public official, after she compared Disengagement Authority Chairman Yonatan Bassi to the *Judenrat*, the Jewish councils that implemented Nazi decrees during the Holocaust. *Arutz Sheva* writers cited the efforts of the prosecution as "pathetic" and stated that "we [the Jewish State] owe her a lot" (*Arutz Sheva,* June 19, 2006). Another article painted Matar as vilified by the Israeli security forces and being held to a higher accountability than her counterparts on the left (*Arutz Sheva,* September 15, 2005).
13. The survey was conducted in February 2006. The data were collected in a telephone survey of a large, random sample of 753 Jewish settlers from the West Bank and Gaza Strip.
14. Other major differences between the behavior of religious and secular settlers included donating money (69 percent of religious settlers vs. 12 percent of secular settlers), face-to-face persuasion (55 percent vs. 12 percent), illegally taking up residence in areas slated for evacuation (25 percent vs. 5 percent), and blockading roads (16 percent vs. 3 percent). The first two fall within the boundaries of moderate actions and the last two are considered radical actions.
15. Although caution is called for, as we had only five older settlers in our survey (aged 71+), the survey showed that moderate activism was equally a characteristic of younger and older settlers, but younger settlers (aged 18–30) participated significantly more in radical and extreme activities (Hirsch-Hoefler 2008).
16. The literature has shown that engagement in radical collective actions, or actions outside routine political channels, is generally carried out more by males, with, at best, marginal female presence. However, the Gaza case study reveals that the well-known pattern of male dominance in collective action, and particularly in unconventional, radical action, does not apply to the Israeli settlers.
17. Women had previously been involved in establishing settlements and outposts in the West Bank, sometimes without any men being present. For example, in October 1991, twenty-five women – most of them Orthodox, all married, and all mothers – founded the settlement Rechalim on a site where a female settler (Rachel Drouk) had been killed by a Palestinian in 1991, during the First Intifada. This event was a prime example of the activism of Orthodox women in the 1990s (*NRG*, October 7, 2011).
18. Note that these outcomes were not inevitable and might have been avoided with stronger movement leadership. As Eitan Alimi (2007) has shown, political opportunities and threats are not objective features of a political environment, but are, instead, constructed by movement activists.

8 Conclusion

1. There are, of course, exceptions to this general assumption. For example, Shaul Arieli argues that the movement should be interpreted as a failure overall, because its numbers have remained small as a proportion of the Israeli population (never more than a few percent), and indeed have never reached the 1 million mark once predicted by movement leaders.

References

Abdullah, D. & Chehata, H. (2011). European public perceptions of the Israel-Palestine conflict. *ICM for AlJazeera Center for Studies*. www.aljazeera.net/mritems/streams/2011/3/15/1_1048050_1_51.pdf

Admoni, Y. (1992). *Decade of Discretion: Settlement Policy in the Territories, 1967–1977*. Tel Aviv: Yad Tabenkin. [Hebrew]

Agus, J. B. (1946). *Banner of Jerusalem: The Life, Times, and Thought of Abraham Isaac Kuk, the Late Chief Rabbi of Palestine*. New York: Bloch.

Alexander, J. C. (2006). *The Civil Sphere*. Oxford: Oxford University Press.

Alimi, E. (2007). *Israeli Politics and the First Palestinian Intifada: Political Opportunities, Framing Processes and Contentious Politics*. London: Routledge.

Alimi, E. (2010). The Relational Context of Radicalization: The Case of Jewish Settler Contention before and after the Gaza Pullout. Paper presented at the International Sociological Association Congress, Goteborg, Sweden.

Alimi, E. Y. & Demetriou, C. (2018). Price tag violence and the dwindling prospects for peace in Israel-Palestine. *Political Insight*, *9*(3), 36–39.

Alimi, E. Y. & Hirsch-Hoefler, S. (2012). Structure of political opportunities and threats, and movement-countermovement interaction in segmented composite regimes. *Comparative Politics*, *44*(3), 331–349.

Almeida, P. & Chase-Dunn, C. (2018). Globalization and social movements. *Annual Review of Sociology*, *44*, 189–211.

Almeida, P. & Lichbach, M. (2003). To the Internet, from the Internet: Comparative media coverage of transnational protests. *Mobilization*, *8*(3), 249–272.

Alvarez, S. E., Dagnino, E., & Escobar, A. (2018). Introduction: The cultural and the political in Latin American social movements. In S. E. Alvarez, E. Dagnino, & A. Escobar (eds.). *Cultures of Politics/Politics of Cultures*. London: Routledge, 1–30.

Amana (2017). "Settling a Million in Judea and Samaria.'" *Amana Website*. www.amana.co.il/?CategoryID=106&ArticleID=522s

Amenta, E. (2014). How to analyze the influence of movements. *Contemporary Sociology*, *43*(1),16–29.

Amenta, E. & Caren, N. (2004). The legislative, organizational, and beneficiary consequences of state-oriented challengers. In D. A. Snow, S. A. Soule, & H. Kriesi (eds.). *The Blackwell Companion to Social Movements*. Maiden, MA: Blackwell, 461–488.

Amenta, E. & Caren, N. (2013). Outcomes, political. In D. A. Snow, D. della Porta, B. Klandersmans, & D. McAdam (eds.). *The Wiley-Blackwell*

Encyclopedia of Social and Political Movements. Hoboken, NJ: Wiley Blackwell, 1–6. https://doi-org.ezprimo1.idc.ac.il/10.1002/9780470674871.wbespm441

Amenta, E. & Poulsen, J. D. (1996). Social politics in context: The institutional politics theory and social spending at the end of the New Deal. *Social Forces*, *75*(1), 33–60.

Amenta, E., Andrews, K. T., & Caren, N. (2018). The political institutions, processes, and outcomes movements seek to influence. In D. A. Snow, S. A. Soule, H. Kriesi, & H. J. McCammon (eds.). *The Wiley Blackwell Companion to Social Movements*. Hoboken, NJ: Wiley Blackwell, 2nd edition, 447–465.

Amenta, E. & Young, M. P. (1999). Making an impact: Conceptual and methodological implications of the collective goods criterion. In M. Giugni, D. McAdam, & C. Tilly (eds.). *How Social Movements Matter*. Minneapolis, MN: University of Minnesota Press, 22–41.

Amenta, E., Caren, N., Chiarello, E., & Su, Y. (2010). The political consequences of social movements. *Annual Review of Sociology*, *36*, 287–307.

Amenta, E., Carruthers, B. G., & Zylan, Y. (1992). A hero for the aged? The Townsend movement, the political mediation model, and US old-age policy, 1934–1950. *American Journal of Sociology*, *98*(2), 308–339.

Amrousi, E. (2009). *Tris*. Shoham: Kinneret Zmora-Bitan Press. [Hebrew]

Andrews, K. T. (2001). Social movements and policy implementation: The Mississippi civil rights movement and the war on poverty, 1965 to 1971. *American Sociological Review*, *66*(1), 71.

Andrews, K. T. (2004). *Freedom Is a Constant Struggle: The Mississippi Civil Rights Movement and Its Legacy*. Chicago: University of Chicago Press.

Andrews, K. T. & Biggs, M. (2006). The dynamics of protest diffusion: Movement organizations, social networks, and news media in the 1960 sit-ins. *American Sociological Review*, *71*(5), 752–777.

Aran, G. (1986). From religious Zionism to Zionist religion: The roots of Gush Emunim. *Studies in Contemporary Jewry*, *2*, 116–143.

Aran, G. (1991). Jewish Zionist fundamentalism: The bloc of the faithful in Israel (Gush Emunim). In M. E. Marty, & R. S. Appleby (eds.). *Fundamentalisms Observed*. Volume 1. Chicago: University of Chicago Press, 265–344.

Aran, G. & Feige, M. (1987). The movement to stop the withdrawal in Sinai: A sociological perspective. *The Journal of Applied Behavioral Science*, *23*(1), 73–87.

Aran, G. & Hassner, R. E. (2013). Religious violence in Judaism: Past and present. *Terrorism and Political Violence*, *25*(3), 355–405.

Arian, A. (1985). *Politics in Israel*. Tel-Aviv: Zmora Bitan. [Hebrew]

Arieli, S. (2008). Convergence with land swaps. www.shaularieli.com/wp-content/uploads/2018/08/itsuv_hamerhav.doc

Arieli, S. (2012). Not to annex the imaginary "Ariel bloc". *Forum for Regional Thinking*, 22 October. www.regthink.org/articles/%D7%9C%D7%90-%D7%9C%D7%A1%D7%99%D7%A4%D7%95%D7%97-%22%D7%92%D7%95%D7%A9-%D7%90%D7%A8%D7%99%D7%90%D7%9C%22-%D7%94%D7%9E%D7%93%D7%95%D7%9E%D7%99%D7%99%D7%9F

Arieli, S. (2013). *Why Settlements Have Not Killed the Two-State Solution*. London: BICOM.

Arieli, S (2017). *Messianism Meets Reality: The Israeli Settlement Project in Judea and Samaria, 1967–2016*. Tel Aviv: Fund for Economic Cooperation.

Arieli, S., Nathanson, R., Rubin, Z., & Tzameret-Kertcher, H. (2009). *Historical, Political and Economic Impact of Jewish Settlements in the Occupied Territories*. Tel Aviv: Israeli European Policy Network.

Armstrong, E. A. & Bernstein, M. (2008). Culture, power, and institutions: A multi-institutional politics approach to social movements. *Sociological Theory*, *26*(1), 74–99.

Aronoff, M. J. (1985). The institutionalization and cooptation of a charismatic, messianic, religious-political revitalization movement. In D. Newman (ed.). *The Impact of Gush Emunim*. New York: St. Martin's, 46–69.

Aronoff, M. J. (1989). *Israeli Visions and Divisions*. New Brunswick, NJ: Transaction.

Aronson, G. (1996). Settlement monitor. *Journal of Palestine Studies*, *26*(1), 128–137.

Association of Hesder Yeshivas. (2019). Hesder Yeshivas List. *Association of Hesder Yeshivas*. https://hesder.org.il/wp-content/uploads/2019/01/contacts-list-2019.xlsx

Auerbach, Y. (2009). The reconciliation pyramid: A narrative-based framework for analyzing identity conflicts. *Political Psychology*, *30*(2), 291–318.

Aviner, S. (2005). Stop dismantling the IDF. *Be'Ahavah Uve'Emunah*, *500*, 2–3. [Hebrew]

Aviner, S. (1990). *Intifada: Questions and Answers*. Beit-el: Beit-el Library Press.

Avraham, E. (2003). *Behind Media Marginality: Coverage of Social Groups and Places in the Israeli Press*. Lanham, MA: Lexington Books.

Balser, D. B. (1997). The impact of environmental factors on factionalism and schism in social movement organizations. *Social Forces*, *76*(1), 199–228.

Banaszak, L. A. (1996). *Why Movements Succeed or Fail: Opportunity, Culture, and the Struggle for Woman Suffrage*. Princeton, NJ: Princeton University Press.

Bar-Siman-Tov, Y. (1994). *Israel and the Peace Process 1977–1982: In Search of Legitimacy for Peace*. Albany, NY: State University of New York Press.

Bar-Siman-Tov, Y. (2009). *The Disengagement Plan The Idea and Its Broken*. Jerusalem: The Jerusalem Institute for Israel Studies.

Barnes, S. H., Allerbeck, K. R., Farah, B. G., Heunks, F. J., Inglehart, R. F., Jennings, M. K., Klingemann, H. D., Marsh, A. & Rosenmayr, L. (1979). *Political Action: Mass Participation in Five Western Democracies*. Beverley Hills, CA: Sage.

Baron, D. P. (2003). Private politics. *Journal of Economics and Management Strategy*, *12*(1), 31–66.

Bartley, T. (2007). How foundations shape social movements: The construction of an organizational field and the rise of forest certification. *Social Problems*, *54*(3), 229–255.

Bauman, Z. (2000). *Liquid Modernity*. Cambridge: Polity.

Baumgarten, B. & Ullrich, P. (2016). Discourse, power, and governmentality. Social movement research with and beyond Foucault. In J. Roose & H. Dietz (eds.). *Social Theory and Social Movements*. Wiesbaden: Springer, 13–38.

Bearman, P. S. & Everett, K. D. (1993). The structure of social protest, 1961–1983. *Social Networks*, *15*(2), 171–200.

Bell, J. M. (2014). *The Black Power Movement and American Social Work*. New York: Columbia University Press.

Ben-Eliezer, U. & Feinstein, Y. (2007). "The battle over our homes": Reconstructing/deconstructing sovereign practices around Israel's separation barrier on the West Bank. *Israel Studies*, *12*(1), 171–192.

Ben-Porat, G. (2008). *The Failure of the Middle East Peace Process. Jerusalem: Van Leer Jerusalem Institute.*

Bendaña, A. (2006). *NGOs and Social Movements: A NorthSouth Divide*. Geneva: UNRISD.

Benford, R. D. & Snow, D. A. (2000). Framing processes and social movements: An overview and assessment. *Annual Review of Sociology*, *26*, 611–639.

Bennett, W. (2003). Communicating global activism. *Information, Communication & Society*, *6*(2), 143–168.

Bennett, W. L. & Segerberg, A. (2012). The logic of connective action: Digital media and the personalization of contentious politics. *Information, Communication & Society*, *15*(5), 739–768.

Bennett, W. L. & Segerberg, A. (2015). Communication in movements. In D. della Porta & M. Diani (eds.). *The Oxford Handbook of Social Movements*. Oxford: Oxford University Press, 367–383.

Benvenisti, M. (1986). *Report: Demographic, Economic, Legal, Social, and Political Developments in the West Bank*. Boulder, CO: Westview.

Benvenisti, M. (1987). The West Bank Database Project, 1987 Report. *Jerusalem: WBDBP.*

Berda, Y. (2012). *The Bureaucracy of the Occupation: The Permit Regime in the West Bank, 2000–2006*. Jerusalem and Tel Aviv: The Van Leer Institute and Hakibbutz Hameuchad. [in Hebrew]

Berger, Y. (2018, November 26). Isolated Israeli Settlements Get Favored Under New Funding List Approved by the Government. *Haaretz*. www.haaretz.com/israel-news/.premium-isolated-settlements-get-favored-under-new-priority-funding-list-approved-by-gov-t-1.6683728

Berman, S. (1997). Civil society and the collapse of the Weimar Republic. *World politics*, *49*(3), 401–429.

Bernard, A. (2014, January 13). Ariel Sharon's Dark Greatness. *The New Yorker*. www.newyorker.com/news/news-desk/ariel-sharons-dark-greatness

Berthomière, W. (2001). Aliya from the Former Soviet Union. Demographic Landmarks Over a Decade of Immigration. *Bulletin du Centre de recherche français à Jérusalem*, *8*, 188–218.

Biggs, M. & Andrews, K. T. (2015). Protest campaigns and movement success: Desegregating the US south in the early 1960s. *American Sociological Review*, *80* (2), 416–443.

Billig, M. (2015). The Jewish settlements in Judea and Samaria (1967–2008): historical overview. *Israel Affairs*, *21*(3), 331–347.

Billig, M. & Lebel, U. (2009–2012). Judea and Samaria Jewish settlers and settlements research study. *Ariel University, Samaria & Jordan Rift R&D Center 5.*

Blee, K. M. & Taylor, V. (2002). Semi-structured interviewing in social movement research. In B. Klandermans & S. Staggenborg (eds.). *Methods of Social Movement Research*. Minneapolis, MN: University of Minnesota Press, 92–117.

Bob, C. (2005). *The Marketing of Rebellion: Insurgents, Media, and International Activism*. Cambridge: Cambridge University Press.

Bookmiller, R. J. (1997). Likud's Jordan policy. *Middle East Policy*, *5*(3), 90.

Bosi, L. & Uba, K. (2009). The outcomes of social movement action: An introduction. *Mobilization*, *14*(4), 405–411.

Bosi, L., Giugni, M., & Uba, K. (2016). *The Consequences of Social Movements: Taking Stock and Looking Forward*. Cambridge: Cambridge University Press.

Bregman, A. (2014). *Cursed Victory: A History of Israel and the Occupied Territories*. London: Penguin.

Breines, W. (1982). *The Great Refusal: Community and Organization in the New Left, 1962–1968*. New York: JF Bergin.

Breuer, A., Landman, T., & Farquhar, D. (2015). Social media and protest mobilization: Evidence from the Tunisian revolution. *Democratization*, *22*(4), 764–792.

Bsisu, N. (2012). Israeli domestic politics and the war in Lebanon. *Lights the MESSA Journal*, *1*(3), 29–38.

Burris, V., Smith, E., & Strahm, A. (2000). White supremacist networks on the Internet. *Sociological Focus*, *33*(2), 215–235.

Burstein, P. (1979). Public opinion, demonstrations, and the passage of antidiscrimination legislation. *Public Opinion Quarterly*, 43(2), 157–172.

Burstein, P. & Linton, A. (2002). The impact of political parties, interest groups, and social movement organizations on public policy: Some recent evidence and theoretical concerns. *Social Forces*, *81*(2), 380–408.

Burstein, P., Einwohner, R. L., & Hollander, J. A. (1995). The success of political movements: A bargaining perspective. In J. C. Jenkins (ed.). *The Politics of Social Protest: Comparative Perspectives on States and Social Movements*. Minneapolis, MN: University of Minnesota Press, 275–295.

Cahaner, L. (2016). From politics ghetto to geopolitics – Ultra-orthodox settlements in the West Bank. *Theory and Criticism*, *47*, 65–87.

Caiani, M. & Graziano, P. (2018). Europeanisation and social movements: The case of the Stop TTIP campaign. *European Journal of Political Research*, *57*(4), 1031–1055.

Campbell, J. L. (2005). Where do we stand? Common mechanisms in organizations and social movements research. In G. F. Davis, D. McAdam, W. R. Scott, & M. N. Zald (eds.). *Social Movements and Organization Theory*. Cambridge: Cambridge University Press, 41–68.

Caniglia, B. & Carmin, J. (2005). Scholarship on social movement organizations: Classic views and emerging trends. *Mobilization*, *10*(2), 201–212.

Caniglia, B. S., Brulle, R. J., & Szasz, A. (2015). Civil society, social movements, and climate change. In R. E. Dunlap & R. J. Brulle (eds.). *Climate Change and Society: Sociological Perspectives*. Oxford: Oxford University Press, 235–268.

Carmin, J. & Balser, D. B. (2002). Selecting repertoires of action in environmental movement organizations: An interpretive approach. *Organization & Environment*, *15*(4), 365–388.

Carothers, T. & Barndt, W. (1999). Civil society. *Foreign Policy, 117*, 18–29.

Carter, J. (1980, March 3). Israeli Settlements and the Status of Jerusalem Statement on the U.S. Vote in the Security Council of the United Nations. *The American Presidency Project*. www.presidency.ucsb.edu/ws/?pid=33094

Castells, M. (1996). *The Information Age: Economy, Society, and Culture, Vol. 1: The Rise of the Network Society*. Oxford: Blackwell.

Castells, M. (2002). *The Internet Galaxy: Reflections on the Internet, Business, and Society*. Oxford: Oxford University Press.

Castells, M. (2008). The new public sphere: Global civil society, communication networks, and global governance. *The Annals of the American Academy of Political and Social Science, 616*(1), 78–93.

Chanley, V. A. (2002). Trust in government in the aftermath of 9/11: Determinants and consequences. *Political Psychology, 23*(3), 469–483.

Chapman, C. & Benson, K. (2015). *Whose Promised Land: The Continuing Conflict Over Israel and Palestine*. Kidderminster: Lion Books.

Cherlow, Y. (2007). The new national religious elites. In E. Ben-Rafael & Y. Sternberg (eds.). *New Elites in Israel*. Jerusalem: Bialik Institute, 334–354.

Chomsky, N. (2006). The Israel Lobby? *ZNET*. www.chomsky.info/articles/20060328.htm

Clemens, E. S. & Minkoff, D. C. (2004). Beyond the iron law: Rethinking the place of organizations in social movement research. In D. A. Snow, S. A. Soule, & H. Kriesi (eds.). *The Blackwell Companion to Social Movements*. Maiden, MA: Blackwell, 155–170.

Cloward, R. A. & Piven, F. F. (1977). The acquiescence of social work. *Society, 14* (2), 55–63.

Cohen, E. H. (2015). Changes among Israeli youth movements: A structural analysis based on Kahane's code of informality. *Cambridge Journal of Education, 45*(2), 223–243.

Cohen, S. A. (1999). From integration to segregation the role of religion in the IDF. *Armed Forces & Society, 25*(3), 387–405.

Cohen, S. A. (2004). Dilemmas of military service in Israel: The religious dimension. *The Torah u-Madda Journal, 12*, 1–23.

Coleman, J. S. (1990). *Foundations of Social Theory*. Cambridge, MA: Belknap Press of Harvard University Press.

Corbett, J. B. (1998). Media, bureaucracy, and the success of social protest: Newspaper coverage of environmental movement groups. *Mass Communication and Society, 1*(1–2), 41–61.

Cress, D. M. & Snow, D. A. (2000). The outcomes of homeless mobilization: The influence of organization, disruption, political mediation, and framing. *American Journal of Sociology, 105*(4), 1063–1104.

Cross, R. (2013). Radicalism. In D. A. Snow, D. della Porta, B. Klandersmans, & D. McAdam (eds.). *The Wiley-Blackwell Encyclopedia of Social and Political Movements*. Hoboken, NJ: Wiley Blackwell.

d'Anjou, L. (1996). *Social Movements and Cultural Change: The First Abolition Campaign Revisited*. New Brunswick, NJ: Transaction.

d'Anjou, L. & Van Male, J. (1998). Between old and new: Social movements and cultural change. *Mobilization: An International Quarterly, 3*(2), 207–226.

Dalton, R. J. (1994). *The Green Rainbow: Environmental Groups in Western Europe*. New Haven, CT: Yale University Press.

Dalton, R. J. (2008). The quantity and the quality of party systems party system polarization, its measurement, and its consequences. *Comparative Political Studies*, *41*(7), 899–920.

Dalton, R. J., Recchia, S., & Rohrschneider, R. (2003). The environmental movement and the modes of political action. *Comparative Political Studies*, *36* (7), 743–771.

Dalsheim, J. (2011). *Unsettling Gaza: Secular Liberalism, Radical Religion, and the Israeli Settlement Project*. New York: Oxford University Press.

Daniels, J. (2009). *Cyber Racism: White Supremacy Online and the New Attack on Civil Rights*. Lanham, MD: Rowman & Littlefield.

Davidovitch, N. & Iram, Y. (2014). Regulation, globalization, and privatization of higher education: The struggle to establish a university in Israel. *Journal of International Education Research*, *10*(3), 201–218.

De Bakker, F. G., Den Hond, F., King, B., & Weber, K. (2013). Social movements, civil society and corporations: Taking stock and looking ahead. *Organization Studies*, *34*(5–6), 573–593.

Della Porta, D. & Diani, M. (1999). *Social Movements: An Introduction*. Malden, MA: Blackwell, 165–192.

Della Porta, D. & Haupt, H. G. (2012). Patterns of radicalization in political activism: An introduction. *Social Science History*, *36*(3), 311–320.

Della Porta, D. & Tarrow, S. (2005). *Transnational Protest and Global Activism*. Lanham, MD: Rowman & Littlefield.

Della Porta, D., Andretta, M., Mosca, L., & Reiter, H. (2006). *Globalization from Below: Transnational Activists and Protest Networks*. Minneapolis, MN: University of Minnesota Press.

Demant, P. R. (1988). *Ploughshares into Swords: Israeli Settlement Policy in the Occupied Territories, 1967–1977*. Amsterdam: Amsterdam University Press.

Diani, M. (1992). The concept of social movement. *The Sociological Review*, *40* (1), 1–25.

Diani, M. (1997). Social movements and social capital: A network perspective on movement outcomes. *Mobilization*, *2*(2), 129–147.

Diani, M. (2013). *Networks and Social Movements. The Wiley-Blackwell Encyclopedia of Social and Political Movements*. Hoboken, NJ: John Wiley & Sons.

DiMaggio, P. J. & Powell, W. W. (1983). The iron cage revisited: Institutional isomorphism and collective rationality in organizational fields. *American Sociological Review*, *48*(2), 147–160.

Don-Yehiya, E. (1987). Jewish Messianism, religious Zionism and Israeli politics: The impact and origins of Gush Emunim. *Middle Eastern Studies*, *23*(2), 215–234.

Dunsky, M. (2008). Pens and Swords: How the American Mainstream Media Report the Israeli-Palestinian Conflict. New York, New York, United States: Columbia University Press.

Duyvendak, J. W. & Hurenkamp, M. (2004). *Kiezen voor de kudde. Lichte gemeenschappen en de nieuwe meerderheid*. Amsterdam: Van Gennep.

Earl, J. (2000). Methods, movements, and outcomes. In L. Leitz (ed.). *Research in Social Movements, Conflicts and Change*. Bingley: Emerald, 3–25.

Earl, J. (2010). The dynamics of protest-related diffusion on the web. *Information, Communication & Society, 13*(2), 209–225.

Earl, J. (2013). Repression and social movements. In D. A. Snow, D. della Porta, B. Klandersmans, & D. McAdam (eds.). *The Wiley-Blackwell Encyclopedia of Social and Political Movements*. Hoboken, NJ: Wiley Blackwell. https://doi-org.ezprimo1.idc.ac.il/10.1002/9780470674871.wbespm446

Edwards, B. & Marullo, S. (1995). Organizational mortality in a declining social movement: The demise of peace movement organizations in the end of the cold war era. *American Sociological Review, 60*(6), 908–927.

Edwards, B. & McCarthy, J. D. (2004). Resources and social movement mobilization. In D. A. Snow, S. A. Soule, & H. Kriesi (eds.). *The Blackwell Companion to Social Movements*. Maiden, MA: Blackwell, 116–152.

Efrat, E. (2010). *Two States for Two People*. Jerusalem: ABC Publishing. [Hebrew]

Eiran, E. (2009). Politics and the 2005 Gaza and North West Bank compensation and assistance facility. *Harvard Negotiation Law Review, 14*, 101–122.

Eiran, E. & Krause, P. (2018). Old (molotov) cocktails in new bottles? "price-tag" and settler violence in Israel and the West Bank. *Terrorism and Political Violence, 30*(4), 637–657.

Eisenstein, H. (2001). Raising consciousness, eyebrows, and hell. *Science & Society, 65*(1), 145–147.

Eldad, K. & Bashan, S. (2011). *Yesha is Fun (Yesha ze Fun)*. Israel: Shahar Lifshitz Press. [Hebrew]

Eldar, A. & Zertal, I. (2004). Lords of the Land: The Settlers and the State of Israel 1967–2004. *Or-Yehuda, Israel: Kinneret*. [Hebrew]

Elitzur, Y. (2006). Summer 2005: The Yesha council does not answer. *Nekuda, 295*, 18–19.

Elran, M. (2005). Disengagement offshoots: Strategic implications for Israeli society. *Strategic Assessment, 8*(2), 6–10.

Elsbach, K. D. & Sutton, R. I. (1992). Acquiring organizational legitimacy through illegitimate actions: A marriage of institutional and impression management theories. *Academy of Management Journal, 35*(4), 699–738.

Emunim, G. (1980). Master plan for settlement in Judea and Samaria. *Jerusalem: Gush Emunim*.

Enav-Weintraub, Y. B. (2009). (Un)settling the West Bank of Israel/Palestine: The anthropology of citizenship in "no man's land". *Anthropology Matters, 10* (2), 1–10.

Engelberg, A. (2017). Fighting intermarriage in the Holy Land: Lehava and Israeli ethnonationalism. *Journal of Israeli History, 36*(2), 229–247.

Eran, O., Feldman, N., & Yashiv, E. (2015). The EU decision to indicate the origin of products from the settlements. *INSS Insight* No. *769*. www.inss.org.il/publication/the-eu-decision-to-indicate-the-origin-of-products-from-the-settlements/

Escobar, A., Dagnino, E., & Alvarez, S. E. (2018). Introduction: The cultural and the political in Latin American social movements. In *Cultures of Politics/Politics of Cultures*. London, UK: Routledge, 30–1.

Etzioni-Halevy, E. (1996). Civil-military relations and democracy: The case of the military-political elites' connection in Israel. *Armed Forces & Society*, *22*(3), 401–417.

Feige, M. (2002). Being more normal than everyone: Identity issues in Gush Emunim settlement. *Alpayim*, *24*, 119–149.

Feige, M. (2009). *Settling in the Hearts: Jewish Fundamentalism in the Occupied Territories*. Detroit: Wayne State University Press.

Filkins, D. (2015, October 26). The assassination that killed peace in Israel. *The New Yorker*. www.newyorker.com/magazine/2015/10/26/shot-in-the-heart.

Fine, G. A. (1995). Public narration and group culture: Discerning discourse in social movements. In H. Johnston & B. Klandermans (eds.). *Social Movements and Culture*. Minneapolis, MN: University of Minnesota Press, 127–43.

First, A. (2009). The Disengagement in the Media Mirror: How to Build Legitimacy for Government. In Bar-Siman-Tov (ed.). *The Disengagement Plan the Idea and Its Broken*. Jerusalem, Israel: The Jerusalem Institute for Israel Studies, 125–146.

Fishman, R. M. & Everson, D. W. (2016). Mechanisms of social movement success: Conversation, displacement and disruption. *Revista Internacional de Sociología*, *74*(4), e045.

Foley, M. W. & Edwards, B. (1996). The paradox of civil society. *Journal of Democracy*, *7*(3), 38–52.

Friedman, A. (2018, 16 April). "Settlers, kibbutzniks and Arabs in the Knesset – what has changed?" Israeli Democracy Institute. [Hebrew]

Gamson, W. A. (1975). *The Strategy of Social Protest*. Homewood, IL: Dorsey.

Gamson, W. A. (1990). *1975 The Strategy of Social Protest* 2nd ed. Belmont CA: Dorsey.

Gamson, W. A. (2004). Bystanders, public opinion, and the media. In D. A. Snow, S. A. Soule, & H. Kriesi (eds.). *The Blackwell Companion to Social Movements*. Maiden, MA: Blackwell, 242–261.

Gamson, W. A. & Modigliani, A. (1989). Media discourse and public opinion on nuclear power: A constructionist approach. *American Journal of Sociology*, *95* (1), 1–37.

Ganz, M. (2010). Leading change: Leadership, organization, and social movements. *Handbook of Leadership Theory and Practice, 19*.

Ganz, S. C. & Soule, S. (2015). *Social Movements as Purveyors of Legislative Expertise*. https://pdfs.semanticscholar.org/4cd9/39860fd2ea007db70fa15c2d2059a976b6c0.pdf

Geddes, B. & Zaller, J. (1989). Sources of popular support for authoritarian regimes. *American Journal of Political Science*, *33*, 319–347.

Gelb, J. & Hart, V. (1999). Feminist politics in a hostile environment: Obstacles and opportunities. In M. Giugni, D. McAdam, & C. Tilly (eds.). *How Social Movements Matter*. Minneapolis, MN: University of Minnesota Press, 149–181.

Gerlach, L. P. & Hine, V. H. (1970). *People, Power, Change: Movements of Social Transformation*. Indianapolis: Bobbs-Merrill.

Gerring, J. (2008). Case selection for case-study analysis: qualitative and quantitative techniques. In *The Oxford Handbook of Political Methodology*. DOI:10.1093/oxfordhb/9780199286546.003.0028

Getmansky, A. & Sinmazdemir, T. (2018). Settling on violence: Expansion of Israeli outposts in the West Bank in response to terrorism. *Studies in Conflict & Terrorism*, *41*(3), 241–259.

Ghert-Zand, R. (August 23, 2011). Settler movement "It Girl" Emily Amrusi speaks. *The Forward*. https://forward.com/sisterhood/141787/settler-movement-it-girl-emily-amrusi-speaks/

Ginges, J. & Atran, S. (2013). Sacred values and cultural conflict. In M. J. Gelfand, C. Chiu, & Y. Hong (eds.). *Advances in Culture and Psychology. Volume 4*. Oxford: Oxford University Press, 273–301.

Gitlin, T. (1980). *The Whole World Is Watching. Mass Media in the Making & Unmaking of the New Left*. Berkeley, CA: University of California Press.

Giugni, M. (2004). *Social Protest and Policy Change: Ecology, Antinuclear, and Peace Movements in Comparative Perspective*. Lanham, MD: Rowman & Littlefield.

Giugni, M. (2007). Useless protest? A time-series analysis of the policy outcomes of ecology, antinuclear, and peace movements in the United States, 1977–1995. *Mobilization*, *12*(1), 53–77.

Giugni, M. (2008). Political, biographical, and cultural consequences of social movements. *Sociology Compass*, *2*(5), 1582–1600.

Giugni, M. G. (1998). Was it worth the effort? The outcomes and consequences of social movements. *Annual Review of Sociology*, *24*(1), 371–393.

Giugni, M., McAdam, D., & Tilly, C. (eds.). (1999). *How Social Movements Matter*. Minneapolis, MN: University of Minnesota Press.

Goldstone, J. A. & Tilly, C. (2001). Threat (and opportunity): Popular action and state response in the dynamics of contentious action. *Silence and Voice in the Study of Contentious Politics*, 179–94. https://doi.org/10.1017/CBO9780511815331.008

Gordon, N. & Cohen, Y. (2012). Western interests, Israeli unilateralism, and the two-state solution. *Journal of Palestine Studies*, *41*(3), 6–18.

Greve, A. & Salaff, J. W. (2003). Social networks and entrepreneurship. *Entrepreneurship Theory and Practice*, *28*(1), 1–22.

Grossman, G., Manekin, D., & Margalit, Y. (2018). How sanctions affect public opinion in target countries: Experimental evidence from Israel. *Comparative Political Studies*, *51*(14), 1823–1857.

Gupta, D. (2002). Radical flank effects: The effect of radical-moderate splits in regional nationalist movements. Paper Presented at the Conference of Europeanists Annual Meeting, Chicago, IL, March 14–16.

Gurr, T. R. (1970). Sources of rebellion in Western societies: Some quantitative evidence. *The Annals of the American Academy of Political and Social Science*, *391* (1), 128–144.

Gutwein, D. (2004). From melting pot to multiculturalism; or, the privatization of Israeli identity. In Anita Shapira (ed.), *Israeli Identity in Transition*. Santa Barbara, CA: Praeger 215–231.

Habermas, J. (1989). *The Structural Transformation of the Public Sphere: An Inquiry into a Category of Bourgeois Society*. Cambridge: Polity.

Habermas, J., Lennox, S., & Lennox, F. (1974). The public sphere: An encyclopedia article (1964). *New German Critique*, *3*, 49–55.

Hadar, L. T. (1992). High noon in Washington: The shootout over the loan guarantees. *Journal of Palestine Studies*, *21*(2), 72–87.

Haklai, O. (2003). Linking ideas and opportunities in contentious politics: The Israeli nonparliamentary opposition to the peace process. *Canadian Journal of Political Science/Revue canadienne de science politique*, *36*(4), 791–812.

Haklai, O. (2007). Religious-nationalist mobilization and state penetration: Lessons from Jewish settlers' activism in Israel and the West Bank. *Comparative Political Studies*, *40*(6), 713–739.

Haklai, O. & Loizides, N. (eds.). (2015). *Settlers in Contested Lands: Territorial Disputes and Ethnic Conflicts*. Palo Alto, CA: Stanford University Press.

Haklai, O. (2017). What do Israelis think about settlements? Turns out age matters. *The Washington Post*. www.washingtonpost.com/news/monkey-cage/wp/2017/01/11/what-do-israelis-think-about-settlements-turns-out-age-matters/

Han, E. & Rane, H. (2011). Australian press and public opinion on the Israel-Palestine conflict. *Media International Australia*, *141*(1), 58–69.

Hanau Santini, R. (2010). European Union discourses and practices on the Iranian nuclear programme. *European Security*, *19*(3), 467–489.

Handel, A. (2009). Where, where to, and when in the occupied territories: An introduction to geography of disaster. In A. Ophier, M. Givoni, & S. Hanafi (eds.). *The Power of Inclusive Exclusion: Anatomy of Israeli Rule in the Occupied Palestinian Territories*, New York: Zone Books, 179–222.

Handel, A. (2013). Gated/gating community: The settlement complex in the West Bank. *Transactions of the Institute of British Geographers*, *39*(4), 504–517.

Handel, A., Rand, G., & Allegra, M. (2015). Wine-washing: Colonization, normalization, and the geopolitics of terroir in the West Bank's settlements. *Environment and Planning A*, *47*(6), 1351–1367.

Happer, C. & Philo, G. (2013). The role of the media in the construction of public belief and social change. *Journal of Social and Political Psychology*, *1*(1), 321–336.

Harpaz, G. (2017). The EU's new approach to the two-state solution in the Israeli-Palestinian conflict: A paradigm shift or PR exercise? *Leiden Journal of International Law*, *30*(3), 603–628.

Harrison, J. L. (2016). Bureaucrats' tacit understandings and social movement policy implementation: Unpacking the deviation of agency environmental justice programs from EJ movement priorities. *Social Problems*, *63*(4), 534–553.

Hart, S. (1996). The cultural dimension of social movements: A theoretical reassessment and literature review. *Sociology of Religion*, *57*(1), 87–100.

Hedström, P., Sandell, R., & Stern, C. (2000). Mesolevel networks and the diffusion of social movements: The case of the Swedish social democratic party. *American Journal of Sociology*, *106*(1), 145–172.

Hellinger, M. (2008). Political theology in the thought of "Merkaz HaRav" Yeshiva and its profound influence on Israeli politics and society since 1967. *Totalitarian Movements and Political Religions*, *9*(4), 533–550.

Heller, J. (2000). *The Birth of Israel, 1945–1949: Ben-Gurionand His Critics*. Gainesville, FL: University Press of Florida, 277–79.

Hendel, Y. (2013, May 29). "National offenders". *Ynet*. www.ynet.co.il/articles/0,7340,L-4385862,00.html.

Hendel, Y. (2014, December 12). The national separation plan. *Ynet*. www.ynet.co.il/articles/0,7340,L-4602756,00.html

Hensby, A. (2017). Open networks and secret Facebook groups: Exploring cycle effects on activists' social media use in the 2010/11 UK student protests. *Social Movement Studies, 16*(4), 466–478.

Herzog, H. (1987). Minor parties: The relevancy perspective. *Comparative Politics, 19*(3), 317–329.

Hirsch-Hoefler, S. (2008). *Mobilizing Politics: The Mobilization Strategies of the Israeli Settlement Movement.* Doctoral dissertation, Belgium: Antwerp University.

Hirsch-Hoefler, S., Canetti, D., & Eiran, E. (2016). Radicalizing religion? Religious identity and settlers' behavior. *Studies in Conflict & Terrorism, 39*(6), 500–518.

Hirsch-Hoefler, S., Kahn, D. T., & Hirschberger, G. (2018). Reactions to imposed political change: A prospective experimental investigation of Jewish settlers' resistance to state contraction. *Peace and Conflict: Journal of Peace Psychology, 25*(1), 13–23.

Hirsch-Hoefler, S., Saguy, T., & Hirschberger, G. (2019). The psychological effects of forced evacuation: The case of Jewish settlers in the West Bank. In G. Golan & G. Sher (eds.). *Spoiling and Coping with Spoilers: Israeli-Arab Negotiations.* Bloomington, IN: Indiana University Press, 133–152. DOI:10.2307/j.ctvj7wnz6.10

Hirsch-Hoefler, S. & Mudde, C. (2014). "Ecoterrorism": Terrorist threat or political ploy?. *Studies in Conflict & Terrorism, 37*(7), 586–603.

Hirsch-Hoefler, S. & Mudde, C. (2013). Right-wing movements. In D. A. Snow, D. della Porta, B. Klandersmans, & D. McAdam (eds.). *The Wiley-Blackwell Encyclopedia of Social and Political Movements.* Hoboken, NJ: Wiley Blackwell.

Hirschberger, G. & Hirsch-Hoefler, S. (2016). Socio-demographic and ideological differences among West-Bank Settlers: A comparison of four distinct groups. (Issue brief). Commanders for Israel's Security (CIS).

Hirschberger, G., Saguy, T., Hirsch-Hoefler, S., & Shani-Sherman, T. (2014). Psychological preparedness for the future evacuation of West-Bank Settlers: An experimental survey. (Issue Brief). Blue & White Future Foundation.

Hirschfeld, Y. (2000). *Oslo: A Formula for Peace.* Tel Aviv: Am-Oved. [Hebrew]

Hirschhorn, S. Y. (2014). Operation 1000 for the settlement of Jewish-American immigrants in the occupied territories. *Israel Studies, 19*(3), 81–107.

Hirschhorn, S. Y. (2017). *City on a Hilltop: American Jews and the Israeli Settler Movement.* Cambridge, MA: Harvard University Press.

Horstink, L. (2017). Online participation and the new global democracy: Avaaz, a case study. *Global Society, 31*(1), 101–124.

Howard, P. N. (2010). *The Digital Origins of Dictatorship and Democracy: Information Technology and Political Islam.* Oxford: Oxford University Press.

Huberman, H. (2005). *Roots in the Sand (Shorashim B'acholot)* Netzarim, Israel: Netzarim library.

Huberman, H. (2008). *Against All Odds (Keneged kol Hasikuyim)* Netzarim, Israel: Netzarim Library.

Huddy, L., Khatib, N., & Capelos, T. (2002). Trends: Reactions to the terrorist attacks of September 11, 2001. *Public Opinion Quarterly*, *66*(3), 418–450.

Inbari, M. (2009). *Jewish fundamentalism and the Temple Mount: Who Will Build the Third Temple?*. Albany, New York, United States: SUNY Press.

Inbari, M. (2012). *Messianic Religious Zionism Confronts Israeli Territorial Compromises*. Cambridge, United Kingdom: Cambridge University Press.

International Crisis Group (2013). Leap of faith: Israel's national religious and the Israeli- Palestinian conflict, *Middle East Report*, 147.

Israeli, Z. (2017). The National Security Index: Public opinion survey 2016–2017. *Institute for National Security Studies (INSS)*. www.inss.org.il/national-security-index/

Israeli, Z. (2018). The National Security Index: Public opinion survey 2018–2019. *Institute for National Security Studies (INSS)*. www.inss.org.il/national-security-index/

Jasper, J. M. (1997). Identity, interest and action: A cultural explanation of Sweden's intervention in the thirty years war. *Contemporary Sociology*, *26*(6), 776.

Jenkins, J. C. (1982). Why do peasants' rebel? Structural and historical theories of modern peasant rebellions. *American Journal of Sociology*, *88*(3), 487–514.

Jenkins, J. C. (1995). *The Politics of Social Protest: Comparative Perspectives on States and Social Movements*. Minneapolis, MN: University of Minnesota Press.

Johnson, C., Dowd, T. J., & Ridgeway, C. L. (2006). Legitimacy as a social process. *Annual Review of Sociology*, *32*, 53–78.

Jones, C. (2013). Israel's insurgent citizens – Contesting the state, demanding the land. In. G. Joffe (ed.). *Islamist Radicalism in Europe and the Middle East: Reassessing the Causes of Terrorism*. London, United Kingdom: Tauris Academic Studies, 200–214.

Jost, J. T. & Banaji, M. R. (1994). The role of stereotyping in system-justification and the production of false consciousness. *British Journal of Social Psychology*, *33* (1), 1–27.

Juris, J. S. (2005). The new digital media and activist networking within anti–corporate globalization movements. *The Annals of the American Academy of Political and Social Science*, *597*(1), 189–208.

Kaase, M. & Marsh, A. (1979). Political action. A theoretical perspective. In S. H. Barnes et al. (eds.). *Political Action: Mass Participation in Five Western Democracies*. Beverley Hoills, CA: Sage, 27–56.

Kanter, J. & Troup, D. (2018). Social movement success as a political process: The case of the 2012 Quebec student protests. *Canadian Political Science Review*, *12*(1), 50–75.

Karapin, R. (2010). *Protest Politics in Germany: Movements on the Left and Right since the 1960s*. University Park, PA: Penn State Press.

Karolak, M. (2017). Social media and the Arab spring in Bahrain: From mobilization to confrontation. In C. Çakmak (ed.). *The Arab Spring, Civil Society, and Innovative Activism*. Basingstoke: Palgrave Macmillan, 81–119.

Karsh, E. (1997). The peace process peace despite everything. *Israel Affairs*, *3* (3–4), 117–132.

Katz, R. S. & Mair, P. (1995). Changing models of party organization and party democracy the emergence of the cartel party. *Party Politics*, *1*(1), 5–28.

Katzenstein, P. J., Keohane, R. O., & Krasner, S. D. (1998). International organization and the study of world politics. *International Organization*, *52*(4), 645–685.

Keane, J. (2018). Structural transformations of the public sphere. In M. Scammelli & H. Semetko (eds.). *The Media, Journalism and Democracy*. London: Routledge, 53–74.

Keck, M. E. & Sikkink, K. (1998). Transnational advocacy networks in the movement society. In D. S. Meyer & S. Tarrow (eds.). *The Social Movement Society: Contentious Politics for a New Century*. Lanham, MD: Rowman & Littlefield, 217–238.

Keinon, H. (1990, February 2). Ariel – in the eye of the storm. *The Jerusalem Post*.

Khalfa, D. (2009). After the Gaza withdrawal. In E. Marteu (ed.). *Civil Organizations and Protest Movements in Israel*. Basingstoke: Palgrave Macmillan, 27–51.

Kielbowicz, R. B. & Scherer, C. W. (1996). The role of the press in the dynamics of social movements. in L. Kriesberg (ed.). *Research in Social Movements, Conflicts and Change*. Greenwich, CT: JAI Press, 71–96.

Kiely, K. P. (2017). *US Foreign Policy Discourse and the Israel Lobby: The Clinton Administration and the Israeli-Palestinian Peace Process*. Berlin: Springer.

Killian, L. M. & Turner, R. H. (1993). *Collective Behavior*. Englewood Cliffs, NJ: Prentice-Hall.

Kimmerling, B. (1993). State building, state autonomy and the identity of society: The case of the Israeli state. *Journal of Historical Sociology*, *6*(4), 396–429.

King, G., Schneer, B., & White, A. (2017). How the news media activate public expression and influence national agendas. *Science*, *358*(6364), 776–780.

Kitschelt, H. P. (1986). Political opportunity structures and political protest: Anti-nuclear movements in four democracies. *British Journal of Political Science*, *16*(1), 57–85.

Klandermans, B. (2001). Why social movements come into being and why people join them. In J. R. Blau (ed). *The Blackwell Companion to Sociology*, Hoboken, NJ: Blackwell, 268–281.

Klandermans, B. (2016). Social movements and political action. In H. Kemand & J. J. Woldendorp (eds.). *Handbook of Research Methods and Applications in Political Science*. Cheltenham: Edward Elgar, 155–168.

Klein, R. & Ansell-Brauner, G. (2005). The Israeli disengagement plan. http://archive.jewishagency.org/disengagement/content/26384

Kolb, F. (2007). *Protest and Opportunities: The Political Outcomes of Social Movements*. Frankfurt: Campus.

Koopmans, R. (1993). The dynamics of protest waves: West Germany, 1965 to 1989. *American Sociological Review*, *58*(5), 637–658.

Koopmans, R. & Olzak, S. (2004). Discursive opportunities and the evolution of right-wing violence in Germany. *American Journal of Sociology*, *110*(1), 198–230.

Koopmans, R. & Statham, P. (1999). Political claims analysis: Integrating protest event and political discourse approaches. *Mobilization: an International Quarterly*, *4*(2), 203–221.

Kopecký, P. & Mudde, C. (2003). Rethinking civil society. *Democratization, 10* (3), 1–14.

Krause, P. J. P. (2011). *The Political Effectiveness of Non-state Violence: Paradox, Polarity, and the Pursuit of Power* (Doctoral dissertation, Massachusetts Institute of Technology), http://hdl.handle.net/1721.1/68930.

Kriesi, H. (Ed.). (1995). *New Social Movements in Western Europe: A Comparative Analysis*. Minneapolis, MN: University of Minnesota Press.

Kriesi, H., Koopmans, R., Duyvendak, J. W., & Giugni, M. G. (1992). New social movements and political opportunities in Western Europe. *European Journal of Political Research, 22*(2), 219–244.

Kriesi, H. (2004). Political context and opportunity. In D. A. Snow, S. A. Soule, & H. Kriesi (eds.). *The Blackwell Companion to Social Movements*. Maiden, MA: Blackwell, 67–90.

Krinsky, J. & Crossley, N. (2014). Social movements and social networks: Introduction. *Social Movement Studies, 13*(1), 1–21.

Kurtzer, D. C. (2009). Do settlements matter? An American perspective. *Middle East Policy, 16*(3), 89–95.

Kymlicka, W. (1995). *Multicultural Citizenship: A Liberal Theory of Minority Rights*. Oxford: Clarendon.

Lebel, U. (2013). Postmodern or conservative? Competing security communities over military doctrine-Israeli national-religious soldiers as counter [strategic] culture agents. *Political and Military Sociology: An Annual Review, 40*, 23–57.

Lebel, U. (2015). Settling the military: The pre-military academies revolution and the creation of a new security epistemic community–The militarization of Judea and Samaria. *Israel Affairs, 21*(3), 361–390.

Lein, Y. & Weizman, E. (2002). *Land Grab: Israel's Settlement Policy in the West Bank*. Jerusalem: B'tselem.

Leon, D. (Ed.). (2004). *Who's Left in Israel? Radical Political Alternatives for the Future of Israel*. Eastbourne: Sussex Academic Press.

Leuenberger, C. & Schnell, I. (2010). The politics of maps: Constructing national territories in Israel. *Social Studies of Science, 40*(6), 803–842.

Lev-On, A. (2010). Engaging the disengaged: Collective action, media uses, and sense of (virtual) community by evacuees from Gush Katif. *American Behavioral Scientist*, 5–3(8), 1208–1227.

Levy, Y. (2007). The embedded military: Why did the IDF perform effectively in executing the disengagement plan?. *Security Studies, 16*(3), 382–408.

Levy, Y. (2016). Religious authorities in the military and civilian control: The case of the Israeli defense forces. *Politics & Society, 44*(2), 305–332.

Lieberman, R. C. (2009). The "Israel lobby" and American politics. *Perspectives on Politics, 7*(2), 235–257.

Lipset, S. M. & Marks, G. (2000). *It Didn't Happen Here: Why Socialism Failed in the United States*. New York: WW Norton & Company.

Lochery, N. (2007). The politics and economics of Israeli disengagement, 1994–2006. *Middle Eastern Studies, 43*(1), 1–19.

Lohmann, S. (1993). A signaling model of informative and manipulative political action. *American Political Science Review, 87*(2), 319–333.

Lovatt, H. (2016). *EU Differentiation and the Push for Peace in Israel-Palestine*. London: European Council on Foreign Relations.

Luders, J. E. (2010). *The Civil Rights Movement and the Logic of Social Change*. Cambridge: Cambridge University Press.

Lustick, I. S. (1982). Israeli politics and American foreign policy. *Foreign Affairs*, *61*(2), 379–399.

Lustick, I. (1988). *For the Land and the Lord: Jewish Fundamentalism in Israel*. Washington, DC: Council on Foreign Relations.

Lustick, I. (1993). *Unsettled States, Disputed Lands: Britain and Ireland, France and Algeria, Israel and the West Bank-Gaza*. Ithaca, NY: Cornell University Press.

Lyman, S. M. (Ed.). (2016). *Social Movements: Critiques, Concepts, Case Studies*. Berlin: Springer.

Maggor, E. (2015). State, market and the Israeli settlements: The Ministry of housing and the shift from Messianic outposts to Urban settlements in the early 1980s. *Israeli Sociology*, *16*(2), 140–167.

Malach, G. (2019, February 6). Ultra-orthodox political parties in Israel—past, present, future. *The Israeli Democracy Institute*. https://en.idi.org.il/articles/25892

Marteu, E. (ed.). (2009). *Civil Organizations and Protest Movements in Israel: Mobilization around the Israeli-Palestinian Conflict*. New York, New York, United States: Springer.

McAdam, D. (1982). *Political Process and the Development of Black Insurgency, 1930–1970*. Chicago: University of Chicago Press.

McAdam, D. (1983). Tactical innovation and the pace of insurgency. *American Sociological Review*, *48*(6), 735–754.

McAdam, D. (1989). The biographical consequences of activism. *American Sociological Review*, *54*(5), 744–760.

McAdam, D. (1996). Conceptual origins, current problems, future directions. In D. McAdam, J. D. McCarthy, M. N. Zald (eds.). *Comparative Perspectives on Social movements: Political Opportunities, Mobilizing Structures, and Cultural Framings*. Cambridge: Cambridge University Press, 23–40.

McAdam, D. (2017). Social movement theory and the prospects for climate change activism in the United States. *Annual Review of Political Science*, *20*, 189–208.

McAdam, D. & Su, Y. (2002). The war at home: Antiwar protests and congressional voting, 1965 to 1973. *American Sociological Review*, *67*(5), 696–721. DOI:10.2307/3088914

McAdam, D. & Scott, W. R. (2005). Organizations and movements. In G. F. Davis, D. McAdam, W. R. Scott, & M. N. Zald (eds.). *Social Movements and Organization Theory*. Cambridge: Cambridge University Press, 4–40.

McAdam, D. & Tarrow, S. (2000). Nonviolence as contentious interaction. *PS: Political Science & Politics*, *33*(2), 149–154.

McCammon, H. J. (2012). *The US Women's Jury Movements and Strategic Adaptation: A More Just Verdict*. Cambridge: Cambridge University Press.

McCammon, H. (2013). Discursive opportunity structure. *The Wiley-Blackwell Encyclopedia of Social and Political Movements*. https://doi.org/10.1002/9780470674871.wbespm073

McCarthy, J. D. (1996). Money for change: Social movement philanthropy at Haymarket People's Fund-Ostrander. *American Journal of Sociology*, *102*(3), 935–937.

McCarthy, J. D. & Zald, M. N. (1977). Resource mobilization and social movements: A partial theory. *American Journal of Sociology*, *82*(6), 1212–1241.

McCauley, C. & Moskalenko, S. (2017). Understanding political radicalization: The two-pyramids model. *American Psychologist*, *72*(3), 205.

McCombs, M. (2013). *Setting the Agenda: The Mass Media and Public Opinion*. Hoboken, NJ: John Wiley & Sons.

McGehe, N. G., Kline, C., & Knollenberg, W. (2014). Social movements and tourism-related local action. *Annals of Tourism Research*, *48*, 140–155.

Mearsheimer J. J. & Walt, S. M. (2007). *The Israel Lobby and U.S. Foreign Policy*. London: Penguin.

Meisels, T. (2015). Settlement in Samaria: the ethical dimension. *Israel Affairs*, 21 (3), 313–330.

Melucci, A. (1989). *Nomads of the Present: Social Movements and Individual Needs in Contemporary Society*. London: Hutchinson.

Melucci, A. (1996). *Challenging Codes: Collective Action in the Information Age*. Cambridge: Cambridge University Press.

Mendelsohn, B. (2014). State authority in the balance: The Israeli state and the messianic settler movement. *International Studies Review*, *16*(4), 499–521.

Mendelsohn, B. (2016). Israel and its messianic right: Path dependency and state authority in international conflict. *International Studies Quarterly*, *60*(1), 47–58.

Mendelson, T. (1975, 5 December). Representatives of Gush Emunim Met with the Labor. *Group of the Jerusalem Conference*.

Meyer, D. S. (2004). Protest and political opportunities. *Annual Review of Sociology*, *30*, 125–145.

Meyer, D. S. & Gamson, J. (1995). The challenge of cultural elites: celebrities and social movements. *Sociological Inquiry*, *65*(2), 181–206.

Meyer, D. S. & Reyes, D. V. (2010). Social movements and contentious politics. In K. T. Leicht, & C. J. Jenkins (eds.). *Handbook of Politics*. New York: Springer, 217–233.

Meyer, D. S. & Tarrow, S. (1998). A movement society: Contentious politics for a new century. In D. S. Meyer & S. Tarrow (eds.). *The Social Movement Society: Contentious Politics For a New Century*, Lanham, MD: Rowman & Littlefield, 1–28.

Meyer, D. S. & Whittier, N. (1994). Social movement spillover. *Social Problems*, *41*(2), 277–298.

Meyerson, D. E. & Scully, M. A. (1995). Crossroads tempered radicalism and the politics of ambivalence and change. *Organization Science*, *6*(5), 585–600.

Michael, K. (2007). The dilemma behind the classical dilemma of civil-military relations: The "discourse space" model and the Israeli case during the Oslo Process. *Armed Forces & Society*, *33*(4), 518–546.

Minkoff, D. C. & McCarthy, J. D. (2005). Reinvigorating the study of organizational processes in social movements. *Mobilization*, *10*(2), 289–308.

Mirowsky, J. & Ross, C. E. (1981). Protest group success: The impact of group characteristics, social control, and context. *Sociological Focus*, *14*(3), 177–192.

Mnookin, R. H. & Eiran, E. (2005). Discord behind the table: The internal conflict among Israeli Jews concerning the future of settlements in the West Bank and Gaza. *Journal on Dispute Resolution*, *11*, 11–44.

Molaei, H. (2015). Discursive opportunity structure and the contribution of social media to the success of social movements in Indonesia. *Information, Communication & Society*, *18*(1), 94–108.

Moin, V. & Sharlin, S. (2005). Reactions of Shomron Inhabitants to Political Uncertainty and Insecurity: Opinions and Attitudes of Veterans, Immigrants from the Former Soviet Union, and "Experts". *Judea and Samaria Research Studies, ed. Yaakov Eshel*, 275–294.

Morris, A. D. (1993). Birmingham confrontation reconsidered: An analysis of the dynamics and tactics of mobilization. *American Sociological Review*, *58*(5), 621–636.

Morris, A. D. (1999). A retrospective on the civil rights movement: Political and intellectual landmarks. *Annual Review of Sociology*, *25*(1), 517–539.

Morris, A. D. & Staggenborg, S. (2004). Leadership in social movements. In D. A. Snow, S. A. Soule & H. Kriesi (eds.). *The Blackwell Companion to Social Movements*. Maiden, MA: Blackwell, 171–196.

Morris, B. (1987). *The Birth of the Palestinian Refugee Problem, 1947–1949*. New York: Cambridge University Press.

Moskalenko, S. & McCauley, C. (2009). Measuring political mobilization: The distinction between activism and radicalism. *Terrorism and Political Violence*, *21* (2), 239–260.

Moskalenko, S., McCauley, C., & Rozin, P. (2006). Group identification under conditions of threat: College students' attachment to country, family, ethnicity, religion, and university before and after September 11, 2001. *Political Psychology*, *27*(1), 77–97.

Moufakkir, O. & Kelly, I. (eds.). (2010). *Tourism, Progress and Peace*. Wallingford: CABI.

Mozes C., Hellinger, M., & Rynhold J. (2014). *Between Legitimate Protest and Price Tag Violence: Religious-Zionist Attitudes to a Potential Large-scale Evacuation of West Bank Settlements*. Ramat Gan: Argov Center.

Mudde, C. (2010). The populist radical right: A pathological normalcy. *West European Politics*, *33*(6), 1167–1186.

Naor, A. (1993). *Begin in Power: A Personal Testimony*. Tel Aviv: Yedioth Aharonoth. [Hebrew]

Naor, A. (2003). Lessons of the holocaust versus territories for peace, 1967–2001. *Israel Studies*, *8*(1), 130–152.

Nathanson, R. & Gazala, I. (2016). *Settlements in Judea and Samaria*. Tel Aviv, Israel: The Center for Political Economics. [Hebrew]

Neidle, J. (2013). Locating the power of the settler movement. *Journal of Politics & International Studies*, *9*, 481–519.

Neusner, J. & Goldscheider, C. (1990). *Social Foundations of Judaism*. Eugene, OR: Wipf and Stock.

Nevo, A. (2010, August 30). Dozens of artists signed a petition against the boycott of ariel. *Mako*. www.mako.co.il/music-news/local/Article-21b22d72202ca21006.htm.

Nevo, N. (1985). Religiosity and community: A case study of a Gush Emunim settlement. In D. Newman (ed.). *The Impact of Gush Emunim: Politics and Settlement in the West Bank*. Abingdon: Taylor & Francis, 221–44.

Newman, D. (1981). *The Role of Gush Emunim and the Yishuv Kehillati in the West Bank 1974–1980* (Doctoral dissertation, Durham University).

Newman, D. (1985). The evolution of a political landscape: Geographical and territorial implications of Jewish colonization in the West Bank. *Middle Eastern Studies*, *21*(2), 192–205.

Newman, D. (1985). *The Impact of Gush Emunim: Politics and Settlement in the West Bank*. Abingdon: Taylor & Francis.

Newman, D. (2005). From Hitnachalut to Hitnatkut: The impact of Gush Emunim and the settlement movement on Israeli politics and society. *Israel Studies*, *10*(3), 192–224.

Newman, D. & Yacobi, H. (2004). The Role of the EU in the Israel\Palestine Conflict. *Beer Sheva: Ben-Gurion University of the Negev*.

Norris, P. (2004). Young people & political activism. *Harvard University, John F. Kennedy School of Government. (32p)*. www.researchgate.net/profile/Pippa_Norris/publication/237832623_Young_People_Political_Activism/links/569153d708aee91f69a50822.pdf

Norris, P. (ed.). (1997). *Passages to Power: Legislative Recruitment in Advanced Democracies*. Cambridge, UK: Cambridge University Press.

Norris, P., Walgrave, S., & Van Aelst, P. (2005). Who demonstrates? Antistate rebels, conventional participants, or everyone?. *Comparative Politics*, *37*(2), 189–205.

Oberschall, A. (2012). Propaganda hate speech and mass killings. In P. Dojcinovic (ed.). *Propaganda, War Crimes Trials and International Law: From Speakers' Corner to War Crimes*. London: Routledge, 171–200.

OCHA (2018, November 16). High level of violence by Israeli settlers; rise in Israeli fatalities. *The Monthly Humanitarian Bulletin*. www.ochaopt.org/content/monthly-humanitarian-bulletin-october-2018

Oliver, P. E. & Myers, D. J. (2003). Networks, diffusion, and cycles of collective action. In M. Diani & D. McAdam (eds.). *Social Movements and Networks: Relational Approaches to Collective Action*. Oxford: Oxford University Press, 173–203.

Olzak, S. (1989). Analysis of events in the study of collective action. *Annual Review of Sociology*, *15*, 119–141.

Olzak, S. & Soule, S. A. (2009). Cross-cutting influences of environmental protest and legislation. *Social Forces*, *88*(1), 201–225.

Pagnucco, R. (1996). Social movement dynamics during democratic transitions: A synthesis of political process and political interactionist theories. In F. D. Weil (ed). *Research on Democracy and Society. Volume 3: Extremism, Protest, Social Movements, and Democracy*. Greenwich, CT: JAI Press, 3–38.

Parinandi, S. & Hitt, M. P. (2018). How politics influences the energy pricing decisions of elected public utilities commissioners. *Energy Policy*, *118*, 77–87.

Passy, F. (1999). Supranational political opportunities as a channel of globalization of political conflicts. The case of the rights of indigenous peoples. In D. della Porta, H. Kreisi, & D. Rucht (eds.). *Social Movements in a Globalizing World*. London: Palgrave Macmillan, 148–169.

Pedahzur, A. (2012). *The Triumph of Israel's Radical Right*. Oxford: Oxford University Press.
Pedahzur, A. (2014). The silent victory of the Israeli settlers' movement. *Current Affairs*, *113*(767), 350–355.
Pedahzur, A. & McCarthy, H. (2015). Against all odds–the paradoxical victory of the West Bank settlers: interest groups and policy enforcement. *Israel Affairs*, *21* (3), 443–461.
Pedahzur, A. & Perliger, A. (2009). *Jewish Terrorism in Israel*. New York: Columbia University Press.
Pedahzur, A., Hasisi, B., & Brichta, A. (2000). A proposed model for explaining political violence in Israel. *World Affairs*, *163*(1), 18–27.
Pedahzur, R. (1996). *The Victory of Embarrassment: Israel's Policy in the Territories after the Six-Day War*. Ramat Gan: Yad Tabenkin. [Hebrew]
Peled, A. (2013). The Israeli anti-boycott law: Should artists be worried?. *Cardozo Arts & Entertainment Law Journal*, *32*, 751–779.
Peled, Y. & Shapir, G. (2005). *Who Is Israeli: The Dynamics of Complex Citizenship*. Tel Aviv: Tel Aviv University. [Hebrew]
Penn, M. J. & Schoen, D. E. (1988). American attitudes toward the Middle East. *Public Opinion*, *11*, 45–48.
Peres, S. (1987). *Tomorrow is Now*. Jerusalem: Mabat. [Hebrew]
Perliger, A., Hasisi, B., & Pedahzur, A. (2009). Policing terrorism in Israel. *Criminal Justice and Behavior*, *36*(12), 1279–1304.
Perugini, N. & Gordon, N. (2015). *The Human Right to Dominate*. Oxford: Oxford University Press.
Perugini, N. & Rabie, K. (2012). The human right to the colony. In T. Sbriccoli & S. Jacoviello (eds.). *Shifting Borders: European Perspectives on Creolisation*. Newcastle upon Tyne: Cambridge Scholars Publishing, 35–56.
Phillips, N. (2011). Informality, global production networks and the dynamics of "adverse incorporation". *Global Networks*, *11*(3), 380–397.
Piven, F. F. & Cloward, R. A. (1993) [1971]. *Regulating the Poor: The Functions of Public Welfare*. New York: Vintage.
Pizam, A., Uriely, N., & Reichel, A. (2000). The intensity of tourist–host social relationship and its effects on satisfaction and change of attitudes: The case of working tourists in Israel. *Tourism Management*, *21*(4), 395–406.
Polletta, F. (1999). "Free spaces" in collective action. *Theory and Society*, *28*, 1–38.
Polletta, F. (2002). *Freedom Is an Endless Meeting. Democracy in American Social Movements*, Chicago: The University of Chicago Press
Polletta, F. (2016). Storytelling in social movements. In H. Johnston (ed.). *Culture, Social Movements, and Protest*. London: Routledge, 43–64.
Polletta, F., Chen, P. C. B., Gardner, B. G., & Motes, A. (2013). Is the Internet creating new reasons to protest?. In J. van Stekelenburg, C. Roggebrand, & B. Klandermans (eds.). *The Future of Social Movement Research: Dynamics, Mechanisms, and Processes*. Minneapolis, MN: University of Minnesota Press, 17–36.
Putnam, R. D. (1993). The prosperous community. *The American Prospect*, *4*(13), 35–42.

Putnam, R. D. (1995). *Making Democracy Work: Civic Traditions in Modern Italy*. Princeton, NJ: Princeton University Press.

Pyszczynski, T., Solomon, S., & Greenberg, J. (2003). *In the Wake of 9/11: Rising Above the Terror*. Washington, DC: American Psychological Association.

Quadagno, J. (1992). Social movements and state transformation: Labor unions and racial conflict in the war on poverty. *American Sociological Review*, *57*(5), 616–634.

Rahat, G. & Hazan, R. Y. (2005). Israel: The politics of an extreme electoral system. *The Politics of Electoral Systems. Oxford University Press: Oxford*, 333–351.

Regev, E. & Gordon, G. (2019). *The Characteristics of the Housing Market and the Geographical Distribution of the Ultra-Orthodox Population in Israel*. Jerusalem: Israel Democracy Institute.

Rochon, T. R. (1998). *Activism, and Changing Values*. Princeton, NJ: Princeton University Press.

Rochon, T. R. & Mazmanian, D. A. (1993). Social movements and the policy process. *The Annals of the American Academy of Political and Social Science*, *528* (1), 75–87.

Roggeband, C. & Duyvendak, J. W. (2013). The changing supply side of mobilization: Questions for discussion. In J. Van Stekelenburg, C. Roggeband & B. Klandermans (eds.). *Dynamics, Mechanisms and Processes. The Future of Social Movement Research*. Minneapolis, Minnesota, United States: University of Minnesota Press, 95–106.

Roggeband, C. & Klandermans, B. (eds.). (2017). *Handbook of Social Movements Across Disciplines*. Wiesbaden: Springer.

Rohlinger, D. A. (2002). Framing the abortion debate: Organizational resources, media strategies, and movement-countermovement dynamics. *The Sociological Quarterly*, *43*(4), 479–507.

Rokach, A. (1978). *Rural Settlement in Israel*. Jerusalem: The Jewish Agency for Israel and the World Zionist Organization.

Rosenthal, M. (2016). Israel's Governability Crisis: Quandaries, Unstructured Institutions, and Adaptation. Lexington Books.

Roscho. B. (1975). *Newsmaking*. Chicago: University of Chicago Press

Roth, A. (2014). *Not at Any Cost. In From Gush Katif to Amona: The Story Behind the Struggle over the Land of Israel*. Tel Aviv: Miskal & Chemed Books [Hebrew].

Roth, A. (2005). *The Secret of Its Strength: The Yesha Council and Its Campaign against the Security Fence and the Disengagement Plan*. Jerusalem: Israeli Democracy Institute.

Rozen- Zvi, Y. (2007). Settler time. *Theory and Criticism*, *3*, 272–282.

Rubenstein, D. (1982). *Mi L'Adoni Eli: Gush Emunim 1 [On the Lord's Side: Gush Emunim]*. Tel Aviv: Sifriat Poalim.

Rubin, D. (2015). Haredi settlers: The non-Zionist Jewish settlers of the West Bank. In E. F. Isin (ed.). *Citizenship After Orientalism: An Unfinished Project*. London: Palgrave Macmillan, 70–97.

Rucht, D. (2013). Social movement structures in action: Conceptual propositions and empirical illustration. In J. Van Stekelenburg, C. Roggeband & B. Klandermans (eds.). *Dynamics, Mechanisms and Processes. The Future of*

Social Movement Research. Minneapolis, MN: University of Minnesota Press, 169–191.

Rucht, D. & Ohlemacher, T. (1992). Protest event data: collection, uses and perspectives. In M. Diani & R. Eyerman (eds.). *Studying Collective Action*. London: Sage, 76–106.

Rupp, L. J. & Taylor, V. A. (1987). *Survival in the Doldrums the American Women's Rights Movement, 1945 to the 1960s*. Oxford: Oxford University Press.

Ruzza, C. (2004). *Europe and Civil Society: Movement Coalitions and European Governance*. Manchester: Manchester University Press.

Saltzman, I. Z. (2017). Not so "special relationship"? US-Israel relations during Barack Obama's presidency. *Israel Studies*, *22*(1), 50–75.

Samson, D. & Fishman, T. (1991). Torat Eretz Yisrael. *Jerusalem: Torat Eretz Yisrael Publications*.

Santoro, W. A. & Fitzpatrick, M. (2015). "The ballot or the bullet": The crisis of victory and the institutionalization and radicalization of the civil rights movement. *Mobilization*, *20*(2), 207–229.

Sartori, G. (1976). *Parties and Party Systems*. Cambridge: Cambridge University Press.

Sasley, B. E. & Sucharov, M. (2011). Resettling the West Bank settlers. *International Journal*, *66*(4), 999–1017.

Scheuch, E. K. & Klingemann, H. D. (1967). Theory of right-wing radicalism in western industrial societies. *Hamburg Yearbook for Economic and Social Policy*, 11–29.

Schnall, D. J. (1984). *Beyond the Green Line: Israeli Settlements West of the Jordan*. Westport, Connecticut: Praeger Publishers.

Schnell, I. & Mishal, S. (2008). Place as a source of identity in colonizing societies: Israeli settlements in Gaza. *Geographical Review*, *98*(2), 242–259.

Schnell., I & Hope., M. (2012). *The Attitudes of the Jewish Public Toward the Possibility of a Compromise Agreement with the Palestinians*. Tel Aviv University: The Walther Institute for Jewish-Arab Coexistence in Israel.

Schudson, M. (2006). The varieties of civic experience. *Citizenship Studies*, *10*(5), 591–606.

Schurman R. (2004). Fighting "Frankenfoods": industry opportunity structures and the efficacy of the anti-biotech movement in Western Europe. *Social Problems*, *51*, 243–68.

Schwartz, D. (2009). *Religious-Zionism: History and Ideology*. Boston: Academic Studies Press.

Segal, A. (2015). The Israeli media between the 2005 disengagement and the 2015 elections. www.amitsegal.co.il/כללי/התקשורת-הישראלית-בין-התנתקות-2005-לבחירו/

Segal, A. (2018, May 7). The Supreme Court of Justice was not there for the weak. www.amitsegal.co.il/כללי/בגצ-לא-היה-שם-בשביל-החלשים-פסקת-התגברו/

Segal, H. (1987). *Dear Brothers: History of the Jewish Underground*. Jerusalem: Keter. [Hebrew]

Segev, T. (1999). *Anemone days. Eretz Israel during the Mandate*. Jerusalem: Keter Publishing House.

Sela, A. (2007). Civil society, the military, and national security: The case of Israel's security zone in South Lebanon. *Israel Studies*, *12*(1), 53–78.

Selander, L. & Jarvenpaa, S. L. (2016). Digital action repertoires and transforming a social movement organization. *MIS Quarterly*, *40*(2), 331–352.

Shafat, G. (1995). *Gush Emunim: The Story Behind the Scenes*. Bet-El: Bet-El Library. [Hebrew]

Shafir, G., & Peled, Y. (2002). *Being Israeli: The Dynamics of Multiple Citizenship* (Vol. 16). Cambridge, United Kingdom: Cambridge University Press.

Shaked, O., Shimony, G., Canetti, D., Hirsch Hoefler, S., & Mansfeld, Y., (2015). The Effect of Tourism in a Conflict Zone on the Tourist's Political Attitude. West Bank Jewish settlements case study. Paper presented at the annual meeting of the *International Society of Political Psychology*, San Diego, CA, USA. www.ispp.org/docs/pastconferences/Program2015.pdf

Shamai, M. (2002). Parents' perceptions of their children in a context of shared political uncertainty: The case of Jewish settlers in the West Bank before and after the Oslo peace agreement. *Child and Adolescent Social Work Journal*, *19*(1), 57–75.

Shannon, D. M. (2011). *Making Culture: Social Movements, Culture, and Food Not Bombs*. (Doctoral dissertation, University of Connecticut).

Sharlin, S. & Moin, V. (2002). Adjustment of Immigrants from the former Soviet Union in Ariel–Research Report. *University of Haifa and the College of Judea & Samaria*.

Shaw-Smith, P. (1994). The Israeli settler movement post-Oslo. *Journal of Palestine Studies*, *23*(3), 99–109.

Sheafer, T. (2005). Detecting campaign effects in imbalanced campaigns: The Likud's intraparty referendum over Sharon's disengagement plan. *Harvard International Journal of Press/Politics*, *10*(2), 85–93.

Shechory, M. & Laufer, A. (2011). Ideological delinquency: Gender differences among Israeli youth during the withdrawal from the Gaza Strip. *International Journal of Offender Therapy and Comparative Criminology*, *55*(2), 326–343.

Sheleg, Y. (2004). *The Political and Social Implication of Evacuating Settlements from Yesha*. Jerusalem: The Israeli Democracy Institute.

Sheleg, Y. (2015). Innocence lost: The impact of the disengagement on religious Zionism. *Jewish Political Studies Review*, *27*(1–2), 52–64.

Shikaki, K. & Scheindlin, D. (2019). Role of public opinion in the resilience/resolution of the Palestinian-Israeli conflict. *Palestine-Israel Journal of Politics, Economics, and Culture*, *24*(1/2), 61–73.

Shlay, A. B. & Rosen, G. (2010). Making place: The shifting green line and the development of "greater" metropolitan Jerusalem. *City & Community*, *9*(4), 358–389.

Shlaim, A. (2015). *The Iron Wall: Israel and the Arab World*. London, United Kingdom: Penguin.

Shoham, U. (1996). The principle of legality and the Israeli military government in the territories. *Military Law Review*, *153*, 245.

Shor, N. & Mansfeld, Y. (2012). Between wine consumption and wine tourism: Consumer and spatial behavior of Israeli wine tourists. *Horizons in Geography*, 79, 100–117.

Shragai, N. (2003). Settlement monitor. *Journal of Palestine Studies*, *33*(1), 139–147.

Shragai, N. (2015). The disengagement: The unanswered question. *Jewish Political Studies Review*, *27*(1–2), 33–51.

Shuman, E., Cohen-Chen, S., Hirsch-Hoefler, S., & Halperin, E. (2016). Explaining normative versus nonnormative action: The role of implicit theories. *Political Psychology*, *37*(6), 835–852.

Singer, L. (2016). *The Israeli Vagabond: An Analysis of Israel's Hilltop Youth Movement*. Syracuse, NY: Syracuse University Honors College Capstone Project.

Skocpol, T. (1992). State formation and social policy in the United States. *American Behavioral Scientist*, *35*(4–5), 559–584.

Smith, J. (1999). Global politics and transnational social movement strategies: The transnational campaign against international trade in toxic wastes. In D. della Porta, H. Kreisi, & D. Rucht (eds.). *Social Movements in a Globalizing World*. London: Palgrave Macmillan, 170–188.

Smith, J. (2005). Globalization and transnational social movement organizations. In G. F. Davis, D. McAdam, W. R. Scott, & M. N. Zald (eds.). *Social Movements and Organization Theory*. Cambridge: Cambridge University Press, 226–248.

Snipes, A. & Mudde, C. (2019). "France's (kinder, gentler) extremist": Marine Le Pen, intersectionality, and media framing of female populist radical right leaders. *Politics & Gender*, *16*(2),1–33.

Snow, D. A. & Benford, R. D. (1988). Ideology, frame resonance, and participant mobilization. *International Social Movement Research*, *1*(1), 197–217.

Snow, D. A. & Benford, R. D. (1992). Master frames and cycles of protest. In A. D. Morris & C. McClurg Mueller (eds.). *Frontiers in Social Movement Theory*. New Haven, CT: Yale University Press, 133–155.

Snow, D. A., Rochford Jr, E. B., Worden, S. K., & Benford, R. D. (1986). Frame alignment processes, micromobilization, and movement participation. *American Sociological Review*, *51*(4), 464–481.

Snow, D. A., Soule, S. A., & Kriesi, H. (eds.). (2004). *The Blackwell Companion to Social Movements*. Maiden, MA: Blackwell.

Sönmez, S. F. (1998). Tourism, terrorism, and political instability. *Annals of Tourism Research*, *25*(2), 416–456.

Soroka, S. N. (2003). Media, public opinion, and foreign policy. *The International Journal of Press/Politics*, *8*(1), 27–48.

Soroka, S. N. & Wlezien, C. (2010). *Degrees of Democracy: Politics, Public Opinion, and Policy*. Cambridge: Cambridge University Press.

Soule, S. A. (2004). Diffusion processes within and across movements. In D. A. Snow, S. A. Soule, & H. Kriesi (eds.). *The Blackwell Companion to Social Movements*. Maiden, MA: Blackwell, 294–310.

Soule, S. A. (2013). Bringing organizational studies back into social movement scholarship. In J. van Stekelenburg, C. Roggeband, & B. Klandermans (eds.). *The Future of Social Movement Research: Dynamics, Mechanisms and Processes*. Minneapolis, MN: University of Minnesota Press, 107–124.

Soule, S., McAdam, D., McCarthy, J., & Su, Y. (1999). Protest events: Cause or consequence of state action? The US women's movement and federal congressional activities, 1956–1979. *Mobilization*, *4*(2), 239–256.

Sprinzak, E. (1981). Gush Emunim: The tip of the iceberg. *Jerusalem Quarterly, 21*, 28–47.

Sprinzak, E. (1985). Kach and Meir Kahane: The emergence of Jewish quasi-fascism I: Origins and development. *Patterns of Prejudice, 19*(3), 15–21.

Sprinzak, E. (1986). *Gush Emunim: The Politics of Zionist Fundamentalism in Israel.* American Jewish Committee, Institute of Human Relations.

Sprinzak, E. (1987). From messianic pioneering to vigilante terrorism: The case of the Gush Emunim underground. *The Journal of Strategic Studies, 10*(4), 194–216.

Sprinzak, E. (1991). Violence and catastrophe in the theology of Rabbi Meir Kahane: The ideologization of mimetic desire. *Terrorism and Political Violence, 3* (3), 48–70.

Sprinzak, E. (1999). *Brother against Brother: Violence and Extremism in Israeli Politics from Altalena to the Rabin Assassination.* New York: Simon and Schuster.

Staggenborg, S. (1986). Coalition work in the pro-choice movement: Organizational and environmental opportunities and obstacles. *Social Problems, 33*(5), 374–390.

Staggenborg, S. (1988). The consequences of professionalization and formalization in the pro-choice movement. *American Sociological Review, 53*(4), 585–605.

Staggenborg, S. (1991). *The Pro-Choice Movement: Organization and Activism in the Abortion Conflict.* Oxford: Oxford University Press.

Staggenborg, S. (2013). Organization and community in movements. In J. van Stekelenburg, C. Roggeband, & B. Klandermans (eds.). *The Future of Social Movement Research: Dynamics, Mechanisms and Processes.* Minneapolis, MN: University of Minnesota Press, 125–143.

Staggenborg, S. (2015). *Social Movements.* Oxford: Oxford University Press.

Sternhell, Z. (1998). *The Founding Myths of Israel.* Princeton, NJ: Princeton University Press.

Stetter, S., Diez, T., & Albert, M. (2003). The European Union and the Transformation of Border Conflicts: Theorising the Impact of Integration and Association. Paper for the CEEISA/ISA Convention. Central European University, Budapest, Hungary, 26–28 June. www.researchgate.net/publication/228916464_The_European_Union_and_the_Transformation_of_Border_Conflicts_theorising_the_impact_of_integration_and_association

Tal, L. (1985, December 27). I live in Ariel, a city that is fun to live in. *Maariv.*

Tarrow, S. G. (1989). *Struggle, Politics, and Reform: Collective Action, Social Movements and Cycles of Protest.* Ithaca, NY: Cornell University Center for International Studies.

Tarrow, S. G. (1993). Cycles of collective action: Between moments of madness and the repertoire of contention. *Social Science History, 17*(2), 281–307.

Tarrow, S. G. (1994). *Power in Movement: Social Movements and Contentious Politics.* New York: Cambridge University Press.

Tarrow, S. G. (2005). *The New Transnational Activism.* New York: Cambridge University Press.

Tarrow, S. G. (2011). *Power in Movement: Social Movements and Contentious Politics.* New York: Cambridge University Press.

Tarrow, S. (2017). "The world changed today!" Can we recognize critical junctures when we see them? *Qualitative & Multi-Method Research, 15*(1), 9–11.

Tarrow, S. G. & McAdam, D. (2005). Scale shift in transnational contention. In D. della Porta & S. Tarrow (eds.). *Transnational Protest and Global Activism*. Lanham, MD: Rowman & Littlefield, 121–150.

Taub, G. (2007). Gods politics in Israel's supreme court: The retreat of theology in religious settlers' politics. *Journal of Modern Jewish Studies, 6*(3), 289–299.

Taub, G. (2010). *The Settlers and the Struggle Over the Meaning of Zionism*. New Haven, CT: Yale University Press.

Tausch, N., Becker, J. C., Spears, R., Christ, O., Saab, R., Singh, P., & Siddiqui, R. N. (2011). Explaining radical group behavior: Developing emotion and efficacy routes to normative and nonnormative collective action. *Journal of Personality and Social Psychology, 101*(1), 129–148.

Taylor, V. (2000). Mobilizing for change in a social movement society. *Contemporary Sociology, 29*(1), 219–230.

Taylor, V. & Van Dyke, N. (2004). 'Get up, stand up': Tactical repertoires of social movements. In D. A. Snow, S. A. Soule, & H. Kriesi (eds.). *The Blackwell Companion to Social Movements*. Maiden, MA: Blackwell, 262–293.

Teece, D. J. (1987). *The Competitive Challenge: Strategies for Industrial Innovation and Renewal*. Pensacola, FL: Ballinger.

Telhami, S. & Rouse, S. (2018). American Views of the Israeli-Palestinian Conflict, *University of Maryland Critical Issues Poll*. www.brookings.edu/blog/order-from-chaos/2018/12/12/americans-are-increasingly-critical-of-israel/

Tenenbaum, K. & Eiran, E. (2005). Israeli settlement activity in the West Bank and Gaza: A brief history. *Negotiation Journal, 21*(2), 171–175.

Jerusalem Institute for Policy Research (2019). *Jerusalem Current Status and Trends*. Jerusalem: Jerusalem Institute for Policy Research. [Hebrew]

Thomas, E. F., Smith, L. G., McGarty, C., Reese, G., Kende, A., Bliuc, A. M., Curtin, M., & Spears, R. (2018). When and how social movements mobilize action within and across nations to promote solidarity with refugees. *European Journal of Social Psychology, 49*(2), 213–249.

Thomas, M. (2007). *American Policy Toward Israel: The Power and Limits of Beliefs*. New York: Routledge.

Thouin, C. (2010). Under a cloud of uncertainty: AIPAC's 2010 policy conference, 21–23 March, *Journal of Palestine Studies, 39*, 60–71.

Tilly, C. (1975). Western state-making and theories of political transformation. In C. Tilly (ed.). *The Formation of National States in Western Europe*. Princeton, NJ: Princeton University Press.

Tilly, C. (1978). *From Mobilisation to Revolution*. New York: Addison-Wesley.

Tilly, C. (1995). Citizenship, identity and social history. *International Review of Social History, 40*(S3), 1–17.

Tilly, C. (1999). From interactions to outcomes in social movements. In M. Giugni, D. McAdam, & C. Tilly (eds.). *How Social Movements Matter*. Minneapolis, MN: University of Minnesota Press, 253–270.

Tilly, C. (2008). *Contentious Performances*. New York: Cambridge University Press.

Timothy, D. J. (2002). *Tourism and Political Boundaries*. New York: Routledge.
Tremayne, M. (2014). Anatomy of protest in the digital era: A network analysis of Twitter and Occupy Wall Street. *Social Movement Studies*, *13*(1), 110–126.
Troen, I. (2011). "Jewish Settlement in the Land of Israel/Palestine." www.jewishvirtuallibrary.org/jsource/isdf/text/troen.pdf
Troen, I. (2016). Secular Judaism in Israel. *Society*, *53*(2), 153–162.
Tsfati, Y. & Cohen, J. (2005). The influence of presumed media influence on democratic legitimacy: The case of Gaza settlers. *Communication Research*, *32* (6), 794–821.
Tufekci, Z. (2013). "Not this one" social movements, the attention economy, and microcelebrity networked activism. *American Behavioral Scientist*, *57*(7), 848–870.
Turner, R. & Killian, L. (1987). *Collective Behavior*. Englewood Cliffs, NJ: Prentice-Hall, 3rd edition.
Uba, K. (2009). The contextual dependence of movement outcomes: A simplified meta-analysis. *Mobilization*, *14*(4), 433–448.
Van Dyke, N. & Amos, B. (2017). Social movement coalitions: Formation, longevity, and success. *Sociology Compass*, *11*(7), e12489.
Verba, S. & Nie, N. H. (1972). *Participation in America: Social Equality and Political Democracy*. New York: Harper & Row.
Verba, S., Schlozman, K. L., & Brady, H. E. (1995). *Voice and Equality: Civic Voluntarism in American Politics*. Cambridge, MA: Harvard University Press.
Vermeulen, F. (2006). *The Immigrant Organising Process: Turkish Organisations in Amsterdam and Berlin and Surinamese Organisations in Amsterdam, 1960–2000*. Amsterdam: Amsterdam University Press.
Waddock, S. (2017). *The Difference Makers: How Social and Institutional Entrepreneurs Created the Corporate Responsibility Movement*. New York: Routledge.
Walker, E. T., McCarthy, J. D., & Baumgartner, F. (2011). Replacing members with managers? Mutualism among membership and nonmembership advocacy organizations in the United States. *American Journal of Sociology*, *116*(4), 1284–1337.
Wallach, Y. (2011). Trapped in mirror-images: The rhetoric of maps in Israel/Palestine. *Political Geography*, *30*(7), 358–369.
Wang, D. J. & Piazza, A. (2016). The use of disruptive tactics in protest as a trade-off: The role of social movement claims. *Social Forces*, *94*(4), 1675–1710.
Wang, D. J. & Soule, S. A. (2016). Tactical innovation in social movements: The effects of peripheral and multi-issue protest. *American Sociological Review*, *81* (3), 517–548.
Wang, D., Piazza, A., & Soule, S. A. (2018). Boundary-spanning in social movements: Antecedents and outcomes. *Annual Review of Sociology*, *44*, 167–187.
Wapner, P. (1995). Politics beyond the state environmental activism and world civic politics. *World Politics*, *47*(3), 311–340.
Waxman, D. (2013). The Jewish diaspora and the pro-Israel lobby. In J. Peters & D. Newman (eds.). *The Routledge Handbook on the Israeli-Palestinian Conflict*. London: Routledge.

Weber, K. & King, B. (2014). Social movement theory and organization studies. In P. Adler, P. du Gay, G. Morgan, & M. Reed (eds.). *Oxford Handbook of Sociology, Social Theory and Organization Studies*, 487–509.

Weisburd, D. (1989). *Jewish Settler Violence: Deviance as Social Control*. University Park, PA: Pennsylvania State University Press.

Weisburd, D., & Lernau, H. (2006). What prevented violence in Jewish settlements in the withdrawal from the Gaza strip: Toward a perspective of normative balance. *Ohio State Journal on Dispute Resolution, 22*(1), 37–81.

Weiss, H. (2011). Immigration and West Bank settlement normalization. *PoLAR: Political and Legal Anthropology Review, 34*(1), 112–130.

Weissbrod, L. (1982). Gush Emunim ideology—from religious doctrine to political action. *Middle Eastern Studies, 18*(3), 265–275.

Weissbrod, L. (2002). *Israeli Identity. Search of a Successor to the Pioneer, Tsabar and Settler*. Portland, OR: Frank Cass

Weissbrod, L. (2009). Reluctant compliance or civil war: Prospects of retrenchment in Israel. *Civil Wars, 11*(2), 158–178.

Weizman, E. (2007). *Hollow Land: Israel's Architecture of Occupation*. Brooklyn, New York: Verso books.

Wiener, A. (1984, January 3). Construction momentum in settlement in Judea and Samaria. *Maariv*, p. 36.

Willems, J. & Jegers, M. (2012). Social movement structures in relation to goals and forms of action: An exploratory model. *Canadian Journal of Nonprofit and Social Economy Research, 3*(2), 67–81.

Wilson, B., Van Luijk, N., & Boit, M. K. (2015). When celebrity athletes are "social movement entrepreneurs": A study of the role of elite runners in run-for-peace events in post-conflict Kenya in 2008. *International Review for the Sociology of Sport, 50*(8), 929–957.

Wolfsfeld, G. (1984). Collective political action and media strategy: The case of Yamit. *Journal of Conflict Resolution, 28*(3), 363–381.

Wolfsfeld, G. (1997). Promoting peace through the news media: Some initial lessons from the Oslo peace process. *Harvard International Journal of Press/Politics, 2*(4), 52–70.

World Public Opinion (2002). The Potential for a Nonviolent Intifada. https://drum.lib.umd.edu/bitstream/handle/1903/10154/Intifada1_Aug02_rpt.pdf?sequence=4&isAllowed=y

World Public Opinion (2009). Growing Majority of Americans Oppose Israel Building Settlements. http://worldpublicopinion.net/growing-majority-of-americans-oppose-israel-building-settlements/

Wrenn, C. (2016). *Professionalization, Factionalism, and Social Movement Success: A Case Study on Nonhuman Animal Rights Mobilization* (Doctoral dissertation, Colorado State University).

Wright, S. C., Taylor, D. M., & Moghaddam, F. M. (1990). Responding to membership in a disadvantaged group: From acceptance to collective protest. *Journal of Personality and Social Psychology, 58*(6), 994–1003.

Yaar, E., & Hermann, T. (1996–2018). *Peace Index*. Tel Aviv, Israel: The Steinmetz Centre for Peace Research.

Yates, L. (2015). Rethinking prefiguration: Alternatives, micropolitics and goals in social movements. *Social Movement Studies*, *14*(1), 1–21.

Yiftachel, O. (2006). *Ethnocracy: Land and Identity Politics in Israel/Palestine*. Philadelphia, PA: University of Pennsylvania Press.

Yishai, Y. (1987). *Land or Peace: Whither Israel?* (Vol. 352). Stanford, California, United States: Hoover Press.

Yishai, Y. (2012). *Land of Paradoxes: Interest Politics in Israel*. Albany, NY: SUNY Press.

Zald, M. N. (2017). *Social Movements in an Organizational Society: Collected Essays*. New York: Routledge.

Zald, M. N. & Useem, B. (1987). Movement and countermovement interaction: Mobilization, tactics, and state involvement. In N. M. Zald & J. D. McCarthy (eds.). *Social Movements in an Organizational Society*. New Brunswick, NJ: Transaction, 247–272.

Zald, M. N. & Ash, R. (1966). Social movement organizations: Growth, decay and change. *Social Forces*, *44*(3), 327–341.

Zald, M. N., Morrill, C., & Rao, H. (2005). The impact of social movements on organizations. In G. F. Davis, D. McAdam, W. R. Scott, & M. N. Zald (eds.). *Social Movements and Organization Theory*. Cambridge: Cambridge University Press, 253–279.

Zanany, O. (2018) From conflict management to settlement management the concept of Israeli security and the Palestinian state. *Molad: Center for the Renewal of Democracy*. www.molad.org/images/upload/files/Steinmetz_OmerZanany_12.pdf

Zertal, I. & Eldar, A. (2007). *Lords of the Land: The Settlers and the State of Israel, 1967–2007*. New York, United States: Nation.

Zimmermann, E. (2015). Social movements and political outcomes: Why both ends fail to meet. *Annales Universitatis Mariae Curie-Skłodowska, sectio K–Politologia*, *22*(1), 31–49.

Zippel, K. (2004). Transnational advocacy networks and policy cycles in the European Union: The case of sexual harassment. *Social Politics: International Studies in Gender, State & Society*, *11*(1), 57–85.

Zukin, C., Keeter, S., Andolina, M., Jenkins, K., & Carpini, M. X. D. (2006). *A New Engagement? Political Participation, Civic Life, and the Changing American Citizen*. Oxford: Oxford University Press.

Zunes, S. (2006). The Israel lobby: How powerful is it really? *Mother Jones*, 18 May. www.motherjones.com/politics/2006/05/israel-lobby-how-powerful-it-really.

Official Documents

Annals of the Knesset (1968). *Annals of the Knesset*. Parliamentary Documentation of the Israel Knesset 3324–3325, 17 August.

Annals of the Knesset (1992). *Annals of the Knesset*. Parliamentary Documentation of the Israel Knesset, 126, 64, 13 July.

Ariel Local Council (1982). Ariel Planning Team Documents, 21 April.

Council of the EU (2012). "Council Conclusion on the Middle East Process, 3209 Foreign Affairs Council Meeting, para. 4". *Council of the EU*, 10 December.

Government Decision no. 1996 (2004, June 6) "Revised Disengagement Plan". *Prime Minister's Office.*

Government Decision No. 3579 (2005, May 2) "The conversion of the Judea and Samaria Academic College in Ariel to the university".

Government Resolution 1561 (2016). "Special assistance for 2016 to the Judea and Samaria Area". *Prime Minister's Office.*

Government Resolution 3738 (2018, April 15). "Defining localities and regions as national priority". *Prime Minister's Office.*

Government Resolution 667 (2013, August 4). "Defining localities and regions as national priority". *Ministry of Construction and Housing.*

Israeli Defense Forces General. HQ (1963). Reg. 33.0133 1963.

Knesset Resolution 360 (1992). "Settlement constructions". *Peace Now.* https://peacenow.org.il/settlement-freeze-rabin

Knesset announcement (2018). "Final approval: The CHE has been given the authority to act in Judea and Samaria as well". *The Knesset Website.* https://main.knesset.gov.il/News/PressReleases/Pages/press12.02.18hs.aspx

Knesset meeting no. 173 (2004). Government Notice of Resolution 1996 on the "Revised Disengagement Plan". *The Knesset Website.* https://m.knesset.gov.il/Activity/plenum/Pages/SessionItem.aspx?itemID=77706

Knesset Meeting no. 223 (2005). Implementation of the Disengagement Plan Bill. *The Knesset Website.* https://main.knesset.gov.il/Activity/plenum/Pages/SessionItem.aspx?itemID=94279

Levy, E., Shapira, T., & Baker, A. (2012). *The Levy Commission Report on the Legal Status of Building in Judea and Samaria.* www.pmo.gov.il/Documents/doch090712.pdf

Ministerial Committee for Settlement. (1978). Decision No. 414 / H. "Approval of the Tel Aviv Group to Settle Haris," *Ministry of Agriculture.*

Ministry of Education (2019). "Pre-military Academies". *Ministry of Education.* https://students.education.gov.il/toward-military-service/pre-military-preparatory-courses

Regulation Bill 2 (2018). "Proposed Law for Settlements and Neighborhoods in Regulatory Processes". *The Knesset Website,* 18 July.

Regulation of Settlement in Judea and Samaria Law (2017). "5777–2017, Book of Laws No. 2604 p. 394, issue no. 2604672". *Ministry of Justice,* 13 February.

Sasson, T. (2005). "Summary of the Opinion Concerning Unauthorized Outposts: An Interim Report". *Israel Prime Minister Office.*

Shahak, I. & Mezvinsky, N. (1999). *Jewish fundamentalism in Israel.* London, United Kingdom: Pluto Press.

Sharon, A. (2003). "Address by PM Ariel Sharon". at the Fourth Herzliya Conference". *Ministry of Foreign Affairs.*

Spiegel, B (2007). "Spiegel Report". *Ministry of Defense.* www.hamoked.org.il/files/2013/1157900.pdf

United Nations (2008). "The Question of Palestine and the United Nations". New York, NY: United Nations.

U.S. Department of States (2002). "Middle East Quartet, Statement of the Middle East Quartet". *U.S. State Department,* 20 December.

U.S. Department of State (2003). *Roadmap for Peace in the Middle East: Israeli/ Palestinian Reciprocal Action, Quartet Support*. Washington, DC, United States: Bureau of Public Affairs.

Zandberg, H. Report (2018). "The Zandberg Report on Formulating an Outline for Constructions in the Judea and Samaria". *Israel Department of Justice*. www .gov.il/BlobFolder/reports/report_11/he/report_11.pdf

Personal Interviews

Ben-Zimra, Gadi. (December 2007). Rabbi and Head of Ulpana in the Ma'ale Levona settlement. Chairperson of Jewish Heart (*Halev Ha'yehudi*).

Ben-Zion, Davidi (April 2014). Deputy Head of the Shomron Regional Council.

Goldstein, Shaul. (November 2007). Chairperson of Gush Etzion Regional Council and Deputy Head of Yesha Council.

Haetzni, Elyakim (November 2007). Former Yesha Council member and one of the leaders of The Country's Defenders (*Meginei Aretz*).

Lieberman, Bentzi (November 2007). Yesha Council Chairman and Head of the Samaria Regional Council.

Matar, Nadia (November 2007). Founder and Co-President of Women in Green (*Nashim Beyarok*).

Melamed, Shulamit (December 2007). Rabbanit and founding head of *Arutz Sheva*.

Smotrich, Bezalel (December 2007). Chairman of the Land Protection Trust Movement and one of the leaders of Sovereignty (*Komemiyut*).

Regev, Eitan (July 2019). Research Fellow at Israel Democracy Institute.

Pinchas, Wallerstein (December 2007). The Head of the Binyamin Regional Council

Weiss, Daniela (November 2007). Co-founder The Land of Israel Faithful (*Neemanei Aretz Yisrael*) and former Head of the local council of Kedumim

Websites

Amana: www.amana.co.il

- "Settling a Million in Judea and Samaria" (2017)

American Israel Public Affairs Committee (AIPAC): www.aipac.org/

Coordination of Government Activities in the Territories (COGAT): www.idf.il /en/minisites/cogat/

Hebron Fund: www.hebronfund.org/about-us/

Israel Central Bureau of Statistics (ICBS): www.cbs.gov.il

- "The Yearly Statistic of Israel"
- "Internal Migration between Localities – Historical Tables";
- "Localities and Other Geographical Divisions"
- "Dwellings, By construction Initiator, Type of Locality and District"
- "Immigrants of the 90s from the former Soviet Union"

– "Source of population growth by district"
– "Population by District and Region"
– "Local government financial data"
– "Population Census"
– "Population and Immigration Authority, Population Register
Israel Department of Justice: www.gov.il
– "Constructions in the Judea and Samaria"
Israel Ministry of Foreign Affairs: https://mfa.gov.il
– "Golan Hights Law" (December 14, 1981)
– "Disputed Territories: Forgotten Facts about the West Bank and Gaza Strip" (February 1, 2003)
– "Exchange of letters between PM Sharon and US President Bush" (April 14, 2004)
– "The Cabinet Resolution Regarding the Disengagement Plan" (June 6, 2004).
Israeli Central Elections Committee: https://votes21.bechirot.gov.il
– "2019 Election Results by locality"
Legal Forum – For a Democratic Zionist Israel: www.haforum.org/
Peace Now: https://peacenow.org.il
– "Ariel and Ariel Bloc" (May 29, 2005)
– "Unlike in Israel Proper – No Housing Crisis in the Settlement of Ariel" (August 18, 2011)
– "Israel 2013 elections"
– "The Price of the Settlements (or) How Israel Favors Settlements and Settlers" (2013)
– "The Settlements in the West Bank: Facts and Numbers" (2015)
– "The Outpost Combina" (March 9, 2017)
– "Constructions in settlement" (August 18, 2018)
– "Illegal Outpost" (August 4, 2019)
Professors for a Strong Israel (PSI): www.professors.org.il/Hebrew/index.html
Women in Green: womeningreen.org/oz-vegaon/
Yesh Din: www.yesh-din.org
– "The Age of Regularization – The Zandberg Committee Expropriation Report for Retroactive Authorization of Israeli Outposts and Illegal Construction in the Settlements: Analysis, Ramifications and Implementation" (April 1, 2019)
Yesha Council Website: www.myesha.org.il
– "About Yesha Council"
– "Settlers on the Net"
Zionist Organization of America (ZOA): https://zoa.org/2013/07/10206934-zoa-key-participant-in-a-roundtable-hosted-by-house-republicans/

Index

Milton Keynes UK
Ingram Content Group UK Ltd.
UKHW020122071124
450579UK00024B/276